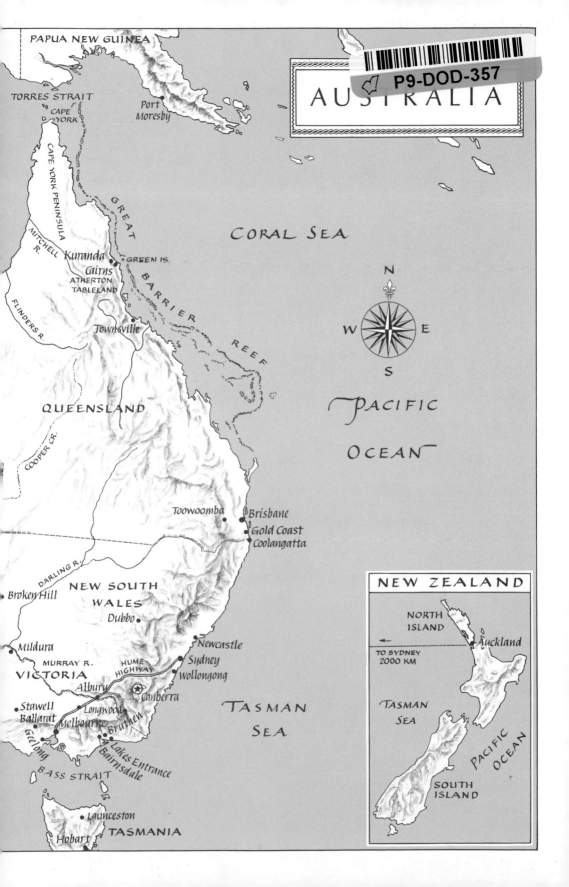

PAPUA NEW GUINEA

AUSTRALIA

P9-DOD-357

TORRES STRAIT

CAPE YORK

Port Moresby

CAPE YORK PENINSULA

MITCHELL R.

FLINDERS R.

Kuranda
Cairns
ATHERTON
TABLELAND

GREEN IS.

GREAT

BARRIER

REEF

CORAL SEA

Townsville

QUEENSLAND

COOPER CR.

N

W   E

S

PACIFIC

OCEAN

DARLING R.

Broken Hill

NEW SOUTH
WALES

Dubbo

Toowoomba   Brisbane
Gold Coast
Coolangatta

Mildura

MURRAY R.

VICTORIA

Stawell
Ballarat

Albury

HUME
HIGHWAY

Longwood
Melbourne   Bruthen

Geelong

Canberra

Newcastle
Sydney
Wollongong

TASMAN

SEA

Lakes Entrance
Bairnsdale

BASS STRAIT

Launceston

Hobart   TASMANIA

NEW ZEALAND

NORTH
ISLAND

TO SYDNEY
2000 KM

Auckland

TASMAN

SEA

PACIFIC

OCEAN

SOUTH
ISLAND

OTHER BOOKS BY ROSS TERRILL

The White-Boned Demon: A Biography of Madame Mao Zedong
Mao: A Biography
The Future of China: After Mao
Flowers on an Iron Tree: Five Cities of China
Socialism as Fellowship: R. H. Tawney and His Times
800,000,000: The Real China

THE

AUSTRA

Ross Terrill

LIANS

SIMON AND SCHUSTER   NEW YORK

Published by Simon and Schuster
A Division of Simon & Schuster, Inc.
Simon & Schuster Building
Rockefeller Center
1230 Avenue of the Americas
New York, New York 10020
SIMON AND SCHUSTER and colophon are registered trademarks
of Simon & Schuster, Inc.
Designed by Eve Kirch
Manufactured in the United States of America

10   9   8   7   6   5   4   3   2

Library of Congress Cataloging in Publication Data
Terrill, Ross.
   The Australians.
   Bibliography: p.
   Includes index.
   1. Australia—Social life and customs.
2. Australia—Social conditions.   3. Australia—
History.   4. Terrill, Ross.   I. Title.
DU107.T47   1987   994   87–4807
ISBN 0–671–54441–1

Contents

THE
AUSTRALIANS

ONE

Memories of Yesterday

United Airlines Flight 815 from New York to Sydney seems to go on forever. The Boeing 747B cleaves through a night and a day that pass too quickly, as if the heavens are making mistakes and hastily correcting them. The Pacific Ocean's vastness saps our energy.

A man sitting beside me, who has never traveled twenty hours in a plane before, misses his birthday when we cross the dateline between Samoa and Fiji and bypass January 17. A hostess, her face puffy as a whore's at breakfast time, brings him champagne and chocolate cake to ease his sense of loss.

The hostesses tell us we are nearing "Sydney, Australia," and that the plane will go on to "Melbourne, Australia." Australian passengers frown darkly, or titter in an attempt at tolerance. "Where *else* could Sydney be!" says a young man, amazed, to no one in particular. "I mean, Melbourne is *Melbourne*," objects a middle-aged woman who has never heard of Melbourne, Florida.

Although I have lived most of my life in Australia, I know this appealing society is in some ways a closed brotherhood; I should change mental gears, now that I am an American, as I enter the Western

13

world's last mystery land. Pre-existent momentum must be checked; only an ear close to the ground can appreciate a fairly inarticulate people. It will take me three weeks to be able to address a man as "mate."

When the jet pulls up on the tarmac we are sprayed with insecticide. Having presumed to come all the way to Australia from "overseas," we must pay the dues of dubious sophisticates entering a healthy land. "Don't Bring In Disease," says a notice about plants and animals in the terminal. "Declare It for Australia"—or pay a $50,000 fine.[1] Do I have any reptiles, the customs man asks me, or turtles, lizards, elephants, or "members of the cat family"? Australia receives us with the self-consciousness of a nation (one of very few) that has no frontiers. Australia's only immediate neighbors are oceans, and no one gets to Australia—not the Aborigines 40,000 or more years ago, not the British two hundred years ago, not the million-plus overseas visitors in 1986—without first being drained by traversing one of them.

As we prepare to reboard for the short hop to Melbourne, a Mediterranean-looking man who does not speak English well is worried about his films being X-rayed. "This machine's different," drawls a gawky girl with lovely skin. "It's not what you're used to in hospitals. Don't worry." The man continues to worry, but the girl grinds him down with obstinacy and patience. The man gives a grunt of resignation, submits to the X ray, and staggers off with his bags. The girl turns to her workmate, a man with short pants, copper-colored legs on which the hairs are as white as an old man's beard, and eyes hidden deep in his face. "You get one every day," she says with a shrug.

I never feel afraid of crashing when coming in to land at Melbourne's bucolic Tullamarine airport—what could you hit: a tree, a cow?—and it is true that Australia is a safe place. Qantas, the Australian airline whose planes now display on the tail a slim kangaroo that looks like a swordfish, has never had a single peacetime fatality in more than sixty years of operation. In Australia it is nature, not man, that is most likely to snuff you out.

As we taxi, I see from my window just one other plane, a KLM 747. It moves beside grass that is bent over in the wind caused by the engines. The jet from Amsterdam seems absurdly out of place against the rolling green hills and twisted trees, like a spaceship that has reached the wrong planet.

Inside the airport terminal the design and fittings suggest London—

1. Throughout this book currency is given in the Australian dollar, which in February 1987 was equivalent to 66 U.S. cents.

even the toilets have a British antiseptic smell—and it comes as a shock to look outside the windows and see glaring light, wide spaces, and gum (eucalyptus) trees with green-gray leaves.

It is the landscape of my childhood, and the sounds of a Bruthen night return in memory's ear as if I had just woken up in that beautiful Australian township. The mellow chime of bellbirds. A sighing wind in the stringy bark trees. The patter, or mad stampede, of raindrops on the green-painted galvanized iron roof of our wooden house, with its five rooms and lovely veranda from which we viewed the world. The sleeper-cutters conversing in shouts as they guzzled beer at the Bruthen Inn down in the valley.

That craziest of laughs, the kookaburra's, as in his fussily feathered bulk he sat smugly among pine cones in one of our backyard trees. The ugly howl of dingoes in the dark gullies beyond the bitumen ribbon of the road north to Omeo. Rippling cackles from our chooks (hens), ducks, or geese, which made me wonder which of the myriad forces of the night had disturbed them. A brown snake was the nastiest possibility.

"Cocky wants a drink," my sister's pet cockatoo would screech as she had taught it to do, if it wanted to plunge its big metallic beak into a jam tin of water or have my sister come and lean her cheek against its white feathers. When she did this, the cockatoo would cease strutting on the perch, tuck its lofty yellow crest to one side, and transform itself from a foul-mouthed disturber of the peace into a smooching lovebird.

These were the years of the middle and late 1940s when my family lived in Bruthen, a sleepy township sitting in a green valley in East Gippsland, a tranquil half-wooded and pastoral stretch of the state of Victoria not far from the Ninety Mile Beach on Australia's southeastern coast. My father was an elemental man with echoes in him of the Australian bushman, a figure becoming rare but still vivid in our imaginations. He was brought up a Methodist, the main religion of the bush, but he threw it off in the debunking style of Australian secularism. Also in the Australian tradition, he hated cops and liked to put down "tall poppies," whether of lineage or achievement. He often used the expression "as game as Ned Kelly," an approving reference to a famous criminal of the bush in northeastern Victoria, where our family had lived during the early 1940s in a scraggy little township called Longwood. But my father wasn't anti-government, as the bushmen were, because chance had turned him into a state schoolteacher.

My mother, born in Victoria as was my father, was not enthusiastic about the bush and wished the family to make social progress. Her own family was more oriented to Britain (though all four of my grandparents were born in Australia), a little more educated, and more in tune with urban life than my father's family. Her family's Presbyterianism did not have bush Methodism's emotionalism and prohibitions.

East Gippsland grew maize and raised dairy cattle. But in my child's mind it was sheep—the economic base of the district around Longwood in the northeast—that ruled the universe of rural Australia. If we believed in anything more abstract than the rays of the morning sun and the power of the fields to provide what was asked of them, it was in the idea of the sheep.

At Longwood, a flat dry place lent character by satin-smooth ghostly gums, we revered the stumbling sheep with their baritone "baas" and their gentle eyes peering from between tufts of thick wool. We had no Australian heroes—only the anti-hero Ned Kelly, our bushranger— and we even lacked proud, strong creatures like the lion or the dragon to look up to. We had only the rather dumb merinos, with their tendency to run the wrong way when the dogs were rounding them up. But Australian sheep—they outnumber the people by about nine to one— provided garments for the world and prosperity for us. Folk we knew around Longwood had lambs living with them in the house.

We learned the stories of the Bible and no less dutifully learned that "Australia lived off the sheep's back." I was particularly impressed—the connection made my world more reasonable—that Jesus liked sheep and held them in his arms. The merinos' stench of dust and grease and pasture-scented turds was, like the aroma of roast lamb from our rambling kitchen, a comforting assurance of being at home.

We children vaguely knew that we were Australians. We felt attached to our place, and across the continent people looked and sounded and behaved just as we did. Yet we were the most unreflective of patriots. Australia for us was indeed a *place*. We loved the green valleys and blue hills. We loved the high wide skies. We loved the wonderful light with its range of moods that was almost like an extra circle of friends. We identified being Australian with the natural world around us.

But a place is not a nation, and we had little sense of our nation. Given largely to outdoor activities, we were like fingers on the body of a creature whose heart was a mystery to its limbs. We were happy pagans far from any Rome.

My father liked Australian literature and history and art, and he liked living close to nature; these enthusiasms all blended into one. From him I learned Banjo Paterson's lines about the man in the outback:

> *And he sees the vision splendid of the sunlit plains extended*
> *And at night the wondrous glory of the everlasting stars.*

And Adam Lindsay Gordon's piece of bush philosophy:

> *Life is mostly froth and bubble,*
> *Two things stand like stone,*
> *Kindness in another's trouble,*
> *Courage in your own.*

And my father taught me Dorothea Mackellar's haunting poem "My Country" (now having a revival in the nationalistic mood of the 1980s), which caught the feel both of Longwood and Bruthen:

> *I love a sunburnt country,*
> *A land of sweeping plains,*
> *Of ragged mountain ranges,*
> *Of droughts and flooding rains.*
> *I love her far horizons;*
> *I love her jewel-sea,*
> *Her beauty and her terror—*
> *The wide brown land for me!*

My mother decided that her children should take piano lessons to fend off bush barbarism with "culture." In our Bruthen lounge room I sat at the ivory keys, my bare legs just reaching far enough to press down the stiff pedals, and wrestled with European sonatas and preludes of another century. In stifling afternoon heat the red velvet curtains of the lounge room were pulled closed to make the genteel music-making seem more real.

Rarely did we fear or confront thieves, but my father kept a loaded rifle in his wardrobe, and there were times when he went out into the yard with it to investigate an unaccustomed noise. Swagmen were the only persons I ever recall being afraid of. A swagman was a wandering beggar, a watered-down heir of the itinerant bushman. These bearded, dirty nomads, each one carrying his billy (a tin to make tea in), would come to our door both at Longwood and at Bruthen and ask for food and hot water. I was worried that a man who did not have a house must be strange. And I was terrified by the appearance of the more raffish swagmen. I felt they would grab us if they got a chance.

Perhaps they looked too much like my father, who loved to make himself as untidy and dirty as possible by way of a change from how he had to look in the classroom, and perhaps I felt disconcerted that any other man could look as disheveled as my father.

On moonlit nights, when the air was soft and gray like the skin of a mushroom, and the command "Go and play" removed us from the adults' indoor world, we stayed out late to play rounders or hidey or tiggy (a chasing and touching game) with the kids next door. If a dispute arose, we pelted each other with dried pats of cow dung or hard little unripe plums. The scent of honeysuckle, wattle, and the violet-colored morning glory that grew over our garden trellis hung as incense upon our rituals.

We took IXL-brand jam tins to the muddy dams of farms near Bruthen to hunt for yabbies. My father drove us in his square black 1928 Chrysler to fish for bream in the Tambo River, where on warm evenings filled with the "baas" of sheep and the buzz of insects we sat patiently with our rods waiting for a bite. More excitingly, he would take us to try for silvery snapper in the saltwater lakes, or for the animal-like gummy shark on Ninety Mile Beach near the resort of Lakes Entrance.

We picked wild blackberries in the smoky-blue hills above our house. We ate as many as we could of these sweet juicy balls and saved the rest in paper bags to take home or give to neighbors. By the time the sun went down, our fingers and mouths were stained crimson, our arms and legs were scratched from the thorns on the blackberry bushes, and our small brown bellies were distended from gorging.

We floated toy bark canoes and skinny-dipped in green twisting creeks where the crack of whipbird and the smell of fresh saplings and wet bark filled the afternoon. Most Australian trees do not shed their leaves, but their bark instead. Bark is a wonderful thing. Its brown and cream patterns are beautiful. With dry bits of bark we could kindle a campfire. From its varied forms we made baskets, propellers for our toy planes, and even small huts to stay in overnight. My mother put twists of bark in the oven when baking her delicious scones to obtain a quick heat.

There was no loneliness in the bush. All of nature conspired to give us company, diversion, and solace. "When you need comfort," another of my father's favorite authors, Alan Marshall, wrote truly, "wrap your arms around a gum tree and all the strength of that tree will flow into you."

The most serious pursuit of my brother and me—more so than our school lessons or the stiff Bible classes at Bruthen's combined Methodist-Congregational Sunday School—was catching rabbits. It was a brutal business. It was also our magic carpet to a tiny realm of economic independence; pocket money came from selling the skins.

The worst animal I know is the ferret. The memory of this lean and vicious creature, ginger in color and faster than lightning, its teeth, claws, and little pink eyes all declaring murder, makes me shudder even now. But our ferrets trapped the rabbits for us. We kept the whining creatures in cages that were always filthy, and as we transferred them to a box with a shoulder strap for their day's work, they tried to bite our hands. Finding a paddock with plenty of rabbits, we chose a clearing and covered all the rabbit burrows we could find with nets secured with iron spikes. Then with a frisson of disgust we pushed a couple of ferrets underground.

Soon rabbits came pounding out—in their defenselessness even more terrified of the ferrets than we were—some of them squealing with pain at a ferret bite. They entangled themselves hopelessly, beautifully in our nets. We pounced. Each rabbit we unsentimentally killed with a firm blow of the side of the hand to the back of its neck. The warm squirming bodies we threw into a hessian sugar bag, counting them with glee as the afternoon wore on.

Skinning a rabbit is like disentangling a fur mitten from the hand of a mangled corpse. We ate so many rabbits it is a wonder we did not grow fur. Our dogs ate even more. Still we threw away most of the rusty-red carcasses. The skins we stretched over a bent wire to dry. When they got to feel crackly like a lampshade we took them off the wires and tied them in bundles with string. I loved the ripe furry smell of the skins at this stage—and also the thought of shiny shillings drawing nearer.

Each month we drove into the neat flat town of Bairnsdale and sold the skins for ten pence each at a warehouse just off Main Street that smelled like women's overcoats. Today I am unable to eat rabbit; the smell of the warm dead bodies and the skinned carcasses, and the sounds of a ferret's attack, are too hard to forget.

Though we were not farmers, we grew or caught nearly all of our food. Now and then my mother put in an order to the butcher, in his blood-stained apron of blue and white stripes, or to the grocer, who wore a tie and smelled of flour. Only the milk—we had no cows—had to come in each day, poured into a waiting bucket at our back door by a neighbor who got tomatoes from us in return. Our vegetable gardens were fertilized in part from our dunny (outdoor toilet), furnished with the rough newsprint of the *Bruthen Times,* cut into squares; no house I knew of in Bruthen had a flush toilet.

The food we ate was wonderful in quality and greasy-British in preparation. The huge brown eggs were fried. Fillets of fish from our trips to the banks of the Tambo were covered with batter as if they were Victorian chair legs that required a decoration before being viewed. Roast beef swam in thick gravy made with flour and arrived with balloons of Yorkshire pudding. Lashings of butter and sugar went into the baked cakes. When money was short, and until postwar rationing of butter ceased, we ate lots of dripping, left over from a roast, spread thickly on toast. This I preferred to most of the costly foods.

Until about 1950 we had no refrigerator, but an ice chest, an invention that came to Australia from the U.S.A. in gold rush times. A large block of ice in the top part of a cabinet cooled the food stored in the lower part. This avoided rottenness, but the flavor of the various foods became collectivized. Butter tasted of meat, milk of fish, and everything of rabbits.

The fridge, long saved up for, arrived from Melbourne like manna for a needy people. Neighbors who did not have one came in to gawk at its smooth green newness and to sniff its strange Bakelite smell. No one knew how to regulate it. Immediately we made ice cream—for my brother and me this was the whole point of a fridge—but it came out as hard as the ice in the superseded ice chest. Even the chooks could not eat our homemade ice cream.

The snacks and lollies (candy) that we devoured were of British type. There were Columbine Caramels and Licorice Allsorts and Fry's and Cadbury's chocolates, which we read in *Boys' Own Annual* were also eaten by London kids. There was coconut ice, pink and white and sugary, as irresistible as it was ruinous to the teeth. There was Violet Crumble, a chocolate-coated stick of honeycomb so brittle that you had to bite it off with the thing well inside your mouth, or else shower the floor with glasslike fragments.

On those happy occasions when my mother's parents came from Melbourne to yarn and inspect, my grandmother would offer "bread and cheese and kisses," a term from the Old Country (as she called Britain) for a thick cheese sandwich. And she would prepare bread and butter covered with hundreds and thousands, a confection of sugar and water in the form of tiny colored beads.

Christmas time was hot, and sometimes we ate the celebratory dinner on the beach at Lakes Entrance, with the legs of a folding card table, and our own feet and ankles, immersed in shallow water. Yet we prepared the meal with slavish adherence to British ways, just as we sent and received London-derived Christmas cards depicting snow-sprinkled carriages and reindeers. In hundred-degree heat we ate a heavy plum pudding covered with hot custard and topped with whipped cream that still smelled of cows, twisting our tongues in search of the sixpenny coins secreted in its gluey depths.

During all meals we had to wave our arms to ward off blowflies. Affectionately known as "blowies," these large buzzing insects were a part of our lives we just had to accept. Wire screens, insecticide sprays, and floppy swatters on a long handle notwithstanding, we could never keep the blowies away from the food, our bodies, and especially the dunny.

In the brown dry sheep country of Longwood, and also to a degree in Bruthen, we lived with an awareness of bushfires. We learned the awful danger signs and the puny precautions. When the paddocks behind our house became tinder dry, the blades of grass brittle enough to snap in our fingers, our parents would become edgy and our dogs restless. If smoke lay on the horizon and dust came swirling from the north, and the water tanks that were fed by pipes from the galvanized iron roof of our house became low, a tight-lipped gloom descended on the household and all of Longwood. Magpies sat on boughs with heads cocked listening for something. My sister's crazily loquacious cockatoo lowered its voice from a scream to a mumble. The cats meowed pitiably. Our goldfish, usually dashing, would look lethargic as the water in their tub became low and as hot as a cup of tea, and we all realized—perhaps even the goldfish—that there was no more water to replenish the tub.

In bushfire weather a day could begin to melt you by breakfast time. We prayed for a "cool change." We took down curtains and other easily ignited items. We burned breaks around the edges of our two-acre property (which was owned by the education authority); these charred bare patches could be effective against a small fire.

Every summer someone we knew got burned out, losing everything, seeing their house and possessions turn into a heap of ash. As a small child in Longwood I saw my school burned to the ground once (our teacher put too many logs on the wood fire in our classroom) and nearly so a second time; I doubt that my experience was unusual.

When a fire was coming—the flames could travel a kilometer a minute—the sky looked as if a war were in progress beyond the next hill. The blue mountains we loved became a menacing orange wall. A magnificent smell of burning, sweating gum leaves filled the nostrils. Some people who had cars and could not stand the heat or the fear packed a few things and drove off in panic toward the sea. Even horse-drawn "jinkers" and buggies, laden up, could be seen heading off in a cloud of dust.

The leaping, strangely insubstantial-looking flames could reduce a timber house to ashes in half an hour. The smell of a burning property—paint and wood and rubber and plastic—was a terrible one. It was hard to believe that the twisted heap of "galvo" on a bed of gray powder had been a family's abode thirty minutes earlier. Only the chimney, tall and alone, a mocking sentry, connected the present with the past.

The fear, chaos, and helplessness of bushfire days are as near to a war experience as rural Australia ever comes. At such a time human beings become as pathetic as insects.

"How changeable this place is!" cries the young woman in the movie based on Banjo Paterson's *The Man from Snowy River* (this river is quite near Longwood) when a fearful storm suddenly arises. "One moment it's paradise, the next it's trying to kill you." We lived with this dual sense of nature as tender and cruel, abundant and destructive. It drew us all closer together.

The townships of Longwood and Bruthen were hospitable and also nosy. "Calling in" was incessant. If no one was home, you went in the open door and made yourself a cup of tea (a pot was likely sitting ready on the side of the never-cold wood stove) and ate a small iced cake or a Vegemite sandwich at the oilcloth-covered kitchen table. Women spent half their lives with a teapot in one hand asking someone to have a "cuppa." They served warm floury scones with jam and cream on them in the middle of the afternoon to all comers.

Families visited each other after tea (dinner) to gossip, play cards, and admire each other's children. At the end of the evening there appeared a supper of English-style sandwiches, filled with Kraft cheese and shredded lettuce, or corned beef and pickle, or nasturtium leaves from the garden, and pavlovas (a dessert of meringue, fruits, and cream) and rock cakes and cream-filled sponge cakes and lamingtons (cake squares dipped in chocolate and rolled in coconut). All this was pressed upon the guests, who protested at the abundance as they ate.

Few people read much—which gave the Bible an influence by default—and this perhaps helps explain why we didn't all get fat. But any scrap of news flew by word of mouth to every kitchen. If someone came down with measles, everyone knew about it. If a man was beating his wife with a branch, the adults knew it and the children could guess it from the adults' whispering.

National events seldom touched us. Melbourne was as remote to me as Moscow is today. In many ways we led a nineteenth-century life. Our universe was nature and a ragbag of local characters pushed close to each other under its dominance. Our Australia was comfortable and healthy. It was also isolated, socially monolithic, and numb to its identity. Our lives took shape from all these traits.

Such an upbringing branded me a country boy for life. I discovered this when we moved to Melbourne. It was still true decades later when, visiting from the U.S.A. to lecture at Australian universities, I noticed how some of the controversies of the day pitted city slickers against country types.

One day in Bruthen my brother came back from a Sunday School picnic by the river and told me he had been defeated in the sprint race by an "Abo." This surprised both of us. The black people around Bruthen were not part of our lives—to us they were more akin to the emus and the gums than to the white people—and we did not expect them to compete with us in a sports event. Our clergyman had seen Aborigines gazing at the picnic from a distance and invited them to have a go at the races.

While in Bruthen to pick beans and sell hand-woven baskets door to door, the blacks slept in tents by weeping willow trees on the riverbank. Sometimes Aboriginal children would attend school for a few weeks, seldom making much progress. My father called the Aborigines "blackfellows." It was not, I think, a term of contempt; but while he welcomed these quiet kids to his school, he did not think they were on a level with white people. Occasionally he would praise one for a hunting feat or a brilliant boomerang throw. My mother simply felt the Aborigines were dirty (which sometimes they were) and told us to keep away from them.

Once or twice a year Bruthen people packed the Mechanics Institute Hall to hear the Aborigines of the Lake Tyers Gum Leaf Band give a concert. Making music by blowing through partly torn eucalyptus leaves to the beat of a wallaby-skin drum, these jet-black visitors from the nearby Aboriginal reserve, fully and gaudily dressed for the occasion, would pierce the night with a mixed program of British and Aboriginal songs.

We were so racist that we were unaware of the possibility of race prejudice. I never had a black friend in Bruthen—around Longwood no Aborigines existed—or imagined I could have one. Nor did a black person ever visit our house. At the lolly shop we bought Niggerboy licorice and never knew the brand name was an insult to millions of fellow human beings.

The Davidson family next door ran a general store that sold liquor in Bruthen's main street. Each year Mr. Davidson or his wife went to Melbourne to renew the store's liquor license, and they were always asked what they would do if an Aborigine came in and asked for beer or whiskey. It was against the law to sell liquor to any Aborigine, and these shopkeepers carefully responded that they would refuse the request. "I knew the rules," Mrs. Davidson recalls today.

At the Bruthen school I did song-and-dance acts with a dark-haired, demure, exquisitely polite girl whom I shall call Agnes. In Sunday School, Agnes and I sat next to each other, which enabled me to smell her spicy-scented hair and the cotton of her frock. Only decades later did I discover that Agnes was half Chinese. Her mother was an attractive scarlet character who had settled down with Bruthen's only Chinese, the local chemist who doubled as the SP (illegal) bookmaker. The "good families," as my mother called them, apparently disapproved of Agnes's father, both for a casual marital situation and for being Oriental.

But my father and the clergyman did not seem to share these feelings; in sparse Bruthen I suppose both of them needed any customer they could get. Perhaps that is why Agnes and I held hands for so many vacant hours after school and Sunday School.

As children we were only dimly aware that Agnes was different from everyone else. Yet for many Bruthen adults an uncomfortableness with that difference was the seed of racism. Looking back, I wonder what Agnes thought of the notices, a common boast of quality and mark of Australian defensiveness at that time, that were branded in purple paint inside large packing cases: MANUFACTURED BY EUROPEAN LABOR ONLY.

It was my mother who pushed for the family to leave Bruthen so that we children could be well educated. My sister attended a teachers' training college attached to Melbourne University. My brother and I won scholarships to Wesley College, a Methodist-sponsored public school (in Victoria that means private school) in the heart of Melbourne.

From Bruthen we now and then had taken the Melbourne train to visit our grandparents. "All aboard!" the blue-uniformed man with a loudspeaker would cry from the wonderfully solid platform, and we felt we were spinning toward another planet. The cry "Gippsland train!" at the Melbourne station would end these dreamlike forays to what my brother called "the Big Smoke." But going to school in Melbourne meant a new life.

My mother as a social romantic liked the shift to Melbourne. She got a job teaching school, and this improved our lives and hers. My father as a bush romantic would have preferred to stay by the hills and streams of East Gippsland. As an urban headmaster he pined for the countryside and lost his health. In Melbourne he could not collect junk—screws, old clothes, clippings, anything that came his way—on the same scale as he had done in Longwood and Bruthen. My sister brought her cockatoo to Melbourne, but it caused havoc by pulling the clothes pegs from neighbors' washing lines and terrifying the city children, and soon she had to get rid of it.

At Wesley College, which was founded in Queen Victoria's time, when Melbourne was booming after the gold rushes, we wore purple caps, gray suits, and purple and gold ties. At first it seemed like the rig-out for a fancy dress party. And wearing shoes nearly killed me. In Bruthen I never wore shoes to school, only to Sunday School. My feet had spread and their surface was a leather sole in itself. They did not fit smoothly into the heavy school-regulation black shoes. Getting home from Wesley in the afternoon, I kicked off my shoes with a cry of relief.

Melbourne as a city of the Victorian era was built around a railway system. And in the expansive mood of the time its streets were laid out wide and straight, permitting a network of green trams, which are loved by Melburnians and laughed at by some other Australians. My brother and I traveled to school by train and tram, a fantastic adventure.

In my first week at Wesley a strike stopped red trains and green trams alike, a state of affairs that is frequent in a nation with haughty trade unions. The strike began at noon. When school got out at 3:30 P.M. all of the Wesley boys, as we were proud to be called, seemed to know how to cope by using buses or other means—except my brother and I. We had no idea how to get to our house, ten kilometers away in the lower-middle-class suburb of Murrumbeena, and we were too scared to ask. So we walked home, following streets nearest to the train line that we knew went by Murrumbeena. The shoes seemed more awful than ever.

Australian public schools were oaks from the forest of British education, transplanted with amazing fidelity on alien soil. "Certain Methodists of Melbourne," began the book of school history given to Wesley pupils, its endpapers of purple and gold in a swirling pattern like those of a butcher's ledger book, "in accord with the interest that John Wesley had shown in the cause of true learning," considered "ways and means of establishing a Grammar School."

It was as if Mr. Wesley were a universal figure whose link with Australia did not need to be explained. Indeed every headmaster of Wesley College until World War Two (with one exception) had been a British import, and those who did not die on the job retired to Britain. Yet Melbourne's many Church of England public schools were even more Britain-oriented than my school. It was rather terrifying to be addressed at school by my surname. When in an informal moment a master would utter the word "Ross," I felt an immense softness.

Wesley College owed much of its handsome physical self to aspirin. Two brothers who had made a fortune from a product marketed as Aspro (its purplish packet bore a resemblance to our Wesley caps) made a gift to the school in the late 1930s. Up went the yellow sandstone pillars and walls, beautifully placed among green playing fields on grand St. Kilda Road, within which I exchanged "nature" for "society."

After World War Two the school broadened as more parents grew dissatisfied with a state education system bursting at the seams. My headmaster was not only an Australian but a "state school boy." Wilfred Frederick built upon a tradition—strenuousness and sentiment were its themes, expressing the earnestness and optimism of the Victorian era—derived from Rugby School in Britain. But not having attended a public school, as his predecessors all had done, Frederick did not want Wesley to be a copy under blue skies of a status-conscious British public school. "Freddy dismantled the sports mystique," one of my teachers recalls today. "There was a nexus between sports and public school snobbism that he didn't like."

As a nation, Australia is more attuned to sports, and generally better at them, than Britain; but a delight in kicking a football, gliding through water, or spinning a cricket ball is quite a different thing from the public school sports mystique. Freddy encouraged boys (there were no girls) to feel that books and the arts and public issues were as important as sports. He also clipped the wings of the military tradition by making the cadet corps voluntary, and setting up a community service scheme for boys who preferred butter to guns.

In my case it was literally butter: I did my community service at an orphanage where, to my shame, I mainly ate the sandwiches that were generously, and hopefully, served to us for afternoon tea midway through our work of cleaning and gardening. Once the sandwiches, with their fresh brown bread, German sausage, and thick layer of strong-tasting bright yellow Australian butter, had vanished from their plates, I seemed able to forget the orphans and think only of going home to play cricket and look at my stamp collection.

The motto of Wesley College, "Dare to be Wise,"[2] will always be part of my consciousness, though I have forgotten the mottos of Melbourne and Harvard universities, from which I later took degrees. Many of us were devoted to the school; purple and gold was my way of life.

Freddy brought to Wesley a master called Morris Williams, a Methodist clergyman's son who did everything with passion. His religion, like that of many children of the manse of his generation, was chipped away by secular pressures until it became an agreeable social idealism. He was a Labor Party member and a rather ferocious pacifist. These enthusiasms rubbed off on a bare slate like me.

There was in the 1950s a tendency to equate scholastic excellence with science. This prejudice obstructed me the more thoroughly because my brother, three years my senior, excelled in science and was bent on becoming an engineer. If I was any good I was supposed to be able to do well what he did well. But the classes in algebra and physics were dull for me. During these sessions some of us masturbated under our desks, competing with each other to see who could do it the most times within the span of a school day (the record was eight).

Morris Williams rescued me from science—and to a degree from masturbation—by showing me that the study of society and of Asia was an alternative path to scholastic excellence. On the topic of Asia, which enlightened Wesley allowed to be taught alongside all the Latin and geometry, Red Morry (as the pupils of high social class called Williams) made a mark even on the boys from the fancy suburbs. He dwelt upon two simple but to me quite new facts: Our nation was located in Asia; and within Asia the era of empires—including Britain's—was ending and a less Europe-centered future was in the cards.

Issues of life-style as well as the study of politics made me more conscious of social class than before. In Longwood and Bruthen I had not been aware that other people had more costly possessions than I.

2. Perhaps better rendered "Have the Courage to Use Your Own Reason," the phrase is from a passage in Horace: "He that begins has half done. Dare to be wise: make a beginning. He that puts off the time for living to right purpose is like the clown waiting for the stream to flow by; but still flows that stream, and still will flow, rolling on forever." (Ep. 1, ii, 40)

But Wesley boys who took the train to and from Toorak or the bayside suburbs talked of habits (their fathers' drinking Scotch) and hobbies (sailing yachts) that were novel to me. Despite Australia's proud egalitarian tradition, a country boy whose father taught school was not the social equal, I found out, of the son of a city lawyer or businessman or professor.

Not to speak of a Jew. "Even after Freddy began to make changes," Red Morry said to me in 1984, "some anti-Semitism remained at Wesley." Williams recalled being criticized in the staff room for "encouraging Jewish boys." Some fellow masters called him "the Jew."

Jews had started to attend Wesley but perhaps not yet to feel completely at home there. Other variations from the Anglo-Saxon norm— southern Europeans, Aborigines, Asians—did not confront us at Wesley in the 1950s. Even Catholics were virtually outside our realm, except when we played cricket or football against Xavier College, and then we were conscious every minute that our opponents were not of our faith and must be treated warily.

As at other Melbourne public schools, Christianity was argued for, not clamped upon the pupils, and its social implications were stressed. The chaplains tended to be mild but intelligent men who could be relied upon to be quietly on your side if you struck trouble.

Occasionally we had a speaker from church circles who was less rational but more arresting. I recall one Reverend Jones, a man who looked like a shriveled walnut, except for a face glowing pink with religious enthusiasm. His topic was happiness. Eyes twinkling, his tiny body bobbing about in a three-piece suit, he told a fascinated if slightly bemused audience that there were three keys to happiness: Get right with God; You can't buy it; Give it away. Before our eyes, doctrinal Christianity was melting away under the Australian sun.

Wesley gave boys an experience of the bush by establishing a log cabin camp in the blue hills above Melbourne, to which classes went in rotation to chop down trees, watch birds, and cook at campfires. But it was playing games compared with living in Longwood or Bruthen. Chum Creek was in the tenacious Australian tradition of trying to keep alive a bush legend long alien to the lives of most Australians ("new chum," an old bush term, was the name used at Wesley for a newly arrived boy).

Sedate ballroom dancing was the accepted social setting for Wesley boys to see girls at night. For a gala we would polish our shoes, struggle into collars that always seemed too tight, and then go—in the family car if we were lucky—to pick up our girl in her rustling taffeta frock. Sometimes we would invest in a frangipanni, meant to bowl the girl over in between dancing the fox-trot and the Pride of Erin. But it was not easy to get through the layers of taffeta. Nor did girls like the idea of their frilly frocks getting grass stains on them in a corner of the back garden. Inside the house, parents stayed awake in bed until they heard their son or daughter come in the front door; its click brought a sigh of relief that danger was over until next Saturday evening.

The streets of Murrumbeena, the Melbourne suburb where I lived with my parents and brother and sister, were bordered with a nature strip, a sliver of public garden between the sidewalk and the road, on which flowering plums with wine-colored leaves rose at intervals from manicured grass. Insects and birds were everywhere: cicadas buzzing from the bushes on hot nights, sparrows dancing on the windowsills, an occasional sea gull soaring up from Port Phillip Bay.

Each home in Murrumbeena was a miniature rural property. One's "block" of land, far larger than the house, was a guarded domain of privacy and a small model of Jeffersonian productivity. In the backyard most families kept chooks, maintained a workshop for doing jobs that in America have long been done by tradesmen, and grew some vegetables. The tomatoes we grew tasted like tomatoes. One's front garden was virtually a religious issue, and people in the street who did not cut and water their lawn, prune their shrubs, and produce a decent show of azaleas or roses or hydrangeas were treated as infidels.

The homes were functional bungalows, with little variation in shape, color, or furnishing from one suburb to another. Red tile roofs. Brick or stucco exteriors (weatherboard in the working-class parts). Small windows heavily shrouded with curtains. Kitchens were large and convenient, with cupboards full of bottled fruit—stewed pears and peaches and plums stored away in glassy neatness for an indefinite future. Living rooms looked unlived in and dining rooms were seldom dined in. There were standard lamps, carpets in swirling floral patterns, and bulky radiograms built not for their sound but for their polished appearance. In our dining room there was a heavy sideboard from which to serve the heavy meals, and a glass-fronted china cabinet where crystal glasses, fragile fruit bowls, and an oval silver meat dish with a high curved cover were kept. A grandfather clock stood sentry in our hallway, and when it chimed I felt like a European in a cathedral.

The ad-fueled craze for consumer goods had not yet arrived. An uncle of mine, a mining engineer, subscribed to the *Saturday Evening*

Post. When the well-thumbed glossy pages eventually reached our household, I was amazed at the world of streamlined cars, ingenious gadgets, and prosperous family life that glowed from its pages. We all assumed this was an American way of life that would never come to Murrumbeena, though we would have welcomed it.

The homes of Murrumbeena were castles of the family. Although they were culturally barren for the most part, despite near-middle-class income levels, they were havens of comfort, privacy, and tranquillity. Housewives spent much time polishing their castles. It was the duty of their station, as assumed in pre-women's-liberation Australia. Houses smelled of wax polish, Brasso, phenyl, and other cleaning products. Front doorknobs gleamed.

The social centers of Murrumbeena in the 1950s were the tightly denominationalized Christian churches, with their twice-on-Sunday services, tennis games, card evenings, and youth clubs—and the milk bar. The small shop was a symbol of Australian suburbia in the 1950s, and the milk bar was the quintessential small shop. A food and newspaper store, it was named for the milk shakes, long and cold and sweet, which were for schoolkids the height of gastronomic exoticism. It smelled of cakes, ice cream, newsprint, and the drying malt-flavored milk left at the bottom of the metal containers in which the milk was "shaken."

For us young people, the milk bar was a badge of our isolation and our hearty enjoyment of life's simpler pleasures. We drank milk, not beer or wine. We had no cars; a Malvern Star bicycle was the limit of our reach for mobility. TV and the cheap paperback had not quite arrived. During school holidays we hung around the milk bar to catch the eye of sheilas, a term for girls that came to Australia from Ireland, and outside the front door, wire-screened to keep out blowflies, the bolder kids of our circle told dirty jokes and showed off French postcards from St. Kilda.

Despite the absence of music, fancy decor, or anywhere to sit, the milk bar was our haven, as the back fence was for our mothers. At intervals we satisfied the uneasy milk bar proprietor by buying milk shakes, Violet Crumbles, lemon tarts, and Cherry Ripes with pocket money that we had earned from delivering newspapers or selling empty lemonade bottles.

A twenty-minute trip in an ocher-red train took us to meet friends under a row of clocks at Melbourne station showing train departure times, a natural rendezvous point in a railway city, and then to a five-o'clock show in the big cinemas of Collins and Swanston streets, with their swishing velvet curtains, pink and blue lights that dimmed gradually, heavily made-up usherettes in maroon uniforms, and mirrored counters at which we bought Black Magic chocolates during interval.

And there was the Royal Agricultural Show, which had begun after the gold rushes of the 1850s as a farmers' showcase and had gradually become a carnival of games and stalls, an arena in which city and country met. You could pick the farm families by the air they exuded of feeling uncomfortable in the clothes they had on, and by the broad-brimmed felt diggers' hats of the men.

The show offered sheepdog trials, wood-chopping contests, and farmers' wives' displays of knitting and baking. There was a Grand Parade of smelly Corriedales, Friesians, cashmeres, and huge black pigs, all done up in colored ribbons, for those intrigued by animals (I no longer was) to gawk at. Now a boy of the Big Smoke, I liked the "city" part of the show: shooting galleries; a sideshow of a House of Horrors or the Fattest Lady in the World; the Big Dipper, which churned my stomach but made me feel very alive and proud when I stepped off it at the end. Especially I liked the "show bags" with their lollies and nicely packaged samples of fancy foods we could not afford to buy in shops. It was in a Royal show bag that I first discovered peanut butter; for some months this product from America seemed to me the most wonderful food in existence.

Great sporting days also took us into town on the train. There were the finals of the Melbourne football season—the game is called "Australian Rules," an echo of the convict-derived stress on regulations of Australian culture—which were a time of collective madness for all who were sane. Clutching a saveloy, crimson with Rosella tomato sauce, lying in a roll of bread as soft and white as a nun's thigh, we took up positions in the outer stand amidst the gesticulating beer bottles and the shouts of abuse ("You weak bastard"; "You bloody old woman"), necks craned to watch each bounce, see each kick and "mark," trying to help by sheer power of attention the fortunes of our team.

And there were cricket test matches, when Australia played foreign teams. On the morning of a test match I found myself glancing at my watch to count the diminishing minutes until the first ball. At noon the magic began. Australian batsmen and bowlers in their green caps were measured against "Poms" or Indians or South Africans or the wizards from the West Indies.

An extremely exciting day dawned for us in 1954. For weeks Wesley College and Melbourne in general had been making practical and mental preparations for it. We rose early and polished the brass lions on our purple caps. Hours before the normal departure time we took the train and tram to school. On this day the Queen of England was visiting Melbourne!

My mother inspected me minutely to be sure that I was worthy of the day. There was a tiny egg stain on my purple and gold tie. It was removed to avoid any offense to our sovereign. As I left the house I said to my father, "By the time I return this evening I will have seen the Queen of England!"

We Wesley boys had the dazzling privilege of lining the royal route between Essendon airport and Melbourne city. For half a day we waited. Our masters taught us to wave and summarized for us the history of the British monarchy. Elizabeth II arrived. In the past she had existed for me as an oil painting and a high-pitched voice on the radio with her Christmas Message; now she was on Australian soil, dropping by, as it were, for a cuppa tea.

Her face pale and smooth, she was wearing a small round green hat. Her husband sat beside her; each of them had a slight smile and one arm bent high as if it had been injured. We had seen our monarch, and it seemed that life could never be the same again.

Now, after twenty years in the U.S.A., much of it spent trying to understand China, I turn my mind again to Australia, retracing old paths and delighting in new ones in several journeys of rediscovery. I return to search for a new Australia bursting from an old skin. I come to see how much of the past British flavor lingers, and how great the American influences are. I wonder if the massive Italian and Greek immigration of some years back has given Melbourne and Sydney a European style, whether the immigrants have begun to reach for political power, and how the more recent arrivals from Asia and the Middle East are faring.

I talk with Prime Minister Robert Hawke and with his two immediate predecessors, Gough Whitlam and Malcolm Fraser, three very different men who together form a political history of late twentieth-century Australia. I call, too, on the premiers of the Australian states and roam their colorful capital cities to hear what people think of their leaders, their nation, and themselves.

In the heart of the continent I see "lakes" that are mere basins of yellow powder, bereft of water for fifteen thousand years, and rivers that do not flow to the sea but start near the coast and flow inland until they disappear. I see kangaroos that live in trees and the lyre bird that builds a trash heap and lays its eggs there, abandoning them to hatch. On verdant islands at the Great Barrier Reef in Queensland, I face the kaleidoscope of color and the symphony of song of scores of different exotic birds, in lush rain forests where man seems irrelevant. Moving to the far north and the far west, I have on my mind the claims of the frontier states of the sunbelt, rich in minerals and tourism potential, to be the center of gravity of tomorrow's Australia, taking over from the cold south with its worn manufacturing base and its lack of entrepreneurial zip.

And what of social values? Have the civil rights belatedly won by Aborigines brought them into the mainstream of Australian life? Is Australia finally coming to terms with the Asian region in social, economic, and security policies, or could the tug between history and geography wrench the nation apart, dividing it by race before it has made up its mind to whom it belongs and for what it stands?

I go back to my home township of Bruthen to see if rural Australia, despite the economic gloom that has replaced the mood of effortless prosperity of the 1950s and 1960s, is still a place of mateship, self-reliance, and a sense of community.

Above all, I wonder as I drive into Melbourne under a high wide sky of blue with banks of silver, if Australia can solve its many problems, truly find itself, and somehow redeem the hopes of the Western world by becoming in the twenty-first century a dynamic new civilization, as America, redeeming Europe's lost hopes, became before it.

TWO

Impressions Today

To realize the sparseness of the sixth largest among the world's nations, the only nation that is also a continent, imagine a land as large as the U.S.A. but virtually without people for the first 3,000 kilometers inland from the west coast—as if in America nothing but sand and spinifex lay in between Los Angeles and Washington, D.C. This is Australia.

The coastline runs for a massive 36,735 kilometers, nearly double that of the U.S.A. The state of Western Australia is eight times as large as Italy. The magnificent northeastern state of Queensland is just about five times the size of Japan. The booming, breezy city of Perth in the west is closer to Bali and Singapore than to the cities of Queensland.

Go to Australia from New York, and the logical way to reach Sydney or Melbourne is through California and across the Pacific, perhaps with a stop in Hawaii, Tahiti, Samoa, or Fiji. But if your destination is Perth, it is as short to proceed through Europe and the Near East and across the Indian Ocean.

I recall my first flight from Melbourne to Southeast Asia many years ago. Several hours after the plane took off on the seven-hour flight to Manila, a Texan traveler boomed to the steward of Philippine Airlines, "What country is that land below?" as he pointed to a parched red expanse.

"That is Australia's Northern Territory," the Filipino steward replied politely.

"Don't fool with me, young man," the Texan snapped. "We've been flying half a day." But the Filipino was right. Any flight from Sydney or Melbourne or Adelaide to Indonesia, Singapore, Malaysia, or the Philippines passes much of the time over central and northern Australia, that "great dry, tawny dog-biscuit of a land," as Ronald Conway has called it.

Most of Australia is dry beyond a European's imagining. Annual evaporation exceeds annual rainfall across 70 percent of the land. Sixty-five percent of Australia's land is used for farming of one type or another, but of this farmland a staggering 96 percent is grazing land; only 4 percent of Australian farmland has enough water to support crops. Death by thirst was as commonplace in nineteenth-century Australia as death on the roads is today; men killed themselves to avoid dying of thirst.

In Alice Springs, a spirited oasis town in the middle of nowhere, an officer of the Royal Flying Doctor Service tells me of a recent death by thirst in central Australia. "An Aboriginal woman. She went walkabout and didn't come back. At times the Aborigines, who know the land well, can get overconfident."

For all of their cherished bushman legend, 80 percent of Australians cluster on the Boomerang Coast, a thin arc around the southeastern seaboard from Adelaide to Brisbane, comprising only one tenth of Australia's area. And 60 percent of that 80 percent live in Melbourne and Sydney. In three of the six states—Victoria, Western Australia, and South Australia—no less than 70 percent of the population live in the state capital city. Few Australians have visited much of their huge sparse land.

Australian culture and politics center upon Melbourne and Sydney, where ideas and the arts flourish and the rest of the world seems within reach. The accessible parts of Western Australia and Queensland form a sunbelt with a resource-rich economy and a desirable life-style; the other parts of these two states, hot and vast, together with the Northern Territory, are so much a wilderness that one can hardly even speak of a frontier—frontier to what?

South Australia is dry, progressive, and urbane, still very pleased that it never had convicts, and producer of 80 percent of the world's opals. Though tucked away at one end of the Boomerang Coast, Adelaide as a place to live is in many ways second to no city in Australia. "If I couldn't live in Sydney," says Margaret Whitlam, wife of the former prime minister, in her Paris apartment, "I'd prefer Adelaide." A city of stone houses and verandas with white-painted posts and wrought iron decor, Adelaide is a soft and rational place and home to a magnificent arts festival. Spurning the norm, the Adelaide Hilton Hotel's restaurants offer oysters in the quantity of either seven or thirteen.

The island of Tasmania is pretty and anti-mainland, and like South Australia, it is different. There is an English flavor given by its cool climate and the relative absence of the Irish race from its immigration history. Old convict jails seem to outnumber factories, and Hobart on Sunday is surely the inspiration for the Australian expression "as dull as a month of Sundays." Tasmania lacks the dingo, since this miserable animal arrived in Australia only after the island had been cut off from the mainland by rising seas, some twelve thousand years ago, and it still possesses the Tasmanian devil, *Sarcophilus,* long extinct on the mainland.

"Tasmania?" exclaims Neil Brown, deputy leader of the Liberal Party (a fairly conservative party), as he offers me a lightning survey of the states. "The Tasmanians grow hops, fart around redecorating Victorian mansions, and make Devonshire teas for tourists." But Tasmania has produced two of Australia's finest poets, A. D. Hope and James McAuley. To a degree South Australia and Tasmania present a sedate alternative to the faster-paced major states and the raw frontier states (though recently Adelaide has been aiming at a trendier image).

The well-scrubbed little non-city of Canberra, Australia's capital, acts as a nonchalant adjudicator of the squabbles between Sydney and Melbourne, and of the larger battles between both these cities and the frontier states.

When the British founded Sydney two hundred years ago, they called the area Botany Bay because a strong first impression was of the flowers and trees, and still today Sydney, Australia's oldest and largest city, seems above all a slice of nature. On rolling hills around a sparkling blue harbor, the red-tiled roofs beneath which 3.4 million people live are softened by green plants and flowering shrubs. Parks are plentiful, and people talk much about boats and gardens and swimming.

In Melbourne, the end of the international road, you find a high vast sky whose light overwhelms, making no compromise with the puny life of men and women below, and a silence that allows you to hear the rustle of a gum tree as you exit from the airport terminal of a city of 2.9 million people.

City train interiors are bare of ads or maps, as if the availability of space exceeds the need for it. Dotting the urban areas are large solid-brick public toilets, like small houses. Australia has never had a revolution, a dictatorship, or a civil war, but it might have one of these things if there were too few toilets.

The cities are clean, I remark to a Chinese student who attends a lecture I give in Melbourne, and he rejoins that it's because there are so few people to spread litter. We discuss the mumbling Australian speech, and again he sees it as space's victory: "Historically, there were few people for Australians to talk to." Coming from China, he was amazed to find in the residential colleges of Australian universities that students have a room of their own. "Living in such isolation, you see why Australians are inarticulate," he remarks. "How are you going?" people ask, meaning how are you *doing*. Perhaps their choice of word reflects a nation's arduous experience of moving across huge distances.

In Europe and America and Japan, cities intrude upon the countryside; in Australia the countryside invades the cities. This was true a century ago, when bush values gave flavor to the cities (large as the cities already were), and it is almost as true today.

Much of Brisbane, the informal and likable capital of Queensland, looks like a horticultural exhibition of the acacia's gray-green boughs and the jacaranda's dusky-purple flowers and fernlike leaves. Within the city of Adelaide, the serene and handsome capital of South Australia, famous for wine and churches, and in recent years for a well-run Grand Prix, you can enjoy the perfume of wattle and the tang of gum leaves.

One can become lost in dreams strolling through Perth's inner-city garden reserve, King's Park. A riot of boronia, orchid, and kangaroo paw spreads beneath magnificent gums, with slim gray trunks that soar up to twisted branches, and peeling bark in strips like smoked glass, and long thin leaves in a shade of green that suggests long years with dust.

In Melbourne on a summer day the north wind is a physical force beating at your body, hardly less so than it is two hundred kilometers away in the wheatfields. For the crowds of shoppers riding trams and licking ice creams in Bourke Street, the dreaded northerly is as tangible as a fire in front of the face.

In Canberra, which has only 255,000 people, you grasp the meaning of the neutron bomb, which kills life but leaves the environment intact. Despite a more established look than twenty years ago, as gums and flowering plums grow taller and office blocks multiply, the national capital still resembles a very large golf course surrounded by hills in seductive hues. It has a few "cared-for streets," the Queensland novelist Rodney Hall observes, "on which its cared-for citizens may occasionally be seen." Its buildings dot the green expanse like animals which have strayed by to feed on the grass.

In few other nations could a realistic novel set in an inner city have a passage such as this one from *The Children's Bach,* Helen Garner's story of love and separation in Melbourne:

> She stood among the rank stalks of the tomato plants. Her legs itched and the sun struck through the back of her cotton nightdress. A bird sat on the fence and trilled madly. It spotted her and flipped away across the vegetable patch to a tree, where it threw back its head, opened its beak like a pair of scissors, and sang tune after tune.

It is no accident that Australia is one of the few countries in the West that has a strong rural political party, or that for many years this party called itself simply "Country Party." Nor can the enviable social peacefulness of Australia be explained apart from nature as a safety valve for urban frustrations; a few hours at the beach, which is often just a stone's throw from office or factory, dissipates a lot of tension.

If Australian faces look set and unused to frequent communication, the words that come out of them are unique in all the world. When an Australian swimmer, Mark Tonelli, won the hundred-meter backstroke at a British Commonwealth Games, he was asked what Princess Anne said when she presented him with the gold medal. "I couldn't understand her," Tonelli replied. "She speaks English and I speak Australian."

An easy way to remember how to pronounce Australia as the locals do (ending in "ail-yer") is to memorize a famous bushmen's chorus:

> *Stringybark and greenhide,*
> *That will never fail yer!*
> *Stringybark and greenhide,*
> *The mainstay of Australia.*

In "Austrail-yern," a good screw means a good wage—nothing else— but being stuffed has a more intimate meaning than eating a lot of food. "Your call has been placed in a queue," says a girl on the phone at an airline office. "Please wait a little while."

The manner of expression can be as blunt as the vocabulary is strange. Cries the ad across the front of a building near Sydney airport: GOT ANY AIR FREIGHT, MATE? At the Todd Hotel in Alice Springs I ask the price of a room. "I'll get someone to sort you out on that," replies the young man at the desk. In Sydney a female taxi driver looks across at me and says, "You look as if you need a good night's sleep." I explain I have been twenty hours in a plane. "Poor wretch," she grunts.

"Two sausage rolls," says a man in a shirt and tie, without any preliminary greeting, as he shuffles into a snack shop in Melbourne's splendid boulevard Royal Parade.

"Sauce, mate?" says the man behind the counter, a Lebanese-Australian, as he reaches for the greasy pastries.

"Yeah."

When he is given his sausage rolls, smeared with tomato sauce of a Technicolor red, the customer grunts, "Ta." Then he slides out of the shop. There are no farewells.

The word "actually" is as overworked as a fridge at an Australian summer party. At times it is a softening word; at other times it is a defensive husk for an obliquely asserted opinion. It can be an Australian's signal that, despite the modest sentiments he is expressing, he thinks he knows better than you do.

Australians are forever making mashed potatoes of words to render them cozy. Years ago the post–World War Two refugees became "reffos," the sustenance workers became "sussos," and we Presbyterians were "Presbos." Today ads on the college bulletin boards ask for a roommate who is a semi-vego (semi-vegetarian). Brisbane becomes "Brissy." Fremantle becomes "Freo." If (with an Australian accent) you say "barbecue" rather than "barbie," many Australians will think you are up yourself (snobbish). Hong Kong is called "Hongkers," as if to make that Chinese jewel less alien to a dinkum Aussie.

I ask Helen Garner, the novelist, about the cozy suffixes. "I think it's a desperate attempt to drag the place down to a manageable size," she replies.

Political debate is extremely raucous. Says the leader of the opposition during 1984: "The prime minister's a little crook." At a dinner party of New Zealanders in Melbourne, one lady from Auckland, asked her first impressions of Australia, says primly, "We were shocked by the swearing in parliament."

Despite the language, a Briton or American can find the cities familiar. Many Australians have the precise gray look and the stiff walk of Britons. The suburban rows of generous plots and gums and terracotta tiles and swimming pools stretch on like those of Los Angeles. Sydney has the look and to a degree the feel of San Francisco. Melbourne's architecture, like Toronto's, recalls the Manchester or Edinburgh of Queen Victoria's time. Queensland lives by a muted Mediterranean rhythm. The daily round in Adelaide suggests provincial England with sunshine added. Perth reminds an American of cities of the southwest U.S. sunbelt.

You can spend a lot of time in urban Australia and find none of the expected romance and rawness. Can this be the bare brown frontier depicted in Nevil Shute's *A Town Like Alice* and its TV adaptation? How could Henry Lawson and Banjo Paterson pluck heart-wrenching stories and verse from this enervating blandness? Where is the beauty and the terror of *The Man from Snowy River;* the dreaming and despair in the paintings of Peter Booth and Mike Parr; the quirkiness and tension of Paul Cox's movies *Man of Flowers* and *My First Wife?* Is all the violence and charm of Australian history over?

The triumph of the automobile, TV, and the multinational corporation make it seem that Australian individualism and amateurism have fallen before the juggernaut of international progress. The car, hailed in the early twentieth century as the savior of the bush, has nevertheless veiled Australia's face. An Australian at the wheel of a Toyota seems less distinctive than an Australian on the back of a horse. Death by drunken driving (more than a thousand die this way in Australia each year) is an ordinary Western death of the 1980s compared with that of Harold Holt, the prime minister who in 1967 stepped into the surf near Melbourne for a Sunday morning swim and disappeared forever.

TV carries so much of the life of the world into Australian living rooms that Australia hardly seems an island anymore. Soap operas are often the same as those in Chicago or London. TV news is less distinctively Australian in content and presentation than radio news was thirty years ago.

Still there are sights and smells and sounds that can be found nowhere else. The squawk of a magpie swooping low to try and peck at my head—on a main street in the national capital! The pungent, dusty odor of the world's best dried apricots and pears and peaches. The rapier reach of Vegemite's smell whipping up to the nostrils from breakfast toast. (This yeast spread was devised by a pharmacist, and many Americans find it tastes like it.) "Orright," said softly at times and with a metallic grind at other times; but always the words "all right" are squashed out of shape with Australian sledgehammer casualness. "Good-oh" spread around like a soothing balm, its suffix giving a complacent "near enough" or "she'll be orright" tone to the term of assent.

The fussy notices, often unheeded, and so revealing of Australian culture, make me feel at home. BOYS OVER SIX YEARS OF AGE NOT ADMITTED, says the sign at the door of ladies' toilets in the British-looking city railway stations, where the number of doors labeled NO ENTRY must set a world record. By the tennis courts at Melbourne University I find the superfluous MISUSE OF RACQUETS CAN CAUSE DAMAGE TO COURT. At the piers that punctuate Melbourne's bay there are notices saying you may not smoke on the pier, nor hold a public meeting there. KEEP WHOLLY WITHIN THE CAR, you are instructed by placards inside trams and trains.

NO FEMALE SHALL ENTER ANY ENCLOSURE SET APART FOR THE EXCLUSIVE USE OF MALES, cries a rule dating from 1980 at the entrance to the Sydney Domain. NO PERSON SHALL CLIMB ANY TREE OR JUMP OVER ANY SEAT OR FENCE, OR LIE UPON OR UNDER ANY SEAT. On it goes, putting ideas into people's heads for bad behavior in this inner-city park. NO STOCK OR POULTRY; NO AIRCRAFT MAY LAND. And then the coup de grace: NO PERSONS OF REPUTED BAD CHARACTER SHALL ENTER OR REMAIN WITHIN THE GOVERNMENT DOMAIN. Even in Melbourne we never had a notice like that.

FROM HERE ON, says a sign by Obelisk Beach in Sydney, a favorite spot for nudists, ACCESS TO MEMBERS OF THE NAVAL ESTABLISHMENT ONLY. A navy man with a gun stands beside it as day by day thousands of people trudge past. Bathers and navy man alike ignore the prohibition.

The wonderful hedonism of Sydney has not fallen victim to the doubts and setbacks of the 1970s. An American is momentarily startled by the newspaper headline BEST WHITES, but the article beneath it is a feature not on race but on wine. FIFTY LOVELY HOT PUDDINGS is the lead story in another Sydney paper. HOBART LEADER OUT, screams a headline, and it refers not to the fall of a Tasmanian government but to the problems of a yacht that had been favored to win the Sydney–Hobart yacht race.

Australians, even the conservative ones, are casual. A businessman can sound as folksy as a worker, and an academic boozing and barracking at a football game can look like a worker. Yet casual Australia—except in the outback—is not very egalitarian.

The egalitarian *style* can still be found. It is an insult to a cabbie for a man traveling alone to ride in the back seat of a taxi. If you do so, you feel like one of the "poofters" or "dagoes" or "long-hairs" that Alf, in Alan Seymour's play *One Day of the Year,* hates and feels threatened by. In one of Helen Garner's novels a middle-class Melbourne woman feels "the small prickle of power that comes to the one who rides in the back seat" of a car. Yet in the newspapers the sports figures on the back pages are Bill and Mary, while the politicians on the front pages are Mr. and Mrs., never omitting a Sir if the monarch's hand has bestowed one, or a Dr. if someone has even an honorary Ph.D.

"I was so furious last night at the interview done during the intermission of *Tosca* on TV," says Helen Garner, who like me attended a rural primary school, as we lunch at an Italian restaurant in Melbourne. "Did you hear those women with graziers' accents!" She mimics plum-in-the-mouth speech. "You see, I was mocked at school for my very Australian accent." (She also lost her job as a teacher in the Melbourne school system for uttering the word "fuck" in the classroom.)

Australian Rules football is a sport of the people, yet at the famous Carlton Football Club in Melbourne there is a pecking order of four grades of accommodation: the glass-enclosed Special Patrons' Room, in which companies (some Japanese) pay thousands for a seat; the opulent Carlton Football Club room, where one day I notice former prime minister Malcolm Fraser; the Members' rooms with a good bistro; a cafeteria for the Australian people.

In Canberra an invitation arrives to a luncheon with the governor general. I know and like this particular governor general—he taught me briefly at Melbourne University—and I accept. The atmosphere in the mansion overlooking Canberra's hills and gums is eerie. Liveried servants receive me with tight lips beneath a British flag in the midsummer heat. Hanging on the walls of the grand salons are paintings and photos of British royalty and the occasional Australian politician.

No women are present, and the men sit down with His Excellency at a table as long as a cricket pitch. We chat stiffly, peering at each other across the great distance. Even after the excellent Australian wines, I feel a dislocation of time or place, as if the decades have been rolled back to the colonial era, or as if I am in London and these windows through which I see the Canberra hills are just framed Australian paintings.

New and welcome is that Australia is not as isolated as before, nor as worried by its distance from the rest of the world. Objectively, Australia becomes less removed as the Pacific area grows in world importance, and as Europe's weight in the scales of world power declines.

In my day as a student, a combustion occurred between original young spirits of the time and Australian society; it sent people spinning abroad under a kind of compulsion, as if insularity contained its own correcting mechanism, a panting for instant cosmopolitanism. None of my teachers felt my education would be complete unless I did a graduate degree abroad, preferably in Britain. At the same time, "going overseas" was an exotic idea for many of the people of Murrumbeena. They saw the rest of the world—"overseas"—as one remote, undifferentiated entity ranged against Australia's separateness. As I prepared to leave on my first trip in 1960, people gathered round as if this were baptism, or marriage, or death.

Australia's "cultural cringe," as one of my teachers at Wesley College, Arthur Phillips, styled the country's inferiority complex, was an unpleasant feature of life in the 1960s. I cannot gauge the sincerity of the words, but what people in intellectual circles *said* invariably mocked things Australian. It was too extreme to be genuine, and when Nino Culotta (actually John O'Grady) wrote *They're a Weird Mob,* a wry, hilarious portrait of Australia through Italian eyes, I think the mirror shocked a little. People laughed at Culotta's transcription of how we spoke ("Yer not right in the scone") but a shade uneasily; perhaps to wallow in self-criticism was more comfortable than to be criticized.

In the late 1980s making a visit overseas has lost most of its wonder and become a majority activity. Australians are less prone than they used to be to cave in before—or else violently reject—foreign ideas. And Australian urban life has become more cosmopolitan with the presence in virtually every suburb of Chinese restaurants, Italian coffee lounges, and Vietnamese, Greek, and Lebanese grocery stores.

Qantas Airways, on which generations of Australians have gone overseas, is almost like a church of the secular age. Its priests and nuns, the staff of the airline, serve and also strut. ("Ladies and gentlemen," intones the steward, "in the interests of safety I *must* have your *complete* attention!") Its believers line up at the check-in counters to feed on the sacrament of travel, washing themselves clean from the stain of Australia's distance from the world.

Qantas began as a lifeline, a tiny airline in outback Queensland—hence its name: Queensland and Northern Territory Aerial Services—in the 1920s. "To Provide a Helpful Service to the People of the Inland," ran its original statement of purpose, "and a Reserve for the Defense of

Australia." It continues in the tradition of transport as a public service, a noble tradition, and in the less noble one of a cushioned institution existing mainly for a guaranteed clientele—plus the convenience of its own employees.

Qantas is comfortable and timid. It gives the impression of being a little removed from the rough-and-tumble of the marketplace. Terrified of competition, it has pressured the Australian government to keep charter flights from Australian shores. Once you are in the plane, Qantas is excellent. But do not expect imagination or any deals from it on the ground. It lives in the dark green shadows of protectionism. A government airline, Qantas has a civil-service mentality. "On arrival at Sydney you must *surrender* your documents to the authorities!" instructs a purser. Its first-class cabins are full of Australian bureaucrats who help keep it comfortable and timid.

The Australian suburban home has been modernized, though it remains a castle of almost rural tranquillity. Kids live by TV, almost as in America, and the VCR makes the property-owning life even less street-oriented than before.

The phone book, sitting beside an instrument whose dial tone is like the purr of a huge cat, suggests Australia's cultural transition. The granny-isms are there: "If you have too few (or too many) copies of this directory please contact the business manager"; "HINT: If friends have moved, write down their new number." The destination for any call outside Australia still is listed under the quaint heading "Overseas countries."

If the state-owned phone company treats its customers like children or potential felons, there is now an overlay of imperious liberationism on the rigidities that stem from convictism. Women's Refuge Referral Service and Gay Line are prominently listed in the front of the book, and you may dial for Holiday Ideas or Massage. It is possible, too, to dial directly to those Overseas Countries.

A society once narrow and traditional has since the 1970s begun to hang free. As a student I joined a university movement against capital punishment and paraded in picket lines outside the state Parliament House to protest the imminent hanging of a murderer. The ruling conservatives felt the death penalty was a test of resolve and civilization. Our Victorian premier, Henry Bolte, a sincere but narrow farmer, summed up a widespread view among older Australians: "Look, on my farm, if I've got an animal that's no good, I kill it. In society it's the same; with a man who proves to be no good, you put an end to him." Today hanging is a relic of a forgotten past.

People flock to classes in exotic philosophies and self-assertion. Middle-class activists guard the rights of possums, kangaroos, and koala bears. Locally made TV serials like *A Country Practice* deal nonchalantly with rape, venereal disease, teenage abortion, homosexuality, and glue sniffing. Human rights commissions advertise to uncover grievances and announce that complaints are welcome "in any language in the world, including braille." Only Tasmania, rich in historical wrongs, lacks a commission to guard rights.

In public policy there is an overdue but somewhat frenetic quest for compensatory justice for every social group (plus animals and trees) that may in the past have suffered. Given the government-mindedness of Australians, the result is a safety-net society, not venturing much to conquer new territory, preoccupied with a redistribution of existing territory.

The wheel of liberty and authority has made a large turn, and sometimes it hits the individual in the throat once more, only from a different angle. Twenty years ago the Melbourne authorities would not let us read *The Ginger Man, Lady Chatterley's Lover, Another Country,* and *Tropic of Cancer* lest we stray from settled values. Attacking demands for a permissive society, conservative politicians used to ask defensively, "Who gave the permission?" The cabinet member in charge of these matters in Victoria banned books as casually as an orchardist might throw out apples that did not meet his standard. Few causes united us in righteous indignation at Melbourne University in the 1960s as much as anti–book banning.

Today a women's lobby in Tasmania demands the confiscation of the Bible on the ground that it is sexist, and authoritarian idealists in New South Wales seek the removal of a biography of Clive of India from libraries because it prettifies an imperialist.

The officially unleashed free-for-all in the realm of values is matched by an unlicensed free-for-all at a baser level. I go to bed in my apartment on the campus of Melbourne University thinking pleasant thoughts about Australian gentleness and restraint. At 4 A.M. I awake; a noise. That must be a squirrel scratching at the window. It is not a squirrel. Two strong arms are trying to pull off the outer wire screen, which is holding on by a millimeter, three feet from my pillow. I am amazed before I am able to be frightened. In Australia this kind of thing used to be virtually unknown.

"Didn't you know," a professor says to me next day, "the crims from the nearby housing estates don't have to go out to the prosperous streets of Kew to rob now. They stay and steal from Carlton's new bohemian bourgeoisie." In Murrumbeena, where in the 1960s we locked the front and back doors of our house only if we were going away for several days, my family's home is the only one in a street of twenty that has not been burgled in recent years.

After she moved to England, Germaine Greer used to say with some justification that Australian newspapers were the world's worst. When we leftist student activists fought against the White Australia policy in the 1960s, not only did conservative politicians call us Communists, and quite a few trade union figures dismiss our student politics as a game—sons and daughters of "privilege" getting worked up about White Australia because we weren't toiling at an honest job—but no newspaper supported us, and virtually none took us seriously until we had manifestly begun to influence public debate.

MUGGED NUN—CITY PRAYS, cries a headline in the *Melbourne Herald* and a whole style of Australian journalism—narrow and mushy—floods back to mind. Still, in recent years most of the press and TV have improved enormously, and at the same time they have become convinced of their own great importance. "The media brought [John] Gorton down," recalls Neil Brown, a former cabinet minister, referring to the freewheeling and personally undisciplined conservative prime minister who followed Harold Holt in office in the late 1960s. "That was the turning point in its rise of power."

The better papers and TV current affairs programs probe, follow through, and even correct themselves on occasion. "Our papers are dedicated to reducing anxiety," the historian Ken Inglis wrote in 1962 in *Australian Civilization,* but today the same papers seem dedicated to skepticism. "It is a hawk-eyed reader who can ever spot a reference to homosexuality in the *Sun News-Pictorial,*" Inglis wrote in 1962, but today this Melbourne tabloid mentions the term "gay"—quite objectively—almost every day. And a Melbourne that has come crashing down from the mountain of puritanism now publishes Sunday newspapers—unheard of in the 1960s.

Alan Seymour's breakthrough play of the late 1950s, *One Day of the Year,* shook my student circle by mirroring generational tensions over the very sacred Anzac Day. We were rebuked by our parents for mocking when veterans prayed at a dawn service at the Shrine of Remembrance and then got drunk, as if the memory of war or the contact with God were too much for them. The Shrine, a beautiful monument in a park on grand St. Kilda Road, inscribed with the words GREATER LOVE HATH NO MAN, its skylights built so that at the eleventh hour of the eleventh day of the eleventh month—the moment World War One ended—the sun's rays strike the word "love" on the plaque, was probably for my parents the holiest place in Melbourne.

Today observance of Anzac Day has shrunk to a quiet minority activity. It is quite a widespread view that all values and traditions are of equal validity and that Australia, like a customer in a supermarket of World Culture, should shop around for a snazzy new collection.

Australian faces are distinctive, and they can be remarkably grim-looking for the faces of a hedonistic people. From a car, the more settled and temperate parts of Australia can resemble California, but if you get out of the car and walk the streets, you quickly realize you are not in California: the faces are too gaunt, the manner is too reserved. Angular features, a big jaw, eyes half closed, and a way of dealing with you that blends humility with a wooden arrogance. The eyes are seldom really open, but when they are the gaze is steady to the point of being defiant. Although there is a sullen look to many faces, recalling the gloom of the Australian bush, and little in them of the sensuality of the Australian body as a whole, when these same faces communicate there is a disarming warmth and candor and even innocence.

The walk of the ordinary Australian is a shuffle, without the style and purposefulness of the American or European or Japanese walk. The self-satisfied walk of the Australian professional class is another thing: a clipped step, the head set slightly down, the jaw firm in a consciousness of important responsibilities.

The Australian is offhanded, as if he or she is either uninterested in communicating or unused to it. When a remark is ventured or a question asked, "ye-es" is said so slowly and hesitantly that you scent reticence or apathy. In an elevator it is not normal to say, "Which floor?" to a fellow passenger, in an effort to help by pressing the button required. "Oh"—the person will be surprised and uneasy, and he will start forward to press the button himself. A compliment, likewise, is more likely to embarrass than please an Australian (abuse is fine, if it is not fully meant). To avoid an open expression of sentiment, the Australian attempts humor.

The convicts in the early days of Australia, says the historian Manning Clark, were cheeky to the jailers when things were going well, but quick to cringe and whine when prospects turned bleak. During World War Two the allies of Australia encountered something of this dualism. The unsettling double reaction can still be found.

Back in the 1840s, a British observer described Australians in terms that modernity has not entirely undermined: ". . . a wild-looking, sunburnt race, strong, rough, and taciturn, they appear as though they had never lived in crowds, and had lost the desire and even the power to converse." Here is the city dweller with a bushman lurking within his breast. Here is the Australian man who some women say only wants to fuck and then depart. Here is the Australian that the foreigner can find dismayingly indifferent, as if the Dead Heart of Australia has entered his or her soul.

At the squash courts in the sports center at Melbourne University, I glimpse in the male students the bushmen of yesterday. Self-sufficient with their little swags, they come in with their racquets and also their own soap and washer (face cloth). The lean and hungry look gives way to a friendly grunt if I speak first. There is no initial smile or greeting; rarely a handshake and no back slapping. There is a cozy habit of asking a question and then oneself immediately proposing the answer to it.

You observe little *enthusiasm* in Australia. Fathers are not to be seen playing in manifest delight with infants. No one curses or sings in the streets, the way someone can generally be found doing on the streets of an American city. Overstatement is always avoided; few people gush.

Australians don't mind silences between each other, as Americans do, as long as a basic rapport has first been attained. In a cab it will not do—for a man at least—to say nothing to the driver beyond the initial G'day; one is after all in the front seat with him. There must at least be an exchange about the weather. But thereafter, once the possibility of unfriendliness has been disposed of, you may if you wish stay silent in these clean and well-maintained cabs.

You feel a strong bias toward finding common ground. Whether the topic is the weather, the stupidity of politicians, or the way the world is going to pot, the Australian tends to want your agreement. The rising inflection at the end of a phrase ("Well, I don't know-oh . . .") suggests a reaching out to try and limit any gulf between viewpoints. If consensus proves out of reach, a dismissive derisiveness takes over, and barroom rudeness is just around the corner.

The sullenness in the Australian mentality comes partly from the lack of civic spirit in Australia, in contrast with the incurable idealism of the U.S.A., where articulateness is a fruit of civic-mindedness. The sullenness also stems from a fear of being "upped," or eclipsed.

The rejoinder "And so are you" (or "And so do you"), with which we school kids used to counter an epithet or criticism, is a very Australian remark. It embodies both the debunking instinct of Australians and their edginess about anyone getting too far out in front. "The others [previous government] did it," say politicians as they put their hands in the cookie jar. The aggressively empty assertion "I don't go to church, but I'm as good as those who do" is a refrain in secular Australia. Ned Kelly himself set the "I'm as good as you, Jack" tone. Sentenced by a judge to be hanged by the neck until he was dead, the bushranger rasped back, "I will see you there where I go."

At school we used to express this same anti-hero tradition when electing a representative of some kind from our ranks by choosing the worst or most unsuitable boy—a no-hoper or a handicapped boy—to show we didn't take very seriously the democratic procedure we were going through. We didn't want any heroes.

When I saw Gough Whitlam occasionally in the 1960s, and later traveled with him in China, I noticed that he was not entirely comfortable with the term "mate," very common in Labor Party circles as a form of address ("Listen here, mate"). Whitlam's half-playful use of "comrade" ("Is that speech ready, comrade?") seemed to be an attempt to fill the vacuum. "Mate" can suggest a veto on difference or distinction, and that did not suit Whitlam, who is by Australian standards an elitist, not very good at swearing and drinking, not fond of the national game of putting down and putting oneself down.

I recently asked Whitlam during a dinner at his residence in Paris if indeed he is uncomfortable with the term "mate." "I don't use it, I suppose, at all," he replied with an embarrassed smile. "And I'm not aware that people use it to *me*." The former prime minister started and left unfinished several sentences—rare for this syntactical master schooled in Latin—and then went on: "It's somewhat archaic, isn't it?" In the course of the evening he addressed me once or twice as comrade, and I quizzed him on the usage. "Oh, among people I know well I use that one frequently. It produces a bit of a frisson among people."

Just as offhandedness masks a leveling impulse, so the leveling impulse is an expression of a fundamental skepticism. The Australian has seldom given himself to big schemes or soaring beliefs. He sees the flaw, the limitation, more readily than he feels an uplifting drive. This has tended to immunize him against envy of the rich; he views the rich as lucky, not as superior.

Ingrained skepticism makes Australians attractively easygoing. It may also handicap them as they face challenges that call for faith and vision, though I believe that in a true national emergency Australian skepticism would evaporate and Australian nationalism would lift every heart.

I find both a skeptical mentality *and* an urge to change and update Australian ways. Is the resistance of Australians to any grand design weakening since Whitlam ushered in his age of reform in the early 1970s, or is the determination to re-examine everything based on something other than idealism?

Among other contradictions I meet is one between complacency and self-deprecation. "My international contacts are priceless," says a Sydney businessman. "I can pick up the phone and ask God for a beer." Yet some Australians still defer with unnatural timidity to any overseas opinion about their country. Is Australian humility only skin deep?

Perhaps it is nature, once more, that makes Australians what they are. The same historical experience that has produced narrowness has also—for nature, which tyrannizes, also commands respect—made Australians fatalistic and self-mocking, which is unusual in the people of a young country.

Australians are an elemental people, yet many of them still possess a derivative self-image. The gum trees and the beach define Australia; I cannot imagine the people aside from such settings. Yet the Australian soul has a need for distant gods and shrines. (And most of the Australians killed in wars lie in graves 15,000 kilometers away.)

Nowhere in the world—not even in France—do I hear more anti-British jibes than in Australia. Yet to this day the Queen of England heads the formal governmental structure of Australia, and the Australian national flag consists of the British Union Jack plus the stars of the Southern Cross—suggesting that Australia is a British outpost under southern skies.

In some ways Australia seems to be at the cutting edge of modernity. This was true of industrial conditions in the nineteenth century. Australia was a world pioneer in achieving the eight-hour working day, and by the 1880s a Saturday afternoon holiday was the norm for city workers—which helped turn Australians into sports lovers. Today Australia seems very modern in attitudes toward leisure (more important than work for many people) and toward the environment (large numbers reject progress in favor of quality of life).

At the same time, Australia is held back by blind spots that are uncommon in an advanced country. There exists in some quarters a sloppiness, an almost Third World lassitude, an absence of will to innovate, and a tendency to bury the head in the sand. The lack of nerve and the flabbiness that are found to a degree all over the Western world in the 1980s are fairly thick on the ground in Australia.

Australian intellectuals talk and drink and spend their leisure like other Australians, yet often their minds are in Europe and their concrete plans (a trip this year, a grant next year) focus on the U.S.A. It is puzzling that at one moment they react as nationalists while the next they speak of Australia as if it were little more than a hotel in which they are for the moment staying.

They can be as fastidious and elitist as intellectuals anywhere in the world. "Have you noticed," says a woman professor with thick glasses and hair over the eyes to her companion in a Melbourne University elevator, "that the students do not know how to use the semicolon?" The companion responds dryly, "I despise all students." In debate among themselves the intellectuals split straws finely and swipe out at each other polemically without restraint.

From a library window I watch a female student stroll across the leafy, flowery campus of the University of Western Australia. With a cascade of blond hair, a modest walk, and smooth nut-brown limbs, she exudes well-being. I scurry down the staircase and she passes close by me beneath wattle trees from which tiny bits of blossom float down to dust us both with gold. Her face seems bare of character, I cannot see her eyes, and she wears a look of strain, even bewilderment.

The nation itself is similarly dualistic. "The smile and the broken bottle," Peter Coleman, editor of the Sydney magazine *Quadrant,* once summed up. In its gentle beauty, absence of freneticism, and good-hearted innocence, Australia can seem a paradise. Then you notice trade union avarice, growing corruption, a drunken brawl that ends in murder, hatred directed toward a tall poppy, a don't care mentality, a cowardly lack of gallantry toward a woman suddenly in need, and the sort of tasteless attempt at humor that I noticed in a sign at the box office of an Adelaide theater: AIDS SUFFERERS USE TONGS WHEN PICKING UP YOUR TICKETS.

"Australian women don't dress for Australian men," says Fraser McEwing, a Sydney fashion publisher, "but for other women. Australian men are embarrassed to recognize that a smart woman is dressed at all." My old school friend's remark reminds me of the male chauvinist tradition, which we took for granted, and which despite enormous changes is not totally dead.

For whatever reason, there is a great deal of the broken bottle in the image of Australian men presented in literature. The drunken, de-structive father in Beverley Farmer's story "Sally's Birthday" suggests a world with no safety valve of civility. So does the violent, negative father in George Johnston's *My Brother Jack* who always has to have something to rant about in order to prove he is master of the house. The pages of William Dick's novel of growing up in Melbourne in the 1950s, *A Bunch of Ratbags,* are full of narrow, cruel monsters of men, includ-ing the leading character's father, who batters his wife and children every time he loses a bet on the races.

I keep thinking of that cry of abuse directed to a player who fum-bled the ball at a football match: "You bloody old woman!" We all ut-tered it, unthinkingly, scores of times, without ever pondering its un-pleasant undertones.

Helen Garner, who was deeply influenced by the feminist movement, has the impression that men and women "live in different worlds." As we lunch in Carlton during the tranquillity of noontime on Melbourne Cup day, she remarks, "Australian men seem so physically uncomfort-able with themselves—always trying to prove something. They have a look of belligerent noncomprehension. They seem to be waiting for something on which they can exercise their force."

Garner, a thin, supple, direct woman whose present husband is French, "can't go into pubs anymore. I can't bear to hear that—what is called laughter"—she winces—"among men. That shattering noise they let out of their mouths fills me with grief. And they stand in a ring, each with his glass of beer, feet far apart, knees tightly pushed back—it's a stance unique to Australians, and I can't take it."

In Alice Springs I drop by the Todd Hotel on a Friday afternoon. In the bar I find a hundred-odd youngish men—very few women—most in tank tops, with hair much longer than the current American norm. They play darts and billiards, lean against the bar, or sit in animated conversation at bare wooden tables under hanging plants. Many of them chain-smoke and some of them laugh the way Helen Garner can't stand.

A boy of Italian origin, olive-skinned, in a white shirt with long sleeves and neatly buttoned cuffs, black trousers, and pointed shoes, rushes around picking up beer cans; his arms are constantly full of them. A redneck throws a can at the boy, striking him on the shoulder. "Ee did it," roars the redneck, pointing to one of his mates, succumbing to the Australian instinct for evading responsibility.

Garner finds the mateship tradition pathetic. "I don't really understand the way men get on with each other. Do they have friends of their own sex or just companions?" She feels mateship is "imbued with a fear of women." One of Australia's most distinguished black writers, Faith Bandler, author of *Welou, My Brother* and other books, becomes uncharacteristically harsh when our conversation in Sydney, where she lives with her husband of thirty-four years, turns to male chauvinism.

"What do you think of the mateship tradition?" I ask, and she replies, "That's a fuck if ever there was one!" She sighs, and her blue eyes cloud. "It made sure the women knew their place. While the blokes were carrying on with their mateship in the bar, getting drunk, the women were home trying to feed the kids, making the last damper." Bandler, a widely traveled woman who was an architect of the campaign that resulted in civil rights for blacks two decades ago, goes on in a quiet but steely voice. "I hate Italian male arrogance, and blasé Austrian men kissing women's hands; I feel I could slap their faces. But it has never been as hard to wear as white Australian male chauvinism. It hasn't been easy to be a black person in Australia—and, oh, it has been that much harder to be a black person *and a woman* in Australia."

Susan Ryan, minister for education, the federal cabinet's one woman and the first woman ever to sit in a federal Labor cabinet, has a different view. "I suppose because of my unusual occupation I've been able to enter the male mateship culture," she remarks in her Canberra office. "The mateship tradition is an authentic way in which people in this country form groups for social purposes."

Margaret Whitlam, wife of the former prime minister, also takes a relaxed, if slightly bemused, view of the mateship tradition. "It's just an extension of the hail-fellow-well-met attitude," she remarks in her Paris apartment, "and those sort of people exist everywhere." She laughs. "Even in France there's a few." Mrs. Whitlam, who is sixty-seven, is detached about Australia's male chauvinist ways. "Boys in the back room with beer, girls out front having tea and knitting. It happened, it still happens, and I think it happens everywhere." She sighs. "In a way I think I prefer it; women would rather talk about recipes, gardens. Anyway I've never worried much about the mateship syndrome. Far worse is the talking-shop syndrome. I met it in legal circles, and it's so boring."

Rachel Faggeter, a museum curator in Melbourne who is a generation younger than Margaret Whitlam, has seen much improvement. "God, when I started school-teaching in 1962," she recalls, "I was paid less than males who had graduated three years after me. One official told me this was because women are 'no good four days out of the month.' That's how bloody primitive things were." She looks out the window of my office at Melbourne University, where once we were classmates, and she laughs gently. "A woman tram driver nearly ran me down today. And I saw a Chinese policeman on point duty. I thought, bugger it, things are improving."

In Melbourne at a great Australian ritual I savor one of the most mysterious of all Down Under's contradictions. Some 80,000 people hunch on benches as at church, except that they are half naked under a blazing sun as they watch a distant ballet of white on green, eleven Australians against eleven West Indians, all wearing long white pants. It is a cricket test match.

The Melbourne Cricket Ground is in the heart of the city—where a cathedral was located in medieval cities—as is the major sports stadium in each Australian metropolis. It is so big that from my bench high in one stand I feel as if I am on a mountain peering at a scene in a valley below.

Out come the umpires—looking like penguins in their black-and-white hats, jackets, and pants—at the precise second they are due. Trains may be late—by days when strikes hit—but not the arrival, or at 6 P.M., as shadows creep across the lovely green field, the departure of the black-and-white test cricket umpires.

A wave of polite applause signals a big hit or the dismissal of a batsman. An occasional roar of formidable Melbourne moral disapproval rises against an umpire's decision. Now and then raucous shouts can be heard—mostly *against* something or someone—and beer cans hit the concrete floors far more often than the bat hits the ball. Yet tension and reverence fill the stadium as the game goes on for four days, six hours a day. This is Melbourne with its mind on the job; this is Melbourne at worship.

Wherever the active, individualistic Australian may be, he does not seem to be here. These pagans have found a God, a surprising one. The earnestness, excitement, and sympathy that the Australian seldom expresses in daily social communication turn up on this hot afternoon at the MCG. Bottled-up emotions are brought to an almost religious pitch in watching the banging of willow against leather.

Having found a God in top-level sport, the pagans are as tame as mice. All of the herd instinct and timidity that produced compulsory arbitration, the White Australia policy, and heavy protection for Australian industry are today utterly believable. A conformist mass is enslaved to the spectacle of "overs" and "teatime," and to the authority figures of the umpires, shouting "No ball" or "Not out" or deciding that "bad light" will stop the game. Yet this Melbourne cricket crowd also brings home to me the camaraderie of the Australians. Radio and TV commentators refer at times to the spectators as "the mob," which suggests the conformism; but no one ever objects to the term, for everyone is included in the definition.

The ritual has not remained untouched by the passage of time. Sport as an exhaust pipe of the emotions no longer serves all sections of the Australian community. There is a traditional British feel to these serried ranks, despite the sunshine and the bare legs and arms. Few Asians, Italians, Greeks, or other foreign-born people (who together make up 28 percent of Melbourne's population) are to be seen. And in the 1980s attendance at test matches started to decline.

On the screen of a TV that a group of people beside me have brought into the stand there is a close-up shot of a black girl in the crowd. The commentator says, "Well, she'll be pretty happy with things here at the MCG today." (The West Indies are beating Australia.) To most Australian cricket lovers there is nothing strange in this ingratiating remark.

These long tough faces, peering into the sun to see what the Windies will try next to undermine the Australian boys, represent a middle Australia that feels little inclination to move over and accept a definition of itself as just one band in a rainbow of diversity. At the end of the day the crowd creeps home to read the *Herald* and watch TV, leaving the drama and rivalry of the game as insouciantly as a snake sheds its skin.

"Jimmy Carter without the modesty," snarls a Liberal politician, in a reference to Prime Minister Bob Hawke's tendency to wrestle in public with his own soul, to speak with a sentimentality unusual in a politician, and even to cry before TV cameras. Many women do not mind the prime minister's crying in public, but many men do. "People say Jesus also wept," remarks Henry Bolte, a former Victorian premier, after one emotional Hawke performance. "But Jesus wept for humanity. I felt Hawke was weeping for himself." In Sydney, the wealthy socialite Lady Mary Fairfax defends Hawke: "I think he's a caring person. True, he weeps in public, but you know the Roman soldiers wept before going into battle." The manifest success—in political terms—of Hawke's public shows of emotion is due, it seems to me, to the spectator character of Australians' emotionalism. Uncomfortable with expressing emotions in daily relationships, they save them for collective occasions. When the prime minister cries on TV, as when a crowd at a football or cricket match is gripped with emotion, it is a welcome release for the repressed self.

Australia, like a roll of silk when viewed from different angles, seems British one moment and American the next. Parliament House in Canberra embodies the dualism. The chair of the speaker is a replica of the one in London's House of Commons, containing wood from Nelson's *Victory* and from the old Westminster Hall. But the two chambers are named House of Representatives and Senate in the American manner, and the seats are not arranged squarely as in the British parliament but in a horseshoe as in Washington.

Places have British names. Kings and aristocrats from the old world have supplied the labels for this new world. Most of the state capitals are named after a British politician (Sydney, Hobart, Melbourne) or a British royal figure (Adelaide). Witheringly hot towns bear names from England's green and pleasant land. Coming out of narrow brown Australian mouths, "Prince of Wales" and "Sandringham" and "Queen Anne" sound strange, even if the associations of these appellations have left the conscious mind.

Each day in the leading newspapers a "Vice-Regal" column lists the activities and visitors at the state and national government houses. On the same page there is sometimes a "Daily Bible Quotation," another echo of *The Times* of London. If someone quotes *The Times,* it is assumed without question that means *The Times* of London.

The British flag flutters from the tower of each state government house. Inside the Queen's representative signs documents and serves as the pinnacle of the traditionalist segment of society—and seems like a dinosaur from a past era to many young Australians.

State and national governments are organized on Westminster lines, with a cabinet drawn from the legislature. Astonishing as it seems, only since the present prime minister, Bob Hawke, made the reform has it been necessary to be an Australian citizen to work in the public service. Until 1984, the requirement was to be a British subject.

"She screws around," a student says of her girlfriend, and I realize that language-wise America has been encroaching on Australia. A moment later she pronounces "schedule" with a "k" in the American way. "Have a nice day" can often be heard in the major cities, as can "You're welcome," though only a decade ago these phrases made any Australian cringe or laugh.

In advertising, American expressions advance like a bushfire. "South

Australia—ENJOY," cries an ad by the tourist authority of this state whose tradition is one of restraint. "Tasmania—BE TEMPTED," says a similar one for the island that, uninstructed by an American-influenced advertising agency, would not likely have seen temptation as among its capabilities. In the universities and the federal public service, American terms (a Human Movement Services department at Melbourne University; "impact" used as a verb in government documents) make such inroads that already people overlook that they are U.S.-derived.

The commercial TV channels are well stocked with *Dallas* and *Dynasty* and similar American programs. American popular music and clothing styles capture youth here as all over the world. It is not uncommon to find within a kilometer of each other a McDonald's, a Pizza Hut, a Wendy's Hamburgers, and a Colonel Sanders.

American ideas of management and problem solving sweep away many cobwebs, as the presence of multinational corporations grows, and as the public service in Canberra (and in some states) shakes off its tradition of amateurism. For one who recalls the Old Boy network of Canberra departments in the 1960s, it is extraordinary to see American management consultants being called in to advise these same departments.

Australian journalism has for some years been moving away from gentlemanly British ways to a more American style of investigative reporting and brightness. Books and ideas from America have made a major advance in Australian intellectual circles since the 1960s. "The journal I get most pleasure out of is the *New York Review of Books,*" says Richard Hall, an influential Labor Party intellectual. "The traditions of American liberalism are very attractive to me." The two major conservative think tanks, the Institute of Public Administration in Melbourne and the Center for Independent Studies in Sydney, both rely heavily on American publications. "We just don't have journals like *Reason* and *The American Spectator,*" says the director of the Melbourne group, who assiduously reads both.

Very often Americans are liked in person, for their dynamism, open-mindedness, and cheerfulness. But Britons know more about Australia than do Americans; not even the most ignorant Briton could make the remark of the well-traveled American lady: "What I loved best in Australia were the lovely little Qantases—you know, in the airline ads, and also in the zoos."

The British know the difference between a koala bear and the Australian airline. Yet British familiarity with Australia, once comforting, becomes irritating when it is combined with condescension. The Briton's half-knowledge, producing the sort of presumption that family members feel toward each other, can be less acceptable than the blank mind of the cheerful Yank.

"Why not?" people say, and Australia indeed is a land of hedonism; its setting of fierce, harsh beauty spurs on the hedonist as risk spurs on a gambler.

The weekend is sacred from the profane intrusion of toil. Saturday arvo (afternoon) in particular is a time of migration from responsibility. Post office service and delivery do not exist on Saturday, and by noon nearly all shops, even news agents, are closed; Australia has entered the magic cave of leisure and will emerge with grumpy reluctance only at breakfast time on Monday. Even the counting of votes after a Saturday national election cannot conquer the Australian Sunday; from Saturday evening the explosive ballots lie around until Monday morning.

Students, bellwether of any culture, take off for the weekend as if books no longer existed and urban life were a dream. Even in sophisticated Melbourne, campus tension evaporates on a Friday night as the great outdoors claims the weekend. Sydney and other cities are remote; nature-oriented pursuits hold sway by default. Students go bushwalking and bird-watching. They drive to the ski slopes in northeastern Victoria. They play tennis or cricket under leafy trees. They put their heads down to the serious business of gardening. Year-round, their weekend has the laid-back feel of midsummer weekends for youth in Boston or Paris or Tokyo.

Here are students with bare bronzed legs hiking along a Victorian bush road one spring Saturday morning. There is a smell of wildflowers, wattle, and honeysuckle. In a swag the students carry fresh bread, steaks to grill, the reddest tomatoes in the world, and a sack of wine enclosed in a box, equipped with a little tap, that Australians call a cask. No one counts the hours, and the progress of the sun in an azure sky measures the day's activity.

In midsummer at Christmas and New Year's the nation virtually stops functioning. Not only do politicians disappear, and newspapers devote their columns to food and drink and the odd report of a bushfire or a shark attacking a swimmer at the beach, but basic services close down for days at a stretch.

Australia's heart is not at its center—a swath of the Northern Territory, Western Australia, Queensland, and South Australia that is, except for the charming town of Alice Springs, virtually a void—but on the beach. The most Australian thing you can do is to lie on a clean, wide, beautiful beach. Here Australian indifference reaches its peak. Here the Australian declares himself as much outside of history as a patient under anesthesia is beyond the conscious world. Even the ugly gray sharks, with their cold eyes and mouths that never close, do not break the torpor. They kill nearly every season, but they are unable to make the Australian beach lover anxious. The beach possesses the Australian soul because it is an unanswerably Australian asset for a people often dismissed—even by themselves—as mere derivatives from cold and distant Europe.

The Australian will often cheerfully admit to being a bludger (a lazy one). He prefers a slow pace and is easygoing except when someone seeks to set a faster pace or behaves self-importantly. His hedonism is seldom loud or violent.

It is quite usual for people lunching in the business districts of Adelaide, Melbourne, and Sydney to drink a bottle of wine each, and for those in Queensland and Western Australian towns to drink a quart of beer each with lunch. Passing the windows of Jimmy Watson's, a popular restaurant in Melbourne's Italian quarter, I momentarily think the place is a glassware boutique as I look through the semicircular windows at a forest of shining green bottles.

When a couple or a group of friends go to a BYO—a bring-your-own-drinks restaurant—they carry as hand luggage a cask or several bottles of wine, or a nest of bottles of the strong, bitter Australian beer. The first order of business, at lunch hardly less than at dinner, is to deploy the various bottles and casks and cans; it is like arranging luggage in a train compartment at the start of a long trip.

Anxiety about diet is growing, but it has not cowed the appetite in Australia as it has in some Western societies. People eat butter with gusto. The saltcellar is not viewed as a dagger pointed at the heart. No one has yet told the truckers who eat huge steaks for breakfast about the dangers of red meat. At discos the entrance fee covers a buffet of food laid out beside the bar. People of all ages smoke without embarrassment or guilt.

Gastronomic fastidiousness has, however, descended on the cities. Australians used to be casual and apologetic about food. A "pie and tea" (the meat pie is largely gravy enclosed in heavy pastry) or fish and chips (fried and greasy in the English way) were a staple viewed as adequate, and in an unspoken way defiantly *asserted* to be adequate "tucker" for any real Australian.

In my youth an exotic item made its appearance under the influence of 1950s European immigration: garlic sausage. A foot in the door for non-British fare, garlic sausage seemed to us a very bold foodstuff. It suggested Roman Catholicism if not downright impropriety. I remember the ripple of excitement on campus when the cafeteria at Melbourne University in the late 1950s added to its menu sweet and sour pork, fried rice, and chop suey. At that time most Murrumbeena people would have declined such Oriental food. They were only starting, gingerly, to digest Italian salami and Greek souvlaki, and to learn from Europeans that "tasty" and "matured" were not the only varieties of cheese.

Today it is different, thanks to the continued flow of immigrants. Diners in Melbourne and Sydney, bare-armed and wearing sandals, will peer lengthily at wine lists, fuss over the right sauce for the duckling, dispute the most appropriate seasoning for the lamb. The yabby, which we kids used to catch in jam tins and did not deign to eat, is now a prized entree (appetizer) at fine eateries. South Australians will drive for half a day to find the desired Chablis for a fish dinner. Victorians will dispute the merits of Sichuan and Hunan cuisine as if arguing about Melbourne football.

If the last moments of debonair Harold Holt as prime minister, spent plunging into the surf, symbolize the Australian's kinship with nature, Gough Whitlam's "last supper" in power expresses the Australian's heartiness of appetite. Confronted with the bombshell of being dismissed as prime minister by the representative in Australia of the British Crown, the elegant lawyer, although fuming, shocked, and in desperate need of a quick plan of counteraction, sat down in the breakfast room of the prime-ministerial residence and ate a grilled steak.

The attractiveness of Australia's space and tranquillity is proved by a million applications each year from around the world to emigrate there. Yet under the surface the nation's problems have been growing more acute.

Mineral riches have proved tougher to deliver to a market and softer in price than expected a dozen years ago. There is serious doubt that the "upholstered island" has the will to make itself competitive in an interdependent world which values Australian wheat, wool, and other agricultural products less and less. Fertility rates go down. The "she'll do" mentality, stemming from Australia's comfortable and leveling way of life, is an enemy of entrepreneurship.

At some point along the way, the land of punishment turned into a land of reward, and the ethic of wanting it all replaced the ethic of mateship. Australia has become a more stratified and selfish society than during my youth. Losers there must be when solidarity crumbles and sectionalism runs riot. A dangerous possibility is a permanent underclass of unemployed youth. A probability is that the pie will not be large enough to meet all the demands upon it.

Australians seldom allow their problems to get them down. Yet they do not always know their own strengths, or deploy them in a far-sighted way. There is at times a lack of resolve to face any unpleasant reality. Better to appoint a commission of inquiry, preferably a *royal* commission, and hope that during the years of waiting for its report the problem will lessen. AVOID HANGOVERS—STAY DRUNK, says a bumper sticker, and such pigheaded evasiveness lurks within even some talented and energetic citizens. Australia has been kept pleasant and peaceable by a practical if sometimes hit-or-miss approach to issues, a lack of powerful and divisive ideologies, and an agreeable climate and stretches of beautiful habitat. Some Australians wonder if all this will be enough for tomorrow's challenges.

THREE

Who Are the Australians?

Modern Australia came into being because Britain had a crime problem. After the American Revolution it was no longer possible to send the undesirables of Britain to the U.S.A. So London pored over maps and noticed the great dimly known land in the south, which since the time of ancient Greece and Rome had been labeled simply *terra australis incognita*. It was at that moment that bells of doom rang over the heads of the Australian Aborigines.

The major themes of the brief but extraordinary Australian past flavor Australian life today: convict origin; advantages and disadvantages of distance from the world's power centers; insecurity about race; lack of a spirit of entrepreneurship; need to woo the right people to Australia and keep the wrong ones out; response to Britain of a lusty son who watches his mother grow old and decline.

Some 40,000 years or more ago—according to prevalent theory—a Stone Age people reached Australia. For an eternity Australia was theirs alone. They revered the land they dwelt upon, but unlike Europeans, they never "occupied" it with fences and houses and rules about property. They lived in caves or tents of leaves and branches. The wheel was unknown to them.

The Aborigines got to Australia by chance, sailing southeastward from some part of Asia. So too did most later arrivals get to Australia through a roll of the legal, climatic, or political dice. All Australians were originally boat people—a term applied to the wave of Indochinese arrivals of the 1970s—and it was probably because European boats were superior to Asian that the long isolation of the Aborigines in *terra australis incognita* was ended by white arrivals rather than by yellow.

For many millennia until the eighteenth century no one tried to take Australia. The Portuguese, looking for a land they could dedicate to the Holy Spirit, and the Dutch, looking for spices and other profitable items, put an end to Australia's suspension in time. Neither grabbed it, but together they smashed the barriers in the way of Britain's later grab. They checked Islam, provided cartographical knowledge, and weakened the resistance of the Indonesian states to European intrusion.

The Dutch, seeking gold in the Indies, bumped into the west coast of Australia early in the seventeenth century. Barren land, fierce heat, and unappealing Aborigines all made the Calvinists shudder. Seeing black swans perhaps clinched the matter; in the antipodes beauty was turned to darkness. They named the place New Holland, but they did not stay.

When the British, plucking fruit from a tree Magellan had planted with his voyage round the world in 1519, in the 1770s sought imperial elbow room, and prison space, they reached the superior east coast of Australia and stayed. James Cook, discovering that Australia was separated by sea from New Guinea, on behalf of the King of England took possession of the eastern part, and on January 26, 1788, a settlement was proclaimed at Sydney. Europeans did not then know whether the west coast (New Holland) and the east coast (New South Wales) were joined or whether they were two separate lands.

The British then began to fill the bright spaces of Australia with their criminals. Each twist of the criminal law in England, Scotland, or Ireland produced heavy consequences in the shape of Australian society. Calvinist repression in Edinburgh gave New South Wales some free spirits. From Ireland's vale of tears came rebels. England contributed thieves, the bulk of Australia's population for the first thirty years. A few convicts had attacked the monarch. One had thrown a stone at King William IV at the races. Another had fired a shot at the young Queen Victoria in St. James's Park.

The convicts got fare, room, and board to go to Australia, just as many later immigrants would be paid to make the trip. The voyage from

Britain was arduous; between 1795 and 1801 about 10 percent of the convicts died on the way. Life at Botany Bay—the first name for the settlement at Sydney—was tough, and convicts sometimes gave as good as they received. "On two occasions," wrote an observer, "I saw men—after undergoing, one a flogging of fifty, and the other seventy-five lashes, bleeding as they were, deliberately spit, after the punishment, in the flogger's face."

The white people of Australia took a bleak view of the place. Its raison d'être was embarrassing, its location was appalling, and its terrain was largely uninhabitable. Morals were judged low in this "second Sodom of the south." Most people agreed with Charles Darwin that the gum trees were "miserable-looking" and "presented the appearance of being actually dead." Here were rivers without water, trees that gave no shade, flowers without perfume, and birds such as the emu that could not fly. As late as 1819 a distinguished Sydney judge, trying to explain Australia's well-known inferiority, put forward the idea that this continent was not planned from the start, when God blessed his work and saw that it was good, but emerged only after the first sinning, when the world was already under a curse. He saw Australia as a punishment for Adam's fall.

At London parties, if a man mentioned he had been in Australia, ladies and gentlemen would move away and check their pockets and purses. The people of Australia, it was quipped, had been chosen by the very best judges in England. When self-governing councils were eventually mooted, Britons split their sides laughing at the idea of lawbreakers becoming lawmakers. "It is the only country in the world," wrote the naval surgeon based in Sydney, "which you are ashamed to confess having visited." Henry Carter's ironic jest suggested Australia's looming identity problem:

> *True patriots all; for be it understood*
> *We left our country for our country's good.*

In the convict decades Australia was a government camp. The French and American revolutions were over, and Australia was to be a place of administration, not class struggle. Europe's usual divisions, with their pull to create and their push to oppress, were absent. The state filled all vacuums. Virtually all economic activity was officially sponsored. Sometimes in Canberra one feels Australia still is a government camp.

Botany Bay society was highly stratified. Sydney had three burying places: one for free people, one for convicts, and one for people who had been hanged. But it was not a society of classes, and this foreshadowed Australia's capacity for cross-class consensus, which so maddens the Marxist pigeonholers. Bureaucrat and thief, being alone, collaborated and eventually produced a framework of class-transcending limited cooperation. Nearly two centuries later, Prime Minister Bob Hawke's consensual "Accord" between business, labor, and government was its latest form. Australians learned to work together, in construction or road gangs, just as later they became good at together refusing to work and came to lead the world in strike activity.

Although Captain Cook had reported that Botany Bay was fertile and abundant, this was an explorer's excess of enthusiasm, and for two decades the struggle for food was acute. Rum helped New South Wales function. An administration desperate to get convicts to work—on the farms of the officers, during hours after prison duties—found that paying them with rum was the sole solution. In one six-month period in 1800, the 5,000 people of the colony of New South Wales imported a colossal 36,000 gallons of spirits. Through all the changes over two centuries Australians have remained keen lovers of the bottle.

The typical founding felon of Australia was an unattached male. Between 1821 and 1830, nearly 28,000 male convicts arrived at the two settlements of New South Wales and Tasmania, the southern isle, and only some 4,000 female. As late as 1830, white males outnumbered white females in New South Wales by three to one. A muster of the Sydney population in 1807 found 807 legitimate children and 1,025 bastards. Today there are Australian women who feel that Australian men don't really like women, and they trace this to convict society, which was largely male, spiced with a few women who were mainly prostitutes.

Botany Bay as a place of bureaucratic fiat began a tradition of fussy rules and authoritarian strutting by paper-shuffling little gods, which is not dead and today fits ill with the easygoing atmosphere of Australian society. Botany Bay as a place of compulsion gave birth to the chip-on-the-shoulder mentality that runs like a rusty streak across Australia's history. Botany Bay as a place of shame began the tenacious career of Australian self-deprecation.

By the time the first governor, Arthur Phillip, sailed back to London in 1792, taking with him four kangaroos and two Aborigines, debate was beginning on basic issues: Who were the Australians? Did Australia have a future beyond the prison doors?

Gradually those born in Australia developed a pride in the country. The first shoot of nationalism came from the inability of the British-born to boast of their birth—as was normal in British colonies—because of the embarrassing fact that the felons too were British-born.

Some wanted Australia to look beyond the prison walls and build a society by making wealth from the land and trading with the world. These people, untraditional in outlook and economic in orientation, had long favored encouraging free settlers to come to Australia. Others were not sure that Australia had any purpose beyond London's desire to get rid of criminals and if possible reform them under azure skies—colossally expensive as it was to run an ever-expanding government prison camp. So began the tension between "development" and "administration" that exists in a different form to this day.

A dilemma was that if New South Wales flourished, a sentence of transportation could hardly remain a deterrent. By the 1820s it was not rare for a person in Britain to contrive to have himself transported. One woman convict in Sydney wrote to her boyfriend in York and asked him to commit a crime so the pair could be reunited. He promptly stole a pair of trousers, was transported to New South Wales, and found sexual happiness if not liberty.

The emerging landed class, called "squatters" after the process by which they obtained land, needed more ex-convicts to work on "their" farms. The free-immigrant workers, on the other hand, feared that a continued flow of convicts would drive wages down. Some people spoke of their fear of the vice and violence of a convict society when what they mostly feared was labor that would compete with their own labor.

The anti-convict forces had advantages. The sheer passage of time. London's budgetary problems. The infuriating image that New South Wales and Tasmania had as Britain's sewer. The reduced terror of transportation in the minds of British criminals. By 1828, when New South Wales conducted its first census, free whites numbered 20,930 and convict whites 15,668, and one quarter of the population had been born in Australia.

From the first days that convicts left the prisons, working for employers who had no other source of labor, Australia was a paradise for the man with labor to sell. Generally speaking, it has remained so, and it is amusing to watch Marxists gnash their teeth in disappointment that revolution has not come to Australia when this simple fact has obviated the need for such strife.

To Tasmania (called Van Diemen's Land until 1855), Sydney spun off its worst convicts, which gave the pretty island an early reputation for vice and murder. In 1830 a convict escaped from the prison in Hobart, the main town of Tasmania, murdered six men, sewed up the body of one of them in the skin of a bullock, roasted it, and ate it.

Today's Brisbane, a hot and friendly city, was founded in 1824 as a place for New South Wales to send convicts who had committed a second offense. The transportation of British convicts to various parts of Australia went on until the 1860s, and the last convicts died only in the 1920s. Some of my grandparents were already at school when the final convict ships reached Western Australia in 1868. I remember my grandmother using the term "convict blood" to explain behavior (generally in Sydney) of which she disapproved. Today it is fashionable to boast of convict blood.

The explorer Matthew Flinders, whose travels proved that no sea separated New Holland and New South Wales, and who suggested the name Australia for the huge continent, in 1802 reached a spot some 1,000 kilometers south of Sydney and noted: "Emus, kangaroos, black swans, ducks, and many varieties of birds abound." This was Melbourne.

Melbourne never received convicts (as my grandmother never tired of recalling) but came into existence because of flickering economic ambitions and because London and Sydney both feared that the French might approach from the south and interfere, as they had done in Canada and India, with the orderly progression of the British Empire.

John Batman, an entrepreneur whose parents both were convicts, made a "treaty" with the Aborigines in the Melbourne area. He told them that although he was a white man, he was "a countryman" of theirs, and he handed out trinkets and put a necklace on each woman and child. By the "treaty," Batman, on behalf of his group of settlers, bought 600,000 acres of sheep and cattle land for £200 worth of knives, looking glasses, beads, tomahawks, scissors, flour, and (for this was Melbourne with its chilly winter nights) blankets. In his diary Batman wrote, "This will be the place for the future village." He instructed members of his party to "build a home and commence a garden," and Melbourne people have been doing that ever since.

Two years later the governor of New South Wales came south to give a name to the village. Once more, as for Sydney and Hobart, the name chosen was that of a British politician. The governor handed out brass plates to thank the Aborigines and invited a crowd to a dinner of kangaroo pie in his tent.

For the time being the western 90 percent of Australia was virtually without whites. The future Western Australia, later to receive convicts, after trying to do without them and meeting disaster because of shortage of labor, and the future South Australia, never to know this stain and the nearest of the Australian colonies to a settlement based on idealism, were still unexplored parts of what the Dutch had called New Holland.

The British did not understand that the Aborigines saw them as invading robbers. No one told the Aborigines that by the yardstick of the British Empire black people were fit only to be dominated. The original Australians' food grew short as the white man caught fish once sought only by blacks, and as his settlements drove away kangaroos. Few blacks could cope with alcohol, vital fuel for white Australia's existence. Smallpox and other diseases from Britain killed tens of thousands of blacks.

Sometimes, when a convict and an Aboriginal woman made love, the half-caste child that resulted was explained by the woman to her men folk as a consequence of her eating too much white bread. The Aborigines, whose view of the cycle of reproduction bore no relation to the facts of life as understood by Europeans, were known to hold a half-caste baby over the flames of a fire to try to darken its skin.

To whites, Aboriginal holy places could not be taken seriously, as they were not man-made but, it seemed, mere swaths of nature. To blacks, the white religion of Christianity seemed trivial because its shrines were *merely* man-made. Few whites could accept black nakedness. Nor were clergy impressed when Aborigines, hearing the promise of Jesus to give them whatever they asked of him, requested boots and dresses.

There were blacks who thought a white man riding a horse was a beast with two heads, one in front and one on top. Others thought bullocks were the white men's women, or saw the whites' ships as birds or fish. Some Aborigines believed that the humans who debarked from these ships were their own dead come back to life in a different form. But the gifts of grubs and snake meat they offered their "relatives" did not win the palates or the hearts of the whites.

Power counted, not philosophy. Because the whites were the more materially resourceful, they after a while could give up the attempt to understand the Aborigines and simply kick them aside. White Australia's opinion of the blacks sank. Cook had been very favorable. "They are far happier than we Europeans," the sea captain claimed. Whereas the "first Parents" of the Europeans "saw themselves naked and were ashamed, these people are naked and not ashamed." Early officials often tried to be kind and even respectful toward blacks. But optimism waned. It was increasingly doubted that the Aborigines could be "civilized," used for labor, or even saved from destruction.

Australia was big enough for white and black to lead separate lives. But both sides tried in mutually uncomprehending ways to relate to the other. The failure was almost total. Each race killed many of the other. The whites killed best and most, and so they inherited the ancient land they named Australia. By 1850 a nation that had been black for millennia was turning white. In Tasmania, where the blacks had lived for five hundred generations, the last full-blooded black died in 1876.

Too late it dawned on the blacks that the intruders were men, not spirits, and that they intended to stay. The relation between people and land was turned on its head; the Aborigine lived in awe of the environment, the white man treated it as an adversary to be subdued. No wonder there is a hardness in the Australian personality, given the history of prison settlement, of subduing an endless and temperamental terrain, and of dealing with black resistance to the white man's possession of that terrain.

The jail is an urban industry, as the historian Geoffrey Blainey remarks, and the convict era set a pattern of heavy urbanization. This was reinforced by the key role of the ports. All six of the colonial capitals were ports. Not far beyond these ports lay inhospitable bush and desert. The two great exports of early Australia—wool and gold—were very valuable in relation to their weight, and shipment from the most efficient port was essential.

So Australia developed as a metropolitan nation and remains so today. Prime Minister Whitlam, coming into office in the 1970s with a brilliant vision of decentralization, tried to force the states to devolve responsibilities to their various provincial areas, but he was defeated by the powerful tradition of centralization in the six ports. Local government was always weak and still is. "Many activities such as schools," Whitlam reflected to me after leaving office, "which in other countries are conducted on a regional basis, are in Australia conducted by the six state governments."

In the first decades the language of public life in New South Wales and Tasmania was breathlessly evangelical. The church backed up the state like a dutiful wife supporting her husband. And it was rewarded: convicts worked in clergy's kitchens and fields. The practice of Christianity, as one observer put it, was "part of the punishment." But the heavy ballast of religion turned out to have little influence on Australia's future course. This religion was almost a branch of law, geared to suppressing bad things, bereft of any vision of good things, except the possible ecstasy of heaven. It was a religion that existed in Australia by default, filling a philosophic vacuum.

The second governor of New South Wales, John Hunter, made church attendance compulsory. The result was arson, and despite the offer of a large reward he never found out who burned down the church. So poor was attendance that the government was driven to tie the issue of rations to church attendance to fend off the embarrassment of empty pews.

The pilgrims came to America praying; the convicts came to Australia cursing chaplain and warder alike. America was settled out of idealism; Australia was settled under compulsion, and to this day Australians are uncomfortable with idealism. But if eighteenth-century Australia lacked idealism it did not lack a spirit of progress. The Australian had to cling to a belief in progress. How else could he face Australia's origins as a prison? If convicts could not reform, Australia could not be built. Few records of progress are more unanswerable than the step from bond to free.

At the start Britain gave Australia little more than religion plus criminals. From this grotesque mix the native-born had to make a civil society; and if they did it without philosophic flourishes, they at least improved upon the ingredients as given.

As religion withered, a secular root of social amelioration came into view. It was Benthamism, based on an unsentimental view that the greatest happiness of the greatest number is the best principle for human society. Australia was a perfect candidate for Bentham's calculus of pleasure and pain. Bare of doctrines, it was unconcerned to inquire into man's theoretical nature and knew nothing of "natural rights." The expressed wants of the people under the gum trees was a sufficient definition of the political good.

In early Australia there was little attachment to liberty. Meetings to further or discuss a cause—even Freemasonry—were forbidden. So was the public practice of Catholicism until 1803, when mass for the first time was celebrated in New South Wales. Australia is in practical terms a wonderfully free country—in a world of few free countries—but it possesses no Bill of Rights, and still today Australians have a weak grasp of the theory of liberty.

I asked Whitlam if he finds it significant that Australia has no statues to liberty or liberators. "You wouldn't expect statues to liberators in Australia," he replied, "because there's never been a foreign occupier—other than the British when they took the country from the Aborigines." Australians are not that attached to liberty because they've never had to fight for it. And they have become Benthamite enough—sometimes being both individualistic and state-dependent—to think that liberty does not matter quite as much as security.

As God was disappointing on Australian soil, so the god of Australia became Nature. Ideologies did not transplant well. What never faded in Australia was implacable nature. So the great festivals of Australia have to do not with religion or politics but with outdoor physical struggle. They celebrate war: Anzac Day. They display bounty wrenched from the land: the Royal Agricultural Show. Or they are spine-tingling sporting battles: the Grand Final of the Victorian Football League, and the Melbourne Cup, a horse race that astonished Mark Twain when he saw it bring a nation to a halt.

If "convict" conjures up Australian history in its first decades, "sheep" does the same for a period beginning in the 1820s. England desired Australian wool; an Australia anxious to wipe away the stain of convictism took the opportunity to open up pastureland—with merinos from the Cape of Good Hope—and supply London with the best wool in the world. "Feed my lambs, feed my sheep," the leading clergyman of Sydney used to read to his flock from St. John, but as the winds of Australian secularism began to smooth his doctrinal edges, the Reverend Samuel Marsden gave the words of Jesus to Simon Peter a literal twist and raised sheep on his own property. It was a symbol of the shift from pious colonial governmentalism to private economic activity on a frontier.

By 1850 Australia had some 18 million sheep (though only 400,000 people) and was on the verge of becoming the world's largest wool producer. Melbourne in 1835 was a sleepy stretch of land with platypuses in the creeks and bellbirds in the wattle trees; by 1850 it was the third-busiest wool port the world had known. Sheep hastened the end of the convict system, opened up many of the readily openable parts of Australia, and made white-black relations even worse than before.

The Swan River settlement, later to be Western Australia, was a colony of free men seeking to raise sheep and cattle. Its settlers brought from England their pianos and silks and Dresden china; but the heat, flies, and dust reduced a genteel class to grubbing paupers. A similar disjunction between European ways and Australian conditions still may be found. Yugoslavs in suits and ties and German ladies in thick decorative frocks meet their match in Perth's 100-degree heat and Brisbane's humidity and Victoria's dust storms. Devout Italian ladies swathed in black dresses, stockings, and shawls sit roasting on Sydney beaches surrounded by half-naked pagan Australian youth.

As the number of free persons outstripped the number of convicts—four to one by 1841—a cry for democracy went up. In this demand the workers and the urban business class often were allies, over against the landed class, which wanted political power to be based on property. "One sheep, one vote" was the mocking cry thrown at the squatters by supporters of individual rights—and a century later the same phrase, hurled by champions of "One man, one vote" in the Labor Party, still had the power to infuriate politicians of the Country Party.

With surprising ease and rapidity the six colonies (the future Victoria, Tasmania, and Queensland in mid-century all became separate from New South Wales; and Western Australia and South Australia were from their beginnings separate) obtained self-government (in many areas) from London, set up elective institutions with manhood suffrage and a secret ballot, and granted their citizens substantial civil liberties.

The squatters had it good, but they did not fulfill their dream of making Australia an aristocracy serviced by ex-criminals; the double threat to other people's wages and morals was too great. And they did not capture the Australian imagination; the bush workers were to do that.

Whereas the Australians once lived mainly in prisons, suddenly in the 1850s huge numbers of them came to live at gold diggings. The fraternity of thieves was reborn as a free-for-all of pre-industrial fortune seekers, and the ethos of both would color Australia for a long time. First in New South Wales, then in a big way in Victoria, the golden specks were found, and the face of Australia was changed within a decade.

Australia needed people. That is why the squatters favored transportation; as the American South felt it could not do without slavery, so the squatters felt Australia could not do without convicts. Far more distant from Europe than was the U.S.A., Australia could not attract immigrants. The fare from Europe to North America was five pounds, but to Australia it was twenty pounds. In 1850, 253,000 emigrated to North America but only 16,000 emigrated to Australia and New Zealand. From 1851, gold brought people at last; the population of Australia trebled during the 1850s, passing one million.

One month after an old man found gold in September 1851 under a wattle tree at Ballarat, then hardly a village, 5,000 diggers were installed under canvas on the lovely plains and hills of Victoria. The poor were on equal terms with the rich, the locals with the new arrivals, all crazed with the hope of sudden wealth. Beards and mustaches flourished, for no one had time to shave. In Melbourne, 120 kilometers south of Ballarat, shops overnight switched from their usual wares to the requirements of the goldfields: pots and pans, boots, blankets, picks, blue flannel shirts, California hats. The squatters were in despair. "Men cannot be got for love or money," one cried.

In search of gold, ex-convicts sailed to the mainland from Tasmania, scaring some Victorian people. Chinese flocked in, and soon formed 20 percent of Victoria's goldfield population. Almost every nation in Europe, where turmoil in the late 1840s gave many people an incentive to leave, was represented on the goldfields. Among the Europeans were radicals who tried to get Australians to think not only of the pay packet but of the rights of man. And for the first time in Australian history, Americans arrived in some numbers.

"There were so many Americans there at first," wrote Rolf Boldrewood of the goldfields in *Robbery Under Arms,* "and they were such swells, with their silk sashes, bowie knives, and broad-leafed 'full-share' hats, that lots of young native fellows took a pride in copying them." Americans ran hotels, introduced denim and the saxophone, brought in coaches, elevators, locomotives, and other new machines, delighted Australians with theater from New York and San Francisco, and taught the locals to mix fancy drinks and put ice in them. Melbourne hotels imported the ice from Boston.

Perhaps it was during the gold rushes that the gambling spirit bored deeply into the Australian soul and the Australian capacity for instant optimism, at times going beyond the known facts, was born. The six colonies desperately needed something to make them believe in the future, and gold provided it for most of them.

The goldfields were a carnival of avarice, drunkenness, social equality, gambling, rich entertainment, interracial sex, and a thunderous profanity of language, even from the lips of little girls. A favorite game during leisure hours was a competition to climb up a greased pole at the top of which bank notes were waiting as the prize. Police were generally hated, an attitude that has not disappeared in Australia. Clergymen were mocked as Australia sloughed off the state-sponsored religiosity of the convict years and settled down to cheerful paganism.

For a chance at the yellow stuff, shepherds left their flocks, servants left their Melbourne mansions, adventurers left their nations, husbands left their wives. The governor of Victoria had to learn how to groom and feed his own horse. Under the gum and wattle trees there grew a society distant from the hand of the state—until the government imposed a flat license fee on each digger, which caused uprisings. By the end of 1851 half of Victoria's adult men were digging. By 1854 Melbourne, exalting in its recent separation from New South Wales, was bigger than Sydney, and upstart Ballarat was bigger than Brisbane or Perth. Over the decade, Victoria's population rose from 75,000 to more than 500,000, and the colony shipped a whopping million pounds' worth of gold to Britain.

Some diggers did well and hardly knew what to do with their money. One man used to go into Melbourne hotels, buy drinks for all comers, and then with a crack of his whip sweep every glass off the counters in order to make the bill worth paying. Another bought a Melbourne hotel's entire stock of champagne, filled a horse trough with it, and invited citizens to have a drink as they passed by.

Others failed utterly and sank into poverty. Among the many at middle levels, quite a few left Australia when the easy finds diminished and gold digging turned into gold mining, to try California. In San Francisco the diggers from the land founded by felons won a reputation for crime; about the same time Victoria passed acts to exclude Chinese as undesirables, California passed similar acts to exclude Australians as undesirables.

The Victoria I grew up in was gold's creation. Up went the solid churches and schools in which I was taught morals and facts (a thousand of each were built in twenty-five years). Gold built town halls, mechanics institutes, libraries, and the reassuringly broad boulevards of Melbourne, with a hotel at each corner.

Gold reduced the power of the squatters as ex-diggers sought land and disputed the squatters' view that property bestowed the right to rule. During the lottery of gold every man jumped into the fray, and this spurred democracy's splendidly smooth Australian career. By 1859 Victoria had a secret ballot and virtually universal franchise for its lower house of parliament. Workers began to enter parliaments all over Australia. In Melbourne a stonemason worked on the walls of Parliament House by day and made speeches inside it for the Labor cause at night.

Gold, which was found to some extent in every mainland colony, by bringing in labor not only put an end to repeated demands from landholders in eastern Australia for the revival of transportation but led to a steady industrialization of Australia. Wool and wheat flowed in abundance from the countryside, but most of the people came to be engaged in manufacturing in the towns.

The term "mate" took root among the gold diggers, spreading there from the workers on the sheep and cattle stations. Soon it moved from the goldfields to the cities. On the Californian goldfields the equivalent term "partner" formed a revealing contrast. "Partners" suggested small businessmen. "Mates" suggested a collectivity of workers.

Of course seeking gold was a highly competitive activity. But it was more akin to buying a ticket in a lottery, which Australians love to do, than to an economic investment which Karl Marx would have recognized as capitalist. The gold rushes had a huge impact on Australia, but they did not turn Australians into fervent capitalists.

In fact Australia would soon become a land of strong trade unions, based on the shearers and other rural laborers. It would see cradle-to-grave welfare state governments, often placed in power by the unions. At the same time it would develop a racial-tribal exclusiveness that tinged the nation with anti-foreignism and made White Australia an article of faith across class lines.

And it would become a land of three distinct physical belts—a vast dead heart, then called the "Never-Never"; a swath of farmland and mines where the nation's wealth was generated; and the tiny Boomerang Coast where 80 percent of the people lived.

The cry "Unlock the lands" went up in the 1850s, but Australia never knew an expanding frontier on the American scale, acting as a safety valve for grievances and a spur for entrepreneurship. Good land did not extend far from the coast, and there were few inland waterways. This ultimately deprived Australia of some of the dynamism and individualism of the U.S.A. The squatters had completed their control of Australian farmland by the 1850s, when gold brought the first large wave of free immigrants. Whereas in America the frontier kept on expanding and new states came into existence, in Australia the basic process of settlement, and the establishment of all its future states, was over by 1860.

Most important for the future of Australian society, the Australian frontiersmen in general were not independent farmers but wage workers for large landholders. They were always too few. So Australian society, although by no means devoid of a spirit of individualism, was possessed from the beginning by an even stronger collectivist spirit and came to be a bastion of powerful trade unionism and of a mentality of depending on the state.

Although the power of the squatters was diluted by the more complex society that arose in the wake of gold, government efforts to throw open land to the small farmer, by selling Crown land at one pound per acre, were not very successful. Farming pioneers in the later nineteenth century often fared poorly. As Manning Clark puts it in his magisterial *History of Australia:* "The lovely valleys and fertile plains of the habitable districts of Australia took on the appearance of graveyards of human endeavor." This was a major reason why Ned Kelly and other bushrangers flourished. They were taking revenge on a culture of poverty which produced them.

Today the legacy of the squatting elite is still to be glimpsed in country towns like Hamilton, Victoria; Toowoomba, Queensland; and Bowral, New South Wales. The graziers hold fast to traditional values and look up to London. At the same time they are genuine people of the soil. Their eyes have a stare like that of their animals; their tweeds seem inspired by the hue and texture of their animals' skins.

The pattern of the graziers' lives is not too different from that of their ancestors a century and more ago: a rigid and yet in its way relaxed life on the land, with occasional expeditions to the capital city to sell the wool clip, attend the Royal Agricultural Show, bet on the horse races, and be seen at a ball or dinner at Government House. The leadership of the conservative parties in state politics often comes from these solid graziers, still dressed in their leather boots and moleskins, but horrified these days at post-1960s values.

By 1890 Australia was a cocky, prosperous place. Distance, so often the arbiter of Australia's fortune, seemed to have shrunk with the coming of the steamship, railways, and the telegraph. Most of the population was Australian-born, and a spirit of the fellowship of the common man, secular, leveling, and racist, was forming into a national consciousness. Gold had loosened Australia up; now the nation re-gelled in novel shape.

Ironically, the new spirit sprang from the bush just when the gap between the cities and the bush was widening fast. Urban Australia, still very British in flavor, was placing faith in factories, technology, and education. At the same time it accepted a self-image from another place and time. Perhaps the bushman was never the typical Australian, but something in the evolution of the Australian mind—maybe resentment against British control and a desire to project an utterly un-British image—led the city dwellers to believe that the bushman really was *them*. The bushman became the image of the Australian. It was as if in the U.S.A. the cowboy rather than Horatio Alger had captured the middle ground of the American self-image.

The most far-reaching value bequeathed by a century of Australian history was fraternity in the face of a hostile environment. The men who battled most intensely against nature—the explorers—became heroes. George Bass and Matthew Flinders, who survived a fierce sea off Melbourne in an eight-foot boat. Ernest Giles, who fought thirst and hunger in the barren center and one day came upon a tiny wallaby that had escaped from its mother's pouch: "I pounced upon it and ate it, living, raw, dying—fur, skin, bones, skull, and all." Edward Eyre, who walked the desert from Adelaide to Perth in a party of five after being fare-welled at a prayer meeting and presented with a Union Jack woven in silk by Adelaide ladies; two of the five reached Perth. Robert Burke and William Wills, who perished on their way back from a south-north crossing of the country. Ludwig Leichhardt, who with his party of seven vanished in that all-devouring center.

To lose out against nature was a failure that in Australia carried the power of national myth. The explorers were trying to do something that transcended economic striving. They were gamblers in the face of fearsome forces, and Australians love a hearty gambler. If the myths Australians have clung to are often sobering—almost as if Australia is a land of dashed hopes—at least these myths have provided an ethos that stems directly from the Australian soil—unforgettably captured by Patrick White in his novel *Voss*.

For us as youngsters the explorers were the most inspiring figures in Australian history, and the runners-up were the bushrangers. These criminals, many of them heirs to the convict tradition of hatred of authority, may seem to us today unappealing candidates for heroism. A well-known early bushranger named Whitehead killed a mentally retarded man by tying moccasins filled with live bull ants to his legs. Ned Kelly at the age of fifteen sent a neighbor's wife a pair of bullock's balls with a note suggesting her husband might find them handy.

But the bushranger was tough. He was courageous (at times). His Luddite streak—Kelly cut down telegraph poles and tore up railways—

appealed to rural people who resented the rise and wealth of the cities. He epitomized the improvisation of rough and ready justice in a frontier society. "A policeman is a disgrace to his country," Kelly spat (he meant Ireland), "not alone to the mother that suckled him." And the bushranger could lay claim to being a nationalist: as a criminal he was anti-British, since authority still stemmed from London. To this day in some cities the tram and train inspectors are called "Kellies," though they are neither heroes nor villains, but green-suited bureaucrats.

The bushrangers were not Robin Hoods. The shearers were not a band of socialist brothers. And the famous rural writers, Henry Lawson and Banjo Paterson and Joseph Furphy, were not proletarians, did not hold socialist values, mostly viewed the squatters favorably, and by today's standards were racist. Yet today many urban Australians romanticize the mateship of the bush, think well of the bushranger, and believe that true Australian values are rural ones. In substantial numbers they tell pollsters they would like to move to the country.

A rather aggressive, narrow, but eloquent literature of defiant egalitarianism was unveiled in Furphy's *Such Is Life,* Lawson's stories, and Paterson's verse. An earlier generation of heroes, the explorers, were often European-born, but the bush characters in the writing of the 1890s cried out their Australian-ness.

Nationalism, at this time, could be quite radical, because it was beginning to be supposed that Australia, long taken to be a southern "New Britannia," might become the world's first true "nation of the common man." Yet the Australian nationalism of the cities was not deeply anti-British. It could not be so, because most Australians still saw their country as an outpost of British civilization rather than as a dependency of Britain.

"The young folk of this country may reflect with pride," said the governor of Queensland in a banquet speech in 1888, when Australia celebrated a hundred years of British settlement with dinners, garden parties, and Church of England services, "that they are not descendants of black Australian natives but of their ancestors who fought at Crécy and Agincourt, who dispersed the Spanish Armada three hundred years ago . . . fought at Trafalgar and Waterloo . . . and built up this province to what it is."

Australians wanted Britain to protect Australia, from the French, from the Russians, and after 1904 especially from the Japanese. For this reason, too, Australian nationalism was not anti-empire, but only anti–*non-British* empires. Australian nationalistic writing of the 1890s was

Kiplingesque in its jingoism on behalf of an uplifting white imperialism, and this spirit intensified after World War One broke out. Australia sent troops to help Britain fight the Boer War; one soldier took with him a boomerang with which to kill President Kruger.

After the gold rushes, to be anti-Chinese was as Australian as the gum tree. Was the "celestial" not teaching Australian children to smoke opium; was he not eating Australian cats? After racial clashes on the goldfields, a widespread urge arose to "drive the yellow bastard out of the Australian bush." "They're nasty *and* they're cunning enough to beat us" was the theme of the sentiment against allowing any more Chinese into Australia, or even allowing those already in the country to stay. The Queensland parliament added a novel twist to anti-Asian feeling by passing an act which denied Asians the right to employ Aborigines. "Our chief plank, of course," said William Hughes, one of the Labor Party's greatest figures, "is a White Australia. There's no compromise about that! The industrious colored brother has to go—and remain away!"

A depression and severe strikes and lockouts in the 1890s cast a shadow over much of Australia, and devastating droughts reinforced the feeling of vulnerability. As banks and building societies crashed, and unemployed workers and panicky bosses snarled at each other, 40 percent of 1893's export income went in servicing loans obtained overseas in the expansive years. Victoria lost population, much of it to Western Australia, which was in the midst of a gold rush. Melbourne's one teachers training college closed because no new teachers could be afforded. In a decade of persistent drought, the sheep population of Australia fell from 106 million in 1891 to 54 million in 1902. For Australia as a whole the optimism of the late Queen Victoria era was gone.

The industrial strife of the 1890s was relatively mild in tone. Only one death occurred during months of confrontation. During a strike in 1891 Lawson wrote a poem about outlaws who come upon a policeman on a horse. They swing their guns into position. Suddenly they realize they know the cop:

> *Then one by one in silence*
> *The levelled rifles fell,*
> *For who'd shoot Trooper Campbell*
> *Of those who knew him well?*

An instinct of accommodation, a sense of being bound together in a small and isolated world, seemed to have entered the Australian spirit.

The feeling of being cast together as common men has never left Australians, and the present prime minister, for all the changes in the tradition over the years, is an embodiment of this generally admired common man. Lawson spoke in solidaristic terms that sounded left-wing, yet he looked up to the squatters and possessed a streak of authoritarianism. Similarly Bob Hawke, a common man in the texture of his life—his accent, his human weaknesses, his ability to talk to anyone—is also a chum of business tycoons, a despiser of left-wing ideology, and a man capable of authoritarianism. "The stuff about the meek inheriting the earth is a lot of bullshit," he once remarked. "The weak need the strong to look after 'em."

The one death from the industrial strife of the 1890s was a suicide, and it inspired Banjo Paterson to write "Waltzing Matilda," later set to music in a lilting song which grabs Australians' hearts. A virtual national anthem, its bush jargon glorifies a swagman's theft of a sheep from a squatter. It centers upon failure and death—the swagman jumps into the river and drowns as the squatter comes to pick him up—as do most enduring Australian symbols and myths.

The most precocious workers' party in the world sprang up at this time. The pragmatic Labor Party men—"ten shillings a day socialists," as they have been called—achieved "one man, one vote," formed governments, and won the eight-hour day (and clauses forbidding the employment of Chinese) decades before such steps were taken in the northern hemisphere.

American books were influential in the early years of the Australian labor movement, especially those with a future-oriented or utopian outlook such as Edward Bellamy's *Looking Backward,* Henry George's *Progress and Poverty,* Lawrence Gronlund's *The Cooperative Commonwealth,* and Ignatius Donnelly's *Caesar's Column.* None of this influence was widely viewed as in conflict with British influence. In fact the Australian labor figures, heavily jingoist on behalf of the Anglo-Saxon peoples, liked to keep a proper order of things by referring to America as "Britain's eldest daughter."

The shadows of the 1890s pushed the six colonies, which were addicted to criticizing each other, to federate (the Australian population now equaled that of the American colonies in 1776) in a murky arrangement that left ultimate power in London's hands. The Commonwealth of Australia came into being in 1901 as a limited contract, after much haggling and without philosophic flourishes. Western Australia had to be bribed with promises of Commonwealth money to link it by rail with South Australia to persuade it to join. "If you vote for the Bill," cried a politician in Tasmania, referring to the measure required to be enacted in each colony's parliament, "you will found a great and glorious nation under the bright Southern Cross, and meat will be cheaper."

The elite of the six colonies, in overcoming their mutual suspicions, were affirming their Britishness as much as their Australian-ness. George Reid, one of the fathers of federation, a typical British-born leader of the Australia of that time, as late as 1905, when as prime minister he gave an interview to Steele Rudd, author of the rural classic *On Our Selection,* confessed he had never *heard* of Henry Lawson or Banjo Paterson. "The crimson thread of kinship runs through us all," said another father of federation, overlooking the Aborigines, whose numbers had been reduced from about 250,000, when the British arrived, to about 70,000.

Still, the federal compact gave a fillip to Australian self-consciousness, put politicians onto a national stage, and spurred industrial growth by rationalizing some previously disparate tariff and trade policies. In its constitution, Australia tried to have its cake and eat it too. It put together American ideas of federalism and separation of powers with a Westminster parliamentary system—and stored up trouble.

That Australia was not ablaze with national consciousness was suggested by the approach of the states to railway building. New South Wales set its rails four feet, eight and a half inches apart, which prompted neighboring states to choose a different gauge, lest the senior state encroach. Victoria, feeling it should have the best railway available, chose the desirable five feet, three inches. Queensland decided on three feet, six inches, which did not make for comfort but was cheap, and kept New South Wales at bay. Western Australia was far enough away from Queensland to be safe with three feet, six inches, as was Tasmania. South Australia created a mess with lines of all three gauges. During my youth we could not travel from Victoria to New South Wales without changing trains at the border, and freight moving from Brisbane to Perth had to be transshipped five times.

Sydney and Melbourne each wanted to be the capital of the new nation, so neither could be. The constitution, which was and remains an act of the British parliament, laid down that a territory for a capital would be within New South Wales but at least 160 kilometers from Sydney. Until a city could be built—no name or site for it yet existed—Melbourne was to be the capital.

Federation's legacy of strife between the Commonwealth and state governments is a daily frustration of Australian political and industrial life. Only very slowly and due to emergencies—above all World War Two—did Canberra acquire the power needed to run the nation. The states still feud and cheat like jealous sisters locked up in a house on a rainy day.

One day in 1913 at an open-air gathering of dignitaries the wife of the governor general pulled a piece of paper out of a silver box. Reading from it in a querulous British voice, she announced that "Canberra" had been chosen as the name for the Australian capital "city." The noble lady could not pronounce the name properly, and no one knew what it meant, but the crowd standing on a hill in sheep-grazing country applauded.[1]

King O'Malley, the minister in charge of arrangements, had wanted to call the capital-to-be "Shakespeare." Some Anglophiles had favored the name of an English monarch or nobleman. "Eucalypta" was suggested but never had a chance. Canberra won by default.

For a city design, the Labor Party government launched a competition and named as judges three men who were not Britain-oriented. London was not amused, and cracks were made at the "foreign birth" of O'Malley; in a Labor Party cabinet full of British-born men, whom no one called "foreign," he happened to be American-born.

The Royal Institute of British Architects advised its members not to submit entries for the competition. Out of 137 designs, the winner was a bold maze of circles and hexagons by a Chicago visionary, Walter Burley Griffin, a theosophist and vegetarian who bore no resemblance to a roast-beef-eating man of empire. The Australian establishment was shocked at the choice of an American, and even more so by the dreamy originality of Griffin's design.

Canberra was not—like Melbourne and Sydney and Adelaide—to begin with the pillars, steps, arches, stained glass, and general gray heaviness of British imperial architecture, but to creep into existence as a scatter of angular and futuristic structures beside an artificial lake.

As a child I often wondered why my favorite uncle was a subdued man. He was kind and he seemed more interested in kids than almost any adult I knew. Only later did I realize that he was deeply cynical and did I learn that he was considered to have failed to fulfill his considerable potential. This uncle at the age of seventeen went to Europe as an

1. Canberra apparently derives from an ancient Aboriginal word, "Kamberra," meaning "meeting place."

Australian soldier. His letters home to another of my uncles ended "From your affectionate brother in great lands." The horrors of the war crushed the kernel of my uncle's spirit. Originally a boy from the bush, he saw things on the battlefields of France that stilled his tongue, without veiling his eyes, forever. He was one of many; no less than one third of Australian male breadwinners were in the armed forces during World War One.

In the Australian spirit there is an easygoing casualness, and there is also a pathos, not always expressed but lining the soul as a residue of sullenness. Historically the pathos is evident in the way Australians have given themselves to distant wars. This dark tradition soared with World War One. It was Europe's war. Australia itself had barely recovered from depression and drought. Yet the Australians, not yet sure of an identity separate from Britain's, threw themselves into the fray with astonishing loyalty and vigor. The whole nation sang the song "Australia Will Be There," which expressed the impulse.

Australians found in World War One a changed form for their nationalism. As the typical admired Australian, the bushman battling against nature's tantrums gave way to the plucky "digger." Named after the man of the goldfields, the Australian soldier, his lean bronzed face grinning beneath the distinctive Australian slouch hat with its brim upturned, did his bit for civilization as defined by British imperialism.

Unleashed, the Australians saw no limit either to the correctness of the cause or to the generosity they owed it. People chopped up their German pianos. Melbourne University dismissed its two German lecturers, the faculty swore itself to total abstinence while the war lasted, and students sang the national anthem (which was the British one) at the end of lectures. On city streets women pulled white feathers, a symbol of cowardice, from their purses and handed one to any young man in sight. In Bruthen a Patriotic Brass Band was formed and half the township's population sought to join it.

The common man found greatness in killing other common men. "Militarism," said the union paper *Worker*, "is less a curse than the armed occupation of your country by invaders—possibly by invaders of an inferior race." No nation had given much thought to invading Australia, but the insecurities of the Australian spirit were gushing forth like beer from a broken bottle. Meanwhile the war blunted the social idealism of both bush and urban workers.

"War has purged us," Prime Minister Hughes declared in 1916, "war has saved us from physical and moral degeneracy and decay." At

the Versailles Conference three years later, when President Woodrow
Wilson put forth his Fourteen Points, "little digger" Hughes in Australian debunking style rasped across the chamber, "God Almighty only
gave us ten." During the conference Hughes on behalf of Australia consistently spoke up for the superiority of the white race, trying to push
Britain and the U.S.A. into anti-Japanese positions beyond their wishes.

Nationalism, which had been leftish in the 1890s, became a more
conservative sentiment as a result of World War One. The evolution of
Billy Hughes reflected the switch. He left the Labor Party over the issue
of conscription—which virtually split the party—and put his rather
negative passion at the service of the right-wing parties. In the end more
Australians (the nation's population was 4 million) were killed in
World War One than were Americans (the U.S. population then being
95 million).

In 1915 at Gallipoli in the Dardanelles, a force including Australians and New Zealanders, the Anzacs, made a daring landing, charging
toward Turkish lines amidst shells and machine-gun fire. In a larger
sense it was not a great success, and eight thousand Australians died,
but in a long man-to-man battle the men fought determinedly, as if in
Turkey they had discovered for the first time in their lives a cause to
lift them out of themselves. Australia had needed an arena broader than
the Sydney–London corridor in which to show its mettle. At Gallipoli
quirks of timing and circumstance, plus wonderful courage and loyalty,
gave the young nation an event to turn into legend.

The Anzac legend joined the bush legend. Both were soon encrusted
with nostalgia for a failed or abandoned cause. Yet to a degree these
legends are still intact and near the heart of any religion the traditional
Australian has. The Australian suspects tragedy, even though he may
seldom have encountered it. Perhaps he feels a guilt within himself that
he personally has never thirsted in a desert or been shot at on a battle-
field. He clasps these two legends that bespeak the pathos of the individual confronted with vast forces likely to make him a victim.

As in the burst of Australian consciousness during the 1890s, Australia during World War One edged sideways toward a mature sense of
nationhood, only to stop short of claiming it, as if Australians were not
yet certain of who they were.

The 1920s in Australia as elsewhere in the West were a time of
buoyancy and improvement in life's texture. There came cars and good
roads, electric trains in the cities, and the quick spread of telephone and

telegraph. Radio, movies, and then in the 1930s talkies and airmail letters, made Australians more lively, pleased with themselves, and connected with a wider universe. Australians looked to Britain for news and to America for movies; to Britain for the steady beat of fundamental values, and to America for exciting flourishes of technology and entertainment.

The depression of the 1930s was severe—unemployment reached 30 percent in some cities—and for Australians with their small, dependent economy it was also a bewildering experience. It put in doubt whether Australia really could go beyond the flaws and dependency of the past and make its own bright future. A slump of 20 percent in the birthrate is frightening in a remote and sparsely populated land.

The ideological bitterness of the 1930s was peculiarly debilitating in Australia because the ideologies were all foreign. Loyalties were to distant gods and shrines, making Australia seem a place for secondhand implementation. To bridge the gulf between Australia and Europe, Australian Communists were prepared to lick Moscow's boots. Some Australian conservatives, to cope with their identity problem, strutted and frothed in a display of super-Toryism or imitation Nazism.

World War Two came as the biggest jolt in Australian history. Australia was even less prepared for it than for World War One. The morale of public life was at a low ebb in 1939. National institutions were still raw—Western Australia had not long before voted two to one for secession from the Commonwealth—and Australia had not seriously begun to think about its place in the world.

So two catastrophic wars, with only twenty years of breathing space between them, dragged a people not yet sure of who they were into the struggles, ancient and new, of world politics. The pre-1890 blend of peace, prosperity, and optimism was to come back only in the late 1940s. Yet fearsome as the cost for Australia was—30,000 Australians died in the war—it was less fearsome than the cost of World War One, and in the end it forced Australia at last to begin to define itself.

American overtures for closer ties with Australia had often been politely rebuffed, but by the 1930s many were starting to realize that Australia, as a Pacific nation, would need American strength as well as British. The "eldest daughter" had become more important than the mother. Japan's attack forced the issue. It also ensured that Asia could never again be overlooked by Australia.

This time, unlike in 1914–18, Australia really was in danger. Citizens built bomb shelters, took the nameplates off streets and railway stations, and lowered lights in brownouts. In the short term, the war unified Australia under a popular Labor Party government, headed by John Curtin, and gave parts of the nation full employment for the first time since the 1890s. Longer term, the arrangements made to meet the danger changed Australia's outlook on the world. In the trenches of World War One, Australian troops sang "Tipperary"; during World War Two they sang the Australian song "Waltzing Matilda."

The Australians saw their prime minister place himself under the command of an American general, and they welcomed nearly a million American GIs to Australian barracks and ports. Since the population of Australia then was about 7 million, that was as if the U.S.A. today were to be host to 30 million foreign troops! The GIs enlivened Australia and introduced new products. For some Australian men, the GIs' free-spending ways made them an object of envy. "The American soldiers could always give the girls superior American cigarettes and a better quality of stockings than we could," recalls an Australian veteran who lives in Brisbane and wears a battered felt hat that may well date from the 1940s. "That caused resentment."

"There were pitched battles between American GIs and Australian men in Queen Street," recalls Stan Mellick, a Queensland literary critic, referring to the heart of Brisbane. "But thanks to the Americans, Brisbane landlords learned how to charge high rents and shopkeepers learned to put prices up."

The wartime envy of the Americans, building on the old chip-on-the-shoulder mentality of some Australians, led directly to some of today's anti-Americanism. Yet the presence of the Americans helped all Australians to become more aware that they were a nation unto themselves. "To be Australian was no longer simply to be a form of Anglo-Saxon," Humphrey McQueen writes of the impact of that experience in *Gallipoli to Petrov,* "it was also to be a particular kind of Anglo-Saxon."

General Douglas MacArthur, reaching Canberra, listened to an hour of parliamentary debate and then remarked, "If Australians can fight as well as they can argue we are certain of victory." By the time victory came, Australia had fallen into the arms of the U.S., and to a degree has stayed there ever since.

In Bruthen during World War Two our numbness to history gave way to an interval of consciousness of the world beyond our blue-and-white beaches. As a toddler I was tossed caramels wrapped in foil of brilliant colors by the American GIs who had arrived to defend us. This was the first dent made on my mind by America. The soldiers, huge in their uniforms that smelled of starch, were cheerful and generous, and I found them reassuring. We began to hear tales of America's wealth and liveliness, and of how it was an even more powerful land (hardly possible!) than our Mother Country.

My mother and sister knitted bulky sweaters and socks from skeins of greasy white wool. The fat ivory-colored knitting needles clicked away like chopsticks—then an unknown item—and my brother and I felt the task must be important to take our mother and sister away from baking rock cakes and lamingtons and feeding the chooks. The sweaters and socks were for navy men going overseas to defend us.

Because it was Mother England and not her dominions who underwent direct war experience, we felt affection for her. From afar we formed heart-warming mental pictures of weeping Londoners forced out of their crowded little houses by German bombing raids; of Churchill conjuring from sheer will a force that would keep the empire intact after temporary aberrations; of undernourished Britons smiling as they opened our occasional parcels of tinned milk and bacon and biscuits; of King George extolling the unity of the English-speaking world, making us feel there was a reliable center to our existence. In a big cinema with fancy lights in the town of Bairnsdale, half an hour's drive away, we were touched by *Mrs. Miniver, White Cliffs of Dover,* and other movies that showed an England reduced in body but shining in spirit, fighting a battle for all of us at the end of the British umbilical cord.

On VJ Day at the Bruthen school we tiny kids followed the older ones in ringing the bell in the yard so recklessly that it broke. My brother and his mates, possessing great authority as nine-year-olds, turned the school's galvanized iron rain tank on its side. We tots crawled into the half-rusty tank. The older boys readied it to be rolled down the hill to the pub in the township's main street. We little ones rattled round like residual peanuts in a jar as the others pushed the steel-gray monster down the dusty road in celebration of British and American success in removing the danger of fascism from Australia's shores.

For us in Bruthen the war had been a fairly distant affair. The township found something to talk about when one day a fisherman at Lakes Entrance said he'd spotted a Japanese dinghy bobbing upon the ocean. But I never saw a Japanese invader, and when in 1942 Japan bombed the northern town of Darwin, 3,200 kilometers from Bruthen, our parents felt anger, I think, but not acute fear.

My father told me that during the war the Australian prime minister, John Curtin, announced that the United States, not Britain, would be Australia's chief rescuer. I developed in my mind a shining image of President Roosevelt, his decision-maker's eyes staring through his spectacles, and of his gray American ships, flying a strange striped flag, busy in the Pacific Ocean, making themselves part of our future. I thought the American accent was funny, but behind those caramels in colored foil there seemed to be strength.

My father's message, however, did not shake my acquired assumption that London was the center of the earth. We felt ourselves to be an outpost of Britain. We realized that with our hot bright days and our kangaroos we were not standard British civilization. But we lacked the airs of a civilization that knows itself to be unique. Narrow, stable, and slow-moving, we were a society unaware of the uniqueness of its physical setting. We did not realize how different nature had gradually been making us.

Our teachers doubted that our own brief history—half as long as America's—was enough to define us; they took it for granted, and so we pupils did too, that the story of Australia had to be tucked into a small pocket of the splendid garment of British imperial history.

The end of the war brought a measured happiness that the world was returning to normal. Yet it was not to be a return but an advance to a new era. Unbeknown to me as a boy, there were great changes in store.

FOUR

Three Tall Poppies

Deep as the lines to the past run, Australia today is in some ways a creation of the years since World War Two. Many Australians expected that the return of peace would mean yet another depression, and when instead there came a comfortable and secure era, much of the time with almost no inflation and more jobs available than people to fill them, the phrase "lucky country" was more than a self-deprecatory quip. People realized as never before what a blessed place Australia was.

Say "Menzies," and I enjoy vivid recall of the relatively calm era between World War Two and the Vietnam war. The world of my government-schoolteacher father—secure, fairly self-sufficient, culturally narrow—reflected the spirit of the age of Robert Menzies, prime minister for sixteen years in a row from 1949.

In those days women were not expected to play a part in public life. When Menzies mocked the Labor Party for being controlled by its thirty-six-seat extraparliamentary executive, his phrase "thirty-six faceless men," electorally a smashing success, made no one marvel that the executive indeed contained no women. Pretty much absent, too, were Jews. Melbourne, the financial center of Australia, had no Jewish stockbrokers. The Melbourne Club at the top of leafy and restrained Collins Street, with its stiff-boned butlers and copies of *The Times* of London on rosewood sticks, had no Jewish members.

When I was about sixteen, I went to an election meeting in the Caulfield Town Hall to hear Menzies speak. He rolled down the aisle, bushy silver eyebrows standing out from a pink face, bundled like a bushel of wheat into his double-breasted suit. He looked part grandfather and part arctic bear. I was surprised at how crudely he roared abuse at hecklers and those who asked hostile questions. Still, at the end, as he answered someone's query near the dais, I moved silently to his side and touched his bulging blue jacket.

"There was something very comforting about those double-breasted suits," a recent cabinet minister, Neil Brown, remarked to me of Menzies's appearance. This silver-tongued lawyer, who could "make the announcement of the opening of a phone exchange sound like a reading from the Book of Prophets," dominated Australia. The nation, despite its traditions of skepticism and independent-mindedness, "clung to him," said the astute political observer Alan Reid, "as a child to its father's leg."

Menzies bestowed a sense of being in charge—even when he was a hemisphere away at Lord's Oval in London watching a cricket test match. Riding wheat trucks around the district of Stawell in Victoria had given him a taste of ordinary people's lives. He knew the weaknesses of the squabbling and backward-looking Labor leaders. And he conveyed that he was standing not for the tycoons of business or the Machiavellians of the trade unions but for the middle layer of "forgotten people" (the title of an influential essay by him), the owners of the milk bars, and the respectable housewives in the bungalows of Murrumbeena. We feared his brilliant success may have put an end to the Labor Party's prospects of ever regaining office.

Yet Menzies had a streak of disdain for Australia. He called himself "British to the boot straps." He "looked as if he were imitating King Edward VII," as John Kenneth Galbraith remarked to me after a visit to Australia. He lacked a keen interest in indigenous Australian art and culture. And Australia's immediate environment—Asia—meant little to him; once Menzies got to Darwin, the next place of interest was London. Beyond the 1960s, it would become impossible for Australia to look up to such a figure, the fount of whose affections seemed to lie not only away from the Australian soil but actually outside Australia.

Menzies wasn't a very ideological conservative, except in his fire-

and-brimstone view of Marxism at home and abroad. He supported public bodies to handle the marketing of important primary products. His political vision amounted to staying in power and keeping the ship of state from doing anything silly or dramatic. When in 1961, to his great surprise, Menzies came within a hair's breadth of losing an election to the Labor Party, he adopted Labor's policy of budgeting for a large deficit to restore employment. At a cabinet meeting one of Menzies's ministers protested, "We can't keep on implementing Labor policies that we condemned at the election."

"If they were good enough for 50 percent of the electorate," retorted Menzies, "they should be good enough for you. Next item, please."

But Menzies did accomplish much in the sphere of education. His program of Commonwealth scholarships made it possible for tens of thousands of us to go to university. We "Menzies students" were a transitional college generation, and the first wave of a huge student army. Pained at the gap between what we read and what we saw about us, we bit the hand of the conservative Menzies generation that fed us.

We were in some ways a fortunate student generation. We were brought up and educated as opportunities had just expanded but before the crisis of values nearly took steadiness and seriousness away. War and unemployment—which had tripped up many of our forebears and would soon trip up a younger group—passed us by. If we were a bit narrow and protected, we had a foundation on which to face the quite different circumstances of the 1970s and beyond.

There was little grandeur about national politics in the Menzies era. Certainly the capital city of Canberra lacked grandeur. Our family drove there once about 1953. My father felt it would be educational, and there was good fishing on the way. But the city eluded us. Driving around in circles, we saw trees, some low buildings, and on the outskirts a couple of kangaroos, but no metropolis. Canberra was a country town amidst the bush with fewer people than a swath of a few blocks in Manhattan. No "dagoes" had yet arrived to bring a flicker of ethnic, cultural, or gastronomic diversity.

The bush had always been at least as much the worker's enemy as any exploiting class; and the suburban-based coziness of the Menzies era seemed to prove that the "middle people" could, once nature's teeth were drawn, find a vague consensus. Sharp edges of conflict had been smoothed. The accommodation had been foreshadowed earlier: The jailer and the jailed were not class enemies. Ex-convicts became policemen without a blush. The state built railways for the country folk. The workers had been given an eight-hour day in Queen Victoria's time and a guaranteed "living wage" just after the turn of the century.

The common man had not really hated his boss, it seemed, but only wanted to emulate him; and if no one soared too high, perhaps no one need feel completely outside the fold. A "fair go" did mean something, and if its context was limited to the white man, as it nearly always was, that only made the fellowship of Australians as common men the more intense.

Where access to opportunity and property is not denied, the radical impulse evaporates, and this is what happened in Australia. There was no conspiracy of "class interests" or "overseas forces" behind the generally conservative consensus of Australia in the 1950s and 1960s. Its logic had been clear long before. Wrote *The Age* in 1855, as it sought to allay fears of democracy: "Where there are no class distinctions, and no aristocratic monopoly of property, democracy itself becomes conservative." It was true. Because nearly everyone had a stake in the existing world, few voted for a new world. As Menzies continued the large European immigration program begun by the Labor government in the 1940s, something of the mateship impulse was expressing itself in a genuine, if still precarious, community of old Australians with new.

It was a long journey from the outback heroics of the explorer Leichhardt, who spoke of spiritual love, hurled himself against the furies of the desert, and sneered at the "fleshpots of Egypt in Sydney," to the supermarkets and the Holden sedans and the TV soap operas of the 1950s. Yet Leichhardt was a loser—nature devoured him—and the suburbanites of the Menzies era were winners. In the suburbs Benthamism thrived, having won a great victory for pleasure over pain. If there was little grandeur, Australia long before chose a bellyful over grandeur.

A "birthday ballot" put me into the small and primitive pre–Vietnam war army midway through Menzies's reign. We unlucky ones—the lord mayor of Melbourne drew marbles from a barrel, each labeled with a date, until the military had enough recruits—were herded to a dry spot north of Melbourne called Puckapunyal for a few months of basic training.

We polished our brass belts, learned to avoid thinking, heard stories about Australian "anti-heroes" killing their officers Ned Kelly–style in the Korean War, and were trained to wield out-of-date weapons (my rifle was a World War One 303).

It was in "Nasho"—as we called this National Service—that I found

out from listening to our officers that Gallipoli was the most sacred episode in Australian military history. No one commented that Gallipoli
was pretty much a defeat, which Australian troops suffered in the course
of a struggle that had little to do with Australian interests.

In Nasho the Australian numbness to history reached a surreal
pitch. Menzies was not a big defense-spender, and we were puppets
going through routines that were not only meaningless for us, but also
without much connection to any grand design for the defense of Australia. But I did learn how to make soup for three hundred people. You
start—or we soldiers on kitchen duty did—by forgetting hygiene, climbing a ladder beside a galvanized iron tank, and filling the tank with
water from a garden hose.

In the army, "church parade" was compulsory; since convict times,
religion had been used this way in an effort to limit vice and disorder.
We shot at trees (to get rid of surplus ammunition, which, if taken back
to headquarters, would require too much paperwork to keep) until
whole clusters of noble gums were set ablaze and many were burnt to
the ground.

By the early 1970s Australia had entered a new epoch, and much
of what Menzies stood for lost out. Australia's mood does not change
rapidly, as America's does, yet Australia can experience abiding change
over a relatively short period because it lacks entrenched institutions
and traditions. This happened in the immediate post-Menzies years.

Perhaps Menzies delayed the changes: from a colonial mentality to
a nationalistic one; from British to American and Asian cultural influences; from a puritan to a libertarian morality; from a Europe-centered
foreign policy to an Asia-centered one; from amateur politics to professional politics; from Canberra as a modest national village to Canberra
as a beehive of powerful bureaucrats.

If Menzies held the tide, he did so only for a while. Two perennial
demons of Australian history—war and economic slump—in separate
dances of destruction ushered in the new epoch. The Vietnam war divided Australia and embittered many of the youth who bore its brunt.
The severe recession of the 1970s added to the bitterness and increased
inequality. Both the war and the recession came at Australia from outside, largely as *faits accomplis,* producing a new bout of agonizing as to
whether Australia ever could be truly independent.

Immigration caused the most far-reaching of the sociocultural
changes. By the 1970s, the non-British immigration from Europe had

diversified the nation. Then the immigration from Asia during the 1970s and 1980s made "multiculturalism" dramatic, and plunged the old issue of Australian identity into deeper waters. In Murrumbeena the milk bar was joined not only by the Mediterranean coffee lounge, but also by the Oriental take-out food shop. An era seemed to be ending; in politics this meant the collapse of the Liberal Party's effort to prolong the Menzies era.

But Gough Whitlam, the dynamic middle-class lawyer who became leader of the Labor Party in 1967, faced formidable obstacles in his effort to reform his own party as a first step toward power. This I knew from my own experiences in Melbourne. One day in the mid-1960s I received a letter from Labor Party headquarters—on its letterhead with an inked sketch of laborers wielding tools—summoning me for a hearing. I was "charged" with having criticized the party in a published article.

My article was tucked away in the obscurity of the *Ormond College Chronicle,* but the Labor denizens of Melbourne were adept at using a hammer to kill a flea. I had written that the Labor Party in Melbourne "will not become strong until it lifts its gaze from the trade unions to the electorate." This was correct but a shade before its time.

I went down to the grimy nineteenth-century bulk of the Trades Hall to face a panel of grizzled sons of the Depression. For these men the class struggle would never be over. I admired their dedication, but everything new in Australian life—whether ideas or the consumer goods appearing in Melbourne homes—seemed suspect to them. The party reprimanded me but allowed me to stay within its ranks. I promised to be more loyal in the future to the party's rules, which were a devil's maze at best.

The Labor Party, especially in Victoria, was in the mid-1960s an anachronism. In an unbalanced way it blended a strong industrial wing of Communist-influenced unions and a weak political wing of Labor Party branches. It was very Australian, and yet its Australia was passing away. "We are Labor because we are Australian, and we are Australian because we are Labor," said Arthur Calwell, Whitlam's predecessor as Labor leader, and the woolliness of the remark expressed a passing generation's uncertainty in the face of change.

One night in 1965 I heard Gough Whitlam speak at a Fabian Society meeting. By now the class-war mentality of the Labor Party in Melbourne had brought the national party to a crisis. Whitlam is a brilliant speaker, erudite, logical, and witty. Early study of Latin gave an exactness and deliberateness to his sentences. I was impressed with his vision of a reasoned social democracy that had an appeal to the middle class. He offered the "revival of enthusiasm for policy" that I had called for in my *Ormond College Chronicle* article. I wrote to him, established a relationship with him, and on intra–Labor Party issues turned against the far left in Melbourne. Thereafter I played a small role in support of Whitlam's efforts to bring Victoria to its senses.

On the holiday weekend of Queen's Birthday I attended the 1965 conference of the Victorian Labor Party as a delegate of the Hospital Employees' Union. I supported this union's industrial interests while being free on broader matters to speak and vote as I wished. The conference was depressing. "War is the result of capitalism," declared our president, who never found fault with the Soviet Union. A proposal to allow movies in Melbourne on Sundays—they did not then exist—was defeated purely on the ground that cinema-industry unionists opposed it. So much for the consumer; so much for the electorate. The sessions manifested distaste for the life and views of ordinary people; love of bitter fighting for its own sake; uncanny skill in avoiding local reality by invoking global abstractions.

The morning after the conference ended I drafted a newspaper article attacking the ruling group in the Melbourne party for its narrow base and its flirtation with Communists through "unity tickets" in union elections. I thought it absurd that the conference treated the press as a sworn enemy of the Labor Party. I thought it ominous that almost a hundred of the four hundred conference delegates represented unions that had Communist bosses. Should I publish the article and be charged by the grizzled sons of the Depression once more? I sent my article to Whitlam and asked his advice. He phoned me from Essendon airport and said, "Publish and be damned. They may expel you from the party; you have to weigh that risk. But we will never get power until the primitives are beaten." The article came out in *The Australian,* Rupert Murdoch's classy new paper, under the heading "Class War Crusaders in the Affluent Age." It carried the by-line "A Special Correspondent," which set the Trades Hall scampering to uncover the writer's identity.

The Whitlam forces within a few years won a handsome victory when the national Labor Party "intervened" in Victoria, spring-cleaned, and so paved the way for the election of Whitlam as prime minister. A hunger for reform was widespread as he made the leap from long years in opposition to power in 1972. His slogan, "It's time," suggested that to a degree he was merely plucking a peach grown ripe on the branch.

Cultural figures flocked to the hustings, telling audiences they had never voted for the Labor Party but now they must. It was an election campaign of tears and laughter and yearning. The crusading spirit was caught by Labor Party leaflets urging the public to give a respectful hearing to the sagging prime minister, William McMahon, last of a quickly passing trio of Liberal successors to Menzies. The left was certain a fair weighing of the issues would give it the verdict.

"Give McMahon a fair go," someone cried, as if somehow the prime minister was already beaten before the vote. "I'm prepared to go halfway," a supremely confident Whitlam quipped in reply. "We'll be fair and he can go."

Patrick White wrote of the Whitlam watershed: "I realised we had reached a stage where a change had to be made if we were to . . . heave ourselves out of that dreadful stagnation which has driven so many creative Australians to live in other parts of the world." None of my teachers felt my education would be complete unless I did a graduate degree abroad. The cultural cringe afflicted us. At Melbourne University our student newspaper fussed about the need to be "conscious" and referred with approval to "the more conscious students" on campus. The key to this strange fear of being unconscious was a nagging feeling that we were lagging behind the world's real centers of thought and action. By 1966 I had left Australia for graduate study and teaching in the U.S.A.

America amazed me for its dynamism, rawness, diversity of people, and blend of the crude and the advanced. Here was a nation where success was not feared, as in Australia, but lusted for. I loved the bright colors of America's vigorous debate with itself.

The impact of the U.S.A. on an Australian student was greater than that of Europe, which seemed like a museum compared with this jumping laboratory of life. I respected Europe as a fount of our civilization, but in the U.S.A. I found a civilization far more enticing and disturbing—parallel to Australia but ahead of Australia. In the U.S. I found sin and idealism—both on a grand scale—and I began to feel Australia was short of both.

America made me see the thinness of Australia but in a positive way. In Europe, Australia meant nothing except in Britain, where Australians were taken for granted as colonials. In the U.S.A., people were just as unconcerned about Australia, yet America's past and present experiences were full of meaning for an Australian.

In New York I attended a meeting in Irving Howe's apartment of the board of the magazine *Dissent* on behalf of a corresponding Australian magazine. I found that in the eyes of these American progressives, including Michael Walzer, who took me to the meeting, Australia was regarded not as part of the new world but, by virtue of its link with Britain, as part of the old! This electrified me. I saw at once that there was some truth to it; the *Dissent* people had identified our past, which we Australians were hardly conscious of. But I was shocked by the implications. And surely, I felt, our immediate future would be different.

Whitlam's election seemed a major deliverance even for an expatriate. "For me as an Australian citizen," I wrote in a starry-eyed diary entry, typical of the spirit of the time, "this is the best day of my life. It is such a satisfaction to see narrowness and banality overcome. Now there is a chance to push for more equality, cut back on foreign control of our country, play a progressive role in Asia, link ourselves with China, give an entirely new deal to the Aborigines, and eliminate racism from our immigration policy."

Written in Boston on a crisp December morning just before I went to teach one of my classes in the Government Department at Harvard, the diary note caught the sense of outsiders coming in: "Throughout my life, ever since I was at high school, the Labor Party has been attacked and vilified. And now we are the government."

Few leaders have deserved office as richly as Whitlam did. The nation, whether it supported his ideas or not, had been reasoned with and taken into Whitlam's confidence. He built a case for reform, fought an open battle to equip his party for office, and told Australia exactly what he intended to do as prime minister and why.

"McMahon wasn't all that bad—not worse than anyone else," Whitlam said to me in Sydney a few weeks after he'd won power, when his staff laughed at the pathos of a phone call that came in from the defeated prime minister about some luggage he had left behind at the prime-ministerial residence. "It's just that he came in at a time when the whole [Liberal] party was breaking up." Whitlam felt that McMahon had been crushed as much by the dead weight of the Menzies legacy as by Labor's new vigor.

Few Australians were in the mood to heed McMahon's words "Do not let the Labor Party put its hand in the till behind your back." Some of the Whitlam team were innocently wide-eyed about governing; they came into office like eager boys exploring a forbidden palace. Almost overnight Whitlam increased the number of federal departments from twenty-seven to thirty-seven, and the percentage of employed persons working for the government shot up from 22 percent to 25 percent.

Whitlam remained somewhat aloof from his difficult pack of ministers. Older and less educated than Bob Hawke's ministers of the same party today, they were reformers who had waited long arid years for the chance to bring in their schemes; fighters who had reached the age of idiosyncrasy and were hungry for a last fling; a group that had been long enough together to despise as well as love each other.

Whitlam believed in a large role for government, and on a variety of ever-wider community services he spent money abundantly. He believed enthusiastically in using government funds on projects such as paying the fares of students from various states to go to Melbourne or Sydney to view an art exhibit from New York. He even wanted to start a government newspaper. Cries in the wilderness of the Menzies era became symphonies of the mainstream in the Whitlam era. Women emerged from their peculiarly Australian cage of timidity and fatalism. Environmentalists jumped on anyone who spoke up too crudely for growth or progress.

A sort of right to be different won an overdue victory in Australian life; indeed permissiveness made such strides that a small political party which specialized in attacking it, the Democratic Labor Party, went up in a puff of smoke at the 1972 election. Sectarianism seemed at last to be dying, as serious religion and ideology both faded. With courage and vision, Whitlam tackled the dragon of racism, and he achieved more on that issue—Aboriginal and immigration policies alike—than all previous Australian prime ministers combined.

Like waters from a burst dam, the Labor reforms came after accumulated pressure. Most of them were clearly needed. Some of them were overreactions to backward policies. They tended also to be one-shot reforms; the shots were fired, the gun was empty, the passion was gone.

If history is a consciousness of the past, Australia prior to the 1970s did not seem to have much history—at least not its *own* history—but from the Whitlam era Australians tasted the excitement, and accepted the shock, of looking at their past. Australians who used to be diffident or apologetic about their past now forcefully asserted Australia's uniqueness by appealing to the past.

Historic buildings were treated like sex symbols. Historians became public figures as historical events sprang to life in moral and political colors. Australians brought up in the slumberous years learned, sometimes from schoolchildren who had listened to a new breed of teacher, that the Aborigines were a proud and ancient people far from being extinct. Left-wingers wrote of the British as imperialists in Lenin's rather than Kipling's sense of the term. Right-wingers, equally fascinated with the past, wrote of the uprisings on the goldfields as the heroic cry of the entrepreneur hamstrung by government regulation.

British flavor faded. British citizens in Australia lost their special privileges. The Church of England, in terms of stated allegiance the largest church in Australia, changed its name to the Anglican Church in Australia. In government and business circles, Britain was taken less seriously than before. Vietnam had been a turning point; there Australia for the first time fought a war that was not also a British war. The entry of Britain into the Common Market in 1973 accelerated the replacement of Britain by Japan and the U.S.A. as Australia's chief economic partners. In Canberra the term for the English, "the Brits," was often uttered scornfully. The Brits have bungled again; what else would you expect of the Brits; the Brits are living in a dreamworld.

Much that Britain did in relation to Australia came up for scrutiny. It was claimed that during wars in which Australia fought for Britain's cause, British commanders at times—at Gallipoli, on the Somme, at Passchendaele—treated Australian lives cheaply. In a recent talk with me in Paris, where he was Australian ambassador to UNESCO, Whitlam looked back on a "very great reassessment of the propriety of what Australian governments aided and abetted during the 1914–1918 war." The films *Breaker Morant* and *Gallipoli* have given brilliant artistic expression to the colder view of Britain's treatment of Australia.

For the most part an attitude of shrugging the shoulders about Britain was probably more widespread than either hostility or support. Few wanted to kick the British in the teeth. Britain just became more and more irrelevant.

Some people linked the decline in standards and civility in Australia to the ebbing of British ways. Says a character in "Shark Logic," an evocative story about raw Australian beach life in Robert Drewe's collection *The Bodysurfers:* "The grubby amorality, the lack of manners, saddens me. If I crystallised my impressions I'd say that all the Englishness has gone." The character goes on to speak nostalgically of New Zealand. "New Zealand is still very English, more so than England . . . [over there they] all wear natural fibres, speak without stridor, play many sports, entertain in their homes, eat roast lamb and mint sauce, go to bed early and read English literature."

A strong American influence in the Whitlam period formed a sharp departure from a tradition. Instead of giving Australia only entertainment and technology, the U.S.A. now bestowed political radicalism.

The anti–Vietnam war movement spread from the U.S.A. to Australia. Australian Aborigines learned from American black and Indian militants. Feminists in Melbourne and Sydney found heroines in America. The Australian left wing, which had been anti-American since the crusade of Senator Joseph McCarthy, became much less anti-American as it discovered that America had a left wing of its own.

"How can an *ally* behave like this?" cried Henry Kissinger, waving a cable from Whitlam to Nixon, as I walked into his White House office on December 23, 1972. I was expecting to talk with him about China. But Whitlam had criticized Nixon's Christmas bombing of Vietnam and all hell had broken loose in Washington. "It's unforgivable for this Australian government to put us on the same moral footing as North Vietnam!" said Kissinger, dressed on this Saturday morning in a greenish tartan jacket and gray slacks, as he bobbed about in agitation. "We are not going to reply to it. We're not going to acknowledge it. We're going to pretend it never came—I didn't even send it over to State."

"Well, they feel strongly about it," I pointed out. "And anyway I want to make it clear that from the Labor Party's point of view ANZUS [a tripartite defense pact linking the U.S., Australia, and New Zealand] is unshakable."

"Well, *can* ANZUS be unshakable?" rejoined Kissinger, who had been among my teachers at Harvard. "You can't apply the alliance on some points and not on others."[1]

A few days later, I went to see Whitlam at Kirribilli House, the prime-ministerial residence in Sydney, with its wide verandas and its velvet lawns curving down to the water's edge. Whitlam was in buoyant mood, making decisions by the minute, more than ever giving the impression of a man who draws in for future use every item that meets his eye or ear.

On this brilliant summer day it happened that a U.S. warship was anchored almost at the foot of the gardens. "It cruised up yesterday," said Whitlam, informal in a floral open-neck shirt, "while I was talking about Australian-American relations with Waller and Plimsoll [two

1. A decade later in Canberra, when I related this remark to Bill Hayden, the foreign minister said, "Kissinger recently told me that at that time we were on the top of the shit list—quickly supplanted by Sweden and one or two others." Hayden stopped and frowned. "If the U.S. were to argue that ANZUS is globally embracing, that would demolish it. Malcolm Fraser once tried to extend the ambit of ANZUS to cover the Indian Ocean, but within a week he drew back. Yes, Ross, you *can* apply the alliance on some points and not on others."

Australian diplomats] and has been there ever since." The ship's air-conditioning was making a roaring noise, intrusive through the open windows of a mansion that lacked air-conditioning.

Whitlam, still in his first month in office, was preparing policy departures on China, Indochina, North Korea, and Cuba; and he was requesting greater information on the activities of the important American military installations in Australia. All of this, he knew, would irritate Washington. But the Nixon-Kissinger attitude had made him not less but more inclined to let the chips of his independent-minded foreign policy fall where they may.

The issue of Australian-American intelligence cooperation bothered him. "My own staff apparently have to get security clearances," he said rather grimly. This seemed to allow Uncle Sam to reach right into his own appointments decisions. "Can't they be trusted," he said of his staff, "after all these years of service?"

In fact Kissinger did reply to the Whitlam cable. "I have never seen such language," said the head of the Australian foreign ministry, Keith Waller, shaking his silver-haired head, "in a cable from one government to another."

"We are not going to say anything about the Kissinger cable," muttered Whitlam. "We are just going to pretend it never came."

I later read Whitlam's cable to Nixon and was surprised at its mildness. "The reason why it was never released [at that time]," a close Whitlam aide, Peter Wilenski, told me, "was that Whitlam felt it wasn't strong enough to satisfy the left wing of his own party."

It was a pity that Washington was not better prepared for Whitlam's accession to power. "I know and like them both," the assistant secretary of state for East Asia and the Pacific said to me at the State Department three weeks after Whitlam's election to office, "Mr. Gough and Mr. Whitlam"—thinking he was referring to the leader, Gough Whitlam, and deputy leader, Lance Barnard, of the Labor Party. In his talk with me the same day, Kissinger at first called the new prime minister "Mr. Whitelaw." Secretary of State William Rogers did not know—until told by Australian ambassador Plimsoll—that under the Australian system the Labor ministers (some of whom were making a merry sport of criticizing Nixon) had not been chosen by Whitlam but elected by the Labor parliamentarians.

As so often in the lurching relations between Washington and the Australian Labor Party, the quarrels were over images, and the crises were ones of nerves. It was far less what Whitlam did than what the

American side feared he might do—but never did—that caused the 1972–73 tension.

Little things, however, came between Whitlam and the U.S. Once he was sent a paper about Laos that was full of references to "enemy [Communist] forces" and "friendly [pro-U.S.] forces." He told an aide to send it back with a notation asking which forces were which. This kind of thing terrified the Americans, as it did the Australian bureaucrats who wrote the paper and were required to rewrite it in objective terminology.

For months in 1973, Whitlam did not know if Nixon would receive him on his impending visit to North America. He contacted me at Harvard to ask me to try to arrange a preliminary meeting between his top aide, Wilenski, and Kissinger because he was afraid that a request for a meeting through the Australian embassy, if refused, would get to the press and make his government seem "isolated from America" or even "anti-American." Whitlam was so concerned that Wilenski see Kissinger that he said to him, "If you see Kissinger, you can take a week getting back to Australia."

Whitlam's anxiety was partly due to his feeling that he may have been snubbed by Kissinger in Washington the previous year. Twice an appointment for Whitlam—then opposition leader—was made and twice it was canceled. Just after Whitlam's election, Kissinger told me it wasn't a deliberate snub, that he regretted the cancellations, and that at the time no one had told him that Whitlam was leader of the opposition. He asked me to convey his respects to Whitlam and to tell him that "in the middle and long range there is no reason why Australian and American strategic attitudes cannot coincide."

Wilenski kept his meeting with Kissinger secret from Australia's own envoy in Washington until an hour or so beforehand. Sir James Plimsoll, not entirely happy at being bypassed, had some last-minute advice for Wilenski. "Argue for our common outlook and solidarity as Anglo-Saxons," the elderly Anglophile said to the young technocrat with a degree from Harvard. Wilenski was born in Poland, and Kissinger in Germany, but the Australian foreign policy of Sir James Plimsoll and his era seemed born and bred in London.[2]

2. I had no doubt that Kissinger would receive Wilenski. Just a few months before he had received, at my request, a far more controversial Australian. Wilfred Burchett, in New York to write about the People's Republic of China's seating in the U.N., expressed interest in meeting Kissinger. Burchett thought Kissinger had shown signs of openness to China and he liked Kissinger's cautious view of Japan. Kissinger, who considered Burchett an intelligent and well-informed man and who was at that time

Looking back on the 1973 incident during our talk in Paris in 1986, Whitlam said, "I took the view that Australia's relations were so constant and close that it was perfectly natural for a prime minister to call on the president without any great panoply." Whitlam compared his relaxed view of the relationship with a "lickspittle tradition" that prime ministers "had to go to Washington to get anointed."[3]

It was in the Whitlam period that the Australian public service found its tongue to speak up to Washington, and also that the U.S. was required to adjust to a maturing Australia. All subsequent Australian governments have benefited from the change.

Despite a few brushes with Washington, Whitlam was pro-American, bearing in mind that his vision of America was mainly of its progressive traditions. "Probably the greatest political influence on me," he remarked during our Paris talk, "was Franklin Roosevelt—very much greater than that of any British prime minister." It did not surprise me that Whitlam sent his son, Nicholas, to be an undergraduate at Harvard; or that as prime minister he contacted me in Boston and laid quiet plans to make an Australian government bequest of $1 million to Harvard as a gift for the U.S. Bicentennial.

When Whitlam was choosing a new governor general in 1973, he wanted to appoint Kenneth Myer, a Melbourne retail magnate of Russian immigrant background who leaned toward the Labor Party. But Myer, in the midst of a marital change, was not available, so Whitlam turned to an old associate from the Sydney legal world, John Kerr.

After quibbling over the salary—Whitlam, not one to count the government's pennies, agreed to double the governor general's salary—Kerr accepted. A working-class product of a tough Sydney suburb, Kerr loved the pomp of being the representative in Canberra of Her Majesty the Queen. With his white hair and pudgy face he looked, in his robes, like a prize merino done up with ribbons and sash for the Royal Agricultural Show.

Two years later the unthinkable happened: In the biggest constitutional brouhaha of Australia's history, Kerr fired Whitlam.

---

hungry to know anything he could about Hanoi's mind, quickly agreed and a breakfast ensued at the White House on October 19, 1971, with Vietnam the main topic of conversation.

3. Whitlam included his Labor successor Hawke in his gentle criticism: "There's this odd sort of attitude by my predecessors and successors [he emphasized the "ors" in the word successors] that somehow there must be a great fuss when they're in the U.S. and available for a summons to the White House."

The Whitlam government lacked a majority in the senate, and in an unusual move the Liberal Party opposition, led by a brilliant young Victorian grazier, Malcolm Fraser, was blocking the passage of the budget through that secondary chamber. Fraser claimed that the undoubted difficulties the government was experiencing, as the oil shock hit and dubious foreign loan schemes were hatched, gave him a moral right to force Whitlam to have an election—or entice Kerr to do the unthinkable.

On November 11, 1975, the governor general summoned the leader of the opposition to his mansion, Yarralumla, told him he was going to fire Whitlam and appoint him, Malcolm Fraser, prime minister. With Fraser secreted in a side room—ready for his immediate appointment—Kerr then received Whitlam and handed him a letter of dismissal.

Kerr then called Fraser out of the side room and made him prime minister. "Malcolm rang me," recalls Mrs. Fraser, who was at her hairdresser's, "and said, 'Gough's been sacked.' I said 'I don't believe you.' "

"Had I known Mr. Fraser was already there," said Whitlam in 1986, "I would not have set foot in Yarralumla. I would have gone straight back to Parliament House." He paused and added with heavy emphasis, "Any communications would then have had to be in writing." Secrecy was crucial, for Whitlam could at any time prior to receiving that appalling letter have fired Kerr, simply by telling the Queen he was appointing a new governor general.[4]

The government leader in the senate, told by his Liberal opponent that the budget bills were going to be allowed to pass at last, received the information with delight—and not a wisp of a suspicion that a virtual coup d'état had occurred, and that the budget was now not Whitlam's but Fraser's.

"You've buckled at last, have you?" said Ken Wriedt, the Labor senator.

"Yes, we have buckled," replied Reg Withers, the leader on Fraser's side.

"Well, I'll be damned. Why?"

"Gough's been sacked and Malcolm's prime minister."

Wriedt roared with laughter. "You're a funny bastard, Reg. I'll say this for you, you keep your sense of humor when you're in trouble."

4. There seemed to be a strange echo of mixed British and American influence on Australia in the crisis of 1975. The governor general was at once a British relic and a check and balance, U.S.-style, on the power of the prime minister and his party in the house of representatives.

From the steps of parliament the secretary of the governor general read a proclamation dissolving parliament—Fraser would be prime minister during the lead-up to an election—and it ended: "God save the Queen." Whitlam addressed the bubbling crowd that had gathered: "Well may we say 'God save the Queen,' because nothing will save the governor general." Whitlam beseeched the agitated crowd to "maintain your rage."

Margaret Whitlam had been in Sydney at a meeting when the blow fell. "Just as well," she recalls in her Paris apartment. "Who knows, if I'd been in Canberra I might have collapsed and died." Looking back, the former prime minister's wife thinks "Gough should have just torn up that piece of paper, and said to Kerr, 'You're full'—which he was—'it's your word against mine, go to blazes.' " She stops and her tone becomes more philosophical. "It's the sort of episode that in many other countries would have ended in violence. And look at us; we're alive, and living in Paris!"

Most of the Australian people, attuned to bread-and-butter issues more than to constitutional ones, did not maintain much rage at the dismissal of an elected government by a ceremonial figure. In the ensuing election Fraser trounced Whitlam.

A year later I slipped into the Melbourne Town Hall for a Citizens for Democracy rally commemorating the first anniversary of the Whitlam dismissal. "If the peaceful path to change is blocked," intoned the historian Manning Clark, "Henry Lawson's vision of 'blood staining the wattle' may come true in Australia."

It was all froth. The Whitlam age of reform was over. The Australian people had turned the page, and the revolutionary talk was as meaningful as a Latin chant to Aussies alarmed by the rapid onset of high inflation and high unemployment. The average citizen had interpreted democracy differently from the Whitlam intellectuals. Nevertheless, Kerr was quite widely hated, and before long the Fraser government found it wise to find a new governor general.

"Of course I still feel angry about November 11, 1975," said then Premier Wran, president of the Labor Party, in his Sydney office in 1984. "The dust will *never* settle on it. That day the well of Australian politics was poisoned. Since then, politics has become a less pleasant calling. We've had some low points in our national politics, but that was the lowest ever. Kerr's treachery, not only to the Labor Party but to Australia's sovereignty, should never be forgiven or forgotten."

Said Tony Staley—who was in the Fraser cabinet—over an Italian lunch in Melbourne during the same period: "I have no doubt that we [Liberals] acted within the constitution. Myself, I feel that Whitlam, who was in so much trouble by November 1975, almost willed his own fate."

Mysteries remain, but it is clear that in the small world of Australian politics Fraser was better connected than the rather isolated Whitlam, for all Whitlam's formal power. The ambitious grazier reaped the benefit of a network of cronyism that included a governor general who had come to dislike the prime minister. It afforded a crucial measure of secrecy; it facilitated within the anti-Labor establishment some useful winks and glances and the ongoing mutual scratching of backs in the alarmingly unpredictable atmosphere created by Whitlam's careening governmental chariot.

The clash revealed how sordid the grubbing over public office can be amidst the beautiful hills of Canberra. Kerr had quibbled over his salary and privileges, and while Whitlam took this as a trifle, perhaps it was part of Kerr's entire motivation. He wanted his governor generalship to be marked by increased prestige and power, some of it at the expense of the prime minister's, and he wanted a second term of office, which Whitlam would not have given him. "Remember," remarked a Melbourne judge, who talked of this drama rooted in Sydney legal life as a bishop might talk of a drunken orgy, "Kerr was a boilermaker's son very excited to get into the establishment."

Royal baubles and gutter-level intrigue. The pride of a Sydney lawyer and the pressure on him of establishment outrage at Whitlam expressed at parties during Melbourne Cup week. The wary eye for pension levels in a society that tends to look to government rather than to enterprise for needed funds. All this underlay the clash. One is reminded of those murder statistics that show it's someone you know rather than a stranger who is most likely to kill you.

Some of it had happened before in the Benthamite outpost where power is like steam in a pressure cooker. In 1808, in the little colony of Botany Bay, Governor William Bligh was surprised to find himself arrested. "He was generally detested," Manning Clark tells us, "by the higher classes of people." He was a man who "craved display and grandeur." The main force that brought down the chief office bearer of Botany Bay was the grazier John Macarthur, "whose great wealth gave him influence, and unbounded ambition made him turbulent, and natural ability [made him] dangerous to the government."

Macarthur, like Fraser, prospered. Bligh, unlike Whitlam, had the verdict against him essentially undone. But Whitlam, who has never spoken to Kerr since that moment in the study at Yarralumla when the letter of dismissal was thrust forward, can joke about the event. "Like the thread of Ariadne," said Justice Michael Kirby while introducing Whitlam at a lecture at the Australian National University some years later, "the law runs through the career of Gough Whitlam."

"What you failed to say," said Whitlam as he rose to begin his address, "was that this set me up to be consumed by the Minotaur."

One evening in Washington during 1974, when Prime Minister Whitlam was visiting and a dinner for him unfolded at the Australian embassy, Secretary of Defense James Schlesinger, one of three members of President Ford's cabinet present at the table, rose to respond to Whitlam's toast to the health of the U.S. president. "To Her Majesty the Queen," intoned Schlesinger. I noticed on Whitlam's face an amused, rueful expression. "Can't you put an end to that!" I whispered to the head of the Australian foreign ministry, Alan Renouf, a Whitlam appointee, who was next to me at the table. Whitlam, who hates monarchical trappings, rose from his chair and in his own dinner speech referred with gentle sarcasm to Sir Patrick Shaw, the Australian ambassador—not a Whitlam favorite—as "among our most regal and imperial representatives."

Whitlam took some steps to strip away Britain's residual authority in Australia, but it was the hurricane of his dismissal that swept him to republicanism. "I remember the Washington dinner," the former prime minister mused in Paris in 1986. "My reaction to such a toast was less untoward than it came to be a couple of years later. Before 1975 I had seen no threat or impropriety in having a monarch and I might have seen some advantages. But after I saw the monarchy abused and manipulated . . ." Whitlam paused and leaned back on the white sofa. "Obviously now the risks are too great for it to be continued."

I asked Whitlam in 1986 if he had any lingering suspicion that the CIA may have played a role in his amazing dismissal by Governor General Kerr. "There have been some clear cases where American agencies have involved themselves in the politics of other countries," Whitlam began circuitously, "but I think we've got to realize that security services do conduct their affairs without their political masters always knowing what they're doing." He went on to observe that "security services do prefer conservative governments . . . even to the extent of compromising the interests of their own countries."

But Whitlam does not really believe the U.S. played a role. "Despite

Kerr's fascination with security services over the years, he wasn't spurred by the U.S. security services to do what he did," he summed up. "It was a purely indigenous conspiracy, and Kerr was looking after his own material advantages." This seems to be the gist of the matter. Richard Hall, who was Whitlam's close aide for five years and who wrote the biography *The Real John Kerr*, recalls sadly: "We destabilized ourselves, helped on by some smart operators."

At his elegant Paris apartment I asked Whitlam if Kerr had envied him. "I guess he did, yes." The former prime minister paused and looked out from the white sofa on which he was sprawled toward the twinkling lights of the Eiffel Tower, framed in the panoramic window against a midnight-blue sky. He turned back to face me and smiled. "I suppose he envies me still more now."

From Whitlam to Fraser was a sharp change. Fraser steadied the nation and taught it lower expectations. After Whitlam's expansiveness came Fraser's admonition that "life wasn't meant to be easy." In the Whitlam years Australia passionately debated the merits and modes of reform. By the end of the Fraser years the nation was soberly focusing on economics.

At the same time, the conservative revolution that many expected in the late 1970s did not occur. In the realm of policy the Benthamite center pretty much held up. Fraser enacted freedom-of-information legislation and appointed the first national ombudsman, steps which would have been unthinkable before the Whitlam era. "Fraser's failure to unlock the two-airline policy was symbolic," says the conservative Greg Lindsay of the Center for Independent Studies in Sydney, in a reference to the Siamese-twin behavior of Australia's two main domestic airlines, which deprives the traveler of varied schedules. "To think that a government supposed to be for a free market in seven years did nothing about this!"

The present leader of the Liberal Party, John Howard, who was Fraser's treasurer, defends to a degree the record of attachment to conservative fiscal principle in the years 1975–83. "In absolute terms, spending went up under Fraser at about two percent per year in real terms," says the opposition leader. "Reagan has done no better than that. The Fraser government wasn't a failure in achieving spending restraint. That's not to say that more shouldn't have been done."

Fraser did not stem the tide of real wage increases that began in the Whitlam years—until too late. His overdue wage freeze of 1982 did not bear fruit until the electorate had replaced him with Hawke. "There's no doubt Hawkie was lucky with the Accord [between government, unions, and business]," the union chief Simon Crean observes, "in that it was built on Fraser's wage freeze."

In foreign policy the continuity from Whitlam to Fraser was more striking than any conservative departures. "The end of foreign policy as a big election issue dates from Whitlam," says Bob Carr, a minister in the New South Wales government, and a rising star in the new-look Labor Party of the Hawke era, when I comment as we lunch at Parliament House in Sydney on the absence of argument over the international scene during the 1984 election campaign. "Whitlam's initiatives were simply absorbed by Fraser." Whitlam's memoir, *The Whitlam Government 1972–1975,* proudly makes the same point.

One of Fraser's greatest achievements, his sculpting of the idea of a multicultural Australia and his stance against racism internationally, endeared him more to the left than to the right. "He feels very strongly about it," says former minister Neil Brown, "perhaps because his mother evidently was Jewish."

Conservatives were sometimes unhappy with Fraser's anti-racist zeal. "I told Mr. Fraser multiculturalism was a lot of nonsense," says Professor Leonie Kramer at Sydney University. "His Institute of Multicultural Affairs is a great mistake," says Greg Lindsay of the Sydney think tank. "If people wish to pursue their cultural identity, that's fine, but it doesn't have to be organized by the government."

On the left the Sydney judge Michael Kirby, a guru to the Labor Party on law reform and social policy, is full of praise for Fraser's stance. "Multiculturalism is one of the great contributions of Mr. Fraser's government to Australia—for a dour Scot to embrace multiculturalism is a very important achievement."

In his paneled Melbourne office, its walls lined with rows of leather-bound volumes of parliamentary debates, Malcolm Fraser talks about his years at the top. "Thirty years is enough in that zoo," he says of parliament as we sink into deep leather couches. "Australian politics is a pretty vitriolic world. People freely call each other liars nowadays." He finds "pleasanter" his active retirement as farmer, businessman, and commentator.

Six feet, five inches tall, with the big square jaw of the rural Australian, dressed in a dark blue three-piece suit, Malcolm Fraser looks and sounds like the Oxford-educated grazier that he is. Family photos are prominent in the suite of offices. Forty-four floors above the hubbub of central Melbourne, the rooms have an air of polished efficiency and quiet discretion. Coffee arrives in fine blue china.

Fraser is quite unrepentant about his role in the fall of Whitlam. "All we were seeking, you know," he says of that torrid spring of 1975, "was the right of the people to vote." He says of the powers invested in the governor general: "That a power deliberately put into the constitution by Australia's founding fathers had not previously been used was not an argument against using it." Such a crisis could occur again, in Fraser's view, "if there is another prime minister who refuses to resign when he can't get his budget through parliament."

Fraser claims that he pioneered the concept of restraint in government spending. "We achieved a total revolution in the economic debate." He sees the current moderateness of Hawke and Paul Keating, the treasurer, as following in the Fraser footsteps. "Before Thatcher and before Reagan," he says as he sips his coffee, "my government was speaking of and practicing restraint."

But the former prime minister—the second-longest-serving one after Menzies in Australia's history—says he should have held government expenditure back more, and earlier, than he did. "We were badly advised by the head of treasury," he remarks, though he acknowledges that he was responsible for accepting the advice. " 'We've got plenty of time—take it gently!' this man urged, but we didn't have time—it was very bad advice."

Fraser admits that in his last couple of years in office "three things happened that blew apart a little of what we'd been achieving." As well as the international recession and the bad Australian drought, which "reduced farm product by forty percent," he points ruefully to the "extraordinarily damaging wages explosion" of 1980–81.

Fraser regrets that after "five years of consultation with the trade unions working well," he did not have a prior power to prevent the wages explosion by simply making strikes illegal, as Canberra can do with federal public servants. "The unions just went in for the kill on higher wages." Fraser pauses, then adds wistfully, "I should have gone for full industrial powers at the start of my government in 1976."

The drought returns to Fraser's mind. "You know, it rained one week after Mr. Hawke won the election," he remarks of his defeat in 1983. "It could easily not have rained for another twelve months."

A secretary puts her head through the doorway to check a date for a trip to the U.S. and Europe, pronouncing Dulles airport "Duels" and Newark airport "New Arc." Fraser often travels to the U.S.A., sometimes in connection with activities of the American Enterprise Institute, and across the room I see a large photo of Fraser and Reagan shaking hands. In many ways, though, his patriarchal political style is less reminiscent of American politicians than is that of Whitlam, who admired and learned from various U.S. Democratic Party leaders.

I observed both Fraser and Whitlam at Harvard. Fraser, who came to Harvard to hand over the gift that Whitlam had made for the U.S. Bicentennial, did not engage much with the environ. Upon his arrival in Cambridge, I took him in to meet President Derek Bok and Dean Henry Rosovsky, but he was not expansive and had little to say.[5] Whitlam, who came to Harvard to lecture after he left office, reveled in the atmosphere and made great use of his three months there.

Fraser is proud of his achievements on issues of race—he criticizes his own party for lagging behind him—and he is an enthusiast for high levels of immigration. He believes passionately in a multicultural self-image for Australia, "within which people from many different origins can feel fully Australian."

"One migrant declared to me," Fraser recalls, "that thanks to the multicultural policy I introduced, for the first time since he came to Australia he no longer felt he had to look over his shoulder all the time." The Liberal leader expresses an extreme hostility to the South African regime, which he has attacked relentlessly in British Commonwealth forums. "I don't know of any other country where the law has been used so vigorously to entrench the position of a minority against the majority."

What of the Soviet Union? "In Russia, if you're prepared to accept the dominance of the Communist Party," Fraser replies to my surprise, "being of one race or another is not going to put you in any trouble."

---

5. "I was underwhelmed by him," Bok told me some months later as we drove from Boston airport to Cambridge after meeting on a plane from New York on June 7, 1977. Dean Rosovsky had his own postmortem: "Fraser simply was anxious to get off to Canada, where he had trout fishing lined up." For Fraser, Harvard was not Oxford. On the other hand, Harvard was far from effusive about Fraser and took a rather take-it-or-leave-it attitude toward the Australian gift. The arrangements for Fraser's arrival at President Bok's office were a little casual. I was in the foyer of Massachusetts Hall chatting with the wife of Richard Leahy, a Harvard dean, when cars pulled up at the door and Prime Minister Fraser strode alone toward the front door. Dean Rosovsky was not in the foyer, as planned, to receive the distinguished visitor. I flew down the corridor toward President Bok's office and cried loudly, "They're here!" Rosovsky, closeted with Bok on some university matter, rushed out. He was just about in time; I had saved half a minute by greeting the prime minister myself. Fraser may well have thought it odd that I—a Whitlam loyalist and associate professor of government at the university—should be the first person to greet him on his arrival for the Harvard festivities.

Fraser today speaks up for individual freedom and responsibility in a world of state paternalism. "Democratic societies have offered more and more services," he observes, referring to electoral pressures to do so. "There has not been enough emphasis on individual and family responsibilities. Every time the government assumes responsibility for something that was once the responsibility of an individual—a mother, a father—some element of self-esteem has been taken away from the individual."

The former prime minister thinks deficits will "destroy democracy" if they are not checked, but he is not exactly a small-government enthusiast. He declines to attack the growth of the public service and he supports state-owned enterprises to develop the country.

"Which world leaders impressed you most during your eight years as prime minister?"

"Helmut Schmidt," replies Fraser, beginning a very short list with a social democrat.

"There are two things wrong with Mr. Reagan," Fraser declares when our conversation turns to current international affairs, "his terrible deficits and their effect on the world; second, while he has made the U.S. strong, he must do more to make the world peaceful." This is not the deferential tone toward Washington that conservative Australian prime ministers have always adopted. "He's an impressive communicator," Fraser adds of Reagan, "but I worry about his fundamental understanding of complex events."

Fraser thinks that "in major power relationships, ideology must be put aside," and he feels Reagan won't do this. "So often," the Australian conservative says, "Reagan seems to talk as though he believes communism is a dying faith, as though rollback in Eastern Europe is a possibility—which it isn't."[6]

Fraser, who like Whitlam appointed an Australian, not a Briton, as governor general, seems anxious to associate himself with the independent foreign policy of his Labor Party successor. "Look, what my gov-

---

6. One international matter on which Whitlam and Fraser diverged sharply was Australia's policy toward Soviet control of the Baltic republics. Whitlam reversed conservative policy by acknowledging Moscow's control of Estonia, Latvia, and Lithuania. I became aware of Fraser's repeal of Whitlam's step at a dinner party at Rupert Murdoch's New York home on June 5, 1978. Prime Minister Fraser, then very friendly with Murdoch, was guest of honor for the small party at the Fifth Avenue apartment near the Guggenheim Museum during his visit to the U.S.A. Seated next to Mrs. Anna Murdoch, who is of Estonian heritage, I heard her thank Fraser for taking the step, which—lacking much practical consequence, as it did—pleased Baltic nationalists. Evidently she had earlier urged the change on Fraser.

ernment did, Hawke is echoing. It was my government that said on behalf of Australia that many issues are just too important to be left to the great powers alone." Whoever is echoing whom, Fraser is quite agitated in asserting Australian independence.

"When I first came into government," he says, "London contacted us about a certain diplomatic initiative they were taking. I did not like the tone of the cable. They were expecting us to support them without even explaining the reasons." Fraser sprawls across the leather couch. "I sent a strong, appropriate reply. Acute apologies were made for having taken Australia for granted. Of course, they said, in future they would do things differently, and explain their reasons. The tone of messages from Britain to Australia altered forever after that incident." It would seem that Fraser did to Britain what Whitlam did to the U.S.A.— jolted it into taking Australia more seriously.

As he shows me to the door, saying he will see me at Harvard when he lectures there on South Africa in 1986, Fraser remarks, "It's not that Australia is being Americanized, you know. What's happening is that we're becoming more distinctively Australian."

Leaving Fraser's office to stroll in Collins Street on a crisp Melbourne autumn day, I reflect that after the Menzies era conservative Australian leaders have not wanted or needed to be strongly pro-British in sentiment or allegiance; and that after Vietnam, conservative Australian leaders have modified their pro-Americanism, from the eager pageboy adoration of Holt to the solid national-interest-based support of Fraser.

Like Menzies, Fraser—who remains an impressive analyst of the political and international scene—doesn't seem very right-wing. "I turned to my shelves," says Neil Brown, a Fraser minister who lost his seat when Fraser fell to Hawke in the 1983 poll and then returned to the practice of law, "to take down the 1980 volume of *Commonwealth of Australia Statutes*. There were *two!* The first year since 1901 that required two volumes! In both acts of parliament and Commonwealth regulations the Fraser government was prolific."

"In his last one or two years," says Brown, who is now back in parliament and has become deputy leader of the Liberals, "Fraser had grandiose visions of government; he started new departments—productivity, special trade negotiations, all sorts of boards and commissions. He had come to think that government—his government—could change things." It was a long road for an admirer of the philosophy of Ayn Rand.

"You see, Fraser had no firsthand knowledge of what it's like to run a business or to work in a factory," explains Brown, who fights an uphill battle for small government. "Developing a product, marketing it, investing—he does not know these things. If Fraser woke up one day and there was no crisis, he wouldn't know what to do—he couldn't handle a regular life."

It is a paradox that Australians despise politicians, yet fail to restrain them—perhaps feeling it is not worth the bother to do so. In practice they tolerate—indeed put in high office—some strong-willed and haughty characters. They elected Menzies repeatedly; even working-class people who were the target of his shriveling, elitist rhetoric voted for the great conjurer. And in electing Whitlam and Fraser, five times in a decade, Australia with its matey and egalitarian traditions chose two more giants—both men are big-boned as well as extremely tall—with an aloof and dictatorial streak.

When Fraser visited Harvard in 1976, I remarked, to make conversation, that it was good for him that he got his trip to China over the previous month—for just that week Whitlam was caught in an earthquake in China and was lucky not to be killed.

"Had I been there, and not Whitlam," replied Prime Minister Fraser, "perhaps there would have been no earthquake."

Two Harvard professors who were listening thought it was an arrogant remark. I whispered to an Australian journalist, "Gough Whitlam could easily have made that same remark."

"But Fraser sounded as though he meant it," whispered back the journalist.

Whether or not they fully mean such quips ("the only interruption I tolerate is applause," Whitlam has said), Australian leaders have sometimes sounded authoritarian. At the top the Australian political style can include, along with soft patches of self-deprecation, a hard streak of unshakable self-assurance. Perhaps a strident assertion of authority masks a doubt as to whether the skeptical Australian people have bequeathed the wholehearted mandate the leader craves.

For all the long shadows they cast, Whitlam and Fraser have begun to recede into an irretrievable history as Menzies did before them. At times they seem like dinosaurs from a past age, so much have the style and agenda of politics changed in the era of today's prime minister, Robert Hawke.

FIVE

A Tale of Two Cities:
Melbourne and Sydney

Melbourne is a flat city, laid out in squares, somber in gray stone. Pervaded by a sense of privatism and restraint, it does not feel like a port, just as London does not. It takes an interest in Victorian provincial centers as a mother in her daughters.

Melbourne knows extremes of weather and of ideology. The summer is the nicest of any Australian city, but the winter is probably the worst. In Melbourne you can have sunshine in Swanston Street, rain around the corner in that belt of style, Collins Street, and a gale up the hill in Exhibition Street, named after an extravagant building thrown up in the heady 1880s to house a show of Melbourne's precocious achievements.

A key to Melbourne—and indirectly to the Melbourne-Sydney relationship—is that Melbourne is a nineteenth-century city. I go into the dining room of the Windsor Hotel and see an era caught in time like salmon in aspic. The heavy grandness of the chamber, with its swirling murals, thick floral carpet, and domes illumined by blue, green, and purple lights. The trickery of a nest of stained-glass windows—the face of Victorian religion—so impressive at first glance but sentimental in motif and contrived in its dependence on light.

Victorian atmosphere and a price tag of $150 for dinner for two do not crush Australian informality. "You've eaten a lot, lady," says a waiter to my companion as he takes away our dessert plates. "I've never seen anyone eat that much in my life."

I go past the fine department stores of Bourke Street, feel the commercial spirit of this impressive avenue, and then look up at the Salvation Army's City Temple. It is a fussily turreted, wonderfully confident-looking structure. Across the lofty facade is a motto: BY LOVE SERVE ONE ANOTHER.

Much in Melbourne still reeks of the religiosity, high purpose, and optimism of Queen Victoria's time, when the hotel and church and Exhibition Building were built. The public-spiritedness, the loyalty, the reserve. The addiction to holding a public meeting on any available issue. The prohibitions not always observed. The wide streets which seem designed to cement conformity and avoid nooks where a sinner may hide. Between its normal city streets Melbourne has "little" streets of the same name, and these are as wide as an ordinary street in Rome or Tokyo or Mexico City.

As it prospered after the gold rushes, Melbourne became a wild place, "the vice center of the continent," as the historian Geoffrey Blainey puts it in *Our Side of the Country,* with scores of brothels within a stone's throw of Parliament House and the Catholic cathedral, and the nearby Exhibition Gardens turning into "a great human bed on warm nights." It was typical of Melbourne that its numberless pubs alternated with the offices of the Religious Tract Society, the Order of Rechabites, the Bible Society, and other such organizations, which, like the brothels, gambling dens, and pubs, were all part of the late-nineteenth-century mix of expansive hope and gnawing guilt. If Melbourne was so sure that the lack of a convict past made it superior, people in Sydney wondered, why did it have to build scores of huge and expensive churches to prove it?

Melbourne, like Boston, is a city with a heavy ingredient of puritanism but also a very civilized city. Rodney Hall, author of the novel *Just Relations,* who was brought up in Brisbane, says people in Melbourne "have an air of preoccupation about them, each appearing to be a person of consequence, right in the middle of conducting some unhurried business." The Brisbane writer puts his finger on the point that makes Melbourne a *challenge* to Sydney: "Something lurks beneath the surface, something Sydneysiders do not have. Crowds intermingle like members of a club."

Hall finds the "club" united by Australian Rules football, a game begun in Melbourne in the 1850s as a means, it is said, for cricketers to keep fit in winter; and by "a kind of faith in the common good," which gives Melbourne people "an everyday reliability, as though someone has said, if we stick together we'll be all right."

In the residence halls attached to Melbourne University, members of the senior common room stride to the high table in gowns, and a Latin grace is boomed across the heads of the hushed standing students. It is still a world of sherry, weekly magazines from England, talk about Oxford and Cambridge, Vegemite served in silver dishes with lids, and hidebound academics in baggy tweed trousers chopping logs for their fireplaces.

Melbourne has long been a base for the "services," members of which—especially navy officers—are fond of British ritual and hierarchy, and over port at their fancy clubs can still be heard to call Britain "home." In all of these circles a Sir John or a Lady Margaret will receive a little more respect than an "untitled" person.

I speak at a luncheon of the Institute of International Affairs and feel engulfed in a polite, measured London atmosphere. The food is English-style sandwiches, soft and dainty, with the crusts of the sliced bread cut off to suit gentle palates, filled with shredded lettuce and processed cheese. "Chatham House rules," says the chairman before I begin my talk on China, in a reference to a British way of conducting an off-the-record meeting where journalists may be present. Chatham House is the home of a London institute on which the Melbourne one is modeled. A gray sternness marks my audience; the men are in three-piece suits, the women are in tweeds and dowdy hats. Questions are put to me with debating society formality.

Melbourne produces theories and extremists, fascist and Communist alike. It is the capital both of creativity and cranks, with a thousand earnest adult education classes in between. Three of Australia's four leading literary magazines—*Meanjin, Overland,* and *Scripsi*—are based in Melbourne; all of them are good, if a bit jumpy and word-sharp at times. Although realities and the theories have sad encounters, which make martyrs or villains of the left-wing members of the Labor Party, Melbourne ideology is a reality in its own right—and quite alien to Sydney.

"My task," says Gough Whitlam—a Sydney man, referring to the late 1960s, when his maneuvers toward the prime ministership included reform of the ultra-left Labor Party in Melbourne—"was to get out of

Vietnam and to go into Victoria." He pronounces "Victoria" with heavier emphasis than "Vietnam," as if Melbourne posed a bigger Communist problem than Hanoi. Vernon Wilcox, a former conservative attorney general in Victoria, has another perspective on why Melbourne spawns fanatics: "I've always believed that the Communists targeted Victoria—through the Labor Party—because Melbourne is so influential in Australian political and intellectual life."

Melbourne's main newspaper, *The Age,* is extraordinarily good, if a little prone to bang over the head with its halo people it does not agree with. Founded by David Syme, "a long-faced theologian who had lost his faith in God," as the historian Blainey describes him, it has crusaded recently against corruption in Sydney.

"Like all serious newspapers we sometimes lapse into pomposity," editor Creighton Burns remarks over lunch on a sweltering December day, a few hours after he has won the Journalism of the Year award. Yet *The Age* has added racy features on life-style and has discovered that the writhings of the counterculture can make as good copy as the steady march of the establishment. Articles on animal liberation and transvestites nestle beside illustrated ads of properties for sale in Toorak and Portsea. Melbourne's old dualism of radicalism and propriety lives on. Burns, with high Melbourne purpose, takes stands on issues of liberty and justice that make some parts of the city's diversifying establishment splutter. "This is a conservative town," he says, "people are resistant to new ideas, nervous about debate over ideas. Melbourne is a place that has to be seduced; pack-raping is no good."

People in Melbourne like to think of Sydney as host to the flippant and the odd. "There's a woman in Sydney who is making a very good living," says Burns, "charging people twenty dollars an hour to come and talk to her." He smiles and turns back to his marinated lamb. "She's booked out for a year ahead. She even has women come and talk to her in a foreign language she doesn't understand, and they pay for this because no one else listens to them."

Burns does not deny that some corruption exists in Melbourne, but he insists that in Sydney it is widespread. "Remember that Sydney is less nonconformist than Melbourne," he observes. "And it's more entrepreneurial. When business gets tough, in Melbourne the tendency is to batten down, tighten up. In Sydney there's a tendency to take risks, tread yourself out of it somehow. The easy-buck mentality is more embedded in Sydney than in Melbourne."

The editor of *The Age,* who in the 1970s reported for the paper from the U.S.A., makes a comparison between Sydney and Chicago. "There was no evidence that Mayor Daley was putting it in his own hip pocket. Daley used corruption to lubricate the party machine. To an extent that's what's happened in Sydney. Both Liberal and Labor governments up there have discovered the therapeutic value of corruption. Rewarding your friends with impunity, and at the same time punishing your enemies."

"Things begin in Melbourne," says Bruce Grant, an author who was Whitlam's ambassador to India in the 1970s, in the slightly gloomy study of his bluestone home. "Later they may percolate to Sydney." Grant, who is now arts adviser to the Victorian government and chairman of the Premier's Literary Awards, continues: "In Sydney there's nothing to grip. Melbourne always had a civilizing mission, and there's a certain tension to Melbourne. The interest in Asia shown by Australians, whether in journalism or foreign policy or defense thinking, has always come out of Melbourne. This is where the split in the Labor Party occurred [in the mid-1950s]. This is where the Australian Democrats [a minor but fertile political party] arose. Sydney is freewheeling and much looser, more neutral, without that tension between the local and the universal."

When the Labor Party split occurred—the Catholic Church turned against the Labor Party over the issue of Communism at home and abroad—the devastation was engineered by Bob Santamaria, a son of Italian immigrants who for decades has maintained his Rome-versus-Moscow worldview. "It's Sydney's problem," says Santamaria, neat in a navy blue sweater and tie at his office desk, his eyes fixing me the same way they used to do when I was a student and he accused me of helping the Communist cause by woolly-minded Protestant leftism. "I have never felt any envy of Sydney." The Catholic activist is not content to let the point rest there: "Ecclesiastically, Sydney was jealous of Melbourne." His voice softens, there is a trace of a smile, and I sense the Santamaria didacticism rising. "Sydney as the first diocese in Australia was not happy when Archbishop [Daniel] Mannix, the Melbourne Catholic leader, became a national figure. From [Michael] Kelly to [Norman] Gilroy, the Sydney archbishops were upset about this." Santamaria looks grave. "One of the three reasons for the whole crisis in the Labor Party was Sydney's jealousy of Melbourne. Because of the defection of the church in New South Wales, I could not carry out the policy I was striving for."

My old adversary, whom I now respect, leans back in his chair at the National Civic Council, publishers of *Newsweekly,* and manages a smile. "The funniest day of my life was when Bishop [James] Carroll [now Archbishop of Sydney] said to me, 'Apparently you Melbourne people think Ian Johnson should be captain of the Australian cricket team!' " The political strategist gives a measured laugh. "I had never thought of our off-spinner [a kind of pitcher in cricket] as a possible Australian captain—but there you are, Sydney sensitivity." Santamaria's tone changes. "Sydney was adamant on practicalities," he adds sadly, "not on theories."

"Anyone brought up in the Melbourne tradition," writes historian Manning Clark, "would not view Rome confronting Moscow as an impasse, but rather as the beginning from which something momentous in the history of mankind might well develop." This misty observation expresses a perennial Melbourne illusion.

Perhaps Latin American intellectuals still imagine that Rome confronting Moscow can produce light, but in Melbourne during the 1960s most people discovered only the impasse. Precisely because in reality, as distinct from in soaring imagination, it *is* an impasse, Melbourne intellectuals have been better at defining challenges than at surmounting them, better at the agonies of analysis than at the ecstasies of synthesis.

For my part, I am grateful to the Melbourne tradition for its impossible challenges, even if the gurus and warriors who threw them up were under some illusions—like the dog in a scene from Camus's *Carnets,* which steals two anchovies from the table of an old woman in a cottage by the sea in the south of France and is defended by the woman's son, who remarks, "Poor dog, he thought he was already in heaven."

"Yes, I've believed in heavens, too," says the mother, chasing the dog away, "but I've never seen them in my lifetime."

The boy persists: "Yes, but he was there already."

Traditionally Melbourne hasn't sold itself as much as Sydney has, and many of its people adopt an ironic posture toward the city. "What I dislike about Melbourne," says Don Dunstan, a former premier of South Australia who directs tourism in Victoria, "is a carping negativism. Melbourne's self-denigration gives me a pain in the ass. In the public service you get a *proprietorship* in negativism."

But the mood may be changing. A radio station gives the suffix "in the world's greatest city" each time it summarizes news and weather. "I think Victoria, the old dear, is gathering its skirts up a bit," says Tony

Staley, a former Liberal minister. "Melbourne's saying, 'Bugger it, we're not going to sit here and see the game taken away by the outer states and by Sydney.' "

When I was a student, the Melbourne city council was one of the most exclusive and undemocratic enclaves in all of Australia. "To be Lord Mayor of Melbourne," as *The Age* put it, "was to be de facto patriarch of Portsea, and archduke of Toorak." In recent years the council has been headed, in the person of its lord mayor, by a wharf laborer and a news agent. The new Labor Party leaders disdain the old formalities of sherries for the ladies in a separate room and gilded robes for the lord mayor that took twenty minutes to put on.

I take a train to the bayside suburb of Sandringham. We pass British-looking stations in solid brick with cream-painted decorations, and we overlook green, precise backyards. On these trains we students used to pore over mathematics and read Dickens and Balzac, sunlight filtering onto our page through plane trees thoughtfully planted along the railway line decades before.

Beside me today are youths from two music groups, all dropouts from school, who seem to have no connection with a staid Melbourne.

"We nearly got sponsored by a sheik. You know what they are—it means an oil sheik."

"Jesus, why didn't it come off?"

"He chopped and changed. I think what the geezer really wanted was Libby [another member of the band]. But he nearly sent us to Fiji. And he was gunna put us onna wage!"

"Actually, Jim and I both got into Libby too."

"I thought she was a mull."

"She is."

A long pause and then: "Those sheiks are dirty buggers, aren't they?" I reach my destination and on the brick station wall is a railways authority poster headed GO TO THE ZOO. Over a picture of an ape it goes on: AND SEE YOUR RELATIVES.

When Melbourne took its personality from the respectability of the Queen Victoria era, the wild side was an under-the-counter compensation. Today the roles are reversed. The city, including *The Age,* seems unaware of its continuing bourgeois solidity—perhaps at last it can simply take it for granted—and is pleased to wave the flag of a regained reformism and even social avant-gardism.

Some attribute the recent loosening up of Melbourne to the coming to power of the Labor Party, which in the 1970s took off its depression mask and replaced it with a trendy one ("Volvo socialists," sneer people—conservatives or "real" leftists—who do not like the new Labor Party trendies). But the causes are not only political. I ask a Melbourne conservative if the city isn't in danger of slipping away from its established custodians. "It's already slipped," the lady replies with a quick shudder. "Look around you. Premier Cain fails to wear a top hat and a morning suit to the [Melbourne] Cup. People commit sexual intercourse in our public parks. The mayor of the city of Brunswick is a homosexual who lives with another man."

She averts her eyes and smooths her frock. "Worst of all, no one is self-reliant anymore, no one shows enterprise. Isn't it strange? The trendy socialists love the historic buildings, but everything else from our past, whether it's traditional clothes or solid values, they attack and throw out the window."

At a small dinner party in a fancy part of Melbourne toward the end of 1984, the talk turns to rumblings of republican sentiment that, like a new episode in a long-running serial, have been coming out of the Labor Party government of Victoria. "It seems Premier Cain does not like the governor," I remark, on good authority, to the tableful of conservatives.

"It's reciprocated," says Hugh Morgan, head of Western Mining Company and one of Australia's most able and vocal business figures, as we eat an appetizer of mango and avocado with ginger. "Every time we go there," adds the elegant Mrs. Morgan, referring to Government House as if it were her beauty salon or tennis club, "you can *feel* the hostility to the Cain government the moment you enter the door."

Premier John Cain has recently said that top hat and morning dress should not be worn for the festivities surrounding the Melbourne Cup. Parts of Melbourne society scoff and take Cain's announcement as a sign of insecurity. "He can wear his dull, ill-fitting suits," says one guest in a half-British accent, her lip curling as she attacks her quail wrapped in bacon, "or anything in the world he likes. He certainly won't stop *us* wearing appropriate clothes as we have always done."

"I simply lay down certain standards," Premier Cain says to me in an office shut off by heavy curtains from Melbourne's beautiful Spring Street, explaining why Melbourne is more upright than Sydney. "That makes us less susceptible to corruption." With no view available from the office, I find myself watching Cain's face intently. It is a lean, creased face. A tough face, except for the eyes, which are soft, almost vulnerable.

Cain is neat and modest and disciplined. He is the kind of person who at the end of the day likes to have half a dozen decisions made which are going to make a difference. "The real action is in Victoria," he asserts as he paints a picture of high tech and revived manufactures making Melbourne the city of the future. "We've done better here with the recovery from the recession than any other state. You'll have a few backwoodsmen and rednecks from other states who will disagree with that, but their bubble's burst."

"The federal intervention [Whitlam's clean-up in Victoria in 1971 which paved the way to his winning national power] broadened the Labor Party here," Premier Cain observes. "It's recognized now that the Labor Party is an umbrella party, and the natural party of government." He says something which is arresting to one who remembers the Victorian Labor Party of the 1960s. The "madder elements" in the party have been passing extremist resolutions, "but I'm not going to follow what they've resolved."

Has the coming to power of the Labor Party transformed Melbourne's establishment? "You never transform the establishment," replies Cain. "There's a grudging acceptance of us." As for whether the balance between political and economic power has changed in the city, the premier measures his words. "Certain things still get done in the Melbourne Club, in the boardrooms. I think we've changed the process of decision-making in economic development—whether that changes the balance between economic and political power is hard to say."

"Irritation over ties with the Crown is overstated," this paragon of civic responsibility goes on to claim. "There's a lot to be said for having a symbol as head of the government. I'd leave it alone." He stops, and I try to read his shrewd lawyer's face. It is late 1985 and just days ago he has forced the resignation of the governor of Victoria, allegedly over perks, but in fact as the culmination of a long, tense struggle over the meaning of the residual role of the British Crown. I am left in no suspense. *"Provided the governors haven't got any power,"* he adds.

"Are the days of the conservative forces using a governor general or a governor in a political power play over?"

"I've no reason to think they are," says the premier, now in full flight. "If what happened in Canberra in 1975 had happened in Melbourne," he says, referring to Governor General Kerr's dismissal of Whitlam, "I'm not sure where it would have finished. I think you would have seen serious direct action in the streets." A touch of steel has entered Cain's voice. "If it happens again, it may well mortally wound the system. If politicians try to use the monarchical thing to foreshorten the life of elected governments, where do you finish up?"

Tomorrow is the 1985 Melbourne Cup, and I ask Cain if he's going.

"Yeah, I'll go out for a while," he says with a little laugh. "I won't stay long; I'm not a racing man." Again he laughs faintly. "I've got some visitors 'from the other side.' They will accompany me to the Cup." It is a reference to Prince Charles and Princess Diana, who have arrived from London to help Victoria celebrate its 150th anniversary.

"What are they like, John?"

"They're all right. Quite interesting. They're doing their job." And Premier John Cain, on "his side" of the political and social barrier, goes back to an orderly desk to get on with his job.[1]

I stroll down to the financial and legal district to look up an old Labor Party friend, a supreme court judge appointed by the Cain government. "Melbourne is the center of idealism in Australia," says this senior judge, "and of new thinking." I ask him about corruption in Sydney. "Convict origins," he replies without hesitation. "The first Sydney police were convicts. And in early New South Wales, law and politics were very close. There were no political institutions, so disputes were fought out in court."

In the judge's chambers we sit in red velvet armchairs and munch sandwiches and bananas. "My goodness, the things people accept up there!" he bursts out. "A judicial vacancy occurs, and open canvassing for it goes on. Never in Melbourne." The judge goes on to analyze a current case in which a justice of the Australian high court and former federal attorney general allegedly used his influence to delay the trial of a friend. "Well, it's not exactly corruption, but it would not happen in Melbourne."

"Republicanism still matters to me," he says, expressing the long-standing tension in Melbourne between Labor and the vice-regal realm. "Especially when I travel in Asia, and people disparage Australia because we seem to have a status something like Hong Kong's. By all means," he adds, "let the *Women's Weekly* continue to fill its pages with pictures of the royal family for those who want to look at them." Up till now there are plenty of Australians—mostly women—who do, and not only in Victoria.

I head for Carlton, an Italian quarter of Melbourne, to lunch with Stuart Sayers, longtime literary editor of *The Age,* for which I began reviewing books twenty years ago. "You know it was awful," Sayers says, "when visiting England after World War Two, my brother and

1. A few months after I talked with John Cain he appointed as the new governor a very unstarchy Presbyterian theologian who was master of Ormond College when I was a tutor in political science there in the 1960s.

I said, 'We're going home.' " Sayers is a discreet and reflective man, with the face of an accountant and the eyes of an aesthete. But he thumps the tablecloth. *"This* is our home!"

"We laugh a bit at the royal family these days," Sayers says as he starts on a grilled flounder. "The Queen came, we saw her, God knows some people touched her. That was enough. When she came a second time it was an anticlimax."

Then in a Melbourne way of speaking, which Americans would consider a near-British accent, Sayers muses, "The British now find Australia a foreign country. But they brought it on themselves to a degree. My daughter suddenly found she couldn't work in London without a work permit. The British began to treat Australians as foreigners too."

Sayers dislikes the colonial mentality that the English sometimes show toward Australia. "Take the London publishers. When something brilliant comes out of Australia, they can't hide their surprise. They're like the first generation of painters in Australia who looked at Australia through English eyes. They did not see our glaring light. They did not see colors other than green—they were not open to the beauty of the Australian soil.

"I remember the Olympic Games in Melbourne," he says, sipping a Seppelt Chardonnay, "just two years after the Queen's first visit. I walked into the press lunchroom one day, and three Fleet Street types were bitching about the arrangements. 'These Australians just don't know how to handle anything,' one said. I resented that because it was wrong."

Sayers, who once seemed to me a somewhat British person—it was through his hospitality that I savored the very British atmosphere of Melbourne's Naval and Military Club—now does not seem so at all. Has he changed? But surely, too, the times have changed. To be very "Melbourne," as Sayers is, no longer carries any pro-British connotation.

Sayers loves Melbourne. "We are the Athens of the south," he observes as we finish a gelato and accept an espresso. "I mean, look at our newspapers—then look at Sydney's." He smiles a boyish, helpless smile. But Sayers sees a shift in Sydney's direction. "Many of the Melbourne writers are aging." Referring to the leading newer Australian writers as "aggressive and cynical," he says they are "mostly found north of the border."

Can Melbourne cope with tomorrow's new social and racial diversity? "Camberwell is a secure world," Sayers says slowly, referring to his own prosperous and respectable suburb as we stroll in Lygon Street and a December sun beats down on the mostly Italian-Australian pedestrians. "People there really do not care what may go on in Carlton or Footscray—let alone in the rest of Australia."

The "Cup" hangs over me, as unavoidable as Christmas, closed shops on Sundays, and the north wind and blowflies in midsummer. "Are you going?" is the only question anyone asks.

The day of the 123rd Melbourne Cup seems out of the natural order from the start. Students at Ormond College, where I am staying, normally informal to the point of slouchiness, bring each other breakfast in bed, with a rose placed on the tray, and champagne to accompany the dining hall's leathery hard-boiled eggs.

Fortified with shrimps and champagne, our party heads for Flemington Racecourse by tram, and at once I feel the puritans-at-play atmosphere of Cup Day. It is a morning of insipid sun, typical of Melbourne spring, but when the high white clouds float away there is a stab of warmth to the sun's rays.

A girl climbs on the tram in swimming costume plus a fur coat, and her boyfriend—on roller skates—wears long red socks and a red cap. There are men in top hats, others in diggers' hats; one has a pig's face as a mask. Boys wear shorts, their beefy legs still white from a long winter. Many women are dressed in swooping black and white garments, faces made up in white and red. Beer, fried chicken, and champagne are being consumed, and a stern Melbourne tram seems to have become a picnic ground.

Yet this is still a Melbourne tram. On climbs an inspector in his green uniform and spectacles. His complexion sallow and his mouth tight and hard, this symbol of Melbourne authority inches down the aisles to make sure we have all bought our fragile paper tickets.

Pensioners show their travel cards, then push their heads back into the racing pages of the *Sun,* where they may find a clue to a winning horse and, who knows, a whole new future in a Toorak mansion or a condo on the Queensland Gold Coast. One old and grizzled lady has a broad hat adorned with felt models of Australian birds, which bob around as her sharp eyes flash down to her racing guide, and as with a trembling hand she marks in red pencil her chosen horses.

People have descended on Melbourne from Sydney, the west, Queensland, and from countries across the globe. TV stations have sent boats up the rivers, and helicopters into the air to get every angle on the events. And if there is something excessive in the air, one feels Melbourne as a town of gray civility should be permitted a compact to be silly within the limits of the day. There is zaniness precisely where it is never found. Perhaps only a city as serious as Melbourne could besport itself so madly on Cup Day.

Flemington is choked with 80,000 people, in a swirl of gaiety and ugliness, a duet of the formal and the bizarre. I am reminded both of the style of Boston's Beacon Hill and the cheerful crudity of England's resort towns. For the first hour the only thing I cannot see is a horse; and only for one brief moment, as I go by the stalls to see the waiting contenders, does the smell of horses eclipse that of food and drink.

Melbourne people tend to stay home in their houses and gardens, but when they do go out it is in extravagant numbers and laden with food to eat in public. Race-goers move about the concrete car park in fancy clothes serving themselves a meal amidst grease and plastic and dust. They have brought chairs, tables, stereos, and much liquor. On the smooth lawns within the members' stand, Toorak ladies in the year's finest gowns are handed tulip glasses of champagne and large oysters on the shell by uniformed waiters they have brought with them for the day. While the rich eat lobster and caviar in uncomfortable conditions, others flock to stands offering Indian curry, the Big Mac, hot dogs, "Australian dim sims," or sixty varieties of pie from a "pieologist."

I see two transvestites dressed in empresses' robes of the Tang dynasty, with pointed shoulders and bodices encrusted with cheap stones. A heavily painted woman labors under a hat from which forty roses rise. A man wears a lampshade on his head. A schoolgirl has chook's feet. There are people from the solid southeastern suburbs in evening dress, and there are other people, younger and not from the southeastern suburbs, who accompany evening dress with tennis shoes and funny hats. Girls from a TV channel, dressed as poodles and dalmatians, are interviewing selected race-goers on their impressions of the clothes and the horses.

Even on Cup Day Melbourne's fussy officialdom—which runs the event with great efficiency—is not silent. "Mr. Stevens of Frankston to the secretary's office please," says an announcer with a touch of impatience. "Ian McLean, aged seven, of Footscray is lost and tired; his parents should collect him at once from the secretary's office." Nor is ideology entirely absent. "Late Scratching" heads the leaflet handed me by a tall angular woman without makeup. Is my horse out of the race? No. "Australia Out of the Arms Race." A button of the Nuclear Disarmament Party stares down at me from the woman's flat left breast.

The leaflet has another section: "The Nuclear Stakes—Time to Be

Announced." It goes on to offer a Form Guide with anti-Bomb quips about the names of the day's leading horses: Second Chance ("non-starter") Black Knight ("will be around for a long time if it wins"); Mushroom Cloud ("has yet to make an appearance here but has shown devastating form in Central Australia").

A girl in a hat three feet wide topples toward me and murmurs, "My sister's seen me drunker than this." A young man who is dressed normally grabs the arm of his girlfriend: "If you stand in one place, Mavis, you miss out on too much." As we rest on a grassy mound, a girl beside me has beer accidentally tipped onto her white dress. She looks to the sky, then at me, and says through clenched teeth, "With relatives like this, you really need friends." I see at last some real racing people, lean and tough like greyhounds, smoking furiously in their nervousness, the women among them seeming to take their manner and coloration from the men.

The elite are here, and the masses are here, and though the two groups are in different enclosures the mixture is part of the excitement of Cup Day. In their dress the elite take a step toward garishness; the masses try formal clothes half in a spirit of caricature. The Cup, a handicap race, gives ordinary horses a chance, and it gives ordinary people a chance too.

The terrain is so flat that the horses—like students at Melbourne University exams they go not by name but by number—are hardly more than a colored string of beads on the horizon. But tension quickly mounts; talk subsides; frenzy grips those who hope or fear. The colors of the jockeys' clothes grow more vivid and the sound of madly galloping hooves reaches our ears. One of my companions, a history professor at Melbourne University, is prancing like a dervish. His horse, Black Knight, is leading and within a flash this graceful animal has won the 123rd Melbourne Cup.

The governor general appears and through a loudspeaker he tells the crowd that this is Australia's "real National Day." He has brought along the governor general of New Zealand; on Cup Day the people of Melbourne are polite enough not to groan. The New Zealand head of state, who like the Australian one is as lean and rangy as a horse, looks mildly surprised that he is unscathed. He dares to say—or is it a protective mechanism?—that many horses in Australia came originally from New Zealand.

The owner of Black Knight is Robert Holmes à Court, a very rich Western Australian tycoon who is at this moment in bed in London. His wife steps up to the microphone in his place, and in a tiny half-British voice says Black Knight is a wonderful horse. At any rate it has won $525,000 for the Perth business couple. The jockey who rode Black Knight is given a moment at the microphones. "I know you're watching, Mum and Dad," he says, "and I want to thank you for everything."

Today the city of solidity and routine has gambled its head off. This most Scottish of Australian cities has spent over $50 million on the Cup. At the payout stands I walk by bookies in hats and cardigans who consult their lists and shout out to their assistants how much is to be forked out to the waiting punters. A young assistant, dressed in brown with a cigarette at the corner of his mouth, holds his money in an old-fashioned Gladstone bag. He is utterly silent, in fellowship with his crackling notes, as his bookie boss calls out the figures in a voice of gravel. The boss cries out $1,040, and for this sum the youth reaches for a rubber band to put around the notes.

Like little Ian of Footscray, I begin to feel slightly lost and tired, and so we depart, to seek normalcy again, to see if there really are people somewhere not dressed like birds and drinking champagne.

Beside the gate, near a stand where fresh crayfish are for sale, a man in a T-shirt marked USA has fallen asleep under a tree, his legs bent up in a comfortable position, a Foster's beer can gripped in his right hand. As we pick our way through the champagne bottles and beer cans I recall Billy Graham's remark: "Melbourne is one of the most moral cities in the world." Next year Foster's beer will sponsor the Cup. Two great cross-class religions of Australia, horse racing and beer, will conjoin.

Tonight there will be a thousand private parties all over Melbourne and people will say, "See you next year." The words suggest the appeal behind the ritual of the Melbourne Cup—a measuring rod for the march of time.

A week later in Sydney I ask a taxi driver which is his busiest day of the year. "Melbourne Cup day," he replies. Are people dashing to and from the airport? "Oh, no, they don't *go* to Melbourne; they are dashing to Melbourne Cup parties around Sydney."

As the key to Melbourne is its nineteenth-century character, the key to Sydney is its magnificent harbor—with 240 kilometers of shoreline—and its sense of itself as the senior Australian city.

Whereas in Melbourne nature has been arranged into parks and avenues lined with oaks and elms, Sydney follows nature's contours. If

Melbourne is ordered into set places for the pursuit of commerce, eating, religion, and family life, Sydney bustles, excites, surprises. In Sydney everything is open, anything can be obtained. While Melbourne's trams, with their stately lines and varnished wood panels, rumble along appointed tracks on broad boulevards, Sydney's functional buses climb and twist in a feverish anarchy. "I think what kills Melbourne is the flatness," says the playwright David Williamson, explaining why he moved to Sydney. "Sydney is all hill and dale and winding streets and harbor glimpses."

Sydney is less ordered and spacious than its sister city (3,160 persons to the square kilometer, compared with Melbourne's 2,537). If Melbourne recalls northern Europe, Sydney can remind a visitor of southern Europe. Its great buildings look theatrical in copper-colored or turnip-colored stone. Addressing an ocean, as San Francisco does, unable to hide its hedonism, Sydney neglects the New South Wales hinterland with a reveler's unconcern.

Sydney is not really less British than Melbourne. A century ago it was considered more so, and Melbourne was viewed as the Yankee upstart; Boston water carts were imported to lay the dust on Melbourne streets, and Boston fire engines to put out Melbourne fires. But in its bones Sydney is older than Melbourne. Melbourne today seems more British because the scars and glories of the Victorian period are particularly enduring and visible.

Sydney is aware of Melbourne's nineteenth-century provenance, and of the way Melbourne rose from nowhere to become Australia's biggest city when gold was discovered. This makes Sydney nervous and rude about Melbourne. It does not seem to satisfy Sydney that it is now more populous than Melbourne, and that in private Melbourne people speak enviously of Sydney Harbor. Two thirds of the American and Japanese firms that operate in Australia have their headquarters in Sydney. The market in New South Wales is larger than in Victoria, the Sydney lifestyle is very attractive for foreign executives, and Sydney's predilection for rapid turnover and quick returns suits many international businessmen better than Melbourne's cautious and consensual approach.

I ask the Sydney journalist Bruce Stannard over breakfast at the Sheraton Wentworth Hotel how he feels about Melbourne. "In Melbourne I just feel I'd like to get back to Sydney." He grins. "Melbourne seems provincial. Look at the low-rise somber architecture; then look at the soar-away glassiness of Sydney buildings. And let's face it, people live well in Sydney. You don't see people around with their arse sticking out of their pants."

It is Sydney Harbor above all that entices Stannard, a specialist on boats and the sea whose live radio broadcasts from Newport of the America's Cup victory in 1983 helped stir patriotic fervor in Australia, and who eighteen months before the event predicted that Dennis Conner's *Stars and Stripes* would win back the Cup for the U.S.A. in 1987. "The harbor is available to everyone," he says. "Melbourne people are watchers; see them in the stands at the football. Sydney people are doers; take a look at the harbor at weekends, and also on Wednesday afternoons."

In Melbourne, where people work on Wednesday afternoons, there is nothing as anonymous and hedonistic as the beaches at which people in Sydney spend much time. With an old school friend I spend Saturday "arvo" at Manly Beach. There is a smell of salt, sand, suntan oil, and fish and chips. Shops are not closed, as they would be in Melbourne because of Victoria's idiotic retailing laws. People are not sitting huddled in a stadium, as they might be in Melbourne. Sydney's big sporting event, the surf contest, doesn't lend itself to enormous numbers of spectators. Here people stroll the streets, gaudily half naked, licking ice creams, coming to or from the blue-and-white magnificence of Manly Beach.

"Life is faster here," says my friend, who long ago moved to Sydney. "People are less law-abiding than Melbourne people, more ready to take a chance, to cut their losses and move on." He remembers the period after we left Wesley College. "It was when I came from Melbourne to Sydney that I had my first fuck, learned to drive a car, and went to work for an advertising agency." As we peel off our clothes he adds: "You left Melbourne for the U.S.A. to find freedom. You need have gone no further than Sydney."

America is many things, and in the Australian imagination and experience only slivers of America are savored. Few Australians know the full range of what America is, and they continue to identify it with fast food, habits of boldness, and certain clothes, songs, and TV programs. In the ways most Australians measure Americanization—pop culture, machines, and life-style diversions—Sydney seems to me almost as American as Boston.

By the main road that separates the beach from the milk bars, restaurants, clothing shops, and fish-and-chip windows there is a notice: PLEASE HAVE CONSIDERATION FOR MOTORISTS. It goes on to ask that you cross the road "briskly" and "in groups when possible." A lifeguard, bronzed to an Aboriginal degree, makes an announcement. "We are looking for a lost boy," he says in that soft, apologetic, almost feminine voice that tough young Australian men often have. "He's got on white pants, and he's possibly wearing a light blue shirt." The gentle giant comes back to his microphone: "I forgot—he's six years old."

Back in the city, at The Rocks, an old spot now beautifully restored, I find a statue to honor the founding felons of New South Wales. "The earliest convicts," claims an inscription, "were treated and worked like animals." No evidence or explanation—did some of them kill like animals too?—just the assertion. Certainly in those days people crossed the road in groups.

"I think I believe in the greatest good for the greatest number," says Lady Mary Fairfax, wife of Sir Warwick Fairfax, a powerful Sydney publisher and one of Rupert Murdoch's main Australian media rivals, "but people want to retain what they have earned." She sweeps her arm toward the far wall of her sitting room, one of Sydney's grandest, from which we can see the Harbor Bridge. "Taking away this house from me wouldn't solve any problems. The money from it would last the poor about two days."

"Last night I gave a dinner party for my husband's birthday," Lady Fairfax explains, "and it was tiring, because my first cook has just died, and my second cook just left for a visit to London—I had to do many things myself."

Gardens sweep down from the house to the edge of the blue water. "It was a ballroom," Lady Fairfax says of the salon in which we sit, "but I converted it into a sitting room. I have concerts here." She sips her coffee. "I'm not one for Big Brother, you know? I like the *look* of the Opera House, but when one is *in* it, with twelve hundred other people, it's not the same as having music in this room."

I ask Lady Fairfax about the new Victorian Arts Center, Melbourne's brilliant answer to Sydney's Opera House. "It will do a lot for Melbourne," she replies in a tone that suggests Melbourne needs it. "But to tell you the truth, I am devoted to Melbourne. They have kept good things from the past. Here in Sydney we slough off a skin every few years. Melbourne is attached to enduring values, and I like that." Her eyes return from looking out the window toward the Harbor Bridge. "Whenever I think I'm going to Melbourne, I start smiling." She smiles and adds, "And I wouldn't dream of not going to Melbourne for the Cup."

Mary Fairfax was a brilliant science student at Sydney University, but found a diverting excitement in an early dress-shop business encouraged by her father. "I'd never met any factory girls before that, and

I thought they were rather nice." She looks back on her success. "Anyone who doesn't like money is either a hypocrite or a saint, because money confers freedom. With money, you can tell people who pressure you to get lost."

"I respect the Queen," Lady Fairfax remarks. "A symbol like that prevents people who just serve special interests from getting to the top. But America is where it's at now." She recalls the experience of her son as a student of philosophy, politics, and economics at Oxford University. "Fourteen of the seventeen in his class were Communists." Her pretty eyes enlarge. If Mary Fairfax sniffs decay in Britain she finds in America—where her son now works for the Chase Manhattan Bank—something that Australia needs. "America has the puritan work ethic—and we lack it. Why do you think I sent my son to New York? I don't want him to catch the terrible Australian disease of 'This'll do, mate.' "

We stroll out of the sitting room, past a work by Rodin and one of Lady Fairfax's own sculptures, called "Lily." "The face shows pain, joy, and accomplishment. The long neck is reaching up to God." As we reach the foyer she adds, "The gap in the back of the neck represents the hollowness of life."

I find the gates of the Fairfax residence unlocked and unguarded. The Sydney rich are not terribly separate. To the degree that they are, they edge toward ordinary company, to make themselves Australian again. It is a conservative worldview, without the European notion of privilege by right of birth, and softened by an Australian spirit of self-help and of "a fair go."

Trevor Kennedy is the highly successful chief editor of a variety of publications owned by Kerry Packer, a publishing magnate whose principal mansion is just down the road from that of Sir Warwick Fairfax, his bitter rival. Originally from Western Australia, the boat-loving, infectiously friendly Kennedy loves Sydney and takes a pretty dim view of Melbourne. "In Sydney you have a greater quality of life than in any place in the world," he declares as we lunch on grilled John Dory and Krondorf Traminer Riesling at Doyle's restaurant by the water. "Sydney offers a champagne life-style on a beer income."

Kennedy, whose hand guides *The Bulletin* as well as *Australian Business, Cleo,* and other magazines, worked in Melbourne for two years after returning from a spell as a correspondent in London. "There's a village atmosphere about Melbourne," he observes. Then he chuckles in a good-hearted attempt to be fair in the presence of someone from Melbourne. "Melbourne is a relatively easy place to work in, a great place to eat in—otherwise it offers nothing. And it has that terrible British reserve about it."

Sydney eclipses Melbourne as a center for magazine and newspaper publishing and for broadcasting, and to Kennedy it seems likely that Sydney will increase its overall dominance among the Australian cities. High tech and the growth of communications make for centralization, he points out. Sydney's life-style continues to lure the businessman. And Western Australia and Queensland remain at the mercy of foreign markets.

The Sydney editor does not approve of the role of *The Age* in exposing corruption in Sydney. "Helping a mate is all right," he argues as Doyle's stirs with the bustle of a Sydney summer lunchtime. "It's taking money for doing something that's wrong. There's too much confusion as between money and favors." Kennedy refuses to throw out the baby of mateship with the bath water of corruption. He feels that "if a minister in the government arranges for his old mate to see the chief planning officer and says, 'Give this bloke a sympathetic hearing,'" this is "the old Tammany style" and should not be called corruption.

"We've been enormously fortunate in the level of honesty and probity of Australian public services," Kennedy says. He sees *The Age* as rather self-important and "to a large extent irresponsible. They published a lot of stuff that assassinated the characters of quite a few people—including Kerry Packer." Was it a Melbourne vendetta against Sydney? "Probably more a drive to build circulation—and, you know, *The Age* always sees itself as very much having an influence on national affairs."

Kennedy has an unsentimental view of Australia's role in the world. His personal preferences are more for American than for British ways, but, he reasons, "To look to either Britain or the U.S. for succor and sustenance is a pretty old-fashioned view. In the final analysis we can't rely on either of them." He turns to the trade disputes that have Australian farmers up in arms against the U.S. and parts of the EEC. "It's pretty hard at this stage to tell either the Europeans or the Americans that they owe Australia a living." Here is the Sydney spirit of pragmatism.

On a sticky, glary, thundery December day I go to see Dame Leonie Kramer, who is professor of Australian literature at Sydney University. Kramer was born and educated in Melbourne, and since 1956 has been a resident of Sydney. She feels deeply influenced by Melbourne. "There was a sense down there of duty to society," she says in her large book-lined office, "a sense that life could be fun, but that it wasn't for frivolity."

"To what degree do you think of yourself as a Sydney person?"

"Hardly at all. I still feel I'm a tourist in Sydney—after twenty-nine years." This tough, spirited woman pauses to sip tea from an earthenware cup. "I don't feel a great attachment to Melbourne either," she adds, seeking to throw me off the track, or expressing the rootlessness that Sydney bestows on people.

Kramer is a member of a conservative Sydney circle around *Quadrant,* a lively magazine that is secular, internationally minded, and funded in part by business. In Melbourne there is a very different conservative circle around *Newsweekly,* the newspaper of Bob Santamaria's National Civic Council, which is lean, religious, and dedicated to stemming the tide of moral as much as political evil. Kramer seems more concerned with culture-in-Australia than with a special Australian culture, and she has been accused by writers on the left of a scorn for "Australianism in literature."

"I regret the decline of understanding of the nature of the relationship between Britain and Australia," she remarks, "and an absolute failure to understand the nature of tradition." She explains: "For years a silly argument went on with some people saying nineteenth-century Australian poets could not write because they used British eight-stanza forms, and talked about 'dells' instead of 'gullies.' People don't understand that an interesting process of *adaptation* was going on—just as before them, English writers adapted in relation to Renaissance Italy."

Professor Kramer refers to the broadcasting authority which she once headed. "The ABC is a case of a successful adaptation of a British model to Australian conditions. But many people just cry for more Australian content."

Leonie Kramer denounces and explains the Australian political style. "There's a total incapacity to engage in proper intellectual discussion, especially in politics. People jump into rigid positions straightaway. It's very serious, because our population is small and we have no metaphysical tradition. There's endless talk about politics but none about questions of the spirit."

Justice Michael Kirby, president of the New South Wales court of appeals, is a calculating and urbane man with a crisp, well-stocked mind, slightly playful in the manner of a clever lawyer. "Sydney lawyers work early, Melbourne lawyers work late," he observes. "I have for twenty years started early. Melbourne rolls into chambers about ten A.M., gets ready to dress up and go into court, and then works into the small hours of the morning." I suppose in Sydney the lawyers are doing other things in the small hours of the morning.

"Sydney is a more rumbustious city," adds the judge, not able to remain evenhanded for too long, "and I think the bar reflects that. Melbourne is a provincial town; Sydney is a cosmopolitan port. The Sydney bench is more aggressive in interrogation," he explains with a small smile. "The Melbourne judges are more gentlemanly. I say gentlemanly because there are no women judges in Victoria." He gazes from the panoramic window of his modern wood-paneled chambers. "Whether you get more out of judges and clients by the aggressive or gentlemanly technique is a matter of debate. I aim at the compromise of a gentle aggression."

George Negus, a TV reporter from Queensland who now lives in Sydney, can see the two cities in perspective. "If you like Sydney's razzmatazz and pace, Melbourne would drive you crazy," he says over a breakfast of tropical fruits at the Sheraton Wentworth Hotel. "If you're a person who enjoys differences, these two cities' opposite character can be appreciated. I do enjoy the contrasts, perhaps because I'm not a Sydney person.

"In Sydney people move in groups," continues Negus, who is constantly on the move between the Australian cities for his TV show *Sixty Minutes*. "There's no Carlton [the Italian quarter where Melbourne intellectuals nest] in Sydney, no place where you can go and run into people who are sitting around talking about the human condition. *Sixty Minutes'* rating in Melbourne is sometimes ten points higher than in Sydney," he adds. "Melbourne people are almost students of TV. There I'm seen as a journalist. Here I'm seen as a celebrity."

Negus cautions that Sydney is no seamless web of glory. "If you could not choose where you were going to live, Sydney would be a dreadful city. Most of the people who sing the glories of Sydney have the money to position themselves in nice spots with a harbor view."

Rippling waters glisten in the sun, blue etched with gold, at Lady Jane Beach, one of several Sydney beaches declared nudist. The hills opposite are covered with rough scrub in the subdued gray-green color of the Australian bush. To one side is the central Sydney skyline, not far distant, yet for the moment a planet away. On the other side, the little streets are choked with cars as people cruise in circles trying to find a place to park. From the nearest street there is a narrow picturesque walkway to Lady Jane, a sort of chastity belt for the beach strip.

It is difficult to climb down to the sand at Lady Jane Beach, and some people stay on the cliff above, either to avoid the walk down a flimsy ladder or to get a bird's-eye view. From below, framed against the sky, arms folded, faces serious, still clothed, they look almost menacing.

"I wish they'd come down," I say to my companion, "or take off their clothes, or go away."

"Perhaps they are not Sydney people," he rejoins.

On the approaching path, where the bathers are dressed, the march is silent and intense. People seem interested to know who else is coming or going, but they do not look too directly to find out. There are numerous Europeans, or migrants not long arrived from Europe, who instinctively walk to the right. As Australians come toward them, they quickly dodge to the left and murmur, "Sorry," in a heavy accent.

Seen from a distance, the bathers climbing rocks at either side of the beach look more like insects than humans. Without the usual "human" colors, people become akin to beetles or grasshoppers or clumsy walking birds. The atmosphere is more clinical than sexual.

Ferries on their way to Manly chug by, and then a smaller boat swings in close. From it two women shout. "You're all ugly!" one cries. "You score one out of ten!" adds the second. The voices have carried to our world of sand and flesh. We may feel offended, but the beach is collectively silent, and no answer goes out to the two fully clothed women who roar with laughter.

From the top of the cliff a demented man cries out that we are all sinners and that Lady Jane Beach is a doomed place. We laugh and go strolling by the rock pools. A large gray rock coated with green moss rises by the water's edge, and beside it stand two young people. The girl, who has a nice smile, is very fair and rather fat. She wears a blouse—perhaps against the fierce sun—but nothing below her ample waist. The man, who has a mop of strawlike hair, is naked and tattooed like an Italian mural. As the girl leans against the rock, the man pushes gently against her, trying with a word here and a movement there to break down her resistance.

"Take that out, Ray," the girl suddenly says. "I don't want sand in me." He obliges. The girl is not angry, but still she is unwilling. Nearby are some mates of the young man, and one of them calls out, "You're halfway there!"

Ray, now very ardent, says to the girl, "I know; we'll go into one of the rock pools."

"No, Ray, then I'd get seaweed in me." Ray's mates laugh, and

Ray seems to give up. Soon his cock is limp and modest like the others on Lady Jane Beach. Perhaps Premier Neville Wran and his trendy, corruption-tinged, but enlightened Labor Party government have after all produced a Sydney life-style distinct from Melbourne's.

Premier Wran, perched on the small chair he has placed beside mine on the visitor's side of his desk, looks on the defensive when I dare to mention Melbourne's capacity to draw gargantuan crowds for political rallies, sports events, and religious crusades. "A big sports event in Melbourne or a religious crusade in Melbourne is all that's *happening* in Melbourne."

Wran looks more comfortable. "Here on a Saturday afternoon people do their *own* thing. They may be distributed between rugby league, Union, soccer, many things. The choice is so much greater here. And in Sydney there's always a percentage who go to the clubs on a Saturday afternoon and play billiards or drink or ogle a barmaid— they watch their sport on TV."

There is a pause as the New South Wales premier perhaps recalls that I am Melbourne born and bred. "I mean the Adelaide Festival, too, is a great event—I'm not against Melbourne—but it's just that here in Sydney we have a festival every *day*." I look around the enormous office, high above the mid-blue water of Sydney Harbor, graced with black leather couches that could seat thirty people.

"Does it bother you," I ask the premier, "when people say Sydney is becoming Americanized?"

"Not a bit. There's nothing wrong with being Americanized," replies Wran in a flash. "The U.S. is the greatest democracy, it's the financial center, and few would dispute that New York is the center of intellectual life and creativity in the world. To revert to our English ancestry, and take a dim view of those bastards who went over and made a revolution, that would be very parochial.

"It's inevitable," Neville Wran elaborates on Americanization. "The Americans speak English. They support the concept of the family. They're Christians, for the most part. We both have a Pacific coastline. We have the same roots in England, followed by broader immigration. All this, coupled with the experience of World War Two, makes it the most natural thing in the world for us to be Americanized."

"We have changed the whole life-style," says Wran, his ruddy face eager, when I ask which of his government's achievements he is most proud of. "We did it in Sydney, and since I believe Sydney is Australia, in Australia in general." Wran begins with alcohol. "We've made liquor a normal part of people's existence. Pubs can be open seven days, and most of each day. This is civilized, and it's been adopted by most of the other states, though I believe Victoria is still dragging the chains a little."

The New South Wales premier, who has been in power for nine years,[2] says that in Sydney the arts have been made more accessible, buildings have been beautified, and Sundays have been transformed. "We started cheap excursion tickets to entice people out on Sundays. We abolished the admission charges to the museums and galleries. We've encouraged people to use the place." I am surprised that he doesn't call the dull old Sunday "Melbourne Sunday," as some Sydney people do. In Melbourne they call "Continental Sunday" that lively version of the day that Wran calls "Sydney Sunday."

"People are difficult to govern here," the premier reflects of Sydney, "because they are independent-minded. I'm not sure why. Maybe it's the climate. Maybe it's our ancestry. We did start off as a bunch of convicts, and there's still a larrikin streak evident everywhere you go."

Just as I feel a pang of pleasure that I did not have to bring up the convicts, the phone rings, and Wran, lean and nimble, goes back to his desk. It is one of the premier's ministers returning his call. "Is that place on the parole board filled?" The minister replies that it is not. "Well, don't fill it," Wran rasps into the phone. "I've got a good guy I want to put on it, so leave it open for me."

The premier rejoins me on the far side of his desk. "I like the larrikin streak, incidentally," he picks up. "I encourage it. I mean, you don't want people who are dull, with hair parted in the middle, who beat their breasts at every small indiscretion that takes place. I don't see life that way, and I don't see Sydney that way." I feel glad my hair is not parted in the middle.

"I'm a self-confessed atheist," adds the charming New South Welshman, as if hurling the remark across the Murray River in the direction of moralistic Melbourne, "and that's done nothing to damage my political life.

"People in New South Wales are more demanding" than Melbourne people, according to Wran, who once practiced as a lawyer. "They have higher standards. And if something is not to their liking, New South Wales people are not slow to voice their disapproval. They know how to demonstrate. They know how to strike." He pauses, as if re-

2. In mid-1986 Wran retired from politics and was replaced as Labor Party premier by Barrie Unsworth.

calling turbulent events. "Sometimes the results are good. Sometimes you get a shocking display of bloody-mindedness."

Quite different, yet cut from the same cloth, Sydney and Melbourne love to hate each other, and indeed people in the two cities *do* things differently and *put* things differently—at least since 1883, when New South Wales and Victoria joined themselves by rail, of varying gauge. The two governors traveled to the border for the festivities. At a banquet for 1,016 guests in a locomotive shed at Albury, there were no fights, but the Melbourne guests wore morning dress and the Sydney guests had chosen evening dress.

In Melbourne I feel impelled toward seriousness of purpose. I go to bookshops, universities, and dinner parties at which politics and ideas are dissected. In Sydney I never quite get away from the feeling that I'm there for pleasure. I go to art galleries, to the beach, and manage to get outside of myself.

Melbourne calls its private church-sponsored schools "public schools," while Sydney calls them "private schools," and calls public schools what Melbourne calls "state schools." In Melbourne you run into an old schoolmate every week, but Sydney is too fluid, too anonymous for that.

Sydney people are into bodies, Melbourne people into hobbies. Melbourne people go out of their shaded bungalows to attend organized occasions; Sydney people dart out of their flats for parties.

The rich parts of Melbourne—Toorak, South Yarra, Portsea on the Bay—are silent; all is secluded behind high fences and tall trees. The rich parts of Sydney—Vaucluse, Point Piper, Double Bay—are lively and even garish by comparison; people show their jewelry, poodles, boats, and suntans. The non-rich in Sydney make quips about "Double Pay," but for the non-rich in Melbourne the exclusive zones are too unknown to evoke quips.

Melbourne consumes a lot of tomato sauce, spread like a crimson blanket on the pies and pastries that give warmth in cold weather, while Sydney consumes more mayonnaise, on the healthful salads that are eaten on sun-drenched patios. Melbourne vehicles smell of gasoline, Sydney vehicles of diesel. Melbourne is plagued with blowflies, Sydney with cockroaches.

Melbourne loves its trams, Sydney laughs at them, and Melbourne resents the mockery. A TV fantasy produced in Melbourne shows trams turning into airborne roving creatures. They fly around Victoria, soaring above beautiful countryside. They reach Sydney, turn into aggressive insects, and begin to play tricks on the sister city. Their wheels acting as claws, they whisk the Opera House (its roof looking like French nuns playing football, as someone in Melbourne once said) from its lovely site. They grab the Harbor Bridge and deposit it on top of an office tower.

Sydney girls use the word "orgasmic" a lot; Melbourne girls say "really amazing." Melbourne money, which is often old, goes heavily on clothes, and charities are not overlooked. Sydney money, more likely to be new, is poured into gambling, and giving to charity is meager. In Melbourne there is a tendency to believe that real power lies behind the gray stone walls of the Melbourne Club; in Sydney there is a tendency to believe that it lies with the crime bosses and their political contacts. Melbourne people think that in Victoria crime is something done in the streets, whereas in Sydney it's done also in boardrooms and even in government suites; Sydney people think Melburnians are hypocrites about this. The crime rate is a bit higher in Sydney than in Melbourne, with the single exception of the offense of being a Peeping Tom, where Melbourne wins pants-down.

When Germaine Greer left Melbourne University to live in Sydney for a while, about 1960, the young intellectuals of the "Sydney push" teased her because she wouldn't say the word "fuck." She recalls: "I thought it was very common." Yet it was in Melbourne that she was raped, by a boy from a church school.

A foreign visitor who stays briefly in Australia will generally find Sydney more worthwhile than Melbourne. Sydney is more instantly cosmopolitan; what goes on internationally is available too in Sydney. But perhaps it is in Melbourne that Australian cultural life is most rooted. My high school teacher Arthur Phillips used to speak of the "easy achievement of happiness" in Australia as being in tension with "our inherited European temperament." He would complain that it was difficult to teach any sense of tragedy to instant hedonists. To a degree, Sydney is the special repository of that easy achievement of happiness, and Melbourne of the grappling with ideas from a larger world.

In my student days, Sydney students seemed to be at university mainly in order to get a job, while Melbourne students seemed to be there either to make themselves socially presentable or to dissect the world. For all the changes since, the distinction can still be found.

The recent discovery each of Australia's two great cities has made of its attractiveness has done nothing to lessen the passionate, hilarious sniping between them. People from the rest of Australia put up with this game; they are used to it, as children become used to the arguing of their parents. "It's mad," says Peter Wombwell, editor of the *Sunday Times* in Perth. "It's like London and Manchester. In fact nobody in Western Australia cares what Sydney and Melbourne do. One reason we've been successful is that we haven't relied on either of them."

For all their differences and rivalry, Sydney and Melbourne sit on a dirty mutual secret: Like two superpowers that bicker as they jointly rule the world, these cities privately believe that the other one counts and that little else in the nation beside the two of them does.

"Really Australia is a mock federation," former deputy prime minister Frank Crean remarks over lunch at his Melbourne home, "because it's essentially Melbourne and Sydney." Population figures are stark in Crean's support: Simply in the drab western suburbs of Sydney there are 1.3 million people, as many as in either South Australia or Western Australia, and three times as many as in Tasmania.

Tasmania is distrustful of the entire mainland, and the quips made about it in Melbourne and Sydney would seem to justify the distrust. "In Melbourne people ask, 'Where do you live?'" it is said both in Melbourne and Sydney. "In Sydney they ask, 'How much do you earn?' In Adelaide people ask, 'What school did you go to?'—and in Tasmania they ask, 'What school in Melbourne did you go to?'"

That Canberra is small and can so reasonably be disdained perpetuates the games Melbourne and Sydney play.

Melbourne and Sydney in fact have a lot in common. Both are cities of good housing, an abundance of fresh food, vigorous culture, little street life, many cars, plenty of space, all encompassed by that southern sky that makes you feel far from anywhere. Both are padded with a sprawling red-tiled ulcerless suburbia, the living evidence of Australians' impulse to avoid going to the bush, and instead to cluster reasonably near to each other on the coast. People of both cities live in similar Californian bungalows, post–World War Two boxes, older homes girdled with verandas and bristling with towers, gables, and conical spires, or in flat ultramodern houses in the outer fringes.

In sober moments the two cities see each other's merits. "The two most atmospheric sports events in Australia," Neville Wran concedes, "are both in Melbourne: the football Grand Final, not to be missed, if you happen to be in Australia when it's on, and the Melbourne Cup."

"When I first used to go to Sydney, years ago," recalls Tony Staley, the former Liberal minister, "I was terrified by the adventurousness of the place, the brashness, the Americanization. But Sydney is curvaceous, it has ups and downs, it's a sexy city." My former Melbourne University classmate laughs. "In Melbourne we see ourselves as more stable, with fewer crooks. Though, my Jesus, we've got our share of crooks now; we don't have a *reputation* for having them. But you know, now, as a Melbourne man, I love going to Sydney."

The love-hate posture may stem from the fact that Sydney and Melbourne complement each other. Sydney's Opera House has a magnificent exterior; the Victorian Arts Center in Melbourne is better inside. Sydney is great for the outdoor life; Melbourne concentrates on the indoor tasks of thinking, cooking, and dressing fastidiously. Sydney solves problems; Melbourne is excellent at analyzing problems. In Sydney, where the stakes are high, you find much crime; in Melbourne, where they are a bit less high, you find skilled crime prevention.

Melbourne generally supplies the conservative political leaders, while Sydney sets the tone for the success-oriented part of the Labor Party. Melbourne upholds a constantly evolving puritan tradition; Sydney expresses a measured hedonism. In complex ways the moralism and the flamboyance have always been linked; there is a bit of Sydney in Melburnians, a bit of Melbourne in Sydneysiders, and a bit of Sydney and Melbourne in all Australians.

SIX

Beauty and the Bush

"I'm in bananas an hour's drive south," says the sandy-haired young man in a Brisbane bar. "I used to live in Melbourne, but after a while I couldn't stand the flat rows of red roofs, everything the same." Queensland, the 2,000-kilometer-long tropical state that occupies Australia's northeast, has gained scores of thousands of people from the Boomerang Coast over recent decades.

To some Australians, Queensland is what Australia once was like and should still be like, just as for some Americans all of Australia—as they perceive it—is what the U.S.A. once was like and still should be like. To other Australians, Queensland public life is backward and its people are yokels. There are southerners who call Queensland "Bananaland," in the same tone—what *is* wrong with the banana?—that the term "Banana Republic" is uttered. Melbourne and Sydney papers publish items that paint Queensland into a corner of right-wing extremism. "Welcome to Queensland," says a cartoon of a scraggy-looking Brisbane in a Melbourne paper. "No Strikes, No Unions—And No Questions." The next frame shows workers with their hands up before a policeman; one worker grunts, "At least the weather is nicer than Poland's!"

144

A column in the Sydney weekly *The Bulletin* chuckles over an account of a Chinese man arriving in Australia without a visa: "Chee hid in a lavatory. Asked why he came to Australia, he replied: 'To see Brisbane.' The immigration officials said this aroused suspicion."

Brisbane was founded, from Sydney, as a place for convicts who committed a second offense, and it remains a great place for an unlikely comeback. A pruned bush will flourish with new growth almost while you wait. A furious rainstorm will be followed by a kaleidoscopic sun that makes the purple jacarandas shine, and the green acacia leaves seem lit from behind by electric bulbs.

The Brisbane River winds through a hilly city of 1.16 million people that has grown higgledy-piggledy. At dusk a fading sun shining through inky clouds in bizarre formations turns the water fish-colored and lights up the angles of a Meccano-set bridge. Most of the houses are wooden, set high on stilts to give ventilation and keep flood waters at bay, with wide verandas to keep out the sun.

As Sydney moves on to weary sophistication, it is Brisbane that is the blowsy sister of the Australian urban family. Like Perth, Brisbane has been transformed by a post-1960s boom, and it looks a youthful, healthy city. Its public buildings are floodlit as if for a permanent festival, not in subtle white lights but in rich gold or blue or green. It is a place of bare legs, big hats, intuitive judgments, and moneymaking. Up here, to keep healthy you swim and fuck; you do not eat nuts and do aerobic dancing. In the city streets nearly everyone is white; Queensland has more Aborigines than any other state, but they scarcely impinge on pink, shiny, bouncy Brisbane.

In front of the impressive City Hall—whose clock tower you may enter, actually walking inside the clock so that its four glass faces surround you like the walls of a room—the atmosphere is that of a country town. Here in the central business district men and women in shorts play a modified form of cricket within improvised nets beneath sprawling Moreton Bay fig trees. I go into a coffee shop run by two ladies who have the casual dignity of fine rural folk. They are almost old world, yet they speak in the broad, slow Queensland way. On the walls they have hung violins, oil paintings of England, and large kitchen utensils. One lady brings me mango, pawpaw, and other northern fruits, together with buttered raisin-bread toast, and as she sets the plates before me she says, "Thanks."

In Queensland people prefer a folksy frankness to a false objectivity. "No rain anywhere through the state today, unfortunately," the weatherman on the usually staid ABC says. Reads a notice from the police about the use of bicycles: "What time is it? You are not stupid enough to ride at night time without a headlight and tail light, are you?" After listing points to watch out for, the notice ends: "Everything OK? Then off you go, Good-Looking—AND KEEP OFF THE FOOTPATH."

As the Northern Territory inspired the film *Crocodile Dundee,* so Queensland a couple of years ago came up with *Coolangatta Gold,* a beautifully filmed movie—not of an innocent abroad like Dundee, but of machismo, dogged family loyalty, and simple moral struggles in a setting of sun and surf.

I drive out by Roma Street station, where silvery trains snake in and out against a backdrop of stone churches and houses with aluminum-colored roofs on surrounding hills, past hotels with wrought-iron balconies brushed by pink oleanders, to the semitropical garden campus of the University of Queensland. In an hour of walking around the campus I see no male in long pants.

"Where you went to school means little here," says a historian, himself a South Australian, as we lunch on rich fare at the faculty club, a round structure reminiscent of an airport terminal restaurant, except that we look out not onto a tarmac but onto leafy hills. "It's the opposite of Adelaide, where even the shop assistants still wear their old school ties." On his campus students pad to classes in bare feet and shorts, like Gold Coast beach boys or waitresses.

"Do ya seat belt up, mate," says the cabbie, a cigarette at the corner of his mouth, as I head for newly minted Griffith University on the city's outskirts. "Otherwise it's a forty-dollar fine and three points off your license." I buckle up. "The other day I had this guy in me cab; he was from Sydney, poor bugger. They fined him the forty bucks. He said to the cop, 'I didn't know about it—I'm from Sydney.' And the cop said, 'Well, now you do know.' "

The cabbie now and then points out to me an unmarked police car. "You can tell them," he explains, "because their stickers are always the tenth month, whereas other people's stickers expire at various months."

"Why so many unmarked police cars?"

"Looking for drunk drivers, sexual perverts—that sort of thing."

"There's an impression that our politicians get round in bare feet, with their trousers open, chewing bones," said a Griffith University economist as we sit amidst the gums of the raw outback-style campus, "yet when you meet them they can exude charm."

"I don't know which is reality, though," chips in a colleague, "the chewing of bones or the charm." In today's newspaper there is a report of the death of a Queensland cabinet minister. He was crushed to death on his farm by a tractor; no effete deaths up here.

Another Queensland cabinet minister, 250-pound Russell Hinze, very much alive and, one would think, uncrushable by any tractor, denounces his conservative colleagues in the south for having "no fire in their stomachs and no steel in their spines." After the conservatives (Liberals) elected John Howard to lead them in the national parliament, Hinze, who rejoices in the title "Minister for Main Roads, Local Government and Racing," said, "Howard has as much charisma as an alley cat."

When Hinze's Labor Party opponents came out with an unflattering photo of his great bulk over the caption "Is This the Shape of Things to Come?" the steel suddenly left Mr. Hinze's spine, and the fire his belly. "It's not only a political matter," he complained, "it's a matter of attitude to the stouter members of the community."

Southern conservatives often think no better of Hinze and Sir Johannes Bjelke-Petersen, the National Party premier of Queensland, than this pair think of them. "Queensland is a mirage," says Bob Santamaria, the high priest of Melbourne's religion-based anti-Communism. "Joh plays as much to TV as Hawke does. And the Gold Coast is a social disaster." Says Greg Lindsay, head of the Sydney Center for Independent Studies: "Alas, Queensland is the most socialist state in Australia."

Queensland's Labor Party produces rough-hewn, generous, hungry pragmatists like "Big Jack" Egerton, who after decades as a labor movement stalwart accepted a knighthood from the Fraser government and was promptly expelled from the Labor Party. Gough Whitlam recalls a meeting in Canberra between Egerton (then still a Labor Party leader) and Queen Elizabeth when Whitlam, as prime minister, had just enacted legislation declaring the monarch "Queen of Australia." The burly Egerton greeted Queen Elizabeth with the words "They tell me, luv, you've been naturalized."

Historically, Queensland has been a state of reform as well as of reaction. A century ago it produced the first Labor government the world ever saw, and the first woman trade union organizer in Australia, and much later it elected the first Aborigine to sit in the senate. It is the only state in Australia that has abolished the upper house of parliament. Decades ago, Communists sat on the Brisbane parliamentary couches beside farmers. Queensland station owners have been known, in response to trade union demands, to install refrigerators stocked with free beer in their shearing sheds.

"It was a desert when we came," says Adrian McGregor, a journalist with the *Courier Mail*, speaking of Brisbane in the 1960s. "We were on holiday up here, and when I saw the rickety city, all timber—I'm from Balmain, where things are bricks and mortar—I said to my wife, 'You couldn't live in this place.'" Two decades later, sitting in the living room of one of these sprawling timber houses, McGregor, dressed in shorts, sandals, and a T-shirt, wonders why he and his wife settled in Brisbane. "I guess I stayed because I thought things would change, and I wanted to be here when they did."

Perhaps Adrian McGregor, an eager, reflective man who has written several books, has changed a bit too. "I rang the Melbourne University Press the other day with a query about doing a biography of a famous scientist," he remarks. "Oh, they said, we only do biographies of people who are already dead. I felt that typified the difference in attitude between things down there and the University of Queensland Press."

McGregor has just visited Melbourne. "God, I felt like a redneck in Carlton!" he exclaims with a schoolboy's chuckle. "A Turkish restaurant one night, a Greek one the next! All these swarthy people around! Everyone nicely dressed; women in high heels!"

Although Adrian McGregor has adjusted to Brisbane and really likes the place, as an intelligent left-of-center journalist he gripes at Bjelke-Petersen's conservatism. "What is it about good climates that attracts such rednecks? I mean, they're not content just to be here; they want to get their claws into it and convert it." Normally a calm man, McGregor is waving his arms. "Sometimes I'd like to throw Fitzroy and Surry Hills at them," he says, naming two bohemian suburbs of Melbourne and Sydney respectively, "and say, take a dose of this and grow up quickly." I think of the observation of Rodney Hall, the Brisbane-raised poet and novelist, that Brisbane people are often sophisticated, if only because they have to refashion the world on their own terms if they are to have it on any.

"You see," claims McGregor, "down south there's a political-cultural awareness such that sometimes people just say no to the politicians. Here it's different. You ask me why land rights [for Aborigines] isn't a big issue here as in Western Australia. Joh just says no to land rights, and that's it. There's a concept in Queensland that justice isn't really being done."

When I hesitate to embrace his negativism, McGregor relates a story about the son of his wife, Helen. "John had a friend at school whose mother was a mad religious fanatic. She thought Helen's son was a bad influence on her son. One day I had a phone call; the cops were searching our house for drugs just on this woman's say-so. I said to Helen, 'Tell the cops the *Courier Mail* is on the way with a photographer, and that it sounds like a fascinating story.' I got home, and they backed off." McGregor smiles. "They did find a bong in John's room, together with his .22 rifle and things."

During one of my visits to Queensland the minister for justice made it illegal for bars or liquor shops to sell drinks to "deviants, child molesters, drug dealers, and sexual perverts." The mind boggles: "I have just molested a child, how about a drink?" Queensland politicians tend to think *their* bartenders can instinctively pick the decent guy from the child molester. Expressing other values of traditional Queensland, the Country Women's Association recently organized a cruise to Fiji. The ladies took paper patterns, buttons, and scissors. They swapped sewing and handicraft hints with Fijian women. They distributed pamphlets on family planning, gardening, and raising pigs.

"How do you go into action, Mrs. Joyner?" I ask the energetic power behind the Society to Outlaw Pornography and the Committee Against Regressive Education, when she bounces into the lobby of my Brisbane hotel for a chat.

"I start with the premier and the cabinet ministers!" replies Queensland's mistress of public morals, a very successful upholder of traditional Australian values, today often thought of as Queensland values. Rona Joyner, a neat, well-organized woman with a gleam in her eye and an armful of pamphlets, is the only person I interview in Australia who requests a fee and asks in advance about my political and religious views.

"The premier thumped the table in support of me," says Mrs. Joyner of one campaign on education, as her teenaged son, Steven, tape records our conversation. "He said he wants teachers to deal with facts, not to raise consciousness. Mrs. Gabler from America was the main reason I succeeded with MACOS," she goes on, referring to a school curriculum proposal, "Man: A Course of Study," which was hotly debated in Queensland. "Mrs. Gabler was visiting in 1977. She knew all about MACOS, which is full of socialist and atheist things."

"I failed over the Intellectually Handicapped Citizens Bill," reflects Mrs. Joyner, who runs a farm and a school an hour's drive from Brisbane and works on her crusades until two and three in the morning. ("Like the premier, I need little sleep.") "It was rushed through when the premier was absent. Had he been present I don't think it would have gone through." She says the legislation allows the children of "extremely spiritual" families to be classified as intellectually handicapped and thus to be "supervised by the state."

Mrs. Joyner's next drive is against "peace education," which is making strides even in Queensland's schools. "I'm not in favor of one-world government, and I know the premier isn't either." She also keeps a wary eye on the environmentalists. "They don't care how many babies are killed," she remarks with an evangelical smile, referring to abortion, which she furiously opposes, "but you mustn't kill a whale, you mustn't touch a snake."

"I'm a little bit disappointed in some of the younger ones coming on," says Mrs. Joyner when I ask if the Society to Outlaw Pornography and the Committee Against Regressive Education have many youth members. As we say farewells, I ask Steven, who is a pupil at his mother's school, what he plans to be. "A computer programmer," he replies.

An hour's drive south of Brisbane lies the Gold Coast, where traditional Queensland seems to have succumbed to the lure of the tourist dollar. By the roadside, which is bright with jacarandas, red poinsettias, and spreading umbrella trees, there are ads like TOP CHOOKS—CHEAP, and motels with garish decor. At the Aussie Resort there is a swimming pool in the shape of a map of Australia, complete with a Tasmania-shaped spa. A Beer Belly Contest is announced. The Gold Coast looks like a pale imitation of Miami Beach and Waikiki—less tall, less lively, but with magnificent beaches.

I dine at Barbarellie's in Broadbeach with a friend who has abandoned Sydney for a nearby farm. Spaghetti You Betti is offered, and also a first course (called "entree" in Australia) called "Skincredibles," of which it is said, "These little buggers are the best drinking appetiser on the menu." A note on the menu says you should feel free to "whistle or shout" to gain the waiter's attention. The list of desserts begins: "By the time you get to the sweets, Chef Barbarellie has destroyed himself on the cooking wine; make it easy for him—have one."

"There's no cultural life on the Gold Coast," my friend remarks. "No auditorium even exists in which to hold a concert. People here would rather spend money on sewage—which doesn't always exist—than on an arts center." The Japanese are moving into the Gold Coast, and in some ways the result can only be an improvement.

On the Gold Coast a "white shoe brigade" of businessmen has joined in the spin-dryer tumble of Queensland society and given a new twist to the National Party. Without roots in traditional Queensland, they have come north for fast bucks. Making deals and sailing yachts, they are polar opposites of the Country Women's Association types who form the backbone of the National Party. But the white shoe brigade have come in the door with huge contributions to the Bjelke-Petersen Foundation, and so their hard drinking, hard gambling style, alarmingly at odds with Mrs. Rona Joyner's values, flavors today's National Party.

Colonel David Hackworth, one of the most decorated heroes of the U.S. war in Vietnam, believing that the U.S. was on a dangerous path of confrontation in various parts of the world, in the early 1970s resigned from the army, left the U.S.A., and came to live and work by the green palms and white sands of the Gold Coast. "I saw Australia as a safe haven," Hackworth explains to me from his farm near the Gold Coast. "Being a white man and speaking English, I felt it was either New Zealand or Australia, and since I was trained in jungle warfare I chose Australia because there's more space."

Feeling that he had learned in the army that good morale is heavily dependent on food, Hackworth, who won ninety-one medals in Vietnam, began as a waiter. By 1981 he was able to sell a restaurant business for $1 million. "An absolute fool can be successful in Queensland," he says. "For someone willing to hustle, there are nuggets lying all over the ground."

Hackworth is amazed at Queensland's laid-back ways. "The police chief can walk down the street, see the most wanted criminal in Queensland, look at his watch, and seeing it's after five P.M., leave the matter until tomorrow." To an American this is a mixed thing. "It's wonderful in the sense that this is a very free place. But it's sloppy; there are no standards. If you're in trouble with the tax people, you just don't answer their letter. They won't bother to write to you a second time."

The American does not think well of the average Aussie worker. "Generally speaking the Australian male does not want to work. I normally rely on females; they come to work at eight A.M., they won't be out drinking all night, they have a sense of responsibility." He sees immigrant males as good workers. "They're the only ones who put their shoulders to the wheel. They see a chance to build a house on the hill."

The colonel, a handyman and entrepreneur as well as a military strategist, has a cultural theory less likely to be expressed in Sydney or Melbourne than in Queensland: "The Australian male is like the black American male. Because of slavery, the black man was always being pulled away and sold; the woman, who stayed and became the baby producer, formed the line of continuity and responsibility. Meanwhile the guy moved from one woman to the next. The Australian man is somehow like that."

It is as far from Brisbane north to Cairns—all within Queensland— as it is from Brisbane south to Melbourne. In Mount Isa, a mining town in Queensland's west, if you ask directions to the Northern Territory, they say, "Drive west out of the town and take the first bitumen road on the right"—that junction is 450 kilometers from Mount Isa.

Years ago I marveled at the distances of the empty north, and at how a flight from Sydney or Melbourne to Southeast Asia flew for hours over an Australia that few ever saw. In those days Qantas did not fly to the Queensland cities of Townsville or Cairns. But now Qantas serves both, and to Cairns planes come in nonstop from Tokyo, Honolulu, and Singapore. Australia is at last claiming its own body.

"Why have you come to north Queensland?" asks the TV host in Townsville when I sit down with her to prepare for an interview on China, as if someone would need a pretty good reason to visit Townsville. I realize I am going to have to supply the questions as well as the answers. "Sugar," I say plucking the word from nowhere, and soon the camera rolls for a conversation about how the masses of China will one day buy out all the sugar Queensland can grow.

It was here on Townsville's clean and modern mall that—in a fairly typical display of Queensland's rip-roaring political style—Prime Minister William McMahon, at an election rally during his campaign against Whitlam, was drowned out by shouts of "Hello, Big Ears" and "Come on, Baldy" from a largely drunk audience as mynah birds chirped overhead. Yet the fingers of fussy authority have not failed to reach north. DANGER, cries a notice in the baggage area at Cairns airport. NO PERSON MAY TRAVEL ON THE CONVEYOR BELT AT ANY TIME. In the *Cairns Post* an expert of the National Parks and Wildlife Service, a Canberra body, is quoted as telling citizens who may find a snake in their home: "Contact the Wildlife Service. And remember that snakes come under the same protection act as other protected Australian fauna." I am hoping I don't find a protected taipan in my hotel room.

In Cairns the average year-round maximum temperature is eighty-five degrees. On these mud flats, dotted with trees that have gleaming white trunks, with round green hills rising to the west, nature dominates life but not as a threat. It has made people laconic without also making them bitter. No one wears a tie to work, and executives stroll under poinciana trees to their homes for lunch. At my motel the public restrooms are labeled "Buoys" and "Gulls."

In Cairns I have left behind the clean-cut bronzed straightforwardness of south Queensland for a tropical zone with something a little off-beat and mysterious about it. The city has many characters, a large dropout element, and a raw black fringe. "The darkies is against the darkies," says a construction worker at the bar of the Barrier Reef Hotel. "The Abos and the [Torres Strait] islanders is as much against each other as the white people is against them. They're bloody beauties, they are." Expressing Queensland's selective racism, this keen fisherman praises Orientals and reserves his criticisms for the "darkies." Ordering two more beers, he sums up: "They're especially bad when they get a few drinks in them. It's unreal, it is."

North Queensland has grown like a mushroom after spring rain. "Before World War Two the visitor to Cairns was a rarity, and he had to come by boat," recalls Sir Sydney Williams, the head of Air Queensland, in his office in the middle of town. "There was no bitumen road on the Atherton Tableland [a fertile belt west of Cairns]—it was the Americans who built our roads, and our airstrips too. Our airline began when a woman was dying on an outback property," says Williams, who fought the Japanese in New Guinea. "There were no roads and the tracks were impassable because of the monsoon. A guy came on the bush radio suggesting they try and cut a little airstrip, and then he would go out in a Tiger Moth. Believe it or not they did, a Tiger Moth landed, the woman was rescued." That was the birth of Bush Pilot Airways, precursor to Air Queensland, and it was a vigorous infant because so many people heard the story of its origins on the bush radio. "People subscribed to the airline for their own protection."

Is there in Queensland a sense of vulnerability to Asian turmoil? "We live in a world of make-believe up here," confesses Sydney Williams. "Life is so casual, compared with the hurly-burly of the south. People just don't think about danger from the Asian area—except a bit about drugs."

I stroll a few blocks to City Hall. The streets are so wide—laid out that way so that the bullock carts could be turned around—that from one footpath I can barely read the shop signs opposite. "Twenty years ago Cairns had no traffic lights," says the mayor, Ron Davis, a former accountant who has lived all his life here. "The highest building was two stories, we were infested with mosquitoes, and the mangroves grew within half a mile of the city center.

"With the Brisbane line during World War Two," says Mayor Davis, "it had been thought that north Queensland did not matter and was dispensable." He waves his hands toward the window, from which we can see new hotels going up. "We had to develop," he goes on, "otherwise we would have been forgotten." Today 70 percent of the Cairns population was born outside Queensland. "I am the first ever mayor of Cairns to be born in Cairns," Davis says.

Although the British national anthem is no longer the Australian national anthem, except when royalty is present, in Queensland "God Save the Queen" is often played on official occasions. "We play 'Advance Australia Fair' at most functions," Mayor Davis says quietly. He smiles as if savoring a mischievous resistance to Hawke's hegemony. "When we can get away with it we play 'God Save the Queen' as well."

North Queensland has a large minority population—10 percent are Aborigines or Torres Strait islanders—but the power structure is monolithically white, and almost totally Anglo-Saxon. At the *Cairns Post* a staff of about a hundred includes no Aborigines or islanders. The school curriculum—even in townships where many of the pupils are non-white—has not yet caught up with the era of multiculturalism as proclaimed down south. Mayor Davis takes the usual Queensland law-and-order approach to minorities: "It's simply wrong that today the Aborigine is being treated better than the white man. Morale among the police suffers. They feel they can't enforce the law."

To the north of Cairns I find Australia's only walk-in dingo enclosure. I watch a crocodile attack show and hear how a girl of thirteen recently saved her friend from certain death at the jaws of a crocodile. On the road to Kuranda, a verdant mountain township on the fringe of the Atherton Tableland, I find a restaurant where the diners climb into actual railway cars from an earlier era, and waitresses with their trays come into the compartments like ticket men. On a roadside tree a sign says VEGGIES, NEXT HOUSE.

On Green Island, a short boat ride from Cairns, I enter a carefree blue and white world. Two youths stand up to their armpits in the china-blue water as they smoke and sip from cans of Swan beer in bamboo holders. I board a glass-bottomed boat to view the marine life of the Great Barrier Reef. Loaves of bread are supplied for us to feed the leaping fish. A blue one with a yellow tail swoops to the surface and tickles my fingers as it gobbles the bread. We glide over giant clams 350 years old. Beneath us is a parrot fish, which at night makes a cocoon out of its own saliva to keep in body odor and thus forestall attack, an orange-colored fish that can hide itself in the sand at night, and a brilliant little creature that simulates open eyes in its tail to mislead potential attackers.

"If you see sharks," says a man who rents me snorkeling equipment, "don't go in alone. Take a friend and you'll have a fifty-fifty chance." In serious vein a local fisherman tells me, "If you see a shark, don't swim away, for it will think you're a fish and take a bite. Stay still, look the shark in the eye, and punch it. You must face it, because your head is not appetizing to a shark—only your white limbs."

Deep within the water a net pattern shimmers on the sandy floor of the sea, reflecting the rippling surface of the water above. Down here the struggles, the fear, the dissimulation, the parade of aggressor and victim make the human society on land seem a Sunday School by comparison.

Flying over this area, from Cairns toward the Reef, you see a patchwork quilt of greenish islands, etched around with white sand, and then outer circles of luminous aqua color where the water is shallow, before all gives way to deep blue—the infinite smother of the Pacific.

Queensland thinks it could develop its way to paradise but for obstacles thrown up by the south. The most recent nay-sayers, like itinerant priests with a message to a flock of locals that feels no need of it, are the environmentalists. "They come and tell us that our life is going to bugger up the birds," observes Sir Sydney Williams. "They say old Mrs. Jones can't throw a line in off the beach because that's someone's holy ground. Some ratbags say the Great Barrier Reef is for scientists, not for visitors."

My mind goes back to a rally in Sydney a few weeks back. Pale girls and grim-looking men hold up pictures of rain forests and banners saying THE WORLD IS ON LOAN TO OUR CHILDREN. An offering is taken up and Bob Browne, an environmentalist leader, rises to say, "This money's going to fight for trees in Queensland. Only six percent of Australia is forest. Seventy-five percent of the forest that existed when European settlement began has been destroyed." The crowd cheers. A cheeky unshaven man wearing a battered felt hat tries to burst the bubble of earnestness. KEEP AUSTRALIA GREEN, reads his banner. HAVE SEX WITH A FROG.

"I decided to go ahead and build the airport," says Mayor Davis of a project that carried some economic risk for the city. "We had to clear some mangroves, but we've got ninety species of mangroves in Cairns, so what was wrong with that?" By American standards Davis is not for development-at-all-costs, but by Australian measure he is pro-growth. "If the environmentalist demonstrators had been in Australia two hundred years ago, nothing would have been achieved."

But Dennis Simmons, an editor at the *Cairns Post* who is the strongest local environmentalist I meet, is cautious. "No one will want to come to Cairns if it's a repetition of the Gold Coast with all those high-rises," he argues. "Some say the Great Barrier Reef is nineteen hundred kilometers long, and surely you can find eighty square kilometers to put down an oil well," says Simmons, who has lived ten years in Cairns and before that three in Townsville. "But I've seen the Long Beach area of Los Angeles, where you've got oil wells right on the beach itself. There's no way in the world I'd accept that as a good thing here."

"Low taxes is the crux of the matter," says Sir Johannes Bjelke-Petersen in his Brisbane office as he looks back over his astonishing success as premier of Queensland for seventeen years. "We started by getting rid of death duties. Cigarette tax, beer tax, petrol tax, sales tax, gift duties—we keep right away from them. If you want growth, you've gotta let the people spend the money instead of governments spending it."

This son of a rural Danish pastor is seventy-four years old, but each day he walks up the stairs to his fifteenth-floor office in a modern tower. He dominates Queensland (the only mainland state not ruled by the Labor Party) as no premier dominates any other Australian state. He laughs as Labor opposition leaders come and go—five in a decade—like showers in the Brisbane wet season.

The office is large, but the premier remains behind his desk. Family photos and piles of documents surround him. "I haven't looked at today's mail yet," Sir Joh says as a clock chimes 6 P.M. across the street. The jacket of his beige suit is on a hanger behind him, a silk handkerchief in its top pocket. He wears a white shirt and a woolen tie of green, yellow, red, and blue horizontal stripes. He's just back from a conference on northern development in Darwin. "We did over the southern politicians," he says like a sportsman telling of a win. "I'd hate to be in their shoes. I got a tremendous ovation."

Speaking of his battle against trade unions in Queensland, the National Party premier remarks, "As with a cement mixer, you don't let it consolidate. Every day I do something to them. I just don't let any situation get accepted." He pauses to move his empty teacup away from the clutter of papers. "In the end they get confused. They jump up and down and shout. And I laugh in front of my TV."

This line of approach brought Sir Joh a spectacular victory over strikers at the state electricity works during 1984. "We have suffered a tremendous defeat," said one of the trade union leaders involved, in a rare admission of impotence. Bjelke-Petersen admires what Reagan did with the air traffic controllers, and he is convinced that by a series of legal steps he has the Queensland trade unions on the run. His record is so impressive that it comes as a shock when he spits at his detractors. The Liberals, until recently his coalition partners, are "spineless" and "trendy," he complains; their leader, a less homespun man than Sir Joh, "travels with his legs on both sides of a barbed-wire fence." He does not denounce the leftists and the wishy-washy Liberals because he still needs to beat them off—they lie paralyzed at his feet— but simply because he is sure they are wrong.

Some people outside Queensland criticize Bjelke-Petersen for throwing open the door to foreign capital, but the premier brushes aside the notion that he prefers to do business with Tokyo than with Melbourne and Sydney. "But for Japan, we as a nation would be in dire straits," he says with a candid shrug.

"Look at the cranes," Sir Joh says, pointing to the windows. "I stood at the window the other day and counted twenty of them." Indeed I see many cranes, as buildings of mixed distinction rise haphazardly all over Brisbane. "Go down to Sydney and Melbourne," says the combative premier, "and with a telescope you wouldn't find a crane." Talking with Bjelke-Petersen leaves an impression that Queensland, which was never very keen about joining the Australian federation, would be better off on its own. But the premier does not embrace the idea of secession, preferring on this topic to hide behind the rules. "We couldn't break it up; the people in Canberra would have to break it up." Meanwhile this political genius wraps himself in the Queensland flag and personally thanks people who move from other states to Queensland.

"People seem to get sick a lot in the Labor states," Bjelke-Petersen says, a look of irritation on his face. "I've just noticed that spending on health in those states is three times what it is in Queensland. It must be horrible to live in a Labor state." The words are like bullets, but the manner is courteous. I recall a moment in Melbourne during the 1984 election, when Sir Joh went south to fight against the welfare state. A plain, zealous-looking woman snarled "fascist" at him by a traffic light in the City Square. "Fascist," she screamed again, poking her thin white face at him. "Thank you," he said, dapperly walking on his way. "Thank you very much."

"People come over our border from the south," Sir Joh says when I ask about the high rate of unemployment in Queensland. "You couldn't keep them out if you stood at the border with a stick." He feels the individual's will to work is as important as the broader economic context. "There's jobs," he says, throwing his hands toward the windows. "The city's singing out for gardeners. I said to a gathering of young people the other night, 'Make yourself presentable when you get interviewed. You can't come in wearing big earrings and stovepipe jeans and expect to get a job.' "

Even in pro-American Queensland, with its wartime memories of Americans and its current desire to lure U.S. tourists, young people are sometimes critical of U.S. policies, and Premier Bjelke-Petersen faults them for it. "I do get annoyed," he remarks, "that some of the young people don't realize how well off we are, or that without U.S. protection we'd be in a sorry state."

How is it that Queensland under Bjelke-Petersen's rule is so different from most of the rest of Australia; is it Sir Joh or Queensland that stands apart?

"The bulk of the rest of Australia sees things as I do," responds the premier, "but there's no leadership down there to achieve their objectives." I ask if he has succeeded by having a finger on Queensland's pulse or by converting Queensland to his views. "Public opinion is the last thing I follow," he declares with a frown. "That's what the Liberals do; they go round like a ship without a rudder."

Having helped bring one national Labor Party government down— he effected a clever senate maneuver against Whitlam that helped precipitate the 1975 constitutional crisis—I wonder if he could do it again.

"Easily—no problem," he replies, as if I'd asked him to chop down an unwanted tree on his farm. "You just watch at the next election." He stops, perhaps surprised at his own candor. "It's not me, really; it's a case of drawing attention to what that crowd in Canberra do and what they don't do. They've dug a hole so deep you can barely see them at the bottom of it." Bjelke-Petersen wants and expects a sharp conservative swing throughout Australia. "We want not just a change of curtains; we want dramatic change." Using an old-fashioned expression, he makes a play on Hawke's first name: "We've had enough of two Bob [shillings] each way policies."

Sir Joh walks me to the high wooden door of his office with the leisurely friendliness of a farmer seeing someone to the property's front gate. "Flo'd be happy to talk with you," he volunteers cheerfully of his wife, who is a national senator, and equally well known for her pumpkin scones. He is shorter than I realized when he sat motionless at his desk, and he is looking up at me as he says by way of benediction, "Put a lot into life and you'll get a lot out of it." He throws me a second philosophic sapphire, as if my return to America will put me in need of some of Queensland's wisdom: "Make yourself indispensable and nothing will stop you."

Down the hall I pass photos of the Queen's visit to Queensland in 1954, showing the then premier, Labor's Vince Gair, tight in his suit like a saveloy. The Queensland of the 1950s seems distant from today's booming state, yet Bjelke-Petersen and Gair are alike in being wily, homespun characters. At the end of the hall I find I cannot leave until I buzz. A guard arrives to inspect me and then let me out.

Inside the handsome sandstone Queensland Parliament the carpets are thick and the maroon leather couches are deep. Oil paintings of all Queensland premiers hang on the walls; only one of them, that of Bjelke-Petersen, is illuminated. Tom Burns, a leading figure in the Labor Party nationally for many years, and deputy leader of the Queensland Labor opposition, regales me with a lunch of grilled reef fish and puts the anti-Joh side of the picture. Burns has a pink, wrinkled face with a mouth slightly indrawn in the Australian manner. He is a straight shooter, talkative and eternally cheerful. He belongs to the Foster's beer left, rather than the dry sherry left. To everyone who enters the dining room he nods or says, "G'day, mate."

"Now don't tell me Joh created the Queensland weather!" explodes Burns with a jovial grin. "Smokey the Bear could have come in when Bjelke-Petersen came in and achieved the boom that we had in the seventies. Joh didn't create the coal. Joh didn't create the machinery—the Yanks gave us much of that. Joh didn't create a demand—that arose in Japan. And when the demand comes, private enterprise will move in," Burns goes on, overlooking that private enterprise has to go and make contact with demand. "But tomorrow there's going to be no jobs for young people. Bjelke-Petersen has failed to use the boom to create a manufacturing base."

"Come back, mate," Burns calls out to a man in a jacket and tie who passes our table. He is the former president of the Waterside Workers Federation, and I ask his view of the conservatives' plan to deregulate labor in the small business realm. "It's probably pretty popular with the average Australian citizen," the union leader, who is younger than Burns, remarks quietly. "The fact is at the moment the trade unions are on the nose."

Burns says nothing. He is a Labor man of the old school, not very happy with the Hawke era—to say nothing of the long Bjelke-Petersen era—and convinced that business and labor must always fight. Yet Burns is as much of a Queensland patriot as Bjelke-Petersen, and this catches him in a political trap. "If I was on the dole in Melbourne and it was thirty-five degrees, I'd come up to Queensland too," he says with a shrug, underlining why Queensland has a sizable unemployment problem—which in public Burns blames on Bjelke-Petersen's policies alone.

He rails against Bjelke-Petersen's "excessive anti-Canberra" stance. Yet a moment later he says, "Gough made Joh," meaning that Bjelke-Petersen got the Queensland people behind him when he fought with Whitlam's Canberra. "Gough was wrong to talk of 'piss-ant states' and 'Queensland hacks,'" he observes of the former prime minister, his good friend.

Burns grumbles that the Queensland flag is everywhere. "In Japan, Australia gets presented as seven separate states," he says. "America doesn't do that. In Australia we say we believe in a centralized government, but I don't think we do." Yet in Queensland only the Labor Party talks in this national way, and the Labor Party hasn't won an election in Queensland since the 1950s.

"Tom, is there any alternative in Queensland to being anti-Canberra?"

"Really, there isn't," he replies thoughtfully, sipping his coffee. "But it doesn't do much for the unity of the Labor Party."

Burns questions whether Bjelke-Petersen is really a free marketeer, despite those ads in the Melbourne and Sydney papers that urge businesses to "escape to the state that doesn't believe in capitalist punishment." "Joh says, I'm against tax—then he races off to Canberra to ask for more tax revenue. The sugar and dairy industries are bound hand and foot by government regulation in Queensland. We had a bloke here the other day who was prosecuted for selling bread under the regulated price."

I tell Burns that when I put the point to Bjelke-Petersen his answer was crisp: "I'd like to see more of a free market, but I'm also a Queenslander." Burns then recounts his own exchange with his adversary in parliament a week or so ago: "Are you for privatization, Mr. Premier?"

"Yes, I am."

"What about the TAA [the government domestic airline] and Telecom services to the west part of our state?"

"Oh, no, I'm not against them."

"But they're socialist, aren't they?"

"Oh, no, there's a lot of good private enterprise people running those services."

Burns smiles wryly. "It's outrageous, but he's very good at it. He's a bloody beauty."

Turning now to international affairs, Burns says, "The people of my generation know that America saved us in World War Two. The Yanks came in, built airports overnight. We'd never seen anything like it. We'd never seen jeeps before. And I think we shouldn't keep punching them in the nose." But he confesses that even in Queensland, as the Coral Sea generation gets older, anti-American views are strong in the Labor Party. "You go to any branch meeting of our party and put up a resolution criticizing the Yanks on Central America and it'll be passed unanimously."

In 1971 Burns and I traveled together in China on Whitlam's first trip there and sometimes yarned on trains and planes about Labor philosophy. I ask what he thinks now of the republicanism issue. "Most Australians want the flag changed," he replies, "but most Australians also like to see the Queen. And you've got to have someone as head of state." Burns's mind turns to his archenemy Premier Bjelke-Petersen as he looks down at his after-lunch Scotch and soda. "I suppose if it's a choice between a president appointed by Joh or a governor appointed by the Queen, I'd go for the governor."

Queensland is a mixture of the informal and the traditional, of the hedonistic and the moralistic. In part this is because Queensland is a rural civilization, the only mainland state where most of the people live outside the capital city. Not only is its governing party a rural party, but its Labor Party began in the shearing sheds and still has deep roots in the countryside. Scratch a Brisbane person and under the surface you often find a country person. Brisbane draws more of its flavor from rural Queensland than any other state capital does from its rural areas. The bush is not eclipsed in Queensland, and will not for a long time be eclipsed. The state dependency and security-consciousness of Benthamism does not, in Queensland, win a clear-cut victory over frontier values of self-reliance and mateship-under-authority.

Queensland is at once old-fashioned and advanced. Brisbane can remind one of Sydney in the 1950s, and Queensland values can recall Australian values of that era. Yet Queensland is the leading state in tourism, devilishly rich in natural resources, and boasts a life-style that most Australians might well covet for the future.

So Queensland can seem schizophrenic. It bans books and magazines and videos that the rest of Australia does not. Yet Queensland delegations go to Europe with films of half-naked girls to lure tourists to the Gold Coast and the Great Barrier Reef. In the outback, Queenslanders hold bulls out to piss, Zola-style, but coming in to Brisbane they cannot handle *Playboy*. Queensland's divorce rate is very high, as is its birthrate among teenagers. But when the Family Planning Association came out with a poster aimed at reducing teenage pregnancy, which showed a waist-to-knee photo of a young man in jeans, over a caption "Open with Caution," pressure from the government and the moral guardians killed the poster.

The duality will not go away quickly, since it does not stem simply from a time lag, or from Bjelke-Petersen. Sir Joh has succeeded because he has embodied bush values. And the triumph of the bush in Queensland is neither a throwback to the past nor a clue to the future, but a fact of geography.

SEVEN

Paradise on the Periphery

"Channel Nine Is Number One," runs a newspaper advertisement of an east coast TV station, continuing in tiny print at the bottom of the page: "And trams will reach Perth before we're number two." One gets the point after crossing the vast and virtually empty Australian continent. My Boeing 747 from Sydney takes four hours and forty minutes nonstop to reach Perth. As we walk onto the tarmac a plane from Bali—this flight takes one hour less than my domestic flight—disgorges Western Australians with their batik and carvings and suntans. "It's cold," squeals a blond girl in shorts, on this October spring day with the thermometer at seventy-two degrees, as she skips to the terminal, with two spears in one arm and an Indonesian boyfriend on the other.

I drive into town past red-flowering bottle-brush trees and glass office buildings of mining companies and multinational corporations. Amidst these shiny badges of Western Australia's newfound prosperity, a homely sign at a roadside restaurant offers SUNDAY ROAST, $6. My cabbie is Greek-born, but he pronounces "day" in the Australian way as "dye"—"yesterdye I didn't been working." Why did he move from Sydney to Perth? "Less bustle, less indifference here," he says.

Perth is a handsome, lively, but still convenient city, well kept if not well planned, and still slightly surprised at its success. A garishness has come to some streets, yet there remain many two-story buildings in colonial style, with wrought iron balustrades and solid veranda posts anchored in broad sidewalks.

Headquarters for the iron ore, natural gas, and other resource industries in the northwest, Perth has developed the cockiness of a Dallas by the sea; and as in Dallas, huge buildings in assorted styles rise in the midst of vast spaces, like shiny-scaled beasts in a desert. Under a china-blue sky that looks touchable through an atmosphere astonishingly clear for a city of one million people, I walk streets where every second shop seems to be a travel agency—an acknowledgment of isolation. I buy a postcard depicting an illustrated map of Australia. The state of Western Australia looks prosperous, its green coastal strip alive with planes, offshore rigs, pleasure boats, and giant fish, and its inland a cluttered abundance of sheep, emus, crocodiles and Aborigines. To the east all the other states are labeled simply "Mainly Unexplored Desert"; snakes and insects dot a yellow expanse. Western Australians like these little jokes. "There are two kinds of Australians," Xavier Herbert, the novelist who was brought up in the west, used to say, "Australians and West Australians."

I go to drink and eat at a two-story brick pub of homely ambience in an inner suburb. The street is almost Southeast Asian with wide verandas and the smell of leaves and flowers, but inside the pub a virtually unbroken sea of white faces anchors me in the Western world. "Ales and stouts" are offered in English style. "The Aussie Job," reads the first item on the dinner menu in the restaurant adjacent to the bar—it is bacon and eggs. Beverages include "Cuppa—Lipton's Tea Bag" and, amongst the coffees, "Flat White." At the tall windows, lace curtains are swept back to hooks at each side, parlor style, as in rural Victoria when I was a child. On each table is a vase of artificial flowers. "We respectfully ask that you don't play with the flowers," says a handwritten notice. "If you must have one they are $10 each, but please ask us first, for they are there for everyone's pleasure."

I go to the gray stone, glass, and chrome museum and gallery and library complex, which embodies the modern, slightly unorganized smartness of Perth. "Life on our tropical reefs," reads the label on an exhibition in the museum. "Life in our western seas," proudly announces another. "The Aborigine skillfully exploited the environment to his best advantage," says a caption on a black history exhibit—not saying whether miners, today, may reasonably be permitted to exploit the environment for *their* best advantage.

The young people who serve me in shops and hotels are well-mannered and clean. Their private lives are flavored by the encroaching international youth culture, but their public sense of duty and respect has not crumbled in the wake of personal liberation, as has begun to happen in Sydney. One feels that sun and space ensure Western Australia against any possible desperation. Yet having sun and space doesn't always prevent people from wanting more. It doesn't make them content with one room and a carpet sweeper.

"Perth's as much an island as Singapore," says Peter Wombwell, editor of the city's *Sunday Times,* as he drives me past the mansions of the west's famous tycoons and the newly arrived Malaysian and Japanese millionaires. "An island between ocean and desert." The nearest big city to Perth is Adelaide (one million people), 2,700 kilometers east across the Nullarbor (No Tree) Plain.

Outside Perth the state of Western Australia, almost double the size of Alaska, thirteen times the size of West Germany, contains a mere 200,000 people. Half of it is an almost flat desert of orange sand and rocks. Thousands of years ago winds blew the desert sands of Western Australia into ridges, and these are held together by spinifex and the few trees that can endure the thirsty heat. Some areas of Western Australia receive no rain for years on end.

Peter Wombwell's fat and prosperous newspaper does not maintain a single correspondent outside Perth. North of Perth I travel for weeks without seeing any substantial cultivation or more than a handful of people together at any one time. I traverse part of a Western Australia coastline which is the same length as the Russia-China border (6,900 kilometers), yet north of Perth find no town of more than 20,000 inhabitants, and many children who are educated by radio and post. The entire northern coastline from Brisbane in the east to the long thin finger of Cape York Peninsula, and then west through Darwin and south to Perth, is 11,200 kilometers long, and in all that distance there is no town of 100,000 people.

"Drug running is widespread," says editor Wombwell, one of whose reporters is just back from a long investigation of it. "Western Australia may be becoming the center of illegal drug importation for the whole nation. Little boats can land at will up there. They also use tiny airstrips that were built during World War Two and are now forgotten about." One problem is that an eleven-gram package of heroin bought in Penang for $180 can sell on a Perth street for $5,250.

Visiting Geoffrey Bolton, a scholar of Western Australia's short but impressive history, at his suburban home, I admire the lean ivory gums, the frangipannis whose perfume fills the twilight air, and the nature strips three times the width of Melbourne's. "The only trouble with Perth," says the author of *A Fine Country to Starve In* with a gentle smile, "is that it's too far from Australia. One of my sons has just moved to Sydney, and the other can't wait to get away from Perth."

The bearded bright-eyed Bolton, who teaches at Murdoch University, sees the lopsided development of Western Australia, in which Perth is like a hen atop chicks, as the product of a series of early political decisions. "Back in the 1880s, Esperance could have become the port for the Kalgoorlie goldfields. Geraldton could have been the port for the Murchison goldfields." The historian smiles. "I think there was a fear people wouldn't want to *live* anywhere else in Western Australia except Perth."

"Our isolation breeds complacency and aggressiveness," remarks Professor Bolton. "The going-it-alone spirit can at times lead to a lack of judgment." He says Western Australia produces entrepreneurs such as Alan Bond, Lang Hancock, and Robert Holmes à Court, because it has a Cinderella complex. "There's the idea that with all this territory, the place has got to prosper, and if it doesn't the reason must be the jealousy or policies of the eastern states (earlier of England). The entrepreneurs are seen as benefactors—for going off to Tokyo or New York and getting people to invest not in the eastern states but here in Western Australia."[1]

"Everything comes from the earth," declares Lang Hancock as I sit before his office desk in suburban Perth. "You either mine it or grow it. The iron you mine makes the plows to dig the soil. You dig or die." On his desk sit folders, maps, and a photo of his Filipino wife; his first wife of thirty-nine years died a few years ago. I notice on the wall a painting of the University of Western Australia and ask Hancock if he graduated there. "I never went to a university," he growls. "I don't know how the hell that picture got there." Dressed in a white shirt with a thin stripe and a white jacket and dark tie, Hancock at seventy-

1. In the east you hear another opinion. "West Australians," says Bruce Grant in Melbourne, "have always suffered from imagining the possibility that the east of Australia had been colonized first not because it had been discovered first but because it was more attractive."

seven is crisp and vigorous. He rasps out pithy maxims and breath-taking generalizations.

One day in 1952, "Bull" Hancock (one of his nicknames) was flying across the Hamersley Range in the northwest in his single-engine Auster. Forced to fly low by stormy weather, he dipped through a deep gorge and noticed an ocher tint to the canyon. He suspected iron ore. He was correct, and the discovery transformed Western Australia and made Hancock fabulously wealthy.

"In the Communist countries, in dictatorships, and in Australia," Hancock says, "minerals belong to the state." They remain useless—"the state cannot mount economic development"—until an entrepreneur wins the permission to mine and the permission to export. For Hancock such struggles have made him as bitter about big government as he is optimistic about his own geopolitical and free-market ideas. He is a genuine right-winger, a bull in the china shop of Australian Benthamism. Would he have done even better if he had been operating in, say, Texas rather than in Australia? "Certainly better, because in Texas the minerals belong to the individual, not to the state."

Yesterday the parliament of Western Australia approved a long-standing Hancock project: a huge deep-water port up the coast at Ronsard, fed by an economical downhill railroad, all made possible by a daring barter deal with Communist Rumania to take iron ore from Hancock in return for light manufactures. "Along the Danube they are currently consuming as much iron ore as Japan buys from Australia," observes Hancock with eyes shining, "and so far not one ton of it has come from Australia." Hancock has spent $25 million on unloaders at the canal that links the Danube and the Black Sea. He pushes maps before me. "We will have ships up to 400,000 tons out of Ronsard!"

"Is it your biggest project, Mr. Hancock?"

"It's probably the biggest project ever in the whole world."

Over the years Hancock has bristled with plans that have for some reason not been realized: using nuclear bombs to blow up mountains of iron ore; linking Queensland's coal and the west's iron ore with a railroad across northern Australia; damming the tides of the Indian Ocean to generate electricity; declaring Australia north of the twenty-sixth parallel a frontier zone with a 100 percent tax holiday; detaching Western Australia from the Australian federation. Despite his personal success, Lang Hancock feels disgusted with the political-economic atmosphere of Australia today.

He is not surprised that Brazil is a threat to Australia's mineral exports. "In Brazil costs are lower," he explains, "and you've got the government behind enterprise, instead of getting in the road all the time, as in Australia." He is scornful of Hawke's plan to restructure the Australian economy to fit in with the Asian region. "Before Australia can deal with Asia, it must bring its costs down." He sees no political will in Canberra to do that. He despises the "buck passers" in the bureaucracy who "hate to make a decision."

"The only way to turn things around," says Hancock as he reaches to a shelf behind his desk, "is to make it impossible for the three levels of government—federal, state, and local—to indulge in deficit spending. They must be forced to live on their income like any good housekeeper." He presents me with a book entitled *The Contribution of Politicians and Public Servants to the Development of Australia*. The author is Lang Hancock. The publisher is Common Sense Publications, and a jacket note states that the book was produced by non-union labor and without the assistance of any grant or subsidy from the Literature Board. The thick hard-bound book consists of blank pages.

Noting that Queensland earns more foreign currency than Victoria and New South Wales combined, and that Western Australia earns almost that much, Hancock suggests how to make the nation more development-minded. "If Queensland and Western Australia were to leave the federation, then the federation would collapse." In the midst of the crisis created by such a step—or threat of it—Hancock envisions a new Australian constitution, inspired by the frontier states, which would outlaw deficit spending. "The other states would have to come under our constitution, because they couldn't exist without us."

But Hancock observes sadly that this plan won't materialize until Australia gets to the verge of collapse, "which can't be far away." He gives a bitter laugh. "In five years Rumania's going to be out of debt. And in five years where the hell will Australia be?"

For Lang Hancock the development of Australia's mineral wealth is not only a question of making Australia prosperous but also of national defense. "At the moment the only defense we have is Japan," he says. "The Japanese are so dependent on us for our products that there's no way they could see Australia be taken over by anybody—except themselves, I suppose." Hancock would like to see this concept of defense extended. "By the development of strategic minerals we also ought to make ourselves indispensable to the U.S.A., West Germany, and Britain. They couldn't carry on civilization—couldn't make a jet—without the stuff that comes out of the earth. I don't give a bugger how many men you've got under arms. If you haven't got the mineral wealth you're finished. Russia's got it. South Africa's got it." Hancock stops and bangs his hand down on the desk. "We've got it, but ours is still in the ground, and it's going to stay in the bloody ground because no bastard's got the incentive to get it out."

As Hancock walks me to the door, he stops in front of a map of Western Australia. "If South Africa goes up, the only alternative source of minerals is right there." His strong hand jabs the Pilbara region.

Western Australia has long been the first or last stopping point for man or beast going by sea between Europe or the Middle East and the antipodes. More than twenty years ago I first saw Fremantle, the port adjacent to Perth, reaching it by ship from India as a student returning to Australia after a hitchhiking trip through Europe. Today I see live sheep being herded onto ships to travel to the Middle East for slaughter and consumption. Barking dogs snap at the occasional undisciplined sheep, just as if the wharf were a farm. It takes two days to board 115,000 sheep onto the specially built cagelike decks. A stone's throw away a vast reconstruction of Fremantle is under way in preparation for the America's Cup. So hectic is the pace that construction and renovation continue on Sundays—a rare sight in Australia. AMERICA'S CUP EMPLOYMENT, says a billboard put up by an agency offering to find workers of all kinds for new enterprises.

"It's the nature of Australia that makes sailing big," observes Noel Robins, executive director of the Australian Defence of the America's Cup, in his wide low office overlooking the water. "We're surrounded by sea; we live on the edge." Constant breezes aid boating and keep pollution away. Half of Perth is always heading for their boats, the quip runs, and the other half is already on board theirs.

"I could get physical with few people," a Scottish-born cabbie of middle age says on my way back to the hotel from Robins's office, "but I could with Alan Bond."

"But I thought he'd helped Perth leap ahead?" I say of the wealthy businessman whose syndicate won the America's Cup at Newport in 1983.

"Perth is going to be a cross between Los Angeles and Miami, with a bit of Hong Kong thrown in. The problems are the Chinks and all that Alan Bond stands for." The cabbie came to Perth when it was small and narrow. He opposes it becoming big and pluralistic, and quite a few of his generation agree with him.

"All we are doing is tidying up Fremantle and creating a wonderful seaside atmosphere there," says Warren Jones, a top executive of the Bond Corporation and manager of the Bond Syndicate's capture of the America's Cup in 1983, when I relay the cabbie's complaint. "And we are creating tourist dollars—the cleanest dollars in the world." Jones, a Christian and free marketeer who was born in Fremantle, pauses and his blue eyes open wide. "The beautiful tourists come, spend their money, get on the plane and leave."

Jones sees benefits in Perth's distance from everything. "When you're young and small you can get away with things," he says with a grin. "As places like Melbourne and Sydney grow older, they become 'establishment,' as do companies that grow bigger. A sixty-year-old entrepreneur doesn't jump up and risk everything he's got—a young man, to whom mountains look like flat roads, does that."

"When we won the America's Cup at Newport," Jones recalls, "we had no idea of what we had done." He shows me a blown-up photo of the 400,000 people who turned out to welcome Alan Bond and the winners back to Perth. "Probably only the victory celebrations after World War Two could be compared with what happened in Australia when we won." After the victory Western Australia changed the motto on its vehicle plates from "The State of Excitement" to "Home of the America's Cup."

"The real Western Australians are ambivalent," says Fay Zwicky, a Melbourne-born poet now rooted in Western Australia, as she sips a Scotch and soda in her well-filled living room in a leafy Perth suburb. "Innocent for a long time, they don't want people coming from outside, yet they welcome the attention they feel they were deprived of for years. People are frightened of the high-flying activity of the entrepreneurs, yet they're also involved in it."

"As soon as I heard we'd won that damned America's Cup," says Zwicky with a throaty laugh, "I thought, Here's trouble. You should have seen the christening of the yacht. Mrs. Bond was led like a prize cow in an ill-cut jacket with a boxing kangaroo embossed on the back." Zwicky, author of *The Lyre in the Pawn Shop,* lights a cigarette. "Nineteen eighty-seven will just bring a lot of five-star hotels that'll be empty ever after. It's going to be a Gatsby story, I think."

Meanwhile Perth's cultural vanguard complain that sport is God. "Perth must be one of the most beautiful places on earth," muses David Blenkinsop, Liverpool-born head of the Perth Festival, as we sit in his office overlooking the Swan River. "This has its disadvantages. In the north of England people were glad to escape from their environment to go to cultural events. Here they're reluctant to leave the yacht, the golf club, the tennis court." But Blenkinsop likes life in Perth and has seen tremendous recent progress. "Ten years ago you couldn't buy a decent loaf of bread," he says. "Today there's no food from any part of the world you can't eat in Perth."

My mind goes back to 1979, when I arrived here from Jakarta to lecture on China under U.S. Information Service auspices. "Beware of Perth's beauty," said a student from Hong Kong who was pursuing accounting at the Western Australian Institute of Technology. "Don't forget it's also pretty boring." He pointed out to me a sign by the bar at the airport: AFTER MIDNIGHT, CURRENT FLIGHT TICKET REQUIRED. Seven years later the student is an immigrant working for a mining company, and he finds the city "not boring at all." In 1986 I find nude beaches, but I cannot find that restrictive notice at the airport bar.

During the 1979 visit, at a dinner party given in my honor by the U.S. consul general, I found myself at a table of a dozen academics, all but one born outside Australia. From them I gained a sense of a city worried by being on the periphery. They exuded embarrassment at having traded proximity to world centers for sunshine and money. They gnawed at the issue of Australian identity like dogs at a shiny bone. It is different in the late 1980s.

"I do respect these buccaneers," says Alan Watson, publications officer of the University of Western Australia. He sees "greater confidence, less parochialism" in Western Australia than a decade ago, and though his politics are far from conservative, he gives credit for it to Lang Hancock, Bond, Holmes à Court, and other entrepreneurs, who breed fast under the western sun.

In the empty west one reflects upon Australia's defense; after all, Hideki Tojo did remark as the Japanese assault on Asia went forward that he was going to be in Perth by January 1943. "During the 1920s and 1930s," claims Peter Boyce, a political scientist who is vice-chancellor of Murdoch University, as we chat in my Perth hotel, "Western Australia was the only state interested in the issue of Singapore's defensibility." In the west there does exist a fear of isolation, though it is rarely spoken about. The proof of it is a closer focus on defense than in southeast Australia and some rather contradictory attitudes toward it. U$A OUT NOW, screams a sign on a Perth factory wall; someone has added USSR OUT NOW—and that pretty much sums up the mood.

A minority cries out against America, then most join ranks and resist that cry. I meet people who make cracks against the U.S.A. yet quietly welcome the American defense umbrella. I meet others who are loudly pro-American, but who over a drink late at night confess anxiety that American military installations make Australia a prime target for Moscow.

"The shopkeepers love the U.S. ships coming in," says editor Peter Wombwell. There is a Dial-a-Sailor phone number. When a U.S. navy ship is due, the newspapers publish the number, and as the vessel docks the line is plugged in. Perth people phone in offering everything from their boats to their bodies.

Professor Boyce welcomes the new stress on Western Australia's defense that has come since Kim Beazley, a Western Australian, became national defense minister, and the state government under Premier Brian Burke began to pursue defense preparation as a springboard for technological advance. "We're hoping we'll get a submarine base," says Boyce. "It would do a lot for Perth psychologically." This thoughtful analyst, whom I have known for twenty-five years, sees a generation gap. "Among the youth there are fewer ideological distinctions than for you and me. Even kids doing a business course can be incipient neutralists. It's as if they've been released from frameworks and are just thinking nationalistically."

"People are equivocal about America," says Alan Watson at the University of Western Australia. "There's some cynicism as to whether the nuclear umbrella is worth much in a crunch, and there's a concern about the U.S. bases making us a nuclear target." Watson pauses and shrugs his shoulders. "Every now and then something reminds us that on the world stage we're not worth a cracker, and that the U.S. could stamp on us if they wished."

Later in Canberra, Kim Beazley, who is from an old Perth family and whose father was education minister in Whitlam's government, explains his anxieties about young people's views of defense. "They don't understand the alliance with the U.S.A. in terms of its concrete benefits. They see only Ronald Reagan's conservative politics—which they don't like." The defense minister's solution is to identify those numerous areas in which the American tie is of specific benefit to Australia's capacity to defend itself, and remind the public of them. "F-one-elevens, the Harpoon missile, and the F-eighteens, reliable strategic intelligence in this region, and so on."

"That's where it all happens," says a cabbie cheerfully as he points to the imposing sandstone Parliament House, showing none of the cynicism toward politics that is normal in Melbourne and Sydney. Gardeners in shorts smile as they tend roses. Silver gums rise high beside the building's golden columns. I go inside to see Premier Brian Burke.

Burke, a former journalist, slightly overweight in his gray suit and maroon tie, resembles an articulate editor or public affairs director projecting an air of reasonableness. "Perth is closer to Singapore than to Sydney," he begins, without indicating whether this is a proclamation of solidarity with Asia or a confession of divorce from the rest of Australia. "The advantage of our isolation," he goes on as he lights a cigarette, "lies in the independence and resilience that have to be developed to counter the isolation. The substantial capital markets in Sydney and Melbourne ignored development opportunities in this state. They thought its distance from them was a good reason not to invest over here." Others, local and foreign, later filled the vacuum.

"Unlike many previous Labor Party governments in Australia," says the young but mellow-looking premier when I ask why the Western Australian economy is doing well, "this government has been able to earn the respect and cooperation of the business community." He gives two more reasons why the state has its first financial surplus in forty years, with a jump in revenue reflecting good business growth, and why for the first time ever the state's per capita debt has fallen. "We've tried to set an example to the private sector in terms of their own efficiency. And we've tried to lessen the burden of government on business—and on the family—by lowering taxes."

If this doesn't sound like Labor Party philosophy, neither does Burke's modesty remind me of many politicians. "And there have been things outside our control—the international recovery, the national recovery, the winning of the America's Cup in 1983, sound policies in Canberra [he is speaking in October 1984]—which have added to the climate of confidence. We've been the fortunate recipient of those."

The premier is one of a new wave of Labor Party leaders of the Hawke era, and his wrenching of the state party from its ideological moorings has won him national prominence. I remark that it seems a long way from Joe Chamberlain, the left-wing King of the West during the 1950s and 1960s—who had Burke's father expelled from the party, and whose influence dominated the Melbourne left in my time—to Brian Burke.

"A bloody long way," blurts out the premier. "Chamberlain's politics was the politics of irrelevance."

"Is the change permanent?"

"We need first to know how long this government lasts, and how long my leadership of the party lasts."

"It has always been the Labor Party's obligation to care for the disadvantaged and less fortunate," the premier observes when I ask him about intra-party resistance to his pragmatism, "but for too long it has pursued that obligation to the exclusion of common sense and relevance." He believes—as Joe Chamberlain never did—that making the pie bigger is the best way to give "our constituency" bigger slices.

I ask Burke about the Labor Party's relations with the vice-regal sphere. "We have an excellent governor, much loved," he replies, referring to the shy ex-academic who is Western Australia's governor, "and no constitutional-type problems." He grins as he recalls the recent conflict in the more tradition-encrusted state of Victoria between Premier Cain and a starched Anglophile governor. Then his tone changes. "But our governor wasn't appointed in the dying days of our opposition's term of office. We appointed him."

The premier is pro-American on defense and foreign policy. "We're more security-conscious out here, being so far from the rest of Australia—and being closer to where the inevitably racist Australian mind has always seen danger emanating from." But he argues for a balance on American cultural and economic influence. "We should maintain as much of our character as we can, remembering that Western Australia is a very young state. Other states had sophisticated economies decades before we did, so arguably the problem of maintaining our identity is greater here."

Premier Burke rejoices in the west's isolation as a crime preventer. "It's simply very difficult to import organized crime from the eastern states," he says as he lights another cigarette. "There's basically one sealed road into Western Australia, one train track, and one airport for the big commercial jets." He brushes aside as a "different question" the exposure of Western Australia's vast northern coast to drug running.

Brian Burke sees Western Australia as more convinced than the rest of the nation that the economic future of Australia lies in the Asian region. Does he fear Japan? "No. The Japanese are redoubtable people with a clear view of their national interest; it's our obligation to develop the same fierce national interest." Burke says of the nation on which Western Australia is overwhelmingly dependent for the sale of its minerals and resources: "I tell you this, Japan's single-minded determination cannot be countered by the traditional Australian attitude of 'Let's have another beer and don't worry about it until tomorrow.' "

Our conversation ends as Burke is called to face an attack by the opposition in the parliament chamber down the corridor. "See you, mate," he says and disappears, cigarette in hand, beyond the wood panels.

"I like Australia because it does not rain," wrote five-year-old Sandra in a school composition exercise. "The heat is very hot," wrote Santeen, age seven. "Here we are at the pitches [movies]; pass the fly spray," ran the poem of eight-year-old Megan. "Cyclone Joan gave Hedland a hiding; Boy, what a hiding. Trees flying, Birds gliding," wrote Natalie. "Have you ever seen a salt pile that looks like a ski slope?" asked little Janine. "I have." Wrote Jodie: "My Grandma died, but it wasn't up here in the Pilbara because she wasn't on her holiday then. It was in Victoria where all the cemeteries are."

These kids all live in a region called the Pilbara, in the northwest, and their perception of things is reasonable.

To alight at the shed which is the Mount Newman airport is virtually to be singed. "It gets to 120 degrees in the summer," says Gordon Godber of Mount Newman Mining Company as he bundles three Japanese miners and myself into his minibus. We cross a bridge which announces the Fortescue River, but its bed is dust and spinifex grass. "In the wet season," says Godber, "the Fortescue can get a hundred meters wide." In the Pilbara, warmth is not a blessing but an adversary. Annual rainfall is 250 millimeters, most of it in one three-month period.

Some two billion years ago, when the entire Pilbara was under the sea, chemical deposition produced rocks full of iron ore. Aborigines lived here unaware of the iron for tens of thousands of years. The first white people reached the coast only in the seventeenth century, and the most famous of them, William Dampier, not noticing the iron ore, pronounced the place "not fit for a dog to live in." A mere 120 years ago whites began to live in the Pilbara.

In the seventeen-year history of the new Pilbara, one billion tons of iron ore have been gouged out of ancient Mount Newman, the world's largest single-pit iron ore mine. Much of it has been shipped to Japan and has ended up in American kitchens and garages. In the entire Pilbara, an area of 510,000 square kilometers, iron ore reserves total 32 billion tons.

In this desolate infiniteness the travel literature has striking listings for each township: "Closest Town," as if acknowledging sparseness; "Transport Availability"; "Emergency Directory." There is a warning: "Always inform someone if you're going into the bush." The flat oasis of Newman consists of a mere 6,200 people, 1,900 of whom work for the mine. The entire Pilbara has no more people (55,000) than half a dozen Manhattan blocks, yet it is on the doorstep of crowded Southeast Asia, closer to Indonesia's 150 million people than to Australia's Boomerang Coast.

Wearing a sky-blue helmet, I follow the shovels and trucks as they move around their ocher domain like rusty dinosaurs, against a skyline of low brown hills, tinged purple by mulla-mulla flowers. The ore, some brown and some the color of curry powder, goes off in trains half a kilometer long, ten a day, 436 kilometers to Port Hedland.

One of the Japanese, who is based in Sydney for his trading company, requests a photo in front of a shovel that lifts fifty tons of ore in one lunge. "Each tire costs ten thousand dollars," says Gordon Godber, banging one with a hammy fist, and the three Japanese nod, standing just half the tire's height. "The truck itself goes for a million and a half." When the trucks were acquired, Gordon explains, they were driven overland the day's ride from Port Hedland. "There's no road; the trucks just crashed through the bush." I lunch with company officials in the Administrative Area, where glass cases of Japanese dolls are a reminder of who makes all this possible.

A Melbourne friend escorting a group of foreign journalists is irritated to find that at Newman's one motel he cannot phone his flock room-to-room. "This is a mining town, luv," says the lady at reception when he complains to her. "If we let people call from one room to another, someone would come in drunk and phone every room in the bloody motel."

The prodigal space of the Australian frontier seems illustrated in my bathroom: the taps are so far from the shower head that I have to walk two paces from under the stream of water to make adjustments. Early in the morning I go out of my room and meet a fierce sun and the mad screech of galahs. Around the low brown motel buildings are high twisted gums with dusty green leaves and a scatter of red azaleas and purple bougainvillea. On the horizon there are red hillocks covered with yellow grass.

"Some of the phones have been playing up," says the lady at reception, who is friendly in a banged-out sort of way, when I complain that

I cannot get through to the U.S.A. A notice says "Visiting Lawyer"; he is up from Perth for a few days to service this town without lawyers. In the whitewashed dining room a scattering of guests, all in town on mine business, devour steak, liver, bacon, and fat Australian-style sausages. "Want more toast, mate?" someone calls halfway across the large room.

"No, there's no roads, you just drive across the country and look for a waterfall or something," explains Shirley, a secretary in the office of Terry McMullan, public affairs officer of the mining company, as she relates a recent vacation trip to the bush with her husband. "When we reached Marble Bar," she says, referring to a town 300 kilometers away that is known as the hottest in Australia and once had 160 consecutive days of 100-degree heat, "we'd been ten days without a shower. We jumped into one and stayed there for two hours." How did they keep food and drink cool in the desert? "You take the innards out of a wine cask, and by fiddling with the transmission of the car, you can make a link and freeze water in the cask innards—put that in an Esky, and you can keep fruit and beer cool for the day." Huddled together in an oasis made secure against the heat, the people of Newman nevertheless feel impelled to go to the frontier.

"Oh, no, the strike wasn't a problem for us," says Shirley, referring to a serious dispute two years ago over whether apprentices were to be guaranteed future work, "because our holidays were due to start just a few days after the strike began." Did she and her husband, who also works for the mine, get "leave-loading," the 17½ percent bonus on top of wages that Australian workers get during holidays?

"Oh, yes, of course, we got leave-loading as usual."

"I came up from Perth to make a few dollars," says John, the tanned, relaxed manager of the town's swimming pool. "I'll go back to Perth after a five-year stint. Here I earn about three times what I would in Perth." Newman people enjoy high wages, low taxation, the purchase of a home with no deposit and no interest, and air-conditioning at company expense. Even cricket is played in an air-conditioned interior. Like Alaskans, they are conscious that they're far from the center of things and that nature is harsh, but they grit their teeth, focus on their perks, and from their isolation fashion a strong local pride. In Newman there is a compulsory chumminess that one might expect to find in a socialist enclave. But this is capitalism; not governments or ideologues but a profitable, benevolent mining company, largely owned by giant Broken Hill Proprietary, has forged this community.

Terry McMullan points across the cafe within the air-conditioned shopping center. "That girl with the three-tone hair drinking a milk-shake, she's ten thousand dollars in debt. It horrifies me, but it's common among the young. They walk into a shop and buy two VCRs." Terry likes the life in Newman but worries at times about his children. "For a while it's marvelous for them—the trouble is they never learn in the Pilbara that twenty dollars is quite a lot of money." In front of us a travel agent has a sign: FOR AS LITTLE AS $523 YOU CAN EXPERIENCE THE EXCITEMENT OF SINGAPORE.

As I lunch with Terry McMullan, a local policeman, Ian Duggan, joins us. Lean, sandy-haired, and cheerful, Duggan says he is one of two policemen in Western Australia who is learning an Aboriginal language. Where are the Aborigines around Newman, I ask, having seen none in the town. "Oh, in Banaga—three days' drive," Duggan says with a quick gesture toward the window. "They're all on welfare; a truck goes out from Port Hedland once a week with stuff for them."

Waiting for my plane at the little airstrip, I meet two female mine employees who at breakfast time on a Friday morning are off to Port Hedland for the weekend. Then the three Japanese miners arrive and peer into the glare looking for a plane. A blond youth in blue shorts and shirt comes over from under a tree and asks me if the Japanese are flying with Skywest.

"All I know is that they're off to Port Hedland," I reply.

"Oh, that's me," he says with a laugh. He strolls over to a tiny yellow and white plane at one corner of the tarmac. It's the Skywest plane, and the blond youth is its pilot. He puts the Japanese in, and the frail craft roars, trembles, and rises into the blue void.

Until the mid-1960s Karratha (an Aboriginal word meaning "good country") was a sheep station. Today this coastal township 400 kilometers northwest of Newman is a gleaming monument to energy. In the 1960s oil was sought, but natural gas was found—in sandstone 375 feet below the sea's surface, in an area off Karratha where waves can rise seventy feet and winds can blow at 220 kilometers an hour.

"The platform is the world's largest in terms of gas production capacity," says Peter Ellery, a well-organized man with a great love of the northwest who is public affairs manager of Woodside Offshore Petroleum, the main company in the North-West Shelf project. "The value output from this one liquefied natural gas plant," Ellery says as he shows me around the spare, high-tech installation, "is expected to be more each year than from the entire Australian iron ore industry."

Eight Japanese gas and electricity utilities will, starting in 1989, be provided with 6 million tons of liquefied natural gas a year.

"Each shift to run the plant," says Cliff Leggoe as we walk into the bomb- and cyclone-proof control room, "consists of five men: an operator at the panels in the control room, a shift supervisor, and three guys actually on the ground of the plant." Chips in Peter Ellery: "And this to supply thirty percent of Western Australia's energy needs." The gas goes south in a pipeline 1,500 kilometers to Perth.

"We advertised for seven electricians for this control room," Cliff Leggoe remarks, "and we got eight hundred applications from all over Australia." The attractions are high wages, wide open spaces, and excitement. "What you get at Karratha," says Peter, "is urban facilities in an outback location."

I stand on a grassy bank dotted with Sturt's desert pea, its petals like scarlet enamel, and look toward the offshore platform, where employees work two weeks, then go for two weeks to the swimming pools and green lawns of their homes in Perth. The average wage for platform workers is between $40,000 and $55,000 a year for twenty-four weeks of work.

Nearby are the duck-egg-blue ponds of the Dampier Salt Company, and the gleaming piles of salt they produce. I climb over red rocks, beating the flies away, past coolibah trees with white trunks to see the Dampier Climbing Men, Aboriginal drawings said to be 30,000 years old.

Peter Ellery drives me by the short-term housing for "people without partners," and the low, verandaed homes of the settled staff. One of these houses costs $110,000 to build, and rents for a ridiculous $120 a month. No fruit or vegetables grow in Karratha; all come in from Perth. The terrain is so rocky that earth, too, has to be trucked in to establish a base for houses and gardens.

Peter and I are joined at lunch at Karratha's International Hotel, the town's one hostelry, where room rates are at New York levels, by Robin Crane, the state government's regional administrator for the Pilbara. "In Perth we were surviving," says this vivacious woman with blond hair in neatly coiffured bobs as we start on a Western Australian white burgundy and platters of cold fish and salad. "Here we're living." Robin Crane has been thirteen years in the Pilbara, which just about embraces its economic history. "When I first came there was nothing but red dirt," she recalls. "I brought a survival kit—saucepans, thermoses, things like that. And now . . ." She sweeps her arm toward the lofty space of the air-conditioned dining room. In one corner is a poster: "Melbourne Cup: Come Join in the Fun and Excitement of Melbourne Cup Fever on November 5."

"My son will soon start work with Hamersley," Robin says, referring to a large iron ore company. "He's a Pilbara breed. He'll make his life here—which people never planned to do in the early days."

"I haven't seen John yet," says the airline official when I ask him to page the mining executive who is coming to meet me at Port Hedland, the Pilbara's biggest town, 200 kilometers up the coast from Karratha. Hedland is that kind of place; most people who use the airport know each other. Outside the terminal window there are palms, oleanders, and frangipannis, and beyond them a pink strip of desert, looking crushed down by the overarching canopy of blue sky. Inside the caravanlike terminal is a sunroom in which sand goannas—a kind of large lizard—move about listlessly to please tourists and children. There is one overseas flight a week; Qantas and Garuda, the Indonesian airline, share a round trip to Bali.

With John Botting I drive around Mount Newman Mining's Port Hedland operation, where trains snake in from Newman and ships of 200,000 tons carry the iron ore to Japan, Taiwan, South Korea, and a few European destinations. I see tires from the huge Newman trucks lying flat and forlorn, full of red dirt and weeds. "They're surrounds for shrubs, put there for Prince Charles's visit seven years ago," says Botting as our car sends up a wall of red dust. "Later, however, someone discovered it was costing fifteen hundred dollars a week to spray the shrubs—so now there's no shrubs."

"The plant goes twenty-four hours a day," John Botting explains as we take an elevator up the tower of the machine that crushes the ore—the height of a twelve-story building—to view the Indian Ocean. "It closes only for Christmas Day, Boxing Day, and cyclones." During the last cyclone the anemometer in the tower registered winds of 270 kilometers an hour "before it blew away out to sea."

The town of Port Hedland with its 18,000 people is lifted above desolation only by proximity to the sea. Like parts of the Moroccan coast, it is a marriage of red earth and blue water. Life in Port Hedland is mining and loading, high wages, VCRs, drinking, sports, cars, air-conditioning, and a love-hate tie with the surrounding bush.

On Sunday morning, along the narrow strip of town that follows the sea, people are slowly busy with preparations for sports on land and water. Many smoke. No one reads a newspaper. A blinding sun on a day of rest does not reduce the appetite for huge breakfasts. "Do ya want a cooked breakie?" asks the manageress of the Hospitality Inn, a cigarette clenched in her brown fingers. As I settle for the Continental, a man beside me, his face as red as the soil outside the window, disposes of steak, sausages, kidneys, bacon, and fried eggs that shimmer with fat.

In the shopping area I talk with children and find them preoccupied with animals, spoiled by air-conditioning, and vaguely aware that Japan is their lifeline. "Rostrum Club," says a notice, blotched from red dust and rain water. "For those who desire to advance themselves in the art of public speaking, and who hold that freedom of speech, loyalty to truth, clarity of thought, and a love of the English tongue are vital elements to that art. Meets Tuesday evenings." Nearby are tombstones, broken and almost hidden by spinifex, whose Japanese characters recall the Pilbara's links with Asia.

As the temperature soars I retreat to the handsome town swimming pool built with mining company assistance. I ask my cabbie, who is originally from Melbourne, if he has gotten used to the heat. "You don't get used to the heat, mate," he replies, "you put up with it." Outside the front door of the pool stands a row of cars, several of them empty yet with the air-conditioner running.

"Port Hedland is better than Newman," says a young man who lounges on the grass. "Much more to do."

"You don't mind the pollution?" I ask, wiping the red dust from my camera.

"What d'ya mean by pollution?"

I ask what people do on weekends. "If it's a long weekend I like to drive to Broome."

"But that's six hundred kilometers each way!"

"No worries, mate." Before diving into the pool he explains that there are fewer people than usual at the pool today. "It's cold. I doubt it's ninety degrees." I dive in too, but do not feel cold.

At my motel a cook, all in white except for his bush boots, tells me it would take an hour to walk to the Esplanade Hotel, "downtown." A moment later a Vietnamese waitress says fifteen minutes would be enough. They all drive cars and simply do not know how long it takes to walk anywhere.

Over a hearty Australian dinner of oysters and steak John Botting remarks, "In the Pilbara, workers are really little capitalists. They're against the capital gains tax, for instance, because they own property themselves." To the dinner Botting has brought a colleague, John Crowley, who after a bottle of Penfolds Cabernet Shiraz expresses his disappointment that he lost Labor Party preselection for the local seat to a Pom. Since Botting is English-born, I wonder whether the dinner will remain amicable.

"I just can't accept it, mate," says Crowley. "A Pom, only five years in Australia, wins against me by twenty votes." He appeals to me: "You see, I love Australia—it's the best place in the world to live."

"Being Australian is not enough of a policy to run on," rejoins Botting. "You have to fine-tune the issues. You have to persuade people about the issues."

Crowley spears another oyster and the wine flows on. Botting turns to me. "It was U.S. money, backed by BP [British Petroleum]," he says, as if to check any incipient Australian chauvinism, "plus Japanese readiness to buy, that got the Pilbara started."

As glasses of port arrive, Botting gloomily muses that he will not be able to retire in the Pilbara. "Couldn't afford it, after the company subsidies come to an end. A lettuce costs a dollar and a half in Port Hedland, forty cents in Perth. Everything's trucked up, you see, seventeen hundred kilometers from Perth, and each time a truck blows a tire, that's four hundred dollars."

At a pub I meet a Yugoslav who works as a driver for Newman Mining. He's been in Australia since 1972, and he's been able to make five trips back to Belgrade since then. After a few beers it is the Aborigines who are on his mind. "Last week five cars were stolen, including one mine car. No arrests. It's the Abos that do it, but the cops make no arrests because they know the Abos have no money to pay the fine. In the bush you see Abos sitting in the sand under a tree eating a hot meal paid for by the taxpayers." Do they have weapons? "No, it's a funny thing," the Yugoslav replies, "the Abos steal but they aren't armed."

In many ways, I feel, race doesn't matter much in the Pilbara. Class matters to a degree—class always matters—but class is blunted by the high wages of the low, the simple conditions of the high, and the smallness of the total community.

"What does a strong wind do to a pile of salt like that?" I ask Roger Windsor, the dry, quietly spoken resident manager of the Leslie Salt Company, which is a subsidiary of the Cargill Corporation of Minnesota. He gives a small wry laugh. "It blows iron ore onto it." The Leslie Company, a giant, along with Dampier Salt, in the realm of industrial salt, in which Australia ranks second in the world to Mexico, made its plans to produce in Port Hedland before it knew the iron ore companies were going to be next door.

Despite the ore dust and what Windsor calls "an environment of militant unionism," Leslie does well because this spot on the Western Australian coast offers all that is needed for an efficient solar salt plant: sea water, space for the concentrating ponds, high temperatures for the evaporation process, low rainfall to avoid interference with that process, a port that can handle huge ships, and a reasonable proximity to the markets of Japan, Taiwan, and South Korea.

"We have a heavy program coming up," remarks Windsor, who by Port Hedland standards is formally dressed, in fawn trousers, a striped red-and-white shirt, and leather shoes, "and last week we put it to the unions that we must have more overtime. They did it. One of their leaders said to me, 'In the end we want the company to do well so we can screw you in the next negotiations for award increases.'"

The scene resembles the U.S.A.'s Midwest after a snowstorm. We watch drag chains, conveyor belts, and cranes, angled and complex like a cluster of praying mantises, poke into the hills of glistening salt to scoop it up and load it onto trucks and later, after draining and drying, onto ships.

Not far away I visit the Goldsworthy Mining Company. "Mining's exciting," says Ian Lancaster as he shows me the plant of a company that was a pioneer among Pilbara iron producers, and whose ore now comes from Shay Gap, 150 kilometers from Port Hedland. Lancaster is a solid, forthright man, born in Britain but a Pilbara addict. We pass the building that used to be the wet canteen of the plant. "In the first years," says Lancaster, "if anyone was speeding, the cops would fine him a jug of beer." On the causeway back toward Port Hedland there is a sign that points toward CARNARVON 860 KILOMETERS.

What is it that makes mining exciting for Ian Lancaster? "Dealing with the earth. Discovery. The element of danger." He recalls of the 1960s: "There was no TV or sealed roads. DC-Threes were still flying. I remember waiting hours at Dampier for the plane. There was no aircon, there was no bloody terminal. You sat there with a canvas evaporation bag of water, and with the flies. The plane would arrive, and the captain would say, 'Sorry, another breakdown, we're going to Tom Price first.'" Lancaster laughs. "Today if the jet is twenty minutes late into Perth it's a major disaster."

Ian Lancaster formerly worked for the Australian Coast Watch.

"In the Coast Watch, if we saw something, there was nothing to respond with," he recalls. "We'd see an Indonesian fishing boat in Australian waters—OK, we'd seen an Indonesian fishing boat; we did nothing." Lancaster is unhappy with such a situation. "I'd like to see a patrol boat base in Port Hedland." Some people in the area believe that the current dredging of the port is being done with half an eye to attracting the navy to build one.

In the 1960s it was a case of getting the ore out, with little quality control, and effortlessly selling it. The 1980s are different. Operations are far bigger, yet the outlook is in some ways less secure. "Wood's becoming more expensive than steel," explains John Botting when I notice that steel sleepers are being laid on Mount Newman Mining's railway line. The reply arrests me. "The world is hungry for steel," runs a line from Mount Newman Mining's video presentation. But how long will the world remain hungry for steel, in particular for steel from Australian iron ore?

"A delegation to Brazil has come back very impressed," John Botting says quietly during our last moments together. "It was thought the operation would be a few guys in the jungle with pickaxes. In fact the Brazilians are using the latest technology, and they have a large amount of high-grade ore." The estimate in Port Hedland is that the cost advantage (labor, freight, and other factors) that Australia has over Brazil, once 14 percent, has shrunk to 3 percent.

Later, in Melbourne, Minister for Resources and Energy Gareth Evans says gloomily that Brazil "has the capacity to knock us right out of some traditional markets." Complacent trade unions did not foresee this development. "Until they actually visited Brazil," Evans goes on, "the unionists tended to think the threat of Brazil was just a bogey being waved around by the mine owners." And as the mines go, so goes the Pilbara, and much of Western Australia.

"Sorry we're late leaving," says the pilot as we taxi at Port Hedland. "The caterers managed to put your meals onto the wrong plane." There are two planes at the airport.

We fly over the mountains and cattle stations of the Kimberleys. Some 500 kilometers north of Hedland we descend into Broome, once the world's largest pearl-fishing center, now a charming spot for tourists. The sea is two shades of blue as clouds cast inky shadows on top of the light-blue expanse. On one side of the peninsula across which Broome sprawls under pale orange roofs, the water is edged with the whitest sand, like a hem of lace on a dress of aqua color. On the other side the soil is red, and the turquoise water as it meets the earth resembles a sunset encounter between blue and pink.

Technology greets space as our jet pulls up in the glare of tiny Broome airport. During the stopover, hostesses hop in and out of the plane as if it were their car at a picnic ground. An Aborigine wheels the cargo wagon from the plane—like a lawn mower slicing through the heat—and a customer in swimming trunks walks out to rummage on it for a package he is expecting. A woman climbs aboard the plane with an Esky portable cooler packed with food and drink and comes to rest beside me. On my other side is an Aboriginal man so fat that his rolling stomach touches the folded tray table in front of him.

Toward Derby, a short hop northeast from Broome, the soil turns from red to cinnamon, and here and there roads stretch out to the horizon like geometric lines on a drafting table. At Derby airport there is on the wall of the terminal a list of phone numbers, a virtual phone book for this little outpost. Outside are low, fat baobab trees, with small spreading branches. They used to be called "prison trees," a local man tells me, because they were wide enough to be cut open and have criminals (Aboriginal) lodged within.

I stay at the Spinifex Motel on the wide red dirt road that is Derby's spine. Walking around sparse, flat Derby is like walking around an airfield. Dinner at the motel's restaurant is a rollicking buffet affair. A group of truck drivers, wearing shorts and smoking, line up at a carvery where a young man with a pink face and a white hat offers beef, lamb, and chicken, and asks, "What is your choice?" One truckie says, "I'll leave it up to you, mate." Another asks, "Make me up a plate, mate." I order the Australian house rosé wine to accompany my lamb, and its pungency gives a whole new meaning to gasoline sniffing. Beside me a man sits down, says, "G'day," and continues: "It's my twenty-eighth birthday. I decided to drink alone at home, and who should come along but my ex-wife. So I've come here to get pissed."

Opposite the Spinifex Motel the red earth glistens with the glass of broken beer bottles and wine flagons. Inside the glass walls of a handsome indoor cricket center, two neatly attired teams vie against each other with total concentration. Out in the street, beyond the cricketers' attentions, there are scattered altercations among cursing but unarmed Aborigines. As I watch from the motel door, a white man comes by on his way to the bar. "Enjoying Derby's entertainment, eh?" he chortles.

In the air again, flying east across the Kimberleys, I look down on tabletop mountains and rivers of a muddy asparagus-yellow color and see the first cultivation I have seen for weeks. It is 108 degrees as I stand before an ad in the hut that is the Kununurra airport terminal: "Kimberley Air Charter. Specialising Also in 4-by-4 Drive Vehicles. Fully Equipped for Mining Exploration and Survey Work. Contact Us in Bandicoot Drive." Kununurra is the leaping-off point for a dramatic but so far unfulfilled irrigation scheme based on harnessing the Ord River, and the creation of a huge storage basin named Lake Argyle. Nearby is the world's largest diamond mine, at Argyle; half the world's supply of industrial diamonds is said to lie in these rugged, colorful hills.

At the Kununurra Hotel I have a drink in the Green Room and am surprised that this bar is all white (40 percent of the Kimberleys population is Aboriginal). A moment later I see a second place within the hotel for drinking; it is largely black and known to the locals I chat with, white and black alike, as the Animal Bar. Port Hedland may seem small and isolated, but here at the reception desk is a notice saying that an optometrist from Hedland will soon visit Kununurra, and that appointments may be made through the hotel.

Attempts to grow rice and cotton around Kununurra have run into problems of bizarre pests and high costs due to remoteness. The market wasn't there at the right time for the sugar (nor did Queensland take kindly to the threat to its sugar market). Hope flickers again as sweet sorghum is being grown for export to Japan, and melons and mangoes and bananas (grown when the south is in its winter off-season) are produced for the urban market. "People are farming and actually making a living," says a government agronomist based in the area. "This is something that has not happened in the past. Peanuts have advanced and cashews are being talked about." Still the Ord area has under crop or pasture only some 7 to 8 percent of its potential, and tourism and diamonds bring in far more money than farming.

I have to tear myself away from the northwest, and yet on returning to Perth I feel a certain relief. The space is awesome and at times liberating, but at other times it is depressing, for vastness can shrivel human beings and make them lost souls in their own land. Many parts of the northwest teeter on the brink of being a land of dashed hopes. Other parts offer the extravagant mining riches which drive Lang Hancock—despite the "socialism" that hems him in—to fresh schemes even in his eighth decade. In the end the northwest, sturdily self-reliant in spirit as it is, depends totally on the ups and downs of world markets.

These past weeks I have felt enormously distant from the triggers that move the world, and so events and issues that normally seem important to me—and are important to the Pilbara and the Kimberleys—have been reduced to triviality. Yet I have also felt buoyed by a down-to-earth outback wisdom that rules out pretense.

"I just could not tolerate us being the Cinderella state," Sir Charles Court says in his office in St. George's Terrace, the only Perth street with a big-city look. "We had to go begging to the grants commission in Canberra for approval to build a school, a hospital, for public works. It just wasn't good enough for a state with our potential."

Court, a grandfatherly figure at seventy-five years, is a giant in Western Australian history. He was for twenty years a minister in the Perth government, eight of them as premier, and in that period iron ore and other resources gave wings to the state. "It is a fairly unique situation," Court says with satisfaction, "for a state with less than nine percent of Australia's population to account for twenty-four percent of its exports. We turned Western Australia from a mendicant state into a contributor state."

"Water and energy," Sir Charles booms as we sit together at a huge jarrah wood table that dominates his outer office. "Everyone told me the Pilbara and the other developments *couldn't* happen because we lacked water and energy." His mouth curls slightly. "Superficially that was correct."

Court is a self-made man who came through the Depression to become an itinerant musician and later an accountant. "I learned a lot in the Depression," he says quietly. "I took over bankrupt accounts and tried desperately to revive them. If the person survived I had a client." Accountant Court watched some of his farming clients get into trouble over water. "You can transport energy, but not water." Premier Court listened to many people with bright ideas—one was to tow in icebergs from the southern seas and anchor them off Fremantle—but in the end the solution was simple.

"Nature has an amazing capacity to provide if only you look hard enough." Sir Charles is on the edge of his chair, his big brown hands anchored forward on the table. "I consulted the best brains, some foreign, and we realized that all our water from those sudden cyclones in the Pilbara and the Kimberleys just rushes into the sea." The answer was to locate and tap underground aquifers.

"At Mount Newman you've seen the long wall which arrests the waters of the Fortescue River," the former conservative premier goes on, "making it soak down into the aquifers which service the mine and the town. You can even have a yacht club up there now. The important thing is to arrest the flow of water instead of having it tear madly down the ravines. By the way, it's an exciting thing in a cyclone to fly over the northwest and before your eyes to see the rivers start flowing, and the fantastic sight of that water moving painlessly to the sea. It's safe to say," claims the man who was told the northwest couldn't develop because it lacked water, "that for the next hundred years there's no identifiable project here which can't be supplied with potable water."

"No one in Canberra ever thought we were going to make it," Court says with a chuckle. "Menzies regarded economic development, which I was obsessed with, as being the rather vulgar side of politics. Yet Menzies was prepared to let us play with our toys. He would pat us on the head, say, 'Keep up the good work, sonny,' and hope we wouldn't worry *him* too much. He didn't realize how much he helped us by leaving us alone." A frown crosses the suntanned knightly brow. "But there were other people in Canberra who said, 'These people are succeeding!' They were shocked, you see, because the iron ore contracts we wrote in the early 1960s were the biggest mineral contracts ever written. These Canberra types said, 'They can't do these things, what do *they* know about it!'"

Sir Charles laughs and leans back in his upright chair. "What amazed them was that we had no money!" He glances at me sharply. "Don't give me a queer look. It's a blessing that we had no money. If we'd had a little money, we'd have tried to build railways, towns, power stations, down to a standard we could afford, instead of up to the standard we needed." Court's eyes twinkle. "We called tenders even when Australia still had an embargo against iron ore export. And we got a peep behind the curtain as to *what the world would pay for Western Australia's resources*. And what infrastructure they would build! And what royalties they would pay for secure access!" He throws up his strong arms. "You've seen the results, the mines, the railways, the towns, the ports, the power stations."

It was then that the Court government's famous confrontations with Canberra began. "Canberra said, 'These people shouldn't be doing this on their own; there must be some way we can get our finger into this pie.'" Perth won the battle to have the embargo on the export of iron ore lifted, but federal-state feuds soared on other issues. "It was with Whitlam," recalls Sir Charles without joy, "that the centralist versus federalist philosophies fight really came to a head. The centralists used their financial powers to try to get control of us. Then they got involved in 'the environment,' and a whole bureaucracy sprouted on that." Court's fight against Whitlam made him popular—"manna from heaven politically"—in a state where Whitlam's haughty style and stress upon redistribution made him unpopular.

To Court's disappointment the Fraser government was only marginally more understanding of Western Australia's developmental politics. "Fraser and Doug Anthony [then Country Party leader] would swear on a stack of Bibles that they're federalists, and probably they mean it." Court looks pained. "Yet they say to themselves, 'But we know better than these wild colonial blokes over in Western Australia. We've gotta help them.'"

A throaty laugh fills the huge office. "And you know when a government says, 'I'm here to help you,' look out. That's when you've really got cause to be frightened!"

The hour is late and the sun no longer beams in upon us. "You've got to believe in some things, you know, and you've got to believe in yourself." Sir Charles rises to return to his inner office. "It's what development means for people that counts," he says, gazing out over the red roofs of the Perth suburbs and the porcelain-blue water of the Swan River dotted with luxurious white boats. As I walk out into St. George's Terrace, I muse that Western Australia is as young as yesterday. Sir Charles Court's life—he was born in 1911—spans just half the years since Governor Stirling sailed up the Swan River with silks and pianos to try to found a genteel, convict-free colony.

Fay Zwicky's skepticism about the America's Cup's contribution to Western Australia may have some justification; certainly the new hotels will have to struggle to fill their rooms and the vehicle plates will have to find another motto to replace "Home of the America's Cup." Yet the great victory of Dennis Conner's *Stars and Stripes* in February 1987 may not have left the West a total loser. Both the Bond syndicate, and even more Kevin Parry's *Kookaburra III* team, which beat Bond's boat and won the right to vie against the technologically superb *Stars and Stripes,* performed valiantly and lost graciously. "My dear Ron," Perth-raised Prime Minister Hawke wrote to President Reagan in a message that accompanied the gift of an Australian outback hat, after Reagan bet Hawke a cowboy hat for an Australian hat that *Stars and Stripes* would win. "Enjoy the hat. You can keep it. Take pleasure in the Cup. That is only a temporary possession. We'll be back for it in 1990."

The America's Cup races put Perth on the world map as never before, and the hospitable Western Australians proved to themselves and
others their capacity to be fine hosts for a complex event. Meanwhile,
as both Conner and Alan Bond know, there is no guarantee the Cup
will remain anywhere for long. Bond has sold his two boats *Australia III*
and *Australia IV* to a Japanese group that will make that nation's first
bid for the America's Cup in 1990. The close links between Japan and
Western Australia with its mines and boats are forever taking on new
twists.

EIGHT

The Last Frontier

Despite Australia's image as an industrialized Western democracy, 40 percent of the nation lies in the tropics and is very undeveloped. The 3 percent of Australia's population that lives in its tropical 40 percent seem the wrong color and size for a sweating existence amidst palms, desert, and Wet and Dry seasons. Xavier Herbert, author of *Capricornia* and long a Northern Territory resident, liked to say that he loved Australia but not necessarily its people; the Northern Territory (it is not yet formally a state) would seem to be a paradise for such a man. It contains a mere 0.8 percent of the Australian population (140,000) spread over 17 percent of Australia's area (1.34 million square kilometers).

Darwin, the Territory's capital, is a raw, humid, cosmopolitan community of 70,000 people named after the famous biologist, some of whose arguments in *The Origin of Species* were supported by Australian data. Australia's northernmost city, it is as close to Vietnam as to Tasmania, and it feels closer. Within an arc 2,000 kilometers north of Darwin there are 200 million Melanesian and Asian people, while within the same arc south there are 15 million Australians.

191

Leaving the plane, I find a loud tropical scene in the ramshackle Darwin airport terminal, whose only decent room is its bar. Men in shorts rasp at each other, their beer cans bobbing to accentuate their words. Says a notice: PLEASE PLACE INTERSTATE FRUIT IN THIS BIN. Today the clocks change for daylight saving—well, some of them change. This nation of 15 million people cheerfully hurls itself into the chaos of five different time zones. As I reach Darwin it is 6 P.M., while due south in Adelaide it is 7 P.M.; in Queensland it is 6:30 P.M., and due south of Brisbane it is 7:30 P.M. in Sydney and Melbourne; while in Western Australia it is 4:30 P.M. The bloody-minded sectionalism that produced the railway gauge fiasco of a century ago hasn't entirely disappeared; certainly in the Northern Territory one hears few good things about "the south."

Architecturally, Darwin looks monotone and prefabricated—like its arch-enemy Canberra—thanks to Cyclone Tracey, whose winds of 220 kilometers an hour one terrible night in 1974 left some fifty people dead and only 6 percent of the city's homes habitable. But under its bland white exterior, Australia's only substantially multiracial city has a mind and charm all its own.

"I was counting the hours till I got on the plane," relates the poet Fay Zwicky, in Perth, of her recent trip to Darwin and other northern points. "I loved the natural wonders, especially the wonderful milky opal blue sea, but, oh, the people . . ." She laughs.

"What's wrong with the people, Fay?"

"Sides of beef supported by long white socks. I mean, how do you talk to a side of beef?"

Yet in few parts of Australia do I find people as pleasant as in Darwin and the rest of the Northern Territory. Most are patient and courteous with each other, however inarticulate they may seem to a southerner, and perhaps this is because of the common enemy of a vicious humidity. During the Wet, the atmosphere outdoors in the Top End (as the area around Darwin is called) is like a laundry in Miami. Only in the Northern Territory do I appreciate why some Americans find my accent unclear; Australian pronunciation can be poor. The farther you go toward Australia's frontiers—and Perth seems the center of the earth compared with the Territory—the less articulate are the people. Space takes a ransom on communication.

The Northern Territory is the land of the friendly larrikin Mick Dundee, created by Paul Hogan in the film *Crocodile Dundee*. The movie flaunts the landscape, as Australian movies tend to do, and of-

fers the humor of the frontiersman: modest, male chauvinist, and showing a wide-eyed wonder when encountering sophistication. Paul Hogan
as crocodile poacher Mick Dundee turns transgression into quaintness
and narrowness into innocence.

Darwin is a laid-back, cheerful, crude place, softened by tropical
plants and bedecked with the Northern Territory flag in black, white,
and red ocher, and featuring Sturt's desert rose. In a restaurant a politician is greeted by a lawyer who says of an issue that crops up, "Aah,
don't give me a hard time about that!" Rejoins the politician with a
lewd grin: "I'll give *your wife* a hard time any day."

SHIRTS OR SINGLETS PLEASE FELLAS, says the pub sign. LADIES
NEED NOT COMPLY. At bars women upturn their beer or wine glasses
to a vertical position to drain them dry. "Do you serve Continental
breakfast?" a traveler asks at a motel. "Yeah, pies." The percentage of
prison inmates in the Northern Territory—73 percent of them Aboriginal—is more than three times the national average. A shop in town
offers the best of both worlds: "Alternative T-shirts at Southern Prices."

At the bar of the Hotel Darwin I have a drink with a local mother
of three who has just knocked off work as a waitress at a neighboring
hotel. With our drinks we eat a Darwin Dog, a hot dog wrapped in
bacon with corn relish and cheese. "I've been to Perth, but there's too
many people there," says the woman, startling a Melbourne-born visitor—and perhaps explaining what Fay Zwicky found wanting up here
in the Top End.

Outside in the mall there are many Timorese and Chinese, and I
think of Xavier Herbert's comment in an interview just before he died
in 1985. "Alice Springs is the place now," said this nativist of the town
he loved, "because Darwin's turned into a sort of Oriental city." As
close to Singapore as it is to Melbourne, Darwin looks like the outer
suburbs of Singapore might look if that city-state had any.

On a silky evening I stroll in the park opposite the Hotel Darwin.
An elderly Aboriginal man is lying on a bench. Could I sit down for a
moment? "Yeah, Darwin's a friendly place," he says, rousing himself.
"Sit down, mate. My name's Mac."

I tell Mac I'm from Melbourne. "Gawd, that's a long way." He rises
from a prone to a sitting position, wiping his eyes, and arranges his
only garment, a loincloth. "Heh, you can sleep in the park if ya don't
have anywhere else to sleep. Or if you don't like the park, the city mall's
nice."

Darwin achieved an overland link to the south—road and rail combined to Adelaide—only during World War Two. It feels at once cheated and ignored by the south—which means not only Canberra but virtually all the non–Northern Territory urban areas, for *every* state and territory capital except Darwin lies in the southern half of the nation. "The policies in Canberra on matters like air fares," says Dr. Jim Eedle at the Territory's university college, "make us feel we are more welcome looking north than looking south." He refers to the artificially high domestic air fares. "It's two hundred dollars cheaper to go from Darwin to Perth via Bali than to go directly on an Australian domestic airline."

"Darwin is different from Melbourne and Sydney in that it's very new," observes the British-born Eedle, who worked in West Africa before settling in Darwin, as we chat on his bare hot campus. "During World War Two the entire civilian population of Darwin was evacuated. By 1974, when Cyclone Tracey hit, the population had grown to forty thousand, almost all of whom were evacuated after the cyclone, and only half of whom came back."

On defense Eedle is fatalistic. "The only way to defend the north," he says with a shrug of the shoulders, "is by an extremely competent intelligence system. By the time we see them coming over the horizon, it's going to be far too late."

Steve Hatton, since mid-1986 chief minister (effectively premier) of the Territory, is candid on the matter. "The north coast of Australia is basically unsurveilled," he tells me. "Drug runners can operate with impunity as long as they're not within a hundred kilometers of Darwin."

The tiny plane buzzes and shakes over Adelaide River, which twists east from Darwin like an intestine, on a flight to the floodplains between the East Alligator and South Alligator rivers. Here, amidst nature's astonishments, three forces in Australian life are locked in an uneasy relationship.

Scientists of Kakadu National Park, famous for its magpie geese (80 percent of the world's population is here), and a recent addition to the World Heritage List, look down their noses on all that falls beyond the boundaries of their brilliant zoology and their sometimes infantile political anthropology. "Fun and modern living must complement the wonders of prehistoric Kakadu National Park," says a Northern Territory government pamphlet. But some of the high priests of Canberra's Office of the Supervising Scientist (OSS) at Kakadu don't agree. If fun means tourism they are suspicious of it. If modern living requires economic development they would prefer backward-ness—except where their personal comfort is at stake.

Uranium miners try to march forward under the banner of progress, fighting off supervising scientists, environmentalists, Labor Party people who don't think Australia should export uranium, and militants who "advise" Aborigines. While the Aborigines themselves, among the few in Australia who still live off the land, smile at the scientists, criticize the miners, and take money from miner and scientist alike—sometimes heeding their advisers and sometimes going their own way.

On top of our four-wheel-drive vehicle we attach an aluminum boat. With the thermometer at 102 degrees on a late October day toward the end of the Dry, I head for the Yellow Water area of Kakadu with Kate Duggan of the Territory's conservation commission and Dr. Bruce Bailey, a zoologist with the OSS. We launch the boat and Bailey, a blond, boyish, taciturn man, immensely knowledgeable about the creatures chirping and grunting about us, drives it with gusto. Now and then we hit a submerged log and he grins; or if it's a major bump he curses. "It might rain next month," he remarks, scanning the wide, high sky as we glide past a cluster of dead trees, smoky gray like a Czechoslovakian glass ornament, on which corcorans perch. "You see," explains Kate Duggan, when she notices the look on my face, "we've only had eight millimeters of rain since May; we're waiting for the Wet."

Almost within reach of the boat is a three-foot-tall pelican, as long from its neck to the end of its amazing beak as it is from feet to neck. Dixon Lanier Merritt's lines indeed seem apt: "A wonderful bird is the pelican, / His bill will hold more than his belican." Half a dozen brown ducks stand by in obeisance to the pelican's superior size and grace.

We chug by freshwater mangroves and paperbark trees, ghostly in their blue-silver hue, as if moonlight is falling upon them in midafternoon. The glare suffuses even the scruffy grass under the bamboo trees on the banks. Few birds are in the air—it is too hot—but dozens of different kinds (there are 260 varieties in the park) stand motionless as if watching each other.

A lily trotter perches elegantly on the green and ivory carpet of water lilies, occasionally stepping gracefully from one flat lily leaf to another, a sharp eye out for food just beneath the water's surface. A long-necked darter swoops overhead gripping a fish in its mouth. A whistle kite flaps down to earth, grabs a snake, and hauls it off into the blue expanse. A platypus runs along the grassy bank and like a World War Two "duck" pushes smoothly at an angle into the water. Bruce

Bailey stops the boat so that we can watch the movements of a crocodile, now stationary like a log, now poking its ugly head into the air,
and the stillness of death engulfs us.

"A woman was recently attacked by a crocodile," Bailey mentions
casually as our little metal boat, which is heating up like a saucepan on
the stove, leaves the crocodile and putt-putts on through warm reedy
water. "Lucky to survive, actually. It was a woman academic from
Sydney. She was canoeing and a croc chased her. Hours later park
rangers found her—buttocks and thighs severely bitten." I scan the
water and feel momentarily glad I am not a Sydney academic.

Bailey insists I see the Aboriginal rock art of the area, and soon we
are peering through a noisy mesh of blowies at Nabulwinjbulwinj, an
aggressive spirit who deals with women by striking them with a yam and
then eating them. Most of the art of Nourlangie Rock I find unremark-
able. None of it is ancient. Most of it is said to have been done in 1964
by Najombolmi, in the area called Barramundi Charlie, after the north's
most delectable fish.

"Did you know," remarks Bailey, "that's it's against the Aboriginal
way of life to become a millionaire?" I say nothing, staring at a ghost
gum, its surface smooth and white like the thighs of a woman, but I
think back to a wealthy black I met in Western Australia. Perhaps to
these high priests of nature a capitalist Aborigine is somehow less of an
Aborigine than one pushed leftward by intellectuals from Melbourne
and Sydney.

"It's a fact of life that this country burns off every second year,"
says Dr. Bruce Gall briskly from behind his office desk at the OSS. "It's
been that way since before the European settlement," adds this senior
supervising scientist. I ask about the benefit of the burning off. "It must
have benefits or you wouldn't have the system." As I leave Gall's office
I pass a poster, "Mining in National Parks Is the Pits," and on a rack
in the lobby of the log-cabin-style building I see a pamphlet on Aboriginal land rights entitled *The Hawke Government's Sell-Out*. I wonder if someone should be supervising the supervisors.

I drive with Dr. Tony Press, a zoologist with the National Parks
and Wildlife Service, past gum forests and sandstone escarpments,
through a land of jabiru (an Australian stork), tree rat, bandicoot,
northern native cat, sugar guider, agile wallaby, antilopine kangaroo, thrush-tail possum, and dozens of other animals and birds. I ask
Press about the philosophy behind the protection of species. "On one
level, we should try to preserve any species in danger of extinction,"
he replies.

"Even if it's a menace?"

"I don't know what you mean by a menace." Do zoologists ever find a species that they judge the world would be better off without? Press is uncomfortable. He concedes that farmers have a certain case against kangaroos and parrots which eat crops. "I suppose there's a conflict of interest," he murmurs, then shifts his ground. "It's aesthetically pleasing to keep all species," he says, "and it's a reference point for the observation of changes."

I probe the contrast between the functional view of wildlife held by the Aborigines, who seem to be his heroes, and his own sentimental view. "Yes," he says at length, "for thousands of years the Aborigines exploited creatures; wildlife was for them a resource"—which seems for a moment to leave him, or the Aborigines, close to the viewpoint of the economic developers.

With Kate Duggan of the Territory's conservation unit, I visit the Manaburduma Aboriginal Campsite, an unadorned collection of khaki-colored buildings amidst the scrub, with a notice at the front: EN-TRANCE BY AUTHORISED PERSONS ONLY. "Many Aborigines go back and forth," explains Duggan, a slim, quiet woman with weatherbeaten skin and a kind face, "between the campsite and the bush, to which they go back for bush tucker, like goanna, and to go to ceremonies."

Has Kate tried goanna? "Yes, it tastes a bit like chicken."

The town of Jabiru is a green, well-watered, and air-conditioned oasis of 1,300 people, almost entirely dependent on Ranger Uranium Mines, an enterprise of Energy Resources of Australia. "Business people want a motel in the town," Kate Duggan says, "but there's opposition." Later I ask Bruce Gall if more facilities may be needed for tourism to flourish. "As far as accommodation is concerned," he says brusquely, "that's up to commercial enterprises to bring forth recommendations." Meanwhile the guardians of the OSS, high above the vulgar level of commerce, with an annual budget of $4.5 million, "supervise" the area and instruct the visitor on what the Aborigines think is "sacred."

I ask Hilary Speat, administrative secretary of the Alligator River Region Research Institute (another arm of federal supervision of Kakadu), if any human beings have been physically harmed in any way by the operation of the Ranger uranium mine. "Nothing outside the mine itself has been affected. There's a small amount of seepage, but it's hardly gone anywhere. We monitor them on dust and on aerial dispersion of acid from their acid plant, but we haven't found anything."

"Nothing has proved a hazard to human beings in Kakadu?"

"No, no, no." I suppose it's worth $4.5 million a year to find nothing.

Ready to fly back to Darwin, I ask the pretty nut-brown girl who works for Arrmunda Airways what time the plane will leave. "Four-forty—in twenty minutes," she says. She looks around the air-conditioned hut. "Let's see, everyone's here, we might as well leave now. Hop in." The Cessna 402 climbs up over the scrubby trees and a hut marked JABIRU GUN CLUB, and soon we are gazing down on rocky escarpments. The only other passenger is a jet-black youth named Angel. "Lots of people around here are called names like Angel or Faith," he says as his large white eyes bore into me, "because of the Christian mission at Oenpelli."

In Darwin I ask the head of the Territory's mines department his opinion of the Office of the Supervising Scientist. "It's a rather oversize watchdog," he notes dryly.

The lord mayor of Darwin, Alec Fong Lim, invites me to lunch at a Chinese restaurant on the attractive city mall. "My wife and I speak Chinese at home only when we don't want the kids to hear us," he says after ordering his favorite south China dishes. Born in Katherine, Fong Lim came to Darwin at age seven; his father worked in a pub and did bookmaking on the side.

The lord mayor, casual in a red open-neck shirt, is just back from a trip to Hong Kong to promote Darwin's new Trade Development Zone, which will offer manufacturers of garments, knitwear, video cassettes, and other goods a duty-free enclave. "The higher labor costs here," he observes, "will be offset by getting around EEC and U.S.A. quotas. The finished goods will count as Australian—not Hong Kong—exports. It's funny the Chinese in Australia don't drink much," he reflects, sipping orange juice, "but in Hong Kong they drink cognac like they're going out of business."

Darwin, a young city, has twice been forced overnight to become even younger. "We were in Katherine," Fong Lim recalls of March 1942. "We'd been evacuated there. One day these nine planes came over, real high, and went away. A stupid uncle of mine said it's OK, they're our Russian allies. Then they came back and started dropping bombs. Just as they finished, the air-raid siren went off. I can still see the American jeeps running around after the planes had gone. In Katherine one Aborigine was killed in the Japanese bombing," says Fong

Lim as we plunge into Cantonese and Sichuan dishes. "In Darwin it was more than two hundred." You can still see marks of Japanese shrapnel bombs on the big tin hut which is the Darwin air terminal.

The lord mayor discounts the blow to the city's morale of Cyclone Tracey, remarking that most of the people who left Darwin after the disaster were not natives of the Northern Territory. "The city is a thousand percent better built than before Cyclone Tracey," claims Alec (as after five minutes he asks me to call him). "Ninety-nine percent of the houses used to be fibro, with roofs that blow off easily."

I ask Alec to characterize the difference in mood between Darwin and Alice Springs, the second-largest population center of the Northern Territory. "They just feel inferior, they feel neglected," he says of the people of Alice Springs. "They always feel Big Brother in Darwin is watching over them. We try to appease them, but that's the way they think, and you can't do anything about it." He shrugs and grins.

Alec Fong Lim thinks constant patrols of the huge northern coastline are impossible and that pragmatism must rule. "What can you do with the buggers," he says of Indonesians and islanders who are found fishing in Australian waters. "You can't send 'em back with empty hands—they live by fish—so we take half their catch and say, 'You naughty boys, don't do it again.' "

The lord mayor doesn't favor a current Labor Party proposal within the city council to make Darwin a nuclear-free port. "That sort of thing is all right for Melbourne to do. They've got no bloody uranium, but uranium is a big part of our economy."

NEW ROAD, says the yellow and green sign as Bert Wiedemann and I drive south from Darwin toward Pine Creek. PAID FOR BY THE AUSTRALIAN TAXPAYER; 0.8 MILLION DOLLARS. Canberra is not shy about its largesse. "The Track," as Darwin people call it, is the Stuart Highway, named after John McDouall Stuart, an explorer who reached the Darwin area from Adelaide in 1862, inspired by a prize of £2,000 offered by the government in Adelaide to the first man to cross Australia from south to north. The Stuart is the one artery leading out of Darwin and the only long good road in the Northern Territory.

We pass anthills as high as an erect kangaroo, brumbies (wild horses), and lumbering buffaloes that sometimes nearly strike our four-by-four vehicle. "At night you have to watch out," says Wiedemann, my driver-companion who works in the chief minister's department. "If your vehicle hits a buffalo, it's him, not you, that walks away."

Near Adelaide River we visit a war cemetery where those who died in the Japanese bombing of Darwin are buried, together with troops who died in the war in the islands to the north. An oasis of memory in the scrub, the simple square of nicely cared for lawn is shaded by umbrella trees and lit up by red and apricot ixora flowers. "We'll be fighting the Indonesians before long," Wiedemann says unexpectedly as we return to our vehicle, "in the same islands where we fought the Japanese. They have maps that show New Guinea as part of Indonesia."

At Pine Creek, where the Northern Territory effectively began with the gold rush of the 1870s, I find a sleepy township of a few hundred people with a museum to recall the past and a high-tech gold mine to broach the future. Pine Creek is the "biggest town" on the road south from Darwin to Katherine, a stretch of 300 kilometers, but it has only one shop, owned by a legendary Chinese family—now Pine Creek's only Chinese family.

In the 1880s, Chinese outnumbered Europeans by six to one in the Northern Territory. Many of them were gold diggers in the Pine Creek area, and among these was the grandfather of Jimmy Ah Toy, owner of the shop where we drop in for a cool drink. "Laws were passed against the Chinese," says Ah Toy, a wizened seventy-year-old clad in shorts and sandals, "and the gold industry declined. By the 1930s there were still many Chinese in Pine Creek, but far fewer than in the 1880s."

"Why did they leave?"

"They didn't leave," he replies, rubbing a sweaty hand down his T-shirt. "They ended up dying."

Jimmy Ah Toy thinks the new mine of Renison Goldfields, whose managers say proven reserves at Pine Creek total 7 million tons and plan to employ 120 men here, "is gunna give Pine Creek a big lift." But he hasn't bought any shares. "It's the sixth mining venture I've seen in Pine Creek," says this walnutlike survivor who long ago turned from mining to cattle, plus the shop on the side.

Ah Toy's son, Eddie, who was born in the house that is now the museum, runs the shop, which is not a grand affair, while Ah Toy himself, who must be a fairly wealthy man, comes in to Pine Creek from his station only now and then. I ask him if his payroll of eight to ten men at the station includes any blacks.

"Yes, as stockmen—they're good at that." Jimmy Ah Toy, who is facing an Aboriginal land rights claim on part of his property, is adamantly against land rights. "It's all gone far beyond the original plan. Sacred sites is all right—that's all." Then this shy man of few words for the first time raises his voice from a near-whisper. "The blacks won't *do* anything with the land if they get it. They're getting too much government backing. Let them go out and do a bit o' work."

The Chinese-Australian station owner is hostile to the Labor Party and the trade unions "because they started the White Australian policy." Did he and his family struggle against the policy? "We had to. My father was a coolie on railway work, and when that was over he had no right to hold land or to work as long as union labor was available." There is an edge to Ah Toy's voice now. "That's why most of us went into private enterprise. It just wasn't funny. I was born in the place—as Australian as anybody else. Even in the 1930s all Chinese were barred from union-controlled projects. So don't ask me why I'm against the Labor Party."

I look across the dusty half-filled shelves of the shop, past an Aboriginal girl in a yellow T-shirt inscribed "Shine On Brisbane," out the window to the bare main street, with its shabby weatherboard houses warding off the sun with verandas and shades. Does Jimmy Ah Toy ever wish there were more Chinese around?

"That's a hard question to answer." He wipes his brow with his bare hand. "Well, I get along all right with the people here."

Bert Wiedemann and I duck our heads to enter one of the world's most unlikely museums. The little old wooden house at first looks like an indoor junk yard, but Mr. and Mrs. Shaw, curators of the Pine Creek Museum, have created a certain order. There are bits of American planes and other items from World War Two that recall the U.S. presence in the Northern Territory. There are notes and coins of Japanese currency. There is a sausage maker used by Chinese gold miners a century ago.

"Some of the half-castes aren't so good," says Mrs. Shaw—a genial, heavy woman in her sixties—of the local Aborigines. "They're a bit cheeky, a bit educated. But the full-blood Aborigine is great. One of my neighbors is Aboriginal—a health worker. For an illiterate, she's absolutely marvelous. As a neighbor I can't speak too highly of her." She chats on about another neighbor who is 104. "He'll be a hundred and five next May, and he does all his own gardening and cooking."

What is it about Pine Creek that makes for such long life? I ask Mrs. Shaw as we gaze at a bedraggled collection of Chinese vases and bowls.

"Peace o' mind. It's not dog eat dog like in the south. You don't walk over the top of anybody up here."

The Shaws—who have bought shares in the Renison gold mine—shop not in Pine Creek but in Katherine, an hour's drive south. "Two dollars and thirteen cents for a tin o' Milo," Mrs. Shaw bursts out in explanation, referring to a breakfast drink resembling hot chocolate that is popular in Australia. "In Katherine, Milo's one dollar and five cents."

Do the folk of Pine Creek respect Jimmy Ah Toy? I ask nonchalantly as I study a photo of primary school pupils from the World War Two era, about one third of whom are Chinese. "He's a very pleasant man as long as you don't have to pay his prices," replies Mrs. Shaw.

"I was in his shop one day and I was talking to Eddie Ah Toy's daughter, Grace [Jimmy's granddaughter]. Upside down in the *Territory News* I saw a photo of a woman and I said, 'Gee, doesn't she look like a Chink?' And Grace just looked at me and said, 'Mrs. Shaw!' Dear Grace—she won the Miss Heartbeat Contest here, you know. Still the penny didn't drop with this old dumbhead. But then I said, 'I'm sorry, Grace, but I don't *think* of you as a Chinese.' "

Mr. Shaw, readying the keys to lock up the museum for lunch, nods as his wife concludes the story. "You see, there's no race or creed here—or there wasn't until these *land rights* came along. I think of Grace as just the same as what we are."

"Use Common Courtesy with Road Trains," says an information booklet for motorists, "Which May Be Up to 50 Meters in Length." Seeing some of these monsters as we drive south from Pine Creek makes courtesy seem an excellent idea. On the side of the Stuart Highway I see bits of house trailers. "Passing road trains can be hazardous," Bert Wiedemann remarks, "and some people with caravans behind their car don't quite make it." We pass workmen who are laying two kilometers a day of the pipeline that will bring gas from central Australia to Darwin, removing the Top End's need for imported oil. Some of the pipe is based in concrete to make sure floodwaters will not lift it.

We whiz by a flock of black cockatoos nesting in a skeletal tree. At the Fergusson River's broad dry bed there is one pathetic pool of water, about a kangaroo's leap long, and a ray of sun catches it, as if to shame it for its puniness. When the Wet arrives next month, the Fergusson will be a major river, its banks jumping with animal life, its waters a threat to highway traffic.

Set on a flat, dry plain, Katherine is a small town of 5,000 people—

the third largest in the Northern Territory—arranged around one commercial street with smart banks, neat gardens, and many Aborigines who do not seem quite to belong. On the side streets are a few motels where tourists stay in order to view the Katherine Gorges, enjoy "Buffalo Burger Bake-Outs," and fish in nearby waters for barramundi, black bream, archer fish, and tarpon.

Bert Wiedemann takes me to meet the conservative local member of the Northern Territory parliament in his office above a shiny glass and marble bank chamber. "Yes, some votes will go back to the Labor Party because of the air base," says Roger Steele, referring to a defense facility to accommodate F/A-18 Hornet fighter aircraft that the Hawke government is establishing nearby, "but Labor has a long way to go before it could beat me. People around Katherine are frontier people. They're used to picking up the phone and solving their own problems. They just want the government to keep out of the way."

"The Northern Territory has two big problems," continues Steele, who has just finished a term as speaker of the Darwin parliament. One of them, he says predictably, is the non-appreciation in Canberra of the Northern Territory's position and needs, but he gives more stress to lack of population. "I have to drive two hundred ninety kilometers to Timber Creek to see forty or fifty people. Nowhere else in the world do you have time and money eaten up like that by sheer distance."

We drop into Captain B. J.'s Bistro for a counter lunch of roast pork, pumpkin, cabbage, and gravy. The friendly locals talk about the air force base, which will double Katherine's size, and about Aborigines. "Pay night and pension night's the worst," says a carpenter into his mug of Northern Territory Draught, complaining of the blacks. "That's when the Abos get rowdy and we wish they'd stay back at the camp."

Wiedemann and I drive in oven-like heat toward the Katherine Gorges. "In Europe men are much happier going out with their wives than Australian men are," says Wiedemann, who was born in Germany and came to Australia twenty-five years ago. "The great complaint of Australian women is that their man is never home—and it's true. Australian men just don't want to be tied down, that's the point." He goes on: "When I worked as a caravan photographer driving back and forth between Mount Isa and the Northern Territory, before joining the public service, I used to be amazed in the house of a married couple when the woman would want a picture taken, and she'd ask the man, and he'd say no, and that was that."

"Why did you come to Australia, Bert?" I ask as we pass the Katherine River, made famous in Mrs. Gunn's *We of the Never Never,* one of the most widely read accounts of the Australian outback.

"For an easier life. Maybe the conditions here are a bit extravagant at times—the holidays, the perks—but why the devil should you work your guts out when there's no need for it?"

As we pull up in the insect-pierced stillness of the park by the gorges, Wiedemann offers another opinion from his vantage point as a German-Australian: "The Australian drunk is the most aggressive in the world. In Europe, drinking generally makes a man happy. But drinking doesn't make an Australian man happy—just the opposite."

We take a tourist boat through the gorges. "This is one of the cleanest parks in Australia," our boatman grunts. "Let's keep it that way. Don't throw things off the boat." To either side are orange rocky cliffs dotted with wild apple. Beneath is clear green water touching banks on which wild passion fruit vines crawl. Above is a relentless baby-blue sky broken by a few curly clouds. The gorges lack height and grandeur, but they have an intimate, harmonious beauty on a clear afternoon. The staggering thing is that all this grace and charm exists absolutely in the middle of nowhere, more than 2,000 kilometers from any sizable city.

"You may swim," shouts the rather authoritarian boatman. "The crocodiles here are only the freshwater type." A woman from Paris screams, but a Japanese and some locals dive into the crystalline depths.

Amidst the sideshows and jollity of the Katherine Show, Chief Minister Hatton talks expansively of the future of the Northern Territory. "Read the history of the industrial revolutions in Europe," he says as we sit on canvas stools in the booth of his Country Liberal Party (a variant on the Liberal Party). Opposite us are shooting galleries, hooplas, a Big Dipper, a stand offering a game of Lucky Ducks, and food stalls with toffee apples, fairy floss, and bright pink saveloys. "Britain started and led the world, and in the latter part of the century the Germans suddenly industrialized, coming in with new technology, not obsolete stuff, and this was an advantage. In the Territory we have the same opportunity."

Hatton, a quiet, chain-smoking man who has been only two years and a bit in politics, invites me to join him and Barry Coulter, deputy chief minister and treasurer, in a chartered plane going back to Darwin. As we leave the Country Liberal Party booth for Hatton's car, which he himself drives to Katherine airport, a party worker dressed in Paul Hogan–style hat and boots hands me a leaflet with a poem about the Labor Party enemy:

Hawke is my shepherd
I shall not want.
He leadeth me beside still factories
And abandoned farms.
He restoreth my doubts in the Labor Party.
He anointeth my wage with tax and inflation,
So my expenses runneth over my income.
Surely poverty and hard living shall follow
The rest of my days,
And I shall pray for the dole
And live in a rented house forever.

From the windows of the Cessna 402 plane Hatton excitedly points to agricultural projects that are succeeding. Treasurer Coulter, sipping a can of Carlton beer, remarks, "Up here we're benefiting from the collapsed Australian dollar. Shoppers from Indonesia are pouring in on shopping trips to Darwin." Hatton chips in: "The two hundred million people who live within two thousand kilometers of Darwin make up the fastest-growing economic zone in the world. We have every chance to build an export-oriented manufacturing base, using the most modern techniques, and get to that market on our doorstep." Coulter gets up to fetch another beer and calls out, a wide grin on his face, "Want a beer, pilot?" As we descend into Darwin, Hatton points down at what he calls "Hawke's folly," the pathetic tower that marks the uncompleted new airport. "Many millions of dollars wasted," observes the chief minister. "They stopped construction after losing the election for the Territory seat in the national parliament in 1984. And they won't let us do it ourselves, because it's defense land and they say that'd be against the rules." As we taxi in toward the terminal, Coulter jumps up with beer can in hand. "The B-fifty-twos are in, and there are the tankers beside them."

We climb out of the Cessna, and the two politicians confer about arrangements for the coming weekend, when Hatton is going to Queensland for a show of solidarity with Premier Bjelke-Petersen at a National Party conference and Coulter will fill in for him. "All the major tourist attractions of Australia are in the north," Hatton says before getting on his jet for Brisbane. "Foreigners want to see Ayers Rock and Kakadu Park and the Great Barrier Reef. Yet all the airlines go into the south. I'd like to see international airlines go straight into Alice Springs and Ayers Rock."

My plane from Darwin reaches the center of Australia, and Alice Springs comes into view as a smudge on the horizon, beyond orange ridges that resemble hand-indented pie crusts. As we descend, a brilliant late afternoon light catches bushes the color of creamed spinach and the ivory trunks of ghost gum trees, which seem in their vividness to leap toward us against the backdrop of a deep blue stormy sky.

Established in 1872 as an overland telegraph station, Alice Springs with a mere 23,000 people has the pace and human sparseness of a country town. Yet it receives Japanese and American tourists who buy toy koalas with jars of Vegemite clutched in their paws; and its strong Aboriginal presence, haunting scenery, and self-image as the real outback where people eat politicians for breakfast lead many Australians to think of the town as the real Australia.

Only five minutes' walk from the pleasant town mall, on the wide and dusty residential streets with their homes in pale pastel shades, topped with silver roofs, the foliage is the same as 1,000 kilometers away. I hear the sigh of a breeze in the gums and the patter of leaves blown around my feet by a gust of wind. A sign beneath my hotel window says 1,535 kilometers to Darwin and 1,648 to Adelaide. Not far out of town is Lasseter's Highway—and Lasseter's Grave—named for a gold seeker who perished in the desert in 1931. "Alice Springs is a wonderful place," says its longtime mayor, Leslie Oldfield, welcoming me to her home and fetching white wine from her fridge, "because we have to make our own fun. The nearest town, Tennant Creek, is five hundred kilometers up the road." One can see Alice Springs as a future Australian-style Palm Springs, but it won't happen quickly, because expansion and tourism make many people in central Australia nervous.

In the rays of a late afternoon sun two artists work on a mural on the wall of Woolworth's in the mall. Against a landscape of satellite photos of the Alice Springs area, a large pair of hands appears, one holding witchetty grubs, the other holding what Australians call takeaway food. As I turn from the mural, the lights flick on at the top of the smart metal lampposts, a brilliant salmon pink like sunset on Ayers Rock, the chameleonlike monolith 300 kilometers southwest of Alice.

Past 8HA radio station, with its motto "Rhythm of the Heart," I head for the Araluen Arts Center, a striking modern building, high and square in gray and white, aptly nicknamed "The Woolshed." I pass a British-style double decker bus labeled "Christian Revival Crusade Bus," and bearing a sign on the front where the bus's destination would be, JESUS LIVES. A train whistle blows; it is the Ghan, named after the former Afghanistan camel drivers of the area, the last of whom died in an Alice Springs rest home in 1971. This train is Alice's link to Adelaide on the southern coast, one of its claims to superiority over Darwin, which has no railway to anywhere.

In the Aviation Museum there are old planes from the pioneering days—the Drover of the Royal Flying Doctor Service, the Kookaburra Glider, the John Flynn "Wackett"—and indoors they look odd, strung up like oversized insects from another planet. FOUR PERSONS ONLY IN THE AIRCRAFT AT ONE TIME, says a faded notice in one plane. REASON: UNEVEN BALANCE, DANGER OF THE AIRCRAFT TIPPING OVER. The museum occupies the site of the former airport, and its curator remarks, "Only one jet ever landed at this site. It was a mistake. An RAAF Canberra Bomber in 1958 mistook this strip for the new, proper airport."

The colorful studios of Alice Springs's School of the Air serve 134 children over an area of 1.5 million square kilometers. On a wall given over to paintings sent in from the stations where the kids receive lessons by radio is one entitled "The Day Daddy Fell into the Pond." A teacher is at her console with books, cassettes, and notes for this morning's class of four-year-olds. "Peter, what is your news today?"

"I've got a new bull terrier, Mrs. Davis," Peter replies from a microphone in his bedroom on a distant cattle station. "I'm going to call him Agro." Adam from a station in the north reports that he has caught a fish. Bronte far to the west has four new kittens. Mandy in the Simpson Desert had a lizard come into her bed in the middle of the night. Stephen near the tiny settlement of Utopia has visited his sister's boarding school.

These children of the outback are as used to radio as city children are to the telephone. Periodically the kids come in to Alice Springs for a few days at a nearby "real" school. "They have social problems," explains the school principal, Fred Hockley. "Bushies tend to believe they are better and stronger than everybody else. Fights are not unknown."

According to Hockley, the children do well when they go on from the School of the Air to high school. "One strength is that Mum has taken a close interest in their studies. You see, in lessons by radio, at the end of the day when Dad asks what did you do today, a kid can't say, 'Nothing,' because then Dad will say, 'Well, what was Mum doing?' and he'll want to have a word with Mum."

I watch the school librarian fill waterproof, dust-proof bags with books to be mailed out to the kids. "Some go to parents too," says the librarian. "At the moment the mums like books on Chinese cookery and do-it-yourself bricklaying."

The weaknesses of the outback kids are in mathematics and social skills. "No idea of distance," explains Hockley. "Ask Mandy how far from Alice Springs she lives and she's likely to say 'twelve hours.' No idea of money. Glen will go to a shop in Alice, hand over a twenty-dollar bill for a lolly, and take the change without counting it." The children also react badly to noise. "Large numbers of people and traffic give them problems."

As I leave, a man is pushing a trolley in the front doorway. "Ah, a child is finishing up!" exclaims Hockley. On the trolley I see a TV, a VCR, and a radio. "We hope there'll be a cassette recorder too," says Hockley, leaning over to look, "and a set of headphones and a film-strip recorder." All these things the school has loaned to a pupil free of charge. "Plus the Esky," adds Hockley with a smile, patting the portable cooler, "which we say is for Dad's beer."

Alice Springs has become a mecca for southern Australians and foreign visitors alike. "Before we went into the tourist industry," relates Miranda Hornsby at the vineyard and restaurant on the town's outskirts that she and her husband Dennis own, "people warned me about loud Americans, rude Australians, and bombastic Germans, but it hasn't been like that. Tourists after all are mothers, grannies, people with families just like me," she continues as we sit in the restaurant within an old homestead with a veranda and a corrugated iron roof that shimmers in a midday sun. "Everyone comes from somewhere else, and coming here they leave something of themselves behind for me. I think we see people at their best because of the surroundings here. Some people just spend a whole day with their feet up enjoying a bottle of wine."

Miranda and Dennis, who are in their forties, began with nothing; now, seven years later, they produce 1,200 dozen bottles of wine a year from 3,000 vines on six acres. "The exact number depends on grasshoppers and birds and other acts of God," says Miranda with a smile. "We both fell in love with Alice Springs. There's a streak of madness in Dennis, and that's probably helped. The Northern Territory is a great place for having a go. Down south we wouldn't have attempted this, being too aware of what we didn't know and feeling too pressured to succeed. Yes, in Alice we're the last frontier." As she speaks, I recall that 80 percent of the people of the Northern Territory are under forty years of age, compared with 65 percent nationally.

"True, some people come to the Northern Territory to escape various problems," observes Miranda, a mother of three, and she mentions semi-hippies and extreme feminists. "Coming here doesn't solve their problems. But other people come to the Territory because they've got a sense of freedom, of being able to determine their own direction." Some people on the Boomerang Coast—and many in Perth and Brisbane—are worried that they live on the periphery of things, but here in the outback, beyond all peripheries, Miranda Hornsby and many others seem free of that insecurity.

Son Anthony, wearing a T-shirt emblazoned "Singapore: Garden City," comes by to say that "everything's gone wrong" with his attempts to make lemonade, and Miranda reinstructs him patiently. Did Anthony get the shirt in Singapore? "No, it's from another family. We inherited it, a hand-me-down. We do that kind of thing here."

At the family-style lunch table, Miranda Hornsby blends a small group of black American tourists with myself and Shaun Wyatt, the representative in Alice Springs of the chief minister's office, caring for us all personally like a mother with her children. On the wall is a photo of Miranda, Dennis, and the children in Victorian costume, taken by a caravan photographer who periodically comes through Alice with his props and the offer of a momentary new look.

"I just had the princess of Thailand here," Miranda says as she tosses a salad of fresh mushrooms, fresh pinapple, red capsicum, and shallots, "and I did a completely Australian meal. The princess ate goanna." Shaun Wyatt adds, "After lunch, when she was presented with a goanna sand painting, the Thai princess said the art took on meaning because of the lunch."

The mistress of Chateau Hornsby brings out a dish of beer bread and a new red wine she is pleased with. "It's a good Territory drink," she says, pouring a glass for Shaun and me (the Americans stick with water), "because you can drink it chilled, for breakfast, with a barbecue, or with a formal dinner."

"Does Alice Springs ever get snow?" asks a man from New York, and Miranda is just back in time with a tray of desserts to hear the question. "No. There was an old-timer who said he'd seen snow, but maybe he'd been in the sun too long."

CLOSE PINE GAP, says a sign in town that I saw before lunch, and I wonder what Miranda thinks of the discreet, highly important American communications base not far from Alice Springs. "It's delightful to have the base," she says, wiping her hands on a tea towel. "It means we're one of the few towns in Australia that has Halloween. And we have tacos—thanks to the Americans—which I don't think Melbourne has."

Miranda Hornsby captures the spirit that makes Alice Springs a memorable town. "There's no established hierarchy here," she says, pouring me one more glass of her red. "Everybody's accepted for themselves. In Alice Springs no one asks you what school you went to—the first bloody question they ask in Adelaide. So many people are here just because they love the place." She looks out over the rolling hills. "It's a town where everybody takes an interest in everybody else. That could be a disadvantage, but a tremendous lot of caring goes with it."

"By the way, Miranda, where did you go to school?"

"I went to a small public school in Melbourne," she replies and goes on to speak of the school's location and character, assuming that a visitor from America will not know it.

"Ormiston!" I cry. This girls' school, the oldest on the Australian mainland, started by two spinsters before the gold rushes, is not far from where I lived and went to school. "I went to Wesley," I say. "We knew all about Ormiston."

Miranda roars with laughter. "My brother went to Wesley," she says, "and my uncle was chaplain at Wesley for years—Leigh Cook."

"He was chaplain when I was there."

"Was he really? He came to Alice Springs, and he couldn't go anywhere without bumping into an old boy from Wesley—it was extraordinary." We smile at our recognition of Melbourne old-school traces. The gap between Alice Springs and America seems to disappear.

Miranda Hornsby tells me she must now work on plans for the next "Take a Camel to Dinner," when patrons begin the evening by riding a camel from town along a dry riverbed to the Chateau Hornsby, where she greets them with a glass of wine as they dismount. Before I leave she gives me the recipe for the beer bread we ate at lunch. "'It must be simple, because Anthony was making it at age two and a half," she says. "On my radio program I gave the beer bread recipe, and some construction workers heard it. Later they astounded their wives by making loaves of the bread."

On the way out we pause in the garden where the annual Corkwood Arts and Crafts Fair is under way. "Spinners!" says a notice at the edge of the lawn. "Add a touch of class to your spinning—try these blended wools, beautiful subtle colors, $5 per bagful." A sweets stall takes me back in time with marshmallows in tiny ice cream cones, toffees in paper patties, and stained-glass-window cake.

But the familiar soon gives way to the bizarre. At the heart of the world's driest continent, in a town 1,400 kilometers from the nearest coast, it is taken as natural that the rivers contain no water. Thus at the annual Henley-on-Todd regatta people "sail" down the riverbed, their feet sticking out from the bottoms of mock boats, framed against smoky-green gum trees as a crowd waves its beer cans in appreciation. "Only once in twenty-five years of the regatta was there a problem," says Jan Lecornu, a well-known local figure who manages a block of flats, as we breakfast at my hotel. "There'd been rain! There was a risk of a lot of water! So they bulldozed an area of the river to stop water coming down to where the boats would be."

Some foreigners stay in the units that Jan manages, and she enjoys contact with them. "Americans love the harshness of Alice Springs," she remarks. "But at first some people would get apprehensive when I'd say, 'Well, what did you do today?' They looked at me as if to say, 'Why is she asking all these questions?' So I ask fewer questions now."

Shaun Wyatt and I drop by the Todd Hotel late on a Friday afternoon. The branches of gnarled trees stick through the roof of the veranda, which has a fringe of wrought iron. In the bar we find an almost all male crowd. Outside at the bottle shop Shaun stops to buy a bottle of Hermitage red wine from a boy who walks back and forth across the Todd riverbed to work each day. Waiting for her, I stand and smell the gum leaves.

Shaun mentions that her two daughters in Darwin are dating a pair of half-Aboriginal brothers. "I wouldn't have qualms about a daughter of mine marrying a half-caste," she says, "but I certainly would in the case of a full-blood. The other thing is, here in the Territory everybody accepts multiracialism, but I worry what would happen if my daughter and a part-Aboriginal husband moved down south."

I go back to the sparkling Sheraton Hotel, set amidst pink soil, mauve hills, and gums with white trunks. Two middle-class Australian men in their forties wait for the elevator in one of the hotel's far-flung wings. Silence. "Not a bad joint, eh, mate?" one man finally says to the other in a casual swagman tone. "I've seen worse," rejoins the second man. In the restaurant the menu includes "Barbecued Kangaroo Meat with Witchetty Grub Sauce" and "Clear Kangaroo Soup with Rabbit Dumplings." I ask if the barramundi is fresh. "No, sir!" replies the German-born maitre d'hotel as if addressing a battalion. "We are in the middle of the desert!"

From the window of my room at dusk I look out through the magnificently clear air and see two mountains. They are conjoined, except for a small angled gap between them where there stretches a sloped rocky plateau. In the twilight the mountains quickly become gray-green, but the little plateau, whose angle makes it still lit by the sun, glows bright like an ocher-colored neon sign.

"We're struggling to release ourselves from seventy years of colonial bondage," says Chief Minister Ian Tuxworth in his Darwin office when I return to the capital. That Canberra is in the hands of the Labor Party makes things worse. "While they held the Northern Territory seat we got good treatment. As soon as they lost it [in 1984] whacko, zappo!"[1]

"Take the Darwin airport," says Tuxworth, a Crocodile Dundee–like figure in his mid-forties, dressed in a pink open-neck shirt and gray bush pants. "Canberra committed themselves to a $130 million project. They spent twenty million and then walked off the job because they lost the election up here. So today you see a half-finished tower and a few slabs of concrete." Meanwhile the Northern Territory's plans for tourism are thrown awry. "We've built all these hotel rooms on the basis of getting more international flights, but the foreign airlines say they can't come in because the airport isn't up to scratch."

Tuxworth leans his shock of whitish hair back on the pink couch. "The Canberra people regard it as their right to trample on us any time it suits them." But Tuxworth is an optimist who believes passionately in the future of the Northern Territory, which he thinks will have 400,000 people by the year 2000. "Letting go is the problem of the people down south. They don't believe anything should happen unless they control it. I say to them, Come up and control it then, but they prefer to live down on [Sydney's] North Shore."

For Tuxworth, as for Charles Court in Perth and Joh Bjelke-Petersen in Brisbane, politics is not just "fancy footwork" (Court's description of Malcolm Fraser's style) but the management of economic development. He talks in terms of mines, oil, gas, fishing, tourism. Of the Benthamite welfare statists in the south who obstruct him he says, "They're yesterday's people."

The head of the Territory government draws a contrast with the United States. "What I like about Americans is their positive outlook," he says. "They believe; they accept challenges; they overcome problems. Contrast that with the politics of envy in Australia, where we always cut down the tall poppies. I think it's important that in America both political parties are capitalist. Here we have the Labor Party . . ." He grimaces.

1. Between my two trips through the Northern Territory, Tuxworth was replaced as chief minister during 1986 by Steve Hatton.

Decades ago a railway was built from Alice Springs to Adelaide, but the rest of the south-north link has been repeatedly delayed. "It's like stopping the Sydney-to-Perth line in the middle of the Nullarbor," observes Tuxworth, "and then being upset that it isn't successful." In his view the completion of the railway will create a whole new world of investment for Australia in Southeast Asia.

On a recent trip to Sydney to speak out against land rights for Aborigines, Tuxworth ran into a business acquaintance, "a brilliant guy," who had declined to come in on the building of the pipeline that brings gas from central Australia to Darwin, a project which now looks very good. "I told him about our railway from Alice Springs to Darwin."

"There just isn't enough traffic," said the businessman, who is chief executive of a major company.

"I'll bet you two grand we'll be laying track in January 1987," Tuxworth rejoined. (Tuxworth lost the bet, but the railway is on the way.)

"What are you going to lay the track on?"

"Go to buggery, take the bet or not, and then I'll tell you how we're going to do it."

"It's just not possible."

"Twelve months ago you were saying that about the pipeline."

I ask Tuxworth if he doesn't have trouble from the trade unions. "We have trouble from everyone!" he says with a big smile. "But that's not a reason not to go ahead!" The phone has been ringing every few minutes but the chief minister ignores it.

"Canberra believes national parks are for wildlife types," says Tuxworth as he moves to the topic of tourism, on which he is a shrewd visionary, "and that the public is a bloody nuisance and should piss off. They put no facilities in Kakadu so the public will have to leave. Parks are for people," Tuxworth says, and the job of the preservation bodies is "to see that the public using a park has the minimal effect on the environment." He laments that "the Commonwealth loves to police people."

Tuxworth sits up on the couch as I tell him of my visit to Jabiru. "Did you see the notice," he asks, "did you *see* that notice the townspeople put up, saying they apologize to tourists that the facilities of the town aren't open! They're so embarrassed that they put up that notice!" Tuxworth raises his voice. "Canberra has determined that Jabiru is a mining town and tourists aren't welcome. The Aboriginal people want to build a motel. We thought that was a fantastic idea and offered to underwrite it. But the Commonwealth won't let them do it."

"We should be planning to bring thirty million tourists a year to

Australia," says the presiding officer of one of the nation's most tourism-worthy areas, "and we should use whatever carriers we can to bring them in. Our whole tourist industry is structured around Qantas and its web of ties with other airlines." He fixes me with his blue eyes as the rays of the sun light up the office's bright green plants. "We can't have a blossoming tourist industry and Qantas—the two are incompatible."

Ian Tuxworth, who was brought up in Perth and later ran a soft drink business in Tennant Creek, lacks the mentality of the political class. He's in politics for as long as it's exciting and he can get things done. "The day I come into the office and find it a drag," he remarks, feet up on a blond-wood table, "I'll move on. Nothing's forever."

He states his philosophy: "I believe in a minimum of government involvement. I believe that the Northern Territory's interests have gotta come before the Commonwealth's interests. I believe that the bottom right-hand corner's gotta be in the black. The Labor Party have a different way of life. They operate under the system of debts due and debts to pay."

The chief minister presents me with a leather-bound volume of a traveler's account of the Northern Territory in the 1880s. "Don't often get a chance to talk like that," he says as we shake hands at the door. "Thanks for coming in."

I go through the ovenlike heat of an October afternoon to the Northern Territory mines department. Mining is the Territory's largest industry, with a gross value of nearly $900 million per year. Already, despite Canberra's reluctance to grant uranium export licenses, uranium production accounts for more than half of the value of the Territory's mining sector.

"Remember," says R. S. Martin, director of mines, "here in the Northern Territory until the recent gas pipeline we had no local energy source. It's easy for people to sit in a house in Melbourne or Sydney and talk of the evils of nuclear energy, when coal is doing the job fine for them."

According to Martin, the losses from the Hawke Labor government's denial of export licenses to non-operating uranium mines include: an export revenue stream of $77 million in 1987, $300 million in 1988, rising to $350 million in 2000 and beyond; royalties to the Territory of $1 million in 1987, $4 million in 1989, rising to $5 million in 2004 and $6 million in 2020; payments to Territory Aborigines of $6 million in 1987, $16 million in 1988, and $22 million by 2010.

"Develop carefully, yes," director Martin adds in summary. "But those who are *against* development are really against people—and the young are starting to realize that."

The mining of uranium in the Northern Territory may be a test case of whether the politics of development will win or lose against the politics of redistribution; and of whether the potential of northern Australia will be tapped, or whether "Develop the north" will remain one of those pathetic cries from the impotent side of the Australian mouth.

Down in Canberra I ask the prime minister about his uranium policy, and whether he is punishing the Northern Territory. "I can understand the Northern Territory view," replies Bob Hawke very slowly. "There's no one in the Labor Party that could say, or attempts to say, that our policy on uranium mining is rational." He sighs. "It's a mixture of principle—against mining—and recognition of a certain political reality . . ."

Will Western Australia, the Northern Territory, and Queensland one day take charge of Australia's future? It does not seem likely, for the needed capital lies in the skeptical south, and the absence of land transportation between Queensland and Western Australia tends to leave the Territory out and makes it difficult for northern Australia to act as an entity.

Despite the bush myth, influence upon the frontier states from the Boomerang Coast outweighs the frontier's influence on the south. In the Northern Territory people feel—clinging to the Paul Hogan image as presented in *Crocodile Dundee*—that their society is the pure Australia. Yet they love to go to Sydney and Melbourne, and they watch all the videos from the U.S.

For many people this has its comforts. The Australian sunbelt does not really have in it the makings of separatism, as some have feared—and others hoped—for decades. This really is one nation, from Cape York to Bunbury, from Pine Creek to Hobart, its heart claimed by Crocodile Dundee, its mind and body mostly at the service of the Big Smoke. It has in common its continental isolation. It pulls together when urgently necessary. There will be no effortless victory for the frontier states, fabulous in potential as they are, over the older centers. The shift of people and economic activity to Western Australia, Queensland, and the Northern Territory is perceptible and will go on, but not as rapidly as many in the north would like.

NINE

Reckoning with Race

"I mean, Australians aren't *used* to having their neighbors kill sheep in the backyard and hang the meat on the clothesline," a Melbourne taxi driver says, a pained look on his blotchy face as he complains of the Lebanese immigrants in his suburb of Williamstown. "I actually prefer the Aborigines," he adds as we drive out magnificent St. Kilda Road past the Shrine of Remembrance.

"The best thing about Australia is the space," says a young immigrant from Hong Kong, a bank clerk, when during 1984 I ask him at the train station of my former home, Murrumbeena, about the good and bad features of Australia. I think of lines from the new national anthem: "For those who've come across the seas, we've boundless plains to share."

"The worst is the recent Blainey debate," adds the Chinese bank clerk, who is carrying a Bible, referring to Professor Geoffrey Blainey's assertion that Australia is admitting too many non-British immigrants, Asians especially, and the furious responses to it. "Every day you open up the paper, you see what some people say about us Asians, you feel, well, uncomfortable." As I alight at a station near the Melbourne city center, I look up to the bricks of the walkway and see a large white-painted sign: STOP ASIAN IMMIGRATION.

"Taxation is killing Australia," says a cabbie in Perth, which has the highest percentage of Asians of any state capital (not counting Darwin), as we whiz between the green foliage of King's Park and the blue water of the Swan River. "The country's so vast and the people so few that services cost us awfully." I ask if massive immigration is the solution. "Not if it's Asian," grunts the cabbie, lips pursed, as he screeches around a bend.

"There are simply too many of them," says a Sydney housewife with a candid shrug. "I've got nothing against the Vietnamese and other immigrants as individuals, but they're changing things too much, too fast." She is shopping in Cabramatta, which has become a little Saigon. "They sleep on the floor, you see, not on beds. And they rent, they don't buy—which is driving rents too high."

"I think it's marvelous that my five-year-old son is being taught Italian at his state school," says Creighton Burns, editor of *The Age* in Melbourne. "I want my children to have a full choice of religions," adds Burns, whose wife is Israeli-born. "My son goes round Williamstown asking people, 'Are you Christian or Jewish?' They look a bit appalled, and he says, 'I'm lucky, I'm both.' " Burns likens people who won't have an Asian doctor to those who won't have a female one—"hog-heads."

In a Greek quarter of Melbourne a man and his schoolboy son stroll by news agents and food shops with windows full of baklava and salads to go, talking to each other mostly in Greek, with English words now and then. Nearby are old women in black shawls and black stockings, and men with large mustaches in shaped satiny white shirts and pointed shoes. Greek songs and the smell of olives fill the summer night. "Daddy," says the boy as the pair looks at a rack of books and magazines, "they have books in English too."

"With your help," runs a letter of support to Professor Blainey, "we may yet stop the do-gooders from ruining one of the greatest countries in the world." Another of the more than 1,600 who poured out their feelings on paper to the Melbourne University scholar during 1984 wrote, "To sum up, we're tired of paying for others." A third: "I wonder which country will take the unhappy Australians?"

I asked Blainey, who kindly showed me the letters, how he would answer this last question. "New Zealand, I suppose," he said.

In Queensland, one of the states least affected by immigration, there is much support for Blainey. "Why won't the people in Canberra let the English come," complains the premier, Sir Joh Bjelke-Petersen, his voice rising, "and the Germans, Danes, Swedes? It's all right to have people from Vietnam and various different countries, but we must not exclude the Europeans, as we're doing now."

"The older people of the Labor Party still believe in White Australia," says Tom Burns, a senior Queensland Labor politician, over lunch at Brisbane's Parliament House. "On the job there's quite a bit of sympathy for Blainey over Asian immigration."

Why do so many Asians want to come to Australia? I ask a Chinese immigrant from Malaysia as we dine in a red-decorated restaurant in Sydney's Chinatown. "Those with money come because of the political security," she replies. "The poorer ones come because of the high wages and good social welfare structure."

"Peking Fuck," says the English-language section of the menu. About half of the diners in the restaurant are Occidentals, many of them using chopsticks. "Ta," says the Chinese waitress, when I hand her back the menu, pronouncing the Australian word for "thank you" with a drooping Australian accent. "I gave the sheila a ring, but she wasn't home," says an Asian man to his friend at the next table, again sounding Australian.

Australia, I reflect, as my Malaysian companion and I munch upon the skin of the Peking Duck, in recent years has been the great immigrant-receiving land of the globe, and its leap from British monolithism toward Eurasian pluralism is one of post-colonial history's biggest. Each year more than a million people approach Australian embassies and consulates around the world, seeking to emigrate to Australia. Well under 10 percent of these are accepted. By the end of 1984, 41 percent of Australia's population of 15 million were either born outside Australia or had at least one parent who was. Twenty-three percent of the Australian population had at least one parent born in a non-English-speaking country. And 1.6 million Australians aged five years and over spoke a tongue other than English at home.

Once the Australians were black only. Then for a long time they thought they were only white. Today they are all colors. So far less than 5 percent of the population are Asian. But more than half the immigrants who come each year are Asian—government statistics include Middle Easterners in this category—which is a dramatic change from the long decades of White Australia.

Whose country is it? Does it belong to the Aborigines, or to the white settlers, or to the post–World War Two European immigrants, or to the new wave of Asian immigrants? All have their claims.

Darwin, the capital of the Northern Territory, in which 25 percent of the people are black, has a Chinese mayor. This humid city, as close to Singapore as to Melbourne, in my schooldays had separate sections of its pubs and hospitals for whites and non-whites. "I've seen a great change," says Charles See Kee, who came to Australia forty-five years ago and after some setbacks became the Northern Territory's first public servant of Chinese race, as we lunch under leafy trees in the courtyard of the Hotel Darwin. "When I arrived in Darwin there were three groups in the city—Chinese, blacks, and what we called Europeans. But later when Italians and Greeks arrived, Australians got a shock. Who were the Europeans? Were the Australians Europeans? What was an Australian? Surely lots of Chinese were Australians.

"When my second daughter was born," continues See Kee, who is president of the Ethnic Community Council of the Northern Territory, "police came to the hospital and pulled off the nappy to look at the baby—an old rule for any Chinese born here. I got upset and told immigration and the police, 'If you're born in Australia, aren't you an Australian; don't you have the same rights?' "

In the air force during World War Two, See Kee, who looks southern Chinese and sounds Australian, was the only Chinese. "One day I was getting a haircut," he recalls as cicadas shrill in the trees above our table. "The barber said, 'When did ya get ya queue cut off?' I said I got it cut off when I joined the air force. 'Do ya smoke opium?' he asked. Yes, I replied. 'Ever been out with girls? Gone to the races?'—so it went on." See Kee spears some French fries. "The person on the other side of me was already giggling. I wasn't hurt. That guy was just ignorant. In the end I made a fool out of him because I didn't take it as an insult. You see, as a Chinese I never felt inferior to these people."

"There are two distinct types of Chinese in Australia," explains See Kee. "The ABC's [Australian-born Chinese], who in the assimilation days nearly lost their identity. And the people who came after World War Two, later the Vietnamese refugees, and up here in Darwin the Timorese. For them it's a different situation."

See Kee's eyes narrow in the Australian way as he looks at me over the top of his fried barramundi. "The government realized that assimilation just didn't work." He pays tribute to Gough Whitlam as the person who "got rid of the word 'foreigner' and brought in the word 'ethnic.' "

How does Charles See Kee feel when Australia is competing in international sporting events? "When Australia plays the Pommies at cricket, I just get carried away barracking for the Aussie side." And when the opponents are Chinese? "You can't say you aren't torn, then, by two loyalties. And gee, I did feel good when China won all those medals at the Los Angeles Olympics."

In many cities and large towns—hardly at all in rural areas—Australia takes on a cosmopolitan look. In Melbourne I find fourteen Chinese schools and a school where twenty-two nationalities are represented. Greeks and Yugoslavs teach classes which are half Vietnamese and Chinese; yesterday's migrants teaching today's, in English, with gum trees outside the windows, meat pies at the lunch counter, and Australian Rules football during the sports hour.

In the Melbourne suburb of Richmond, on the long strip of Victoria Street, its spine a tram-line, I come upon Little Egypt, a firm of Malaysian lawyers, a German club, Italian coffee parlors, and Vietnamese and Chinese groceries and restaurants. The pubs are filled largely with Anglo-Saxon drinkers, some of whom grumble ritualistically about Richmond's changing face.

A restaurant is labeled "Great Wall" in Chinese and Vietnamese, but the only English name offered is "Chinese Take-out Food," as if the owners feel a full rendition is not of interest to most Australians. On a warehouse wall a nativist Australian voice cries out, "Real punks can't spell cappuccino."

Newcomers seek what they cannot find at home. Britons settle in Perth and Adelaide for the sun. Asians eschew the vast swath of Australia which is tropical and crowd into the industrial cities of the temperate Boomerang Coast. Greeks, turning their backs on blue, make a beeline for gray Melbourne and fill its tradition-encrusted Methodist and Presbyterian schools with their well-rounded sons and daughters. Pale, diffident New Zealanders gravitate to Bondi Beach in Sydney, where they drink in the sun and throw off all restraint.

Much of the public transport in the cities is staffed by Vietnamese, Malaysians, and other Asians. The Lebanese and Vietnamese grocery store has spread as quickly through suburbia as the Greek-run milk bar did some years back. In Melbourne and Sydney a new and moderately popular TV channel, paid for by governments that have marched with shouts and smiles into the misty cave of "multiculturalism," devotes itself entirely to ethnic programs. The fare of global news, European and Japanese movies, and documentaries of migrant Australians returning to the lands of their origin to find out if "home" is still home, is punctuated in summer by fire warnings given in six languages. My parents' generation, once very suspicious of Asian food, now discuss the fine points of Hunan versus Sichuan spiciness as if Chinese food had arrived with the First Fleet. "Eating with chopsticks was thought to be a lark," observes the Brisbane-raised novelist Rodney Hall of the 1950s. "Next it was thought normal; now it is almost a statement."

Upscale, the shadow of Japan falls selectively. Banks and trading companies have set up offices, with Sydney their favored base. Technical and sales personnel make an appearance in those mining areas where Australia is being gouged to supply Tokyo's industries. Japanese honeymooners come in white hats and impeccable shorts to see Queensland's beaches, Melbourne's penguins, and Sydney's Opera House and Harbor Bridge. Rich Japanese invest millions in the creation of holiday resorts.

"I'm violently opposed to having foreigners buy up our land," says Tom Burns, the Queensland Labor politician, "but there'll be more and more of it because old Joh spends half his time over in Japan, asking them to come here." I ask Burns, with whom I traveled to China on Whitlam's first trip there in 1971, about the mysterious explosion at a vast beach resort south of Brisbane which a Japanese tycoon is developing. "It was probably ex-servicemen [veterans] that did the bombing," he replies quietly.

"I don't bear any grudge," says Sir Sydney Williams, chairman of Air Queensland, who fought in two campaigns against the Japanese in New Guinea, in his office in exotic Cairns. "I'd go out to welcome any Japanese who comes to north Queensland, though I know what an atrocious bugger he was in war."

Public debate about race and immigration has at times been alarmingly uncivil. On TV during 1984, politicians of varying views discussed the issues in a tone of schoolboy brawling. Many university teachers and students who think Blainey is wrong felt the need to insult him. Recalls Hazel Hawke, wife of the prime minister, as we chat before a fire in the prime-ministerial residence: "It was unpleasant to see how quickly and easily racist feelings surfaced with just a scratch. They always said, you know, scratch an Australian and you'll find a racist. For a week or so there [in 1984] it was quite disturbing."

ADVANCE AUSTRALIA FAIR—NOT YELLOW, scream signs in country towns. Sexual innuendos are made against Asians that are almost as mindless and nasty as those from gold rush days. In Sydney the ethnic liaison officer of the New South Wales police says "gook," "wog," and "slopehead" are not necessarily racist terms. "It's a convenient method of identifying groups of people," he explains.

At a party in Melbourne to launch a museum to be built in Chinatown, Don Dunstan, former premier of South Australia and now in charge of tourism for Victoria, speaks eloquently of the "Chinese contribution to Australia," which the museum will enshrine, but he does not mention any contribution by Australia to the lives of the Chinese who came for gold and business and adventure. Dunstan keeps calling it a "Chinese museum," when surely it is an Australian museum.

The first director of the museum is not an Australian citizen, and Wellington Lee, a fourth generation Australian-Chinese, complains about this as we nibble Chinese pastries during the party. "The multiculturalists always turn to overseas-born Asians, never the Australian-born ones. And many of the overseas Chinese are in it for what they can get out of it—the Hong Kong mentality, you know, pure materialism."

The police chief in Melbourne says in a speech to a gathering of thirty-three migrant groups that have presented him with a brass bust of himself, "I beseech you not to develop the bad habits of the rest of the Australian community." The tone is odd. Perhaps an enthusiastic vanguard, admirably determined to slay racism, but unstabilized by guilt, is out of touch with ordinary people, and practicing a new form of the old cultural cringe.

Racism, as Hazel Hawke says, has been baked deeply into Australian society, and at one level multiculturalism is an overdue effort to eradicate a dark side of the Australian soul.

In 1788 the First Fleet arrived in Sydney with twelve nationalities represented on it. But New South Wales was to be British, and the other eleven peoples took their place within the folds of the Union Jack, and no one ever thought of them as ethnics.

In the 1860s on the goldfields of New South Wales diggers formed a Miners' Protective League. "We invite men of all nations," began the prospectus, "except Chinamen, to enrol themselves." The miners went on to embrace the principles of the French Revolution, and call for "fair play for all," a summation of Australian-style social justice.

In 1918 the Australian Federation, one purpose of which had been to reduce the danger of Asiatic invasion, was seventeen years old, and "Australian" and "white man" were inseparable terms. The minister for home affairs declared, "The policy of the country is that the Chinese population shall gradually become extinct."

When I was at school in the late 1950s, I attended a birthday party of a girl I was friendly with and took as a gift a carefully chosen vase for holding a rose. The party was a happy occasion until the girl's father, admiring the array of gifts, looked at the bottom of the blue china vase and saw "Made in Japan." He hurled it to the floor. As it shattered, this veteran of World War Two who had been a prisoner of the Japanese in New Guinea said he could not bear to have a Japanese product in his house.

Race and immigration became large issues for my student generation. My upbringing at Bruthen had not led me to treat Aborigines as equals. When I served in the Australian army it was commonplace for our officers to make racist remarks about their Korean War experiences. The year I became a first-year student at Melbourne University, *The Bulletin,* the leading weekly magazine of Australia, still carried on its masthead the motto "Australia for the White Man." "Don't you realize," a cousin said to me recently, "why you became a specialist on Chinese affairs?" I could not guess. "At Bruthen you were friends with Agnes. And in Melbourne your grandfather taught English at night to Chinese merchants from Chinatown."

That explained, at least, the carved cork Chinese landscapes that hung by a thin wire at a forward-tilted angle in our living room at Murrumbeena. These pictures of hills and willows and lakes in south China, bordered in sky blue and dominated by overly large frames of beige-colored wood, were gifts from the Chinese to my schoolteacher grandfather for his English teaching.

Until I went to university my sense of the Orient was laughably primitive. At school we tortured each other with a twist of the wrist called a "Chinese burn." Walking along Swanston Street we peered into Chinatown—never eating there—and thought ill of those shady Chinese people smoking opium and killing our cuddly Australian cats to make their dim sims.

As students we had a new starting point on Asia. We had not seen Japanese atrocities, and in our midst were thousands of students from Singapore, Malaysia, Indonesia, and Hong Kong. We were the first Australian student generation to sit in class with even a scattering of non-whites. We rapidly became the most internationally minded segment of Australian society. From the Asian students I learned to find diversity not threatening, as I think my father found it, but intriguing. All this foreshadowed major change, because among the linchpins of Menzies's Australia were social monolithism and isolation from our regional environment.

One morning in 1961 my parents and their neighbors realized that my education was having an impact not only on me but on them. I went to the front gate to fetch *The Age* and the pint bottles of milk that were delivered daily. ROSS TERRILL IS A NATIONAL PERIL, ran the huge letters in white paint outside our home. TRAITOR was scrawled in even larger letters on our low red brick front fence. It was frightening to see my parents' name under attack and to realize that I was the cause. TERRILL WANTS BLACKS TO STAB WHITES IN THE BACKS, the writing continued (oddly, because there were very few blacks in Melbourne). From the spots on the pavement and the road where the writing appeared, a row of white-painted arrows pointed into the driveway and up to the front door.

This embarrassment resulted from my activity in a Melbourne University group called Student Action, which attacked White Australia, policies toward Aborigines, and the Australian government's racism generally; and in particular it stemmed from a letter I had just written in *The Age,* headed "Time to End the Color Bar."

Australia's immigration policy, although modified away from racial exclusivity, still treated most non-white applicants for permanent entry into Australia less favorably than Europeans. Asians could not get their fares to Australia paid, for instance, as immigrants from Europe could. It shamed me that students from Asia had to undertake not to have a child while in Australia. I was appalled when an Australian government spokesman stated in writing that a certain British citizen (Thomas Palmer, born in Singapore of an English father and Ceylonese mother, a marine engineer on the freighter *Kookaburra*) was to be deported from Australia because Canberra had discovered that he was "predominantly non-European in appearance."

And the Labor Party, to which we young idealists were drawn, still used the term "White Australia" in its statement of policy. The party's leader at the time, Arthur Calwell, had some years before made a quip that summed up his belief that Australia should stay racially homogeneous: "Two Wongs don't make a white." He told me in the mid-1960s he did not regret the remark.

The Labor Party made me choose between my membership in its ranks and my agitation against White Australia. I received a letter giving me a certain number of days to make a choice. As a tactical matter, I resigned from our immigration reform group and stayed to fight within the party.

In those days many young Australians went overseas as soon as possible. On the face of it, we rushed away to get educated, but really it was because we felt suffocated in Australia. Looking back, I think race frequently was the core problem. To finger a wider world was to defy Australia's entrenched racism. And having left, no matter how much Australia was to change, we found it too hard to go back.

"No feathered goods allowed into Australia," cries the customs inspector in *Silver City,* a recent movie which evokes the world of migration to Australia in the 1950s. "The war's over" another inspector snarls when he finds in a European's luggage photos of wartime grief that puzzle or disturb him. "What sort of nuts are we bringing into this country?" he remarks to a colleague, loudly enough to reach the ears of a line of anxious Europeans spending their first moments on Australian soil.

"What would you say if you came face to face with Adolf Hitler?" asks an Australian government official in *Silver City.*

"I'd shoot him dead," replies the migrant.

"Troublemaker," the bureaucrat writes in the dossier.

We felt so good about receiving those migrants. Stationed in aluminum igloos the shape of half jam tins, the migrants in these silver cities waited for Australia to grant them a job. For two years they were required to work in jobs and areas selected by the government. Meanwhile they learned to empty their minds of the past, love Australian meat pies, and make their tongues produce the Australian accent. They owed us much, we felt, and they certainly owed us the shedding of their prior cultural identities, and the burying of cantankerous troubles from their decaying world.

William Dick's novel *A Bunch of Ratbags,* a vivid story of growing up in the Melbourne suburb of Footscray in the 1950s, conveys a strong dislike of immigrants. "We had some terrific street brawls with the dagoes that the government had started bringing out," says the main character, a young larrikin. "Our boys hated these dagoes and bolts [Baltic immigrants]." The larrikin's father's generation was at least as prejudiced against the new arrivals as his own. "My father would say, 'We won't have a bloody country if they keep bringing them out. We'll all be a mongrel-bred race,' he would say."

In the 1950s Asians were punished by the law for eating cats and dogs, olive oil was something you bought only at a pharmacy, and souvlaki was, I thought, the name of a Greek football player. I shared in the widespread jokes and slurs directed against dagoes. For some time—until I developed a craze for Italian food—I simply accepted the view of my elders that dagoes were likely to be dirty, lazy, and uninterested in trying to become "real Australians."

Yet the post–World War Two migration program was an economic success, providing a key ingredient in the prosperity of the Menzies era, and also a substantial success as a process of assimilation. There was pain for Europeans coming up against our Australian narrowness and indifference, but I saw almost no violence, and little serious tension. The crime rate among immigrants has consistently been lower than that among the native-born (still true, with the partial exception of Greeks).

The European immigrants changed the nation. At the same time the great cross-class Australian consensus sucked the immigrants in; a new infusion somehow proved the power of an old formula. The post–World War Two immigrants eventually helped "old Australians" find out who they were. The immigrant mentality, the drive to better oneself, had after all historically been the Australian mentality. Most of the immigrants were paid to come, and that had long been the Australian pattern. Except during the gold rushes, the enticement of people Down Under had usually required subsidy.

Australia was indifferent to the new arrival—it had always been so, ever since nature threw its massive indifference at the first settlers—but there was a welcome in the very dullness. No one enthused, but no one was really against you. And the immigrant found that the key to Australia as a stable democracy is property. The mentality of the immigrant probably is closer to the impulses of capitalism than it is to the aspirations of socialism. As people in the suburbs of Melbourne and Sydney and Adelaide and Perth built their homes in the 1950s and 1960s, they were the gold diggers all over again, and they were the selectors nailing down a piece of land.

Australians didn't realize that they would be changed by the coming of some 2 million Europeans in the 1950s and 1960s. This unawareness made it possible for Australia to accept enrichment, as a child's inattention allows a parent to slip a spoon of medicine into its mouth. Later the nation woke up and saw that something had happened to the Australian way of life.

"Multiculturalism came from the underemployment of the deputy leader of the opposition in the 1960s," says Richard Hall, author and Labor Party stalwart, in the study of his Sydney home. "Invitations to speak came to Whitlam from migrant groups. He accepted because he really does respect other cultures, and because it was a way of campaigning.

"It was all so easy," explains Hall, a Falstaffian figure with a dramatic flair, who in those years was on Whitlam's staff. "The editor of the *Maltese Herald* is always pleased to see you; and, you know, it's good campaigning. 'The Labor Party's stolen the migrant vote,' people said. What Whitlam really did was to stem the erosion [from Labor] of the middle-class migrant vote."

Hall continues: "Then Fraser comes in, and that fucking genius [X], together with [Y], devise a plan to 'get the migrant' vote, and they scheme for multiculturalism, writing a *Quadrant*-type paper on it." Hall's beer glass rises toward me as he spreads his bare arms wide. "So a vast superstructure arose."

Hall sums up the genesis of multiculturalism: "What was a perfectly normal and healthy part of the political process was turned into a theory; multiculturalism came from the right as a way of countering Whitlam's electioneering."

What Whitlam and Fraser did—leaving aside the exact blend of politics and idealism in their moves—was made possible by some long- and short-term changes in Australian society. The post–World War Two European migration was itself a major step, as Australians became accustomed to new arrivals with different food and speech and values. And there was occurring a steady growing together of Australia with its Asian environ.

In my student days, hearing about repression in the Old World— such as the Russian move into Hungary in 1956—I reacted only at an intellectual level. Such events were remote. By contrast, Australian racism and blindness to the Asian region seemed to me truly unavoidable issues. My first trip to China in 1964 was very "Australian" in that, planning my return to Melbourne from Europe, I looked at a map and saw it would be logical to pass through China. The experience, traveling through Siberia, from north China to Canton, and from China to Southeast Asia and Melbourne, did more to teach me the geopolitics of Australia's existence than a hundred lectures.

I saw China as the heart of Asia, yet in Australia we seemed to be repressing the very fact of China's existence. I began to reflect on the practical and spiritual costs of Australia's isolation. And I began to suspect that if we white Australians were to discover our own identity, we would have simultaneously to confront our Asian environment and the racism within our own history and society.[1]

---

1. I wrote a six-part series based on my trip to China for Rupert Murdoch's new paper *The Australian*—the first-ever truly national daily newspaper in Australia—and

Twenty years later, tourist travel by Australians to Southeast Asia and Japan has liberalized Australian race attitudes, as has the presence and good behavior of the scores of thousands of Asian students who in recent decades have graduated from Australian universities. Whereas thirty years ago only 20 percent of Australia's exports went to the Pacific countries, today 60 percent go there. In Australia's foreign policy, Indonesia and Japan outweigh in importance any European country.

In the past Asia, like Australia, was colonial. When it ceased to be so, and the British, French, and Dutch retired to Europe with their memories and souvenirs, Australia lost the cultural protection of its Britishness. Having tried to ward Asia off, Australia in the end could not resist geography and began to accept interaction with Asia on the basis of mutual benefit.

"The idea of a threat from Asia is just a lot of nonsense," says George Negus, a TV reporter who is in his forties, during our breakfast in Sydney. "It goes back to Menzies, and it has been kept going by defense chiefs to keep themselves in a bloody job." Few Australians under middle age have any sense of a threat from Asia. Lack of wrenching controversy, so common from the Chinese Revolution to the Vietnam war, allows Australia to wrestle with the octopus of race free of overwhelming political, military, or ideological pressures.

As usual in Australian history, ad hoc responses to unexpected events played a role. When Vietnamese boat people began to fill the oceans, the widespread unease at Australia's role in Vietnam created a strong pressure to be generous.

Some Vietnamese were handed maps by Singapore authorities, who suggested that Australia was big and waiting, and that they had only to keep floating southward and they would strike it. In a number of talks with Prime Minister Lee Kuan Yew I have found him acerbic about Australia, but seldom has he been as malicious as over Australia and the boat people. "There's the great, wealthy continent of Australia," the longtime Singapore leader said while visiting the U.S.A. in 1975. "They have a very sympathetic prime minister who believes that the White Australia policy is most deplorable and damnable, and here is

---

when the *New Zealand Herald* reprinted the articles apparently without permission from *The Australian*, Murdoch personally tracked the matter down. "I must say we are as concerned about this as you are," he wrote to me on August 30, 1965, after I had drawn his attention to the series' appearance in Auckland. On September 21, he wrote to say "we have extracted some money from the *New Zealand Herald* . . . I hope the enclosed check for twenty pounds will make you feel happier." Murdoch was losing money on his excellent new paper and didn't feel he could spend much on outside contributions. Some magazines and papers paid for my articles in guineas, but Rupert had no time for such British affectations.

his chance." Australia under Whitlam, and later equally under Fraser, took that chance and accepted more than 70,000 Indochinese. I wonder if Lee admires, or despises, Australia for doing so?

"I have never been so proud of being an Australian," says a supreme court judge with Labor affiliations, "as when we took in all those Vietnamese in distress." From the other side of politics, John Howard, the opposition leader, tells me that receiving the Vietnamese "is probably the proudest legacy of the Fraser government." Australia rose to the occasion, discovering that it had changed and matured, that racism had declined, and that multicultural currents were enriching Australia.

Amongst the Maltese, Poles, Yugoslavs, and Vietnamese on the bus headed for Footscray, hardly a passenger is speaking English. Except once or twice in Harlem, I have never felt so self-conscious as an Anglo-Saxon in a city of the Western world—and this is my own home town of Melbourne. A wall of graffiti greets me near the Footscray railway station, all in Greek and Vietnamese save one English entry, which jumps toward an Anglo-Saxon eye: "All cops are cunts."

In the business district of tough, local-spirited Footscray—the setting for Dick's *A Bunch of Ratbags*—as on the bus, about one in every three or four people is Vietnamese. Some 20 percent of the pupils in the suburb's primary schools are Vietnamese. A few years ago there was not a single Vietnamese business in Footscray; today there are scores, and virtually every shop changing hands is going to a Vietnamese family. So in this Melbourne suburb I confront a further factor—the most recent—that has led to Australia's day of reckoning with race: the Asianization of the immigration flow to Australia.

John Cheng, a science student at Melbourne University who is from Hong Kong, joins me for dinner at a Chinese restaurant called Fairy Dragon in one of Footscray's main streets. We sit under gaudy lights with our elbows on red tablecloths. "Five years ago," says the owner of Fairy Dragon, "it wasn't rare for an Australian gang to pull a gun on us when it came time to pay the bill. No longer." I suppose there is strength in numbers.

"The best immigrants are the Italians," says one of the Chinese waiters, after taking our order for some Chinese dishes under heavy Australian influence. "They are open-minded, they are cultured." This young man, who studied chemical engineering in Taiwan but gave up that career for the security and adventure of Australia, does not praise the Greeks.

"May I ask you," says another Fairy Dragon waiter, after we have chatted in Chinese, "were some of your ancestors Chinese?" I laugh and ask the young man, who is from Hong Kong, if his good English means that some of his ancestors were British. "Materially Australia is fine," the waiter from Taiwan says in Mandarin as he puts a flambéed ice cream encased in batter on the red cloth before us, "spiritually less so."

Science student John Cheng, who lives with his sister and her husband and children, likes Melbourne, but as we walk about Footscray I detect at times a slight wariness in his eyes. "The race atmosphere is good," he says, "but it has got poorer since the Blainey controversy got rolling." A couple of weeks ago, while he was waiting for his bus, two Australian girls stared stonily at him. He says he tried to be pleasant, but one spat at him, "Get away, fucker."

After dinner, strolling through a shopping mall under yellow lights, we come upon the rhythm of Greek songs and the smell of cappuccino. In a single food shop there is souvlaki, lasagna, dim sims, cabana roll, roast beef sandwiches in the American style, schnitzel, pizza, and the eternal Australian pastie. "Next door to my sister's house," Cheng says between tugs at a pinball machine, "lives a retired Australian couple who have been very nice. They ask us many questions about Hong Kong." He turns away from the cacophony of the machines, in front of which several languages blend with the language of electronics, and looks at me with a frown. "On the other side is a Yugoslav woman. Recently the side fence broke, and she asked my brother-in-law to mend it. When he refused she got angry, and shouted, 'You Asians get out of here!' "

Does John Cheng get upset by epithets? "The one I really hate," he replies, tight-lipped, "is 'Charley.' "

Racially different as Footscray is from most other suburbs of Melbourne, its curbs and pavements and lighting and plumbing are identical. The same trams and trains, like steel fingers reaching out from the Victorian bureaucracy to lay a claim to the least as well as the greatest of its suburbs, run to Footscray as to Murrumbeena and Sandringham. Even the houses follow fairly standard Melbourne patterns. The fruit and vegetables are as fresh and abundant in Footscray as they are in Toorak and Balwyn. The Australian mold, one feels, is pretty firm and should be able to hold this racial diversity.

"He's a real little Aussie," a worn-looking Vietnamese woman of about forty says of her Australian-born son, in the wide asphalt spaces of Cabramatta, the heart of Indo-Chinese society in Sydney. "He's going to turn out much better than us." Here is a news agent selling papers in fourteen languages, a gambling den in full flight at 11 A.M., and a Buddhist temple. I come upon four hairdressing salons; three are Vietnamese and a fourth, until recently Australian, has in its window a notice saying the lease is available. The notice is in Vietnamese, Chinese, Thai, and one other tongue which I do not recognize, but not in English.

"Vietnam is more beautiful than Australia," says the Vietnamese woman, "but Australia is free of war." A garment worker in a factory owned by an Italian, she regrets that many Australians are moving out of Cabramatta. "It misses the chance for the races to understand each other better." But she herself has recently moved out of Cabramatta, climbing up the social ladder in the classic immigrant way. Today she has come back to Cabramatta to shop.

"Eight or ten Vietnamese live in one room," complains Bill Jenkins, a sixty-four-year-old retired builder wearing brown shorts, a striped fawn knit shirt, and a straw hat, as we drink bitter Australian beer in a corner pub. "It's unhygienic; and they don't put the rubbish out tied up in plastic bags the way Australians do." Jenkins is a veteran of World War Two, when Americans impressed him by introducing turkey and ice cream. "The Vietnamese have no sense of direction," he goes on, expressing what seems to be his major complaint. "When they drive, they veer left, right, and center—and on the footpaths they walk so fast they run into you." The people he feels most sorry for, Bill Jenkins says, pointing his narrow, slightly tapered beer glass toward a billiard table around which young men crowd, are the young Australians who've never had a job in their lives.

"The Vietnamese women all work," Jenkins remarks, adding in an irritated tone that he often sees Vietnamese at the post office sending envelopes fat with money back to Vietnam. "To me a woman's job is in the home." It is less race as such, perhaps, than a process of social change at whose cutting edge the Vietnamese are visible that brings on Bill's fairly mild anxiety. "They never come to the pub," he adds in another crack at the Vietnamese lack of social solidarity and their presumed economic gains, "because they find it cheaper to drink at home."

Are there any Vietnamese policemen, I inquire. "No, and we don't really need them. The Vietnamese are pretty law-abiding, you know that?"

Indeed in Cabramatta I feel an air of immigrants on the make, however modestly, without palpable tension, dangerous-looking mobs, or derelicts hanging around at corners. I see streets that are lively and people with a spring to their stride. It is the young, concerned about jobs, and the elderly, worried about the eclipse of familiar values, who are least happy at the arrival of the Asians.

"It used to be so nice when there were just Australians here," an elderly Cabramatta woman told the *National Times*. "We'd call out 'yoohoo' over the fence if we had a leftover bit of pineapple or cake." The lady, who lives in a block of twenty apartments, fifteen of which are occupied by Indo-Chinese, went on: "One of the flats is empty just now, and I say to myself every day, *Oh, I hope a white person moves in there.*"

I leave Cabramatta for the center of Sydney, full of thoughts and questions and memories, and call on the premier of New South Wales. "The migrants have given Australia a great lift," Neville Wran tells me, "in culture, skills, tradition, in general diversity."

"Ten Cabramattas, ten years from now—would that bother you?"

"Not a bit," Wran shoots back. "Not a bit," he repeats more slowly, as his eyes look straight into mine. "Sometimes in the silence of the night, or the isolation of your own company, you start imagining what it may be like . . ." Wran's voice trails off in a way unusual for him. He looks out the window to the blue magnificence of Sydney Harbor. Then he turns back. "I don't mean there won't be racial tension and racial conflict. There will be.

"But when you go to Cabramatta and mix with the people and eat with them and talk with them," the premier goes on, regaining his momentum, "and when you see the kids running around, and understand that they are genuinely making this their home—when you do this you feel Australia is big enough and malleable enough to accommodate them. Once you come to terms with the slanting eyes and the yellow skins, the Asians have the same feelings, apprehensions, ambitions as everyone else—don't they?"

Another force behind Australia's reckoning with race—together with recent Asian immigration, the postwar European immigration experience, and Australia's ties with its region—is economic. In the 1970s the Australian economy ran into uncertain waters. Inequality grew. A threat has arisen of a permanent caste of bitter unemployed youth.

At a residence hall of Melbourne University I ask a student of commerce what his salary is likely to be immediately after graduation. "Eighty-eight dollars a week, probably," he replies, naming the amount of the dole for a single person aged eighteen to twenty. "If I should manage to avoid that, perhaps eighteen to twenty grand."

"Without economic growth," asks Bruce Grant, author of *The Australian Dilemma,* whose links are with the left, "might not multiculturalism be a dream from which old racist Australia will one day awake, shouting its ancient imprecations?" No one can say, but there is some resentment of immigrants on the part of young unemployed Australians. The point is that in Australian history immigration has always had a close relation with economic ups and downs. It has been high, and welcomed, when the economy was buoyant; it has contracted and been criticized when the economy was lagging.

From Perth to Brisbane to Hobart, I find many young unemployed who feel, with whatever justification, that a reduced immigration flow would add to their own chances of finding work—those who want to work. Such a line of thinking can make fair-minded people seem racist; their own survival as self-respecting Australian citizens becomes entangled with the tangential issues of skin color and cultural difference.

Tension between the old Aussie and the immigrant is made the more likely by the superior drive of the immigrant. "The only people who put their shoulders to the wheel are the immigrants," says David Hackworth, the American war hero turned businessman, who has employed both native Australians and immigrants in his Gold Coast enterprises. "They see a chance to build a house on the hill, which they couldn't do back home."

"They don't regard it as servile to serve," says Sir Charles Court, the former Western Australian premier, speaking of the recent arrivals, especially the Asians, "whereas the average Australian tends to think it *is* servile to serve."

"Let's face it," says the lord mayor of Darwin, Alec Fong Lim, whose father came to Australia from China, "most people who emigrate to Australia have led a harder life than most Australians. Immigrants don't just sit and wait for things to come to them."

The Cafe Sport in Carlton, where Professor Geoffrey Blainey and I are headed for lunch, is a "BYO" restaurant, so we stop at a bottle shop to buy wine. The salesman in this Italian quarter of Melbourne addresses Blainey as Geoff and asks him for his prediction on Saturday's football match.

"Have you got a table for us?" Blainey asks the lady who welcomes us from behind a gleaming coffee machine at the Cafe Sport.

"Even if we didn't," the lady replies with a lovely smile, "we'd *find* one for you."

As we take our seats beneath a garish mural of Naples, a kitchen hand waves a greeting to the history professor, who is the author of *The Tyranny of Distance, A Land Half Won,* and many other books on Australian history, as well as dean of the faculty of arts at my old university.

"Multiculturalism has gone mad," Blainey says, attacking a crisp loaf of bread. "An immigration system is supposed to serve the nation, but now it's the nation that exists to serve the immigrant." He senses an "aggressive multiculturalism" in the air. "Students can learn their history and geography in Turkish if they wish to."

Blainey is a gentle, courteous man, with a face that is at once open and shrewd. In his walk, his smile, and his mind there is something of the farmer, but also of the bohemian. He is very Australian, not in a chauvinist way, but in that he is a man of local attachments.[2]

"The idea of [Arthur] Calwell's magnificent immigration scheme," Blainey remarks of the post–World War Two years, "was that the migrants were to become Australians, equal Australians. It was assimilation, yes. But does an immigration policy have to be a manifesto on race?" he asks me rhetorically. "Should it be so any more than a trade policy should be?" Blainey feels the government is out of step with public opinion on immigration and multiculturalism, and in this period—1984—he is probably right.

Geoffrey Blainey has been hurt and surprised by the hostility of many academics and some media people to his assertions, more so than by the disruptions to his lectures by students. "The *Sydney Morning Herald* says my reputation is in tatters," he remarks and a faint, not happy smile appears at the corners of his mouth. Now I understand why as we met for lunch he said, "Let's not go over there," nodding toward the university faculty club as a farmer might point out a treacherous marsh, and why he suggested the Cafe Sport instead. A few weeks before, Blainey's daughter was stabbed in the street. "She's recovering well," he tells me. He pauses. "We just don't know who did it."

"If we go on taking between thirty percent and seventy percent of our immigrants from the Third World," reasons Blainey, as a lunchtime crowd of mostly Italian-Australians fills the restaurant, "we ought to do

2. I learned—not from Blainey—that recently when his local supermarket was rebuilt, Blainey, who shops there for his family, was invited to be guest speaker at the reopening festivities.

research on why some multicultural societies fail and others succeed." Nowhere in the various layers of the multiculturalism bureacracy can I find any long-range planning, or even forecasting, on Australia's racial composition.

"Environmentalists are worried by changes to the landscape," the historian remarks as we begin a red Chianti. "A lot of our people are equally worried by changes to society." He points out that Australians "haven't been consulted" on the changes in immigration policy. "The decision was made by professional politicians who do not suffer job competition from Asian immigrants." With the Liberal Party opposition unwilling to make an issue of immigration policy, and the Canberra bureaucrats lost in their "daydreams," a gap opened up between the views of the political elite and those at the grassroots—for whom Blainey spoke up.

"If unemployment in Australia was only one percent," Blainey says as veal and pasta arrive, "the present level of Asian immigration would present no problems." Indeed, although the rhetoric is about race, in many ways the heart of the issue is economic. Blainey sees the value of Asian immigrants to Australia. "They work harder than young Australians." He stops and laughs quickly. "If they didn't, we wouldn't have so many tensions. The point is every section of Australian society should be made to feel the competition of Vietnamese and Chinese— not just those people who have most to fear from the future."

We leave the Cafe Sport and go out into the wide, bright space of Carlton. "Our policies on citizenship and immigration are more tolerant than those of any country in Asia," Blainey observes, "yet our government never criticizes the restrictive policies of others—China, Japan, Pakistan—while it responds sensitively to their unspoken criticisms of our policies."

Blainey says his views have been influenced by his experience as chairman of the semi-official Australia-China Council. "At first I was too reticent in saying to the Chinese what I thought—that's typical of Australians dealing with Asia." As he takes his leave to go to a committee meeting, Blainey mentions his worry about the future of Hong Kong, which he calls "one of the glories of the modern world." He does not blush to praise the achievements of European civilization, whether in Hong Kong or in two hundred years of Australian history.

Blainey invites me to browse in the bulging files of letters he has received and one afternoon I do so. "You have no idea how much support you receive from 3rd and 4th generation Australians," writes an ex-serviceman from a New South Wales country town. A British woman living in Adelaide declares, "If the UK had had a Blainey in 1945 much muddle and strife would have been avoided." Inquires an unemployed man in Melbourne: "I wonder what your academic critics would say if they had lost their job to a Vietnamese, as I just have?" A man writes from the quiet blue Victorian coast: "Thank you for speaking out in defense of our heritage."

A reader of these hundreds of letters must say that some contain narrow, bitter, backward-looking, and selfish sentiments. Blainey concedes that most of his letter writers are older people; half over fifty, he guesses. It is clear, too, that many are rural folk, British-born, or ex-servicemen. The letters contain an outpouring of touching solidarity with a fellow Australian under attack. "If you're ever driving along the Hume Highway [linking Melbourne and Sydney] you are very welcome to drop in." "Please don't let TV stations show you with your car and number plate any more."

At times Blainey may romanticize established Australian traditions and underestimate the constant evolution in any tradition, and some people wish he would use his influence to actively combat the knots of racism that make Asians already in Australia uncomfortable. At the same time, as a senior multiculturalism official admits to me, "Blainey struck a chord."

In many respects Blainey's courageous efforts during 1984 won his point; during 1985 the government quietly modified some aspects of its immigration policy which Blainey had called anti-British and pro-Asian.[3] He predicted this to me in 1984, both before and just after the election, and he was correct. "The two parties made an informal agreement," he claimed, "that in return for the Labor Party quietly modifying the policy after the election, the opposition would refrain from making it an issue during the election." The excesses of the immigration debate were sobering, but Blainey was not discouraged. "I believe in the democratic process more now than I did when I started the whole thing," he remarked to me as the dust began to settle.

Few Australians, and perhaps none who are over thirty-five and native-born, can avoid a tangle of mind and emotion on the race question. "I approve totally of the multicultural path," says a Sydney pub-

3. In 1985, the intake of Asians was 25,000, down sharply from 34,800 in 1984; for the same years the intake of Europeans, including Britons, dropped less sharply, from 21,000 to 16,300.

lisher who is an old school friend of mine. "Our parents' generation missed a lot, which we have got from the migrants." A moment later he remarks, "But, you know, I don't *like* seeing all these Chinese kids running round with my kids."

"You go into the swimming pool," says a distinguished professor of Asian studies in a large city over a bottle of Moselle, "and you can hardly make your way through an Asian crowd." This man, whom I consider among the more cosmopolitan of native-born Australians, then remarks, "You hear more and more people say that perhaps White Australia wasn't so wrong after all."

I myself have stiffened upon seeing a large group of Asians happily treating Australia as home, as if this native land of mine were their kitchen table. Given a majority, I say to myself, with a certain sadness, they will naturally and rightfully take over the direction of the country. In America I never experience such racist pangs. In America the immigrant comes to a society that is sure of itself (at times perhaps too sure), and possessed of a tradition of independence and liberty that gives Americans a definition of themselves. In Australia the Asian immigrant enters a more inchoate realm.

The American takes it for granted that the immigrant will become Americanized; many Australians in the late 1980s are not sure that the immigrant to Australia will—or even ought to—become Australianized. To an Australian, the sight of a black American athlete standing with his gold medal on a dais at the Olympic Games, his face shining with pride as "The Star-Spangled Banner" is played, is a remarkable one. The strong, open love of country, even on the part of groups not always well treated in America, is a thing of awe to a traditional Australian.

Americans might smile to hear Australian discussions of multiculturalism. Doesn't everyone do it? Why the self-consciousness? Perhaps Australia is not really ready for multiculturalism. But if Americans are hardly aware of multiculturalism, for Australians it is a deadly serious business. No one tosses it off. The Volvo socialists shout its praises. Many conservative Australians denounce its social engineering aspects. Everyone has a strong view. For Australia—this long ago ceased to be true for the U.S.A.—immigration is perhaps the core of public policy. It is so important that at elections no one mentions it.

On election day in 1984, noticing that the Labor Party's how-to-vote card has instructions on the back in eight languages, I ask a Liberal Party official in the electorate of Melbourne Ports why his party's card gives instructions in English alone. "There is a reason," replies the middle-aged man, a company director, with a trace of a smile, "and I'm not going to tell you what it is."

One cannot rule out severe future racial trouble, given geography, history, and human nature. The population of Australia is still tiny compared with that of neighboring Asia. Australian history is brief and lacking in great moments that are a nation's sources of self-confidence. From English convicts to Vietnamese refugees has been a bare two hundred years. A British outpost that came close to equating national feeling with whiteness, Australia has been unused to the peculiarly biting challenges of racial diversity, and now faces them suddenly, acceleratingly, and indefinitely.

A deep self-examination and an embrace of diversity are being undertaken simultaneously, and it is not certain that the Australian way is yet firmly enough rooted to make these processes character-building, as they ought to be, rather than demoralizing, as they could be.

In one sense Australians are great lovers of liberty, the liberty of the open road, and of self-expression through owning property. The Australian tradition of a fair go is a weapon of liberty; it speaks, however shyly, of each person being free to fulfill himself.

Yet Australia has never had a basic discussion of the rights of man, let alone a battle on their behalf, and one can only speculate at the blend of open-mindedness and narrow panic that would attend the sudden onset of a divisive social struggle involving old rights and new rights, the established heritage and rationalistic claims made against it. Half-thought-out efforts to ban the Communist Party and institute a sweeping crimes act during the Menzies era, and the oscillation over Aboriginal land rights in very recent times, suggest how much at sea Australia is in weighing fundamental issues of rights and duties.

If one day a majority of the population should be foreign-born, it seems possible that today's guilt could become tomorrow's impulsive effort to reclaim bits of a mauled heritage.

The cultural romantics and the social engineers do not strike me as being great champions of the freedom of the individual. In some of its expressions, multiculturalism is a clear-cut enemy of the fair-go tradition. Group quotas are incompatible with equality of opportunity for the individual. The power struggle of ethnic communities is not as sure a facilitator of democracy as the simple mirror of representative democracy based on one person, one vote.

There is a kind of Volvo socialist who cannot distinguish between loving another culture and hating his own. To show his tolerance of

Asian or Aboriginal culture, he feels it necessary to don the costumes of that culture and express apparent regret at the entire European endeavor in Australia. Some even denigrate the English language as inadequate for a new era. "English is a fine instrument for celebrating snowdrops or daffodils or skylarks," writes Mark O'Connor, "but it is tongue-tied when faced with some polyp or reef fish that is a dozen times more beautiful and intricate, but has only a jaw-rattling Latin name." This is sad, defeatist nonsense.

One suspects that some of the trendy middle-class progressives see Asians less as human beings than as decorative furniture with which to jazz up Australia, less as individuals with foibles and hopes of their own than as a category required for the overall design of multicultural Australia.

There is an odd dualism of an exaggerated put-down of Australia's white past and—beneath the surface—a desperate and bitter cultural nostalgia. On the one hand the open smile of multiculturalism; on the other the broken bottle of "What's wrong with us as we are?" Narrowness is the great problem, for it is the subsoil in which racism puts down its tough and ugly roots. The Australian tends to deal straightforwardly with what he comes upon, and is in that sense generally an open-hearted humanist. But traditionally his sphere has been small and remote.

"Not long ago Australia was a wonderful place to live," wrote a Tasmanian to Blainey. "One could travel 1,000 miles in any direction and be sure of being welcomed by the delightful Australian drawl. But not any more." Is the letter writer a racist? Not really, but the eclipse of his narrow, comfortable world provokes in him a hostility to both Asian and non-English-speaking European Australians.

Happily, grassroots race tension is not widespread, and there are voices of refreshing steadiness and good sense. "Most cultures need to change," says Patricia Caswell, a rising trade union official in Melbourne who has lived in Darwin and in Cleveland, Ohio. "Look at the Middle East cultures and their present attitude to women. I'm not going to take foreign cultures as models. But no culture should be done in as a culture—that's what racism is."

"I'm rather against multiculturalism," says a cousin of mine with a smile in the greenhouse of her home in bayside Melbourne. "The world I like is here." She points through the shrubbery to the rows of discreet villas, all with well-tended gardens, in rows leading down to the sparkling blue sea; the world of Martin Boyd's novels. "The soft blue unthreatening world that extends down our coast to Wilson's Promontory," my cousin goes on, "is my moral and practical universe. Apart from here, what I like is the south of France." Although she is against multiculturalism, my cousin will never complain vociferously about it. Certainly she will never discriminate against Asians, to scores of whom she has taught Australian novels and poetry in high school. To a degree one can feel confident that in tomorrow's Australia most people will feel, as my cousin does, that there is room even for what is not particularly esteemed.

Would the head of a conservative think tank mind if Australia came to have a non-white majority? "Not if it was in line with the views of the people at that time. What I care about is shared values. At the moment there's no doubt that many of the Asians coming in are hardworking, free enterprise type of people."

"Yes, there's racism in Australia," says a taxi driver, a mixed Chinese-Thai from Malaysia, as he drives like a demon in busy Melbourne streets. "But, mate, there's racism everywhere, including Malaysia."

"One thing you can say about this bastard of a country," Richard Hall bursts out over a few beers on a warm evening in his Sydney home, "the record on race over the past two decades isn't so bad." He irreverently dismisses Blainey. "Just as Jim Cairns [deputy prime minister under Whitlam] discovered sex in middle age, so Blainey discovered the yellow peril in middle age. Blainey drives home from Melbourne University," says Hall, "and he goes through Carlton and Fitzroy, which are full of ethnics. But ordinary Australians never see a Vietnamese, and what they don't see they don't care about."

Hall, a man of the left, is vehement against the guilt-ridden far left. "One thing infuriates me about the left," he says. "With their half-baked knowledge of Australian history, they stare you in the face and say all Australians are racists." Hall is also critical of many British-born residents of Australia. "Apart from the Vietnamese," he claims, "the most violent immigrant group in Australia is the British."

In the more affluent suburbs of the big cities, Asian doctors, architects, stockbrokers, and teachers increasingly are to be found along the rows of villas with clipped gardens. "Most people want to conform," says a Chinese physician who lives in the outer Melbourne suburb of Doncaster, his pale hands gesticulating in front of his expensive leather jacket, "and in Doncaster there's a middle-class aspiration to conform to. That quest unites us all.

"Asians out here have never lived in a place like Footscray," the physician goes on, "and fortunately we don't have Vietnamese in Doncaster." In a comfortable place like Doncaster, and in dozens of similar places around Australia, the middle-class handshake between Asian and Anglo-Saxon is quiet and effective. Here you feel that perhaps race doesn't matter much after all.

"You know," says an immigrant from Hong Kong as he smiles tentatively, "it's really the Vietnamese, not the Chinese, that Blainey is against, don't you think so?" That various of the non-white groups which today live beneath the broad umbrella of the Australian way of life at times snipe at each other may forebode some future trouble, but it also suggests that there is no iron wall between "them" and "us"—the native-born or white Australians, and those without Australian roots.

Wellington Lee, a fourth-generation Chinese-Australian, was born in Darwin and went to school in Queensland, where his main defense against racist taunts was his skill as a fistfighter. Did he ever wish he could get the hell out of Australia? "No, I was too Australianized," he says. "But there were times I wished I wasn't Chinese. I tried not to be Chinese."

Lee, today a leader of Melbourne's Chinatown, tells me about his friendly struggles with the Victorian chief of police. "The guy said with pride that the force was now fifteen percent ethnic. I said, What about Asians? He said, We'll recruit from the Vietnamese. I explained to him that the Vietnamese aren't *big* enough!" Lee's round, open face becomes animated and his eyes bulge. "In a country like Australia you can't have small people as police. I told the commissioner we need some Chinese police, not Vietnamese."

Lee dislikes the gurus of multiculturalism. "That outfit [the Australian Institute of Multicultural Affairs] is all Greeks and Italians. Generally speaking, I would prefer experienced Anglo-Saxons in these government posts having to do with multiculturalism than European ethnics like [X and Y]. All the committee appointments they make are *overseas* Asians," he complains. "OK, someone's a professor, but if he's just come from Malaysia, what the hell does he know about our Chinese community here? You can't understand the Chinese in Australia unless you've lived here."

In the frontier states the Asian race issue presents itself differently (and much more benignly than the Aboriginal issue). "The best comment on the import of the Blainey debate in the Northern Territory," comments Charles See Kee in Darwin, "is that during all the fuss we had an election for lord mayor of Darwin and a Chinese won."

"Very few people in Darwin," observes James Eedle, a professor at the Northern Territory university college, "have a stake in the land, in organizations, or any wealth that goes back more than ten years." To British-born Eedle this explains why in the Northern Territory "there's very little feeling that people's ground is being intruded upon by immigrants the way people in Melbourne and Sydney may feel."

From a Malaysian mining engineer in Perth, where racism in speech is perhaps more common than on the east coast, I hear a strong defense of Australian society. "In Australia people say what they think," says the engineer, who lived in London for some years. "The British are less likely to *express* a racist sentiment than someone in Western Australia, but there's more racism in Britain." Adds the engineer, who works for Western Mining Company, "And the racism in Australia is not government-sponsored. It is in Malaysia; that's why I left and came here."

"You can't eliminate racism," the premier of New South Wales remarks to me as we talk of Cabramatta, "but you can make it socially unacceptable." That has not yet happened in Australia, though Wran, Whitlam, Dunstan, Fraser, and other leaders, as well as thousands of influential private citizens, have made a contribution toward it. Yet something else, of great importance, has happened.

"The moral position taken by Whitlam on race issues was great," observes the Melbourne author Bruce Grant. "Fraser continued that tradition. He shifted the focus from Asia to Africa, but it was the same. Now it's true also of the Hawke government—they won't give in to racist pressures. Today when people get into influential positions," Grant goes on, "they come with this progressive view, rather than the old view. Oppositions still play the racist game, because they know there's a streak to appeal to. But governments, of all shades of opinion, don't anymore."

"Where are we going to get the capital to develop this place?" says the Melbourne newspaper editor Creighton Burns. "The U.S.A. is now a net importer of capital—it's going to have to come from Korea, Taiwan, Japan, Hong Kong. Can we really tell these people, who'll be supplying the capital, 'No, your grandson can't come and be a doctor here?' " Burns speaks also of labor. "Tell me, in the growth states, the northern part of Queensland, the Northern Territory, and the northern part of Western Australia, who is going to do the hard yacker [work]?"

"There's nowhere to go but to become multiracial like California," says Queensland Labor politician Tom Burns. He acknowledges the strength of pro–White Australia feeling in his state, but he does not agree with it. "I believe in immigration for this country. It's no good hoping for a manufacturing base when you've got no people here to sell the bloody products to."

"Australia can only grow if it takes itself as a part of Asia," says Singapore-based tycoon Jack Chia with unusual passion at his Melbourne headquarters, the magnificent former home of the early prime minister Alfred Deakin. "They've only got fifteen million people—how can they compete with the U.S.A.? The best is to get along with Asia, and grow with Asia." His arms come down on the sides of a Queen Anne chair, and for the only time in a long talk he touches on a current political issue. "Blainey was wrong! And I will say this: If there's going to be racism I would pull out of Australia. I like Australians, but I operate in ten countries. I do not want to be here as an underdog."

Multiculturalism is at its best a principle of tolerance, and it promises a truly mature Australia. At the same time, during the realization of multiculturalism's promise it will be important to maintain a continuity of established Australian values and institutions, and a clear-eyed commitment to liberty. The process is only beginning; so far, Australia has been engaged in overcoming past narrow prejudices, not in a leap to full-scale institutionalized cultural pluralism.

Thoughtful Australians see that in the long term the nation inescapably will become "Eurasian"—Foreign Minister Bill Hayden's approving term. Multiculturalism is a tightrope on which Australia walks to its only possible future. Public opinion, according to repeated polls, expects future race tension, even as the public in general behaves with restraint and good sense. The graffiti are hair-raising, but the streets are calm.

My old school friend, the Sydney publisher, looks at me after his remark about Chinese kids running about with his, and our eyes meet as if in a recognition that we in our forties are a transitional generation, for whom reason and emotion do not always march in step. "The bottom line," he says quietly, "is that a multiracial Australia is absolutely inevitable."

Perhaps the very young in Australia will grow up to take racial diversity for granted. At a cricket test match in Melbourne, as the game ends with a win for the West Indies over Australia, people rush onto the green field, feeling the pitch, searching for a souvenir, trying to talk with a player. "Only the kids are blind to race," a Chinese friend says as we watch. "Look at how those Australian kids are mobbing the West Indian stars. They don't care who is black and who is white."

TEN

Aborigines and the Land

Gough Whitlam remarked to me in the late 1960s before he became prime minister that he considered the Aborigines "our true link with our own region" and that "treating them properly is the best contribution to racial peace in Asia that Australia can make." Today, an anguished postmortem on Australia's treatment of Aborigines—together with the immigration issue and the nation's growing integration with Asia—forms part of the attempt to come to terms with racism.

When I grew up in the Victorian countryside during the late 1940s and occasionally saw blacks at the fringes of our township, I knew nothing of the gulf of values between their world and my own. I did know the Aborigines were not extinct; moving to Melbourne, I met city classmates who thought the Aborigines had died out. But I had not been told that the Aborigines believed man was created from totemic spirits' interaction with the environment in an era called "Dreamtime"; or that to the Aborigine the land is a living being, and that to deprive him of his homeland may be to cut him off from his ancestors and cast him into a void. These things my generation did not know. We had not inquired. It was the blacks who had to adjust to us, not we who heeded the blacks.

During Queen Elizabeth's great tour of Australia in 1954, in an era prior to the impact in Australia of the rise of Third World nations and of American blacks, an Australian governor general for the first time received an Aborigine at his residence in Canberra. The artist Albert Namatjira was introduced to the woman visitor who had become Queen of the land Namatjira's people had lived in for tens of thousands of years. But Namatjira, who like all blacks was a ward and not an Australian citizen, was not permitted to drink at the governor general's garden party, not even a glass of beer. Later that year the artist was arrested for supplying alcohol to fellow Aborigines.

About the same time that I woke up to the sad history of black Australia, through my encounter with black America in the late 1960s, several factors led Australians to a rediscovery of the Aborigines: the impinging on Australia of Third World issues; Gough Whitlam's age of reform; the effect of greater Asian presence on Australian racial attitudes; the appreciation by environmentalists of blacks' reverence for the land. Since the Whitlam era the federal government and some state governments have put much effort and money into an attempt at redressing Aboriginal grievances. "This is a decade of getting scores on the board," says Charles Perkins, head of the Department of Aboriginal Affairs in Canberra, and one of Australia's most prominent Aborigines, in his office adorned with Aboriginal art and the Aboriginal flag. "In a few years we've gone from a budget of six million dollars to one of two hundred and ninety million."

After the granting of full civil rights in the 1960s, governments in the 1970s went on to launch land rights legislation. Public land—not houses and farms and shops—can be claimed by blacks who demonstrate a historical link with it, or its sacred importance to them. Despite intense controversy, and furious opposition from mining groups, much land has been turned back to Aborigines.

"I refused to go along with an assimilationist policy," recalls Don Dunstan, a former South Australian premier who was a pioneer of the change from the 1960s. "I felt the Aborigines should live according to the future *they* choose," says Dunstan, a progressive and debonair man who speaks in the slow, slightly superior Adelaide way. "They should not have imposed on them the materialist European culture that happens to surround them."

The parched brown site of the controversial British atomic tests of the 1950s, Maralinga, west from Dunstan's home city of Adelaide in South Australia, has been turned back to the Aborigines who were at

once endangered and driven off that land at the time of the testing. I ask
Foreign Minister Bill Hayden if the British testing was wrong. "With
the benefit of hindsight very wrong," he replies quietly. "The security
on toxic waste was quite defective." Some 32 percent of the area of the
Northern Territory, whose tiny population is 25 percent Aboriginal, is
under black control, including Ayers Rock, the spectacular outcrop in
the dead heart of the continent, and a further 16 percent is under claim.

Along with land rights has come a totally new respect for Aborigines on the part of opinion leaders on the Boomerang Coast. "Aboriginal culture to me represents the integration of art and life," says Andrea
Hull of the Australia Council in Sydney. "I love the oneness they have
for themselves, the land, the materials they use. Everything is placed
well, and on time." Pronounces Patrick McCaughey, director of the
National Gallery of Victoria in Melbourne: "Aboriginal art has the
grandeur of the primitive."

Back in 1949, Arthur Calwell as minister of immigration cried in
parliament, "We can have a white Australia, we can have a black Australia; but a mongrel Australia is impossible." Such offensive words
from a government minister are out of the question in the 1980s. What
Calwell feared and disliked as mongrel is today fairly widely welcomed
as multicultural. And it is the interaction of the black issue and the
Asian immigration issue that gives to multiculturalism in Australia both
its apparent triumph and its aspect of brittleness.

Attitudes on the frontier are different from those in Melbourne and
Sydney. "My Aboriginal stockmen don't know the first thing about land
rights," claims Jimmy Ah Toy, the Chinese-Australian station owner
at Pine Creek in the Northern Territory. "It's all being done the wrong
way," complains Charles See Kee in Darwin. "They're creating a useless
race of blacks reliant on government handouts. The people who need
help, the full bloods, are not getting it. The stirrers, the half-castes are
getting it. The full bloods get only the white man's vices!" A quiet man,
See Kee becomes slightly agitated. "They talk of sacred sites. Have you
seen a sacred site? Full of beer cans. It means nothing. And Dreamtime,
I tell you, is something the white stirrers told them about; now they find
it very useful. If an Aborigine is drunk in the street, the police are
afraid to touch him. In the schools the Aboriginal kids are allowed to
do anything—no one dares to speak up about it."

"We had a family relationship with the Aborigines on our stations,"
claims Dame Mary Durack, a novelist and historian whose father
owned stations in the northern part of Western Australia. "My sister-in-
law ran a school for her own five kids together with all the Aboriginal

kids. It was a happy arrangement. The Aborigines were our stockmen," she explains. "It was a healthy, happy life, and the Aborigines felt important." She sighs. "That station has now been bought by the government and made an Aboriginal property."

Dame Mary leads the way from her study, an enclosed veranda of her sprawling home in suburban Perth, to show me copies of her early publications (the first in 1934) and photos of Aborigines in her circle. "That's Chunama, my tribal son," she says, pointing to a picture taken in her garden. "He calls me 'Mummy,' and his mother is my sister. Tribal sister, you know."

For Mary Durack, the coming of "equal wages" has ended the family relationship between outback whites and blacks and brought to the blacks booze and unemployment. "They've been told they ought to demand land rights," objects Durack. "People are manipulating them." She reflects on the handing over of Ayers Rock in 1985: "Symbolically it's not a bad idea—to give them the heart of Australia." She pauses and gazes out over the riot of shrubs beyond her study window. "But to break Australia up into a whole lot of little nations—that's just frightening."

"Before World War Two," remarks Sir Sydney Williams, chairman of Air Queensland, who has long experience of the northern outback, and who like Durack is critical of the Boomerang Coast's schemes for redressing Aborigines' grievances, "I never saw an Aborigine who drank. Now my DC-Threes are going out from Cairns [to the Aboriginal areas] full of beer."

"The Aborigines think their system and values are pretty good," says Ian Tuxworth, chief minister of the Northern Territory, in his Darwin office. "We should have allowed those who wanted to change to change, and we should have allowed those who wanted to continue being traditional to do that. There would have been a lot less trauma." Of the tragically high crime rate among Aborigines as white and black Australia deal clumsily with each other, Barry Coulter, treasurer in Darwin and formerly minister in charge of the Aboriginal portfolio, observes: "A lot of Aborigines like going to jail. If you're lying in the Todd River bed at eight in the morning and it's thirty degrees and you're not getting any breakfast, it's quite a good idea to throw a wine flagon through a shop window and get yourself arrested and carried off to jail."

Do the Aborigines fit in with the multicultural vision of Sydney and Melbourne and Canberra, or have the stirrers gone too far and changed too much too quickly? Can Aboriginal culture have any future, and can there be any solution to the multiple problems of guilt and disesteem, of land and inequality, when the whites number 15 million and the blacks—most of them detribalized part-Aborigines—number only about 200,000? Answers to these questions are not easy to find.

"There *is* a hotel there," a Sydney taxi driver says, when I ask about a pub near the Redfern station, "but you wouldn't want to go there. It's where the blacks drink." He is not pleased—am I breaking some bond of white solidarity or is he simply concerned for my safety?—when I insist on going to the Railway View Hotel in this broken-down inner suburb.

Redfern is a suburb of few trees, much concrete, and many places and things that do not function. Abandoned houses alternate with houses painted and decorated in all the colors of the paintbox ("School Sux" is scrawled in purple crayon on one front door). It is a world of smashed-out cars, adult men idle at midmorning, pay phones where you can't see the instructions for graffiti, and a scattering of white people who are here only because they are poor and the rents are low.

"I'm history," gurgles a man who brushes past me in the doorway of the Railway View. "Come home with me," says a woman as she grabs me to her rolling mountain of a body. From a jukebox blares a song by No Fixed Address, a fine black group. Beer is guzzled from cans or plastic glasses. "The cops won't allow real glasses," a bartender tells me, "after so many fights and stabbings." Drugs are in the air, being used and traded. In the toilet a man sits on the floor near the urinals with a whiskey bottle clutched in both hands, and another is curled up inside one of the cubicles, his feet protruding under the door.

A young black man called Steven, smartly dressed and much less drunk than anyone else in the pub, tells me he's just out of prison. My companion, a Chinese-Australian, is anxious to talk to anybody, lest we seem like exhibits or spies, so I ask Steven if he regrets his crime. "Not really, because I made $68,000 out of it. It was armed robbery, you see." Steven upturns his beer can. "If we Aboriginal people are bad," he says, "it's because you white folks made us that way."

He soon tells us more. "My wife's in the hospital having our second kid," he says gaily. "She's not a real wife. You know, a de facto." Steven's "missus" is British, and the pair of them recently made a visit to the UK. "England's the best country in the world." He laughs and turns to tell a friend about the baby, which is due tomorrow. "It's going to be an Abo-Pommie."

Steven and his friend—like nearly everyone else in the pub they have long since ceased to be tribal Aborigines—try to interest us in some grass. Steven's friend starts to talk about fighting, showing his muscles as he prattles. Is it a warning? No, thinks my Chinese companion; he is trying to establish some grounds of manly solidarity with unexpected arrivals. Or it may be a display of defensive guiltiness, a half-conscious defiant message to us that we should not expect the blacks in Redfern to be just like us.

"Blacks outnumber whites eight to one in this neighborhood," the bartender, who is white, tells me as I fetch more beer for Steven and his friend. "Most of the remaining whites are trying to move out. They're sick of being robbed and bashed."

In Western Australia urban black life may be less sordid and less politically manipulated than in Sydney and Melbourne, but extra numbers do not seem to reduce the sadness of the Aboriginal plight. Judy Watson, an old friend from Melbourne, long a Perth resident, drives me to see a young white man who with his mother forms a friendly bridge to the Aborigines at nearby Lockridge Camp, and offers the family house as a kind of base. On the veranda we see chooks, a broken bed, bits of vehicles, and a statue of a brightly dressed Mexican. Behind an upended mattress Judy finds a faded placard: "We the Aboriginal people don't know why the public are belly-aching us, the fringe dwellers of the Swan Valley, being here a mere twenty days when they've been here 150 years destroying the country, desecrating the Aboriginal sacred sites, littering the highways with beer cans and waste from their factories."

Before we go further into fringe dweller territory, Judy needs a drink. "A Shirt or Singlet Must Be Worn in the Hotel at All Times," says a notice at the door to the bar of the mostly white Rangeview pub. Beside us at the wet counter is an Aborigine in his thirties who can barely stand erect, but who is friendly. "I said to the sergeant, I said, '*I'll* fucking well say when I'm drunk.'" Apparently he lost the argument and was on that occasion arrested. "Why don't you have a real drink?" he says to Judy as she sips a lemonade.

"Anything else would make me thirsty."

Drunk as a fowl, the man pushes his grinning face close to Judy's. "Then you'd need a fire extinguisher." He goes over to join his mates, who are playing billiards, navigating unsteadily between square tables where bronzed whites in shorts and sandals toss back the amber fluid.

We leave the pub and head for Lockridge Camp, passing by a newish middle-class white neighborhood, whose neat paved streets end abruptly at a farmlike fence. Judy's chunky station wagon rolls past the fence and through a paddock to the huts of the camp. The black, red, and yellow Aboriginal flag (its colors stand for the black man, his blood, and the sun) rises above uncared-for shacks. "Land Rights" is carelessly scrawled on prefab walls. Here and there are battered cars, like beached whales, and in them sit Aboriginal men with big stomachs and beer cans clutched in spiky fingers.

Judy lets out a scream; she has locked the ignition keys in the station wagon. Two black boys of about fifteen come out of a hut and offer to help. They cannot pick the lock, but one boy, eyeing the trap-door on top of the vehicle, fetches tiny boys to try to climb through it. Two fail to squeeze in, but a third, yet smaller, gets through and comes out of the station wagon triumphantly handing the keys to Judy.

We drive away from Lockridge and find another pub. It has a sign on the door: TRY OUR TASTE-TEMPTING GRILLS AND SEAFOODS. Opposite is a railway line, fringed with graceful gums. A blue-and-orange train carrying commuters from Perth offices whines by, just two carriages, orphanlike, as if a complete train has been sliced into sections. Adjacent is an English-looking locale where many English settled because of the foliage and moderate clime. The space and languor and racial feeling recall a U.S. southwestern town with its sprinkling of Indians, but the crack of cricket bat against leather ball can be heard from down the street.

Inside the pub a mostly black crowd is drinking Swan or Emu brand beer. Judy Watson and I perch on stools under a high smoke-stained ceiling. "You're a perfect couple, you know that," says an Aborigine on the next stool. Judy hastily explains that I'm a visitor from the U.S.A.

"Yeah, you sound a bit like a Yank, too," says the black man, neat in beige cord pants and a T-shirt.

"Don't you like Americans?" I ask, starting my glass of Riesling.

"No, I don't, mate, because they come here and take all our women." Judy stares into her Cinzano white. "Why don't you send over a boatload of women, instead of men all the time? American forces fighting in Central America have women in them. I seen 'em on TV. I think your ships coming into Perth ought to have women on 'em too."

"My name's Delray," the man says as we introduce ourselves. Originally from Kalgoorlie, the fabulous gold town of the 1890s, where some gold still is mined today, he was brought up in the Kimberleys, where his father was a stockman. "We lived north of Derby, where there's a Catholic church done in pearl shells. Them divers, you know, that get the pearls, made a whole church out of it."

"Delray's a nice name," says Judy, who is warming up.

"I was born in 1935. That year the Melbourne Cup was won by a horse called Delray. My father bet on it and won a quid, so I was called Delray. Me mum's still alive in Kalgoorlie. She likes a bit of booze now and then, but no more men."

"I tell ya, Lockridge is a bad place," says Delray in a standard rural Australian accent when I mention our visit to the camp. "Half of them people is into dope. They're all fucking boozin' up—sorry ma'am, I forgot myself—and they're all on the dole. Father's out drinkin'. Mother's out gamblin'. Girls end up getting pregnant. Father comes home, gives the missus a bit of a beatin'. It's not worth it, that life."

Delray, a Catholic, opposes land rights and believes the way out for blacks is through jobs. He works at an emu farm—"eggs to feathers, we do the lot"—for eight dollars an hour. The feathers, like so much else from Western Australia, are sold to Japan. "The emu farms are just about the only places where the black fellas are well off," comments Delray as he starts another beer. "The other places are awful. It's all land rights."

Judy stiffens, for she favors land rights. "What do you mean, Delray?"

"It's a lot of shit—sorry, Judy—I mean land rights makes no sense. If there's a piece o' land, and I'm there before you, and I work my butt off and make somethin' of it, then it's mine. You come along and say you want it—no way." He lights a cigarette and gives Judy a charming smile. "Everyone's equal, right, Judy?"

Even the handover of Ayers Rock to some Aborigines, which is imminent, does not stir this emu farmer. "One damn lousy rock in the middle of nowhere. I don't see the sense." Judy delivers the left-wing white point of view, but Delray is unmoved. "You don't need a thousand fuckin' acres—sorry, Judy—a man just needs *one or two* acres, then 'e can do somethin' with it."

Delray tells us segregation in the pubs of the district has become more pronounced since a recent murder at a nearby pub called Albert's Tavern. "A white girl came in and called the blacks names. They punched the piss out of her. Later people tried mouth-to-mouth resuscitation, but it was too late. A black guy and his wife were arrested." Delray pauses, pensive, and the click of billiards echoes across the saloon. Through the open double doorway I see smoky blue hills, and above them scoops of creamy clouds.

"Now I wouldn't go into Albert's Tavern. You two could go in, but not me. Actually our black women are allowed in, but not our black men. I seen it many times."

Delray accepts the offer of a ride into town. "You get a black man from the bush," he says as Judy swings onto the highway, "and he says what he thinks, and does what he wants. Up there round Ayers Rock, they don't argue the point, they put it straight. Here in Perth black people's got nothin'. There's so many half-castes."

"Would you rather be here or in the bush?"

"In the bush, any day. But I can't leave; I gotta go to the damn court." We fall silent as the lights of Perth skyscrapers come into view on this brilliantly clear night. "The whole damn lot of us 'a' got criminal records," Delray says. "But this time all I am is a witness."

Judy is gripping the wheel tightly, and I reach forward from my seat behind the two of them to light her cigarette. Delray continues: "This girl I used to live with, she got stabbed by an Italian, a taxi driver, and I was there."

We reach the City Square, where Delray is to get off. We stop, he puts his hand to the door, but he sees a police car beside us. "I'll wait a minute." When the lights turn green the police car turns left and speeds away. Delray gets out.

"By the way, Ross," he says through the station wagon window. "When you go up to Derby, don't camp outside your car. Sleep either on top or inside. Otherwise you'll be eaten by crocodiles."

As the F28 jet nears Yulara airport after a 320-kilometer flight from Alice Springs, the massive hulk of Ayers Rock, which looked orange from a distance, turns purple. Ayers Rock and the nearby Olga Rocks, gracefully curved like clusters of clouds, are the tops of a mountain range most of which is now below the earth's surface. Eight kilometers around the base, the Rock is not like a hill, not like a building, but a stunning offense to all categories. Geologists know it as an inselberg. From a kilometer distant its surface looks not rocklike but soft like a heap of ocher sand. Closer up, the texture is that of reddish-brown paint streaked over with a brush. There are breaks in its curved smoothness, like a monster's bites.

"The Rock is like a book to me," says Yani Lester, Aboriginal chairman of today's big event, who is blind and claims the cause was fallout from the British atomic tests at Maralinga in the 1950s. "A big book with a lot of pages and a lot of stories." To the Aborigines each "bite" out of the Rock has its explanation from the Dreamtime; one hero embedded his boomerang in the side of the Rock, and in trying to pull it out made a hole. The whites named Ayers Rock after a governor of South Australia and they identify its features in their own way: the Wine Glass, Napoleon's Hat, Joe's Hole.

Over Yulara the earth is like a Persian rug, with patches of orange soil and blue-green scrub. At the Sheraton Hotel some twenty kilometers from the Rock, the air is clear and dry and the scene recalls a Moroccan oasis. The hotel has pink walls, silver roofs, and gleaming white sail shades, high and broad like bed sheets on a clothesline, to deflect the heat and promote air circulation.

By the pool I see Clyde Holding, today's star as minister for Aboriginal affairs, dressed in a lettuce-green shirt and holding a baby, and in the water I find Susan Ryan, the minister for education, frolicking in a purple swimsuit. A large Aboriginal lady passes across the lawn in a T-shirt with "You Are on Aboriginal Land," written on its bulging front. An Aboriginal man, playing with his son beside the pool, has on the back of his shirt "Aborigines Discovered Captain Cook." The black crowd, in groups larger than family size, mostly not staying at the hotel, do not mix with the officials who have flown in from Canberra and who are staying at the hotel.

I go through the literature that Holding's department has provided for the information of its invitees. "The settlement of Australia by Europeans has not always been successful," begins one leaflet entitled *Welcome to Aboriginal Land: History*. I chat with a black boy of fourteen who has come down from the Queensland mining town of Mount Isa. What's it like for black people in Queensland? "Mount Isa's good; there's much more green there than around here," the boy says, answering the question in terms not of race but of the natural environment. "I want to move to Brisbane later," he continues, "and maybe go to college."

The Darwin government is bitterly opposed to "giving away the Rock." It objects to a further loss of Northern Territory land both to Canberra and to Aborigines who already hold or claim so much of the Northern Territory. It has forbidden any Northern Territory civil servant to attend today's event.

Out in the open, not far from the Rock, I stand amidst 2,500 people, all black except for a few hundred—the Holding invitees—as Yani Lester comes through the red dust to a makeshift podium to welcome the governor general of Australia, Sir Ninian Stephen. In the country fair atmosphere the whites are like guests in an alien place. Beside me are naked kids, burly cops, and women dancers with white stripes painted on their breasts for their performance later. Behind me a woman lifts her child high as Sir Ninian stands up in his white suit to speak for the nation. "Look, see the king," she says to her child in the broadest of Australian accents.

The governor general hands over a piece of paper to the traditional elders of the Pitjantjatjara and Yankuntjatjara tribes, granting them inalienable freehold over Ayers Rock, which they call "Uluru." They are to hold it for five minutes before documents will be exchanged leasing it back to Canberra for ninety-nine years at an annual rent of $75,000 plus 20 percent of the entrance fees paid by visitors to the surrounding park.

As the governor general holds the paper triumphantly over his head, a senior civil servant whispers to his companion, "Peace in our time," and gives a cynical chuckle. Yet I find the day moving, a welcome contrast to the bleak scene of blacks in Sydney and Perth. Never have I seen so many Aborigines together before. Never have I seen whites so outnumbered at an event by Aborigines. The day symbolizes, in however token a form, a reversal of the inexorable pressure put upon blacks by whites.

Just as Sir Ninian hands over the title a light plane roars overhead trailing a banner: AYERS ROCK FOR ALL AUSTRALIANS—Northern Territory code for opposition to handing over the Rock to *some* Australians. Seven minutes elapse as the noise goes on and the crowd cranes skyward to read the banner. The traditional owners' moments of control of Ayers Rock are extended from five to twelve.

The Australian anthem "Advance Australia Fair" is announced, but most people do not know when to stand and when to sit, or what the song is about; the singing collapses amidst embarrassed laughter. Lester's translation into an Aboriginal tongue of the governor general's speech gets out of synchronization. "You've done that bit," interjects the governor general. "I'm not finished yet," he snaps when the translation begins while he is still in mid-sentence. "A little bit of shush, please," cries Lester when the governor general cannot be heard above the hubbub.

Dances are performed and then a buffalo steak dinner is served on paper plates. The former governor general of Canada, now Canadian ambassador in Canberra, introduces himself as I toy with my buffalo. "It takes me back to Indian treaty days in Canada," he says. "There's the same weird combination of people here. Even some cowboy hats. I'm not sure what you call them in Australia." (A stockman is more or less a cowboy.)

"I've waited twenty years for this," says Mungo McCallum, a left-wing journalist, when we meet at the barbecue table. He goes on to sneer at the rent as being "enough to buy a second-grade house."

The dignitaries return to the Sheraton and black kids play Frisbee with the paper plates. A rumble of drum music rises into the night. People come to the microphone to announce or ask about a lost child. Under nearby scraggy trees I see youthful gasoline sniffers; for them death is just around the corner.

Heading back from Ayers Rock, past the desert oaks with their needlelike leaves, and the sprawling gray-green mulgas, our bus faces directly toward the Olgas, an inky blue cluster of loops and curves, darkly intruding into a fading blue-white sky. At the resort complex in Yulara I drop by the Giles Tavern, named after the white discoverer of Ayers Rock, and for the first time in Australia I find a large crowded pub somewhat evenly divided among whites and blacks. The party by the Rock this afternoon was dry—the traditional owners insisted on it—but tonight another tradition holds sway.

On a wall is a drawing of a grinning Aborigine and on the ground beside him is a white man gasping with thirst. In the background is Ayers Rock and nearby an Aboriginal family whose only possession appears to be a refrigerator. The Aborigine is lifting a can of Swan brand lager high in the air. The drawing's caption says, "This Is the Life and This Is the Beer."

I play darts with some Aborigines from Alice Springs. Jeffrey, with a Jamaican gollywog haircut, is a construction worker. Rex, fat and friendly, works for an organization that builds houses for people in the countryside. "I don't build the houses," Rex explains. "I sit in an office. Other people do the building. The money comes from the government." Out in the car two girls wait for Jeffrey and Rex to call it a day and begin the return trip to Alice. They are on the pill. "Half-blacks like us are nearly always on the pill," Rex says. "Tribals do not use the pill." These men have essentially left the traditional life. "I go back to my people sometimes," Jeffrey says vaguely. "But not very often because it's a long way from Alice Springs."

As I pay the five-dollar deposit necessary to get more darts from the barmaid, Jeffrey and a third man quiz me about the U.S.A. Is it cheaper there, or dearer? Are the Americans like Australians? As Jeffrey drinks one more Carlton draft, and Rex one more Victoria bitter—both Melbourne beers—I ask them about the day's events. "Look, it's great," says Rex. "We're OK now. We got the Rock. We'll take it from there."

"We'll have to stop," says Rex when I say it's time for me to go. "What for?" objects a friend. "It's this guy's five dollars," says Rex. "He paid the deposit for us. We'll have to give the darts back now because he's going." I say it doesn't matter, but Rex insists on collecting the darts, leaning down unsteadily to find one or two on the floor. He gets back the money and presses it into my hand.

Next morning I breakfast with Galarrwuy Yunupingu, chairman of the powerful and wealthy Northern Land Council in Darwin, and one of the nation's leading Aborigines. Arriving more than an hour late, Yunupingu, a solid man of medium height, is dressed casually but stylishly in a blue-and-black floral shirt and gray trousers. As we settle into the coffee shop of the Four Seasons Hotel, I ask him if the hand-over was a big victory. "I don't call it a victory," replies Yunupingu. "I'd only call it a victory if we took Australia back; if the governor general came and gave us title to the whole land, and we leased *that* back to the Commonwealth."

Galarrwuy Yunupingu doesn't mean whites will ever leave. "We have to live with the situation." Isn't 1 percent a depressingly tiny proportion of the population? "Look, it's not easy to walk away from your background," Yunupingu responds. "I don't care who tells me who owns my land," he goes on, slowly sipping his coffee, "for I know, myself, that I own every inch of it. I was taught that I own it, every rock, every blade of grass."

Yunupingu was brought up in Protestant Christian circles, but these days he is independent of all creeds. Is there any value to Christianity? "I suppose for people who haven't got anything else to do."

Turning to the subject of mineral resources on Aboriginal land, he says, "Mining has to go on. Maybe I've been brainwashed, but I think it's got to go on. The question is who will benefit from the mining." A group of Aborigines shamble into the coffee shop and sit down across the room. "You blokes sober?" Yunupingu calls out with a grin.

Galarrwuy Yunupingu, who has two sons from previous unions with black women in remote Arnhem Land—the boys now study at Scots College in Sydney—and who lives with a white woman in Darwin, says he is detached about his high post as head of the body which represents militant Aborigines in the north. "My power is out in the bush. Heading the Northern Land Council is important *on the day.*" He thinks his sons will have a better life than he has had. "My strength has only been due to my personality and my traditional background. They'll have education."

"The Aborigines were lucky," says a redneck interviewed on a TV documentary which I see later in the day, jolting me with another point of view. "Had it been the Germans that conquered Australia, it would have been the concentration camps for them. Had it been the Russians, it would have been Siberia. Had it been the Japanese, they would have been bred out. But it happened to be the silly Pom with his do-goodism."

At Yulara airport, waiting for my plane by a row of bright green chairs under pictures of flowers and birds and kangaroos, I am joined by Gordon Bryant, who held the Aboriginal affairs portfolio in the Whitlam years. "Yesterday's ceremony was the culmination of a long haul by the Aboriginal people to establish a national identity," he observes. "Probably there has never been a gathering of Aborigines as large as yesterday's since the white man arrived in Australia nearly two hundred years ago."

Up comes Senator Jo Vallentine of the Nuclear Disarmament Party, and I ask her what is the connection, if any, between her peace movement and yesterday's event. "A very close connection," chirps this Quaker from Perth, a vegetarian who has said that Jesus Christ, were he alive, would be a member of her party. "People must be able to take control of their own lives. That's the point. *Participatory democracy.* Uranium, land rights—both are about the individual taking his own life in his hands." Senator Vallentine hops on her plane to Perth, headed for her next rendezvous with relevance. On my plane back to Alice Springs, I try to work out what her words mean, but enlightenment does not come.

Beside me in the plane is a white bureaucrat from deep in the bowels of the Aboriginal industry. He is reading a typed paper entitled "Looking at Aboriginal Women and Power; Fundamental Misunderstandings in the Literature and New Insights." He acknowledges, as we chat and the plane glides high over the empty center, which resembles a battered brass dish, that public opinion is now in general against land rights, and that further land rights legislation is unlikely. His conclusion is not that he should follow public opinion but that he should change it. It is an interesting approach to democracy.

At the office of the Central Land Council in Alice Springs, where I go to obtain a permit to go into Aboriginal territory west of the town, a sign sits on the front desk: "Journalists shall respect personal privacy. They shall not place undue emphasis on race."

On a gray, cool, utterly still afternoon, accompanied by Meredith Campbell of the federal Department of Aboriginal Affairs office in Alice Springs, I drive in a four-by-four stocked with food and camping gear toward hills which look marbled, pink and blue swirling together as in a medical painting of the anatomy. There are mulga trees bearing lettuce-green leaves and some bush plum and prickly paddy melon. I spot a few dingoes. The Australian government has amusingly provided road signs like PASSING LANE AHEAD.

We cross the Finke River, which Meredith says is the oldest river in the world, but today its bed is a carpet of gray-green leaves on which an old car rests with a severed gum tree lying flat across its top. Every ten kilometers or so an abandoned Toyota sits by the wide, red road. Aborigines who suffer a breakdown do not find it worthwhile to arrange repairs and simply hitch a ride with someone else and leave the car to nature's hot embrace. "Toyota" has passed into the language here and become as local as "tucker," "pension," and "grog." As the quip goes, "There aren't any deserts in Japan, but there's a lot of Japan in the desert."

Stopping for a snack of Vegemite sandwiches and orange juice from our supplies, we see a cairn surrounded by tiny tombstones with crosses, beneath the headstone IN MEMORY OF EARLY MISSION PIONEERS, a reference to the historic Lutheran mission of Hermannsburg not far down the road. A sign forbidding liquor signals that we have left the area of pastoral leases and reached Papunya, an Aboriginal community that reflects a movement of recent years to resettle remote homelands. It is a dusty spectacle of cars that work and others that don't, dogs, broken glass, strewn cartons, and empty drums. Most of the equipment in a playground is broken, but a paddock of white-painted half tires forms a BMX track for kids on bikes. There are homes but no gardens, streets with no names to them, young men with no work to do.

Many of the simple houses with galvanized iron roofs are either unfinished or empty. "Our council building was just burned down by a bum," says Alison Anderson, a bilingual woman of the Loritja tribe who heads the Papunya council. "He was angry that he hadn't received his unemployment check: actually he'd forgotten to fill out his continuation form." Some 200 of the total population of 490 that have a relation to Papunya are on the dole (another 100 are on pensions). In her forties, with curly hair, wearing black cords and tennis shoes stained pink from the dust, Anderson says it was a mistake to build houses in a row. "When a person in one house died, everyone moved out of their house." As she speaks I look over at an empty house where a family has chosen to camp beside it rather than live inside. "Allotting houses we never repeat history," Anderson says of the 100 percent government-funded housing program. "If a person's demolished a three-bedroom brick house, we never give them another one."

A famous white Australian band, Midnight Oil, has arrived today, tired but exhilarated on a Blackfella-Whitefella tour undertaken jointly with the black band Wurumpi and backed by Canberra. In the evening, "Bread Line," "Why Don't You Give Up Drinking," and other songs erupt into the desert night as shafts of golden light rise up from the silver microphones and drums. A crowd materializes out of the gloom, kids at the front, jiving and rocking with delight in perfect rhythm with each song, adults standing quietly at the back. The country music style of Wurumpi pleases the adults; the loud, fast, confrontational style of the Oils appeals less.

We light a fire to cook a bush meal and to keep warm. Aboriginal children with runny noses gather round. Friendly and guileless, they laugh at my dish of spaghetti and whisper to each other that it's "snakes."

Although Papunya is dry, some people become drunk during the evening. Anderson, who chain-smokes and has a white husband, says liquor is the community's biggest problem. "The going price from the grog runners is fifty dollars a cask of wine from Alice Springs." Traditional culture is only thinly alive at Papunya—it is stronger further west at Kintore—with the VCR big and TV on the way, but Anderson says traditional law eclipses European law. "People usually get a spear through the leg, and their wives get hit over the head, you know, if there's a crime."

Camping together with the musicians on Papunya's fringe, I chat with Peter Garrett, lead singer with the Oils. "I enjoyed tonight much more than I do the Sydney Entertainment Center," says the tall, bald crusader for nuclear disarmament and land rights. "It's real."

Next morning I awake to the sound of crows singing and light a fire to boil the billy for tea. For the Oils' breakfast, Anderson has sent around witchetty grubs, which are prized out of the roots of the acacia by Aboriginal women. Garrett declares them delicious and says each one has as much protein as two pork chops. We go to see Papunya sand paintings, done these days in waterproof acrylic on canvas, at the community's art shop. Reggie, brightly dressed in a black track suit with a yellow stripe, accompanied by his father, Mick, comes in with his painting of nearby Haast's Bluff. Annette, a white exile from Sydney who runs the shop, likes its style and brilliant hues. "What do you think it's worth?" she asks. Reggie looks sheepish. "Two," says Annette. "Two-fifty," suggests father Mick. Annette writes out a check for $220. Later she tells Meredith that Reggie's painting will go to a shop in Alice Springs for $400 and retail there for about $500.

Papunya is a welfare society, on which a layer of rentierism has been added as gas and oil royalties flow in. Perhaps it is better for government funding to facilitate an experiment in bush community than for Aborigines to live near cities as fringe dwellers in limbo between two worlds. Still, Papunya does not work very efficiently. Some say too many tribes are intermixed here—Loritja, Aranda, Wailpri, and Pintupi—and others say royalty money has brought corruption. Certainly one trouble is that the Aborigines have been influenced by the Australian mentality of depending on the government, and lacking the training and capital for economic enterprise, they sadly perpetuate it. Into the vacuum of passivity flows grog.

Alison Anderson knows of Papunya's mixed reputation—some see the settlement as the rotten fruit of throwing money at the Aboriginal problem—but it doesn't bother her much. "The stirrers in the cities are the problem," she says in farewelling me. "As for us, we're just a quiet bunch of Aboriginal people in the desert."

Back in the cities of the Boomerang Coast, I try to sort out the mix of reason and emotion, rights and duties, knowledge and ignorance, progress and tradition, in the question of Aborigines and the land. John Howard, the conservative leader, who opposed the handover of Ayers Rock, puts to me a basic fact about the matter: "Look, ninety to ninety-five percent of Australian kids grow up without having met an Aborigine." White Australians, with few exceptions, almost all in the frontier states, do not know any Aborigines well, and have felt no impact from Aboriginal culture.

Has Professor Leonie Kramer ever been enriched by Aboriginal culture? She murmurs about its "contribution to anthropology." Bruce Stannard, a writer for *The Bulletin*, recalls of his upbringing in suburban Sydney: "As kids we saw the blacks making boomerangs or charming snakes at La Perouse, but they didn't impinge on our consciousness." Does Rachel Faggeter, curator of the Children's Museum in Melbourne, who is strong for feminism, the environment, and race equality, have any Aboriginal friends? "No, no I do not. Where I live you do not see them." Have Aboriginal designs made any contribution to the fashion industry? Fraser McEwing shakes with laughter, then adds soberly, "It has no fashion value at all. It's basically brown and beige, and that's it. The motifs are primitive. Once you've done the Aboriginal look once, what next?"

The disturbing truth is that people who live far from the Aboriginal areas, knowing little of Aboriginal life and culture, are more supportive of compensation for Aborigines than those who live in proximity to them. To fly the Aboriginal flag from state buildings in Sydney and Melbourne and to erect a plaque in the Melbourne City Square to a famous early Victorian Aborigine does not cause pain. "The federal decision to grant huge tracts of land to Aborigines in the Northern Territory," observes Geoffrey Blainey, "was in effect a tax imposed on the rural north by southern city Australians."

"I wonder," asks a letter writer to *The Australian,* commenting on Malcolm Fraser's crusade against apartheid, "if Mr. Fraser is going to bring home a few hundred of South Africa's blacks and settle them at Nareen [the former prime minister's farm west of Melbourne]."

It is an old story. Just as Australians as a whole support the demands of black South Africans, and more recently of the Kanak rebels in French New Caledonia, while the South African and French whites closer to the scene tend to oppose them, so within Australia it is not whites on the front line who back the wave of compensatory justice for Australian blacks but the Volvo socialists in their villas on the Boomerang Coast. The multiculturalist intellectuals are far from South Africa, on which they preach, quite far from New Caledonia, for which they have clear-cut solutions to offer Paris, and even thousands of kilometers distant from the Northern Territory, where the whites who actually live beside blacks feel many emotions, of which guilt is not one. Their very remoteness from any front line may tend to make them excessive in their commitments, and to close their minds with a combative click against any gray area of the issue.

Are the Australian blacks, a tiny 1 percent or a little more of the population, to join in the modernized, largely urban white society, or are they to remain rural and traditional? Are they to become economically independent, which perhaps can only occur if they play the game of the capitalist economy for themselves, or are they to be eternal mendicants of the state, with all the resentments on both sides that such dependence spawns? The future holds more than one possibility.

"We will celebrate," says a Victorian Aboriginal leader, Alan Brown, referring to the state's 150th anniversary, "only when governments concede sovereignty of [our] land, and pay rent to the Aboriginal people." He adds, "A hundred and fifty years is but a hiccup in our existence."

Few issues in Australian life over many years have seemed so unhinged as land rights. After vagueness and perhaps excessive enthusiasm during the 1970s, there occurred in 1984 and 1985 a severe backlash against land rights, triggered in part by mining groups. Hugh Morgan, the bright and confident chief executive of the formidable Western Mining Company, tells me at a Melbourne dinner party that the advisers to the Aborigines, and also the environmentalists, are being "sentimental" about the land and its early inhabitants. They are possessed of a "bitter hostility to modernity." They are "as Luddite as Ned Kelly, who pulled down telegraph poles a century ago."

Morgan is not against the granting of inalienable freehold title over land claimed as sacred by Aborigines, but he is scornful of granting them in addition the power of veto over mining on that land. "More than forty percent of Australia's exports are from mining," he points out. He is so frustrated by the "new religion" of the environmentalists and "culture bearers" that he looks favorably on Brazil, Fiji, and other alternative sites for mining investment. Hugh Morgan objects to making land the pivot of compensatory justice for Aborigines. "Australian society should treat them as a disadvantaged group and give them help," he sums up, "but to tie that up with land as if the Aborigines are going to be kept in the ancient mode is nonsense."

Land rights are based on a recognition that the Aborigines were in possession of Australia when the British arrived, yet Australian law is based upon *terra nullius,* a view of Australia as unoccupied when the whites arrived. How could a conservative government pass land rights legislation? At the same Melbourne dinner party I put the question to Tony Staley, a former minister in the Fraser government which passed the bill.

"The legislation slipped by cabinet without most of us paying attention," replies Staley, a tall, energetic man who was a classmate of mine at Melbourne University, speaking of the first land rights act, for the Northern Territory, in 1976. Staley now opposes nationwide land rights legislation, as do his former colleagues in the Liberal Party. And he regards the Northern Territory pattern, whereby the Aborigines own not only the surface of the land but everything below it and can refuse permission for any visitor to cross it, as a mistake which should be rectified.

I put the same question to the officeholder who bears the brunt of the land rights act. "You will understand the guiding force that led Malcolm [Fraser] into that land rights legislation," Chief Minister Ian Tuxworth says in his Darwin office in October 1985, "if you look at his activities on South Africa over the past two weeks." To the Northern Territory leader, Fraser's step was taken for "vague spiritual reasons" and "had no objectives." Tuxworth gazes with an air of patience-at-stupidity out the panoramic windows of his office. "We've had ten years of it—and there's twenty more years of claims to process. We're in and out of court every day fighting over what the act means."

No less than 48 percent of the Northern Territory—an area larger than Victoria and Tasmania put together—is under claim to Aborigines or already granted to them. Mineral exploration on Aboriginal land "has been virtually halted since 1972," according to the Northern Territory Development Corporation.

"People would punch you up the nose thirty years ago if you called them an Aborigine," observes the lord mayor of Darwin, Alec Fong Lim, "while today anyone who's slightly sunburnt calls himself one." Fong Lim feels land rights are "OK for the traditionals, but when you get your Redfern bloody Aborigines, who've never seen a kangaroo in their life, except in a bloody zoo, and know nothing of Aboriginal culture, *determining* what Aborigines should be thinking and doing, it gives me the . . ."

The contradictions in Aboriginal policy came home to roost after Brian Burke's Labor government took power in 1982 in Western Australia—which is 2.5 percent Aboriginal, more than twice the national average. Burke had pledged to follow Labor policy and enact land rights. Yet in 1984 he abruptly reversed himself. Some people blamed the mining companies for Perth's panic, but this is not the whole truth. Less than 20 percent of Australians, according to 1984 polls, were supporting Aboriginal land rights.

"I'm against land rights," says Ian Duggan, a policeman in the remote mining town of Mount Newman. "Out here, one group of blacks makes a claim, and it turns out another group of blacks are now living on that land. What sort of solution is that?"

In his wood-paneled office at the Western Australian parliament, Premier Burke in late 1985 is adamant against land rights in full-fledged form. "I don't agree with the concept of carving off part of the nation's wealth," he says spiritedly, "and passing it over to you because you happen to be an Aborigine—or to someone else who happens to be particularly disadvantaged."

After Premier Burke—aided by Prime Minister Hawke—backed down on land rights, the chairman of the National Aboriginal Conference, Bob Riley, said bitterly, "Our future well-being should not depend on favorable public opinion polls, nor should our rights be jeopardized by the desire for political parties to gain or maintain office."

In Queensland land rights have not become a big issue because

Premier Bjelke-Petersen has simply said no to the whole concept. "And you mark my words," the premier says to me, "the land that's been transferred will be handed back after the next election, because we're going to have a new government down there [in Canberra]. Whitlam said to me, 'Joh, there's more votes going for the Aborigines than against them, and I'm going with them.' Fraser had the same philosophy." The Brisbane leader sees another solution: "The Aborigines have to work, that's it. Some people say it spoils their sacred feeling to expect them to work. Well, we'll see about that."

"Some Aborigines play the role of Black Panthers," says Richard Hall in Sydney, touching on the absurdity that often marks the politics of Aboriginal affairs, "and these are probably in the pay of the [anti–land rights] Chamber of Mines. The press laps it up, and the Chamber of Mines and people like Hugh Morgan say, 'Look at that,' to prove their point that the blacks are irresponsible."

Others on the conservative side of politics blame the white lawyers and idealists who serve the Aborigines and stir the public to pro-Aboriginal positions. "There's nothing wrong with the Aboriginal people," says Bjelke-Petersen, who for many years had close ties with Aborigines in the Cooktown area of Queensland, "it's their leaders and advisers."

"The Aborigines were the original inhabitants of this country," says Leslie Oldfield, mayor of Alice Springs, sitting on a couch in the living room of her simple home. "It was unfortunate for them that we came. But now we're here. Every country has its invaders. Look at England; I'm never too sure who is English and who is not. Does England still belong to the English?" Mayor Oldfield, a vivacious, practical woman who defied her own town council to attend the handover of Ayers Rock ("I don't believe in boycotts"), touches on the corruption that results as land and government money and mineral royalties flow to those of Aboriginal race. "I've got black friends to whom I say, 'You used to be bloody white, and now you're bloody black.' They say, 'Shhhhhhh.' "

Gough Whitlam, from Paris where he was Australia's ambassador to UNESCO from 1983 until late 1986, criticizes the Labor Party's retreat from his own Aboriginal policies. I ask him if he was perhaps ahead of public opinion in the early 1970s. "No, we gave a lead, and then public opinion caught up." The former prime minister speaks with passion. "Subsequent prime ministers have not given a lead. They've allowed the mining interests to monopolize the propaganda field." In apparent response to Hawke's reported view that idealism toward the Aborigines has faded in recent years, Whitlam retorts, "It's a complete distortion to say that the Australian public are less idealistic now than they used to be."

At the same time Whitlam speaks guardedly of "advances" rather than "solutions" when discussing the Aboriginal problem. "I don't assert that there can be eternal solutions to such problems," he says slowly. "There'll always be new conflicts of interest. You solve some problems and new problems will arise."

The smell of tropical flowers and wet leaves fills the night as I walk through the streets of Cairns to meet a man who believes he sees a solution to the Aboriginal problem. "When I took office two years ago," says Bob Katter, the Queensland minister for Aboriginal affairs and for northern development, "you had within Queensland a giant socialist state of 300,000 hectares, with 30,000 people, all belonging to the government, where no individual could own anything. There were only two private businesses in this whole reserve area!"

Katter, a lean white-haired man in his forties, was brought up in the outback. An evangelical Christian, he believes in self-management rather than paternalism from government, and in privatization of the land as against the communalism implied by land rights, in order to advance self-respect and economic independence among Aborigines— who are more numerous in Queensland than in any other state.

"When I took office," Katter says as we chat in the lobby of his hotel, "the police, nurses, and teachers were all threatening a walkout from the reserves. Such was the rioting, drunkenness, and violence that no one was prepared to service the Aboriginal reserves. Twice a year, on the average, we had to fly people in to quell rioting." Katter, who says he has been influenced by Robert Ardrey's *The Territorial Imperative,* the Lincoln Homestead Act, and the American sheriff system, decided to give the Queensland Aborigines a choice between the Land Council concept and a new plan for individual land ownership.

"The Land Council concept," he says, "is a communistic notion, foisted upon the Northern Territory. I once asked Galarrwuy Yunupingu if anyone actually owns anything up there. He replied, 'If I let you own something that means it's being taken off the people'! That's how the act works. Recently I heard Yunupingu say he wasn't interested in cattle, and he wasn't going to be forced to develop." Katter looks grim. "As long as he has his cultural purity, that's all he cares about. It makes me angry. There just isn't such a thing as a free lunch."

Katter says he put the choice to the Aborigines on the Queensland reserves at public meetings: Should the land go to the traditional owners, "whoever the hell they are," or should it go to private ownership? The minister is on the edge of his armchair. "The vote was three thousand to two for private ownership.

"We have not flown in any police into any community in the past eighteen months." Bob Katter stops and grins. "That is a peculiar yardstick, perhaps, but it's magnificent for us. There's been no rioting anywhere. The crime rate—we're not allowed to keep separate figures, but unofficially we monitor it—has dropped more than clean in half. Alcoholism has dropped to the point that the councils are financially embarrassed. Drink's been their income."

Minister Katter's luggage was lost on the flight from Brisbane to Cairns today, and at intervals he gets a progress report on efforts to track it down. Suddenly a grinning young aide comes by with a piece of paper. Katter looks at it and cries, "Jesus, they found me bag!"

Returning to the subject at hand, Katter says, "In this same short period, fishing revenues in the Torres Straits have leaped from $50,000 a year to $1.6 million, and cattle income from $200,000 to $1.2 million." The student of the Lincoln Homestead Act knows that traditional Aboriginal culture will suffer. "The Japanese had to get rid of their feudal culture," he points out, "to succeed with private enterprise." The minister looks across the hotel lobby, where another visitor has arrived to see him. "You know, I reckon that under our system, Galarrwuy Yunupingu would be a top operator!"

I walk out into the languor of the Cairns evening, which is pierced by laughter and shouts from the open-air public bar of the Barrier Reef Hotel, wondering whether Katter may have the answer, or whether, beyond Queensland, the political opposition to his private enterprise plan would be too strong. Certainly the test of any enduring new deal for Aborigines will come in economics. The Aborigine as a producer will find his way in society. The Aborigine as a mendicant may not even hang on to the psychological and administrative gains of the recent past.

"This is our country," says Winnie Quagliotti, spokeswoman for the Wurundjeri tribe in Victoria, in her office at an Aboriginal co-operative society on the outskirts of Melbourne. "I don't care what white, brindle, or any ethnic groups says, Australia doesn't belong to anybody but the Aborigines—by birthright.

"Aboriginal people used to share," continues Quagliotti, a coffee-colored mountain of a woman, joyous and candid, as she leaves her desk and sinks down onto a wooden chair beside mine, "but when the white man came he destroyed that; he brought greed. The land that should be beautiful has been eroded by cattle, cement, cars."

"Cars are a bad thing?" I inquire.

"Cars are a bad thing for everybody."

"Have you got a car?"

"Two cars," she says with a laugh, lighting a cigarette. "Well, Paul [her husband] has one and I have one." There are no tribal Aborigines left in Victoria, and Winnie Quagliotti's people are torn between wanting to progress and wanting to summon back tradition.

Quagliotti, dressed in a gray dress trimmed with red, matching her well-groomed gray hair, is putting in a land claim on behalf of her tribe and linked tribes. What land is she claiming? "Melbourne—the city of Melbourne," she cries, and as her arms wave I fear she may fall forward off her small chair. "Where Batman got the Jagga Jagga brothers to sign," she adds, referring to the "treaty" between Victoria's founder and the Aborigines of the area. "Everything on that land is ours—Government House, the Melbourne Cricket Ground, the Windsor Hotel, the Rialto . . ." The effervescent Quagliotti lists half the landmarks of Melbourne. "I'll sue the Queen if I have to," she declares, her face alight, and then she stops. "We realize we can't get that land back, but we want compensation, that's what we're on about. I don't want to live in bloody Government House. I want help with our health and housing and welfare."

Quagliotti denounces Premier Burke of Western Australia for his climb down on land rights. "He's a real burker." When I look perplexed, she laughs and explains this is Australian slang for an idiot who covers things up. "You've been away in America too long. Let's just say Burke is a dickhead. What I hope is that one day we will be a separate nation," she says. And when I say it is hard to see how that could be, she declares, "You shouldn't be scared of it. You've already got your nation, and we're not scared of you."

I ask Quagliotti if religion is important in her life. "No. Religion means nothing to me. I don't knock the Almighty, but sometimes I wonder why's all this happening to my people. Why's all this happening in Ethiopia? I cried when I saw it on TV. These babies and women who could hardly stand. This should never happen in the twentieth century—especially in Africa!"

Quagliotti is torn at the prospect of dilution of Aboriginal blood. "Our race is dying out," she says, the whites of her eyes riveting me. I point out that the black birthrate is far higher than the white. "But you people are *marrying* us," she cries.

A man appears at the door. "Come in, Paul," she says and introduces me to her Italian husband before she goes on: "My own grandchildren are part Scottish and Italian and so on, and when they marry they'll be even less Aboriginal.

"Would you like tea or coffee?" Winnie Quagliotti asks me. When I decline, she says, "Coffee for me, Dad," to her husband, who leaves the room to fetch it.

"Is the intermarriage regrettable?"

"Very regrettable. Because if someone's face and hair is like a white person's, who's going to believe that they're really Abo?"

"Did you try to persuade your children not to marry non-blacks?"

"Certainly not. That's their choice." She stops, and we listen to the scrape and clatter of dishes in the kitchen, where a group of young people of various colorations—but all self-designated as Aborigines—are cleaning up. "That's why we must have a nation," she goes on, "so that our traditions can be saved."

As Quagliotti walks me to the door, I ask her what she thinks of Charles Perkins, the highest-ranking Aboriginal public servant in Australia. "He's a man who likes power," she replies with a frown. She reaches up to a bulletin board and pulls down for me a poster. It has a picture of Perkins and from the balloon at his mouth come the words "I'll look into it." The poster has the heading: "Charlie's Law: I'll Look into It." Quagliotti laughs. "When we need something, Charlie says, 'I'll look into it.' And that's all that happens—he looks."

"Where did Charlie Perkins go off the rails?"

She laughs again. "When he became a bloody bureaucrat in the bloody Department of Aboriginal Affairs!"

At the gate of the suburban house that serves as the cooperative's offices I ask Winnie Quagliotti about immigration policy. "The immigrants don't know anything about us," she says quietly. "And with all the turmoil going on overseas, who's got time to listen?" Quagliotti goes further into this troubling issue: "If immigrants don't know about our struggle, then I say they shouldn't be in Australia." She pauses, as if taken aback by her own remark. "But who am I to say that. I'm only one person. And you know, perhaps people coming to Australia might teach old Australians that there's a place for everybody on this earth."

"The handover of Ayers Rock is a turning point in Australia's race relations," remarks Charles Perkins as I sit beneath the Aboriginal flag in his Canberra office. "It's a recognition that Aboriginal people were the original owners of this country. Also it will save Australia hundreds of millions of dollars—in jails, murders, frustrations, anxieties."

A handsome man with a warm manner, Perkins was born around 1937 ("Nobody knows exactly when") in Alice Springs. He went to high school in Adelaide—where he never entered a white home—and in the 1960s became well known as a radical student protester in Sydney. "When I told my mother I was going to receive my degree at Sydney University," he recalls with a quick laugh, "she said, Where's Sydney? I said it's a big town. She said, Is it bigger than Alice Springs?" Perkins smiles. "What my mother enjoys most in life is watching the cattle come in to drink."

Charles Perkins has a vision of Aboriginal culture enriching white Australian culture. "Future generations will say Australians of the sixties and seventies and eighties must have been an ignorant bunch, not seeing the jewel in front of them. All they had to do was to incorporate Aboriginal culture into Australian culture—giving Australian culture a uniqueness that it has lacked."

For Perkins it's not too late. "Instead of being pseudo Yanks and pseudo British, we could pick up some of the beautiful things in Aboriginal culture—kindness to others, respect for the aged, non-militarism—and really be Australians."

Can you do this when you are only 1 percent or so of the Australian population? "Well, look at Brazil," Perkins rejoins, then stops and stares at me. "It's not just numbers but commitment to the idea."

Although Perkins was once a fiery radical, he praises Malcolm Fraser on policy toward blacks. "People who rubbish Malcolm don't know what they're talking about. The man is very sensitive. We wouldn't have got anywhere if he hadn't run over the Country Party and his own cabinet [and passed the land rights bill in 1976].

"When he was prime minister," Perkins goes on, "I said to Fraser, 'Come up to the Northern Territory and have a look.' Well, we were in Alice Springs in a creek bed with a huge group of eighty to a hundred Aborigines. There was an old man who was head of a clan of the Aranda people, and since it was his area, he was the boss. Fraser's entourage from Canberra came along the creek bed like a swarm of bees. I said to the old Aranda man, 'This is an important man, I'm going to introduce you to him.'

" 'How're you going?' he asked Fraser. Fraser said in that crisp way of his, 'Who are you?'

" 'Well, I'm the boss of this area and these are my people. And who are you?'

" 'Well, I'm the prime minister of Australia.'

" 'What *job* have you got?' the old Aranda man insisted. 'Are you a ringer or what?' " Perkins explains that the old man thought Fraser might be a stockman. "So Fraser puts on a kind of smile and comes back with 'I'm the number-one guy.' " Perkins laughs. "Jesus, the old Aranda man was not happy with that. *He* was the number-one guy!"

Perkins goes over to a coffee machine and invites me to come with him and help myself. I turn a lever marked "coffee," but see nothing in my cup. Expecting liquid, I keep turning. Perkins is at my elbow. "Jesus, you take a lot of coffee, Ross." Powdered coffee has been pouring into my cup, and it is now half full; a separate lever produces hot water.

The head of the Department of Aboriginal Affairs does not accept that progress and tradition are in total conflict. "There's no contradiction between being a professor of philosophy at Sydney University and a traditional Aboriginal person," he claims as we resume our armchairs. "It's been done in Africa, the Jews have done it, that's what multiculturalism is all about. The trouble is in Australia everybody thinks you've got to be a white blackfella—and you don't have to be. It's no good telling an Aboriginal that he's a white person when he knows that really he's not. Why should you throw away your ancestry just to suit other people?"

Perkins understands the problem of power, even if he seems too optimistic about transcending it. "Australia has never been faced with a race thing that's not been at the whites' own convenience," he says as he sips his coffee, "with the whites setting the rules. The whites have got to learn that multiculturalism is more than shaking hands with an Indian and having a Chinese meal. A black person can be a good bloke, or he can be a nasty shit. Whites have got to relate on that basis." He gets up from his chair to sign for me a copy of his memoir, *A Bastard Like Me*. "Aboriginal people are here to stay. White Australians will have to relate to them, not in a missionary manner, or a government manner, or by being too kind, but judging people as they find them."

Charles Perkins wants an end to Asian immigration. "We're getting some rubbish from Southeast Asia—people who are running brothels at King's Cross [a night spot in Sydney]," he complains. "Why should we take just anybody who rolls up in a boat? And if we were serious about multiculturalism, we'd have fifty thousand black Africans here."[1]

Is Perkins nostalgic for the struggles of the 1960s? "That had to happen. It's good that in Australia we can yell and scream at each other and then sit down with a cuppa tea and work things out. That's the beauty of this country above all others, that we don't have to kill each other to achieve things." He comes with me to the door. "Yeah, the saving grace is that basically Australians are good people."

Richard Hall, who worked on Aboriginal affairs during the Whitlam years, sees excesses on both sides of the Aboriginal issue. "The Hugh Morgan stuff," he claims over a drink in the study of his Sydney home, "is nothing more than the very rich trying to defend what it has." But Hall is not among the Labor Party people who romanticize Aboriginal culture. "You get all this crap," he says, "about the blacks being the first true cooperative people, and about Aboriginal society being a community of true peace."

The silence that befalls many urban Australians when the Aboriginal issue is raised suggests that it's a mirror for white Australians. A mirror does not lie; a mirror gives one pause. A consciousness exists— perhaps it is the root of Australians' ambivalence toward their harsh, beautiful terrain—that the nation was forged through the dispossession of its previous occupants. "But there's no pragmatic gain in the Aboriginal issue," laments author Bruce Grant as we chat in his bluestone home in Melbourne. He contrasts it with anti-Asian racism, which has been nailed in part because "Australia has so much to gain from its relations with Asia. With the Aborigines one can't but feel guilty," Grant goes on. "The trouble is there are no *advantages* in the Aboriginal question, as there are in the Asian issue."

Among foreign leaders only France's President François Mitterrand in recent years has assailed Australia on the Aboriginal issue. "If there is no longer a problem of the original people in Australia," he snarled in 1984, when Australia criticized French policy in New Caledonia, "it is because they were killed. That is not the way chosen by France."

With nothing to justify pragmatic reform, the redressing of Aboriginal grievances is a moral absolute for Australia. Yet the path to a happy future in white-black relations looks rocky. Most of those self-designated as Aborigines walk steadily into the white man's society where the

1. Today blacks are as free as Asians and Europeans to become immigrants to Australia, but the number of black applicants is relatively small.

white man is in control. Nearly every Aborigine I met believes earnestly in education as a way out of Aborigines' interlocking problems, but education is often an enemy of tradition. Intermarriage proceeds apace by free choice of the individual. Some Aborigines try to hold fast to their traditions, but they cannot isolate themselves successfully. And as traditionalists they are unlikely to make it economically unless propped up by the white man's government, which would seem to make a sham of neo-traditionalism.

Toward Aborigines, Chief Minister Ian Tuxworth has the warm, realistic, if perhaps slightly patriarchal attitude that is common in the frontier states and unknown on the Boomerang Coast. "I tell them," he says, "decide whether you want to be a white black man or a black black man, then I'll tell you how I can help. How many Aborigines come through that door," Tuxworth adds, throwing an arm toward the lofty pale wood entrance to his Darwin office, "and say, 'Government gimme'?" Says this politician—almost the only one in Australia—whose electorate is fully 50 percent Aboriginal, "Very few. In fact in the ten months of this year—two."

The mistake, the chief minister thinks, is for whites to drag blacks into their own way of life. "If you and I go bush or canoeing, that's all right. But when the Aborigine wants to do it, all the busybodies say there must be something wrong with him." I wonder aloud if it isn't too late to preserve the Aboriginal way of life, and if the Aborigine can both progress and hold on to his traditions. "You have a point," says Tuxworth, "but the decision should be his. The trouble is we're making all the decisions."

"The detribalized blacks are still suffering the effects of the destruction of their culture," Labor stalwart Don Dunstan says in his office at the Victorian Tourist Commission, "and of their non-acceptance of ours as an alternative. It's going to be a long-running sore, for most of them are now imprisoned in a culture of poverty. One can do one's best to ease the pain—that's about all."

Conservative Perth businessman Warren Jones seems to agree. "Politicians—all of us—assume a job can be done by oneself, within one's own time span," says the Bond Corporation executive. "But our Aboriginal problem is not going to be solved in twenty, thirty, or fifty years. We destroyed the happy Aborigine. We thought we were doing him a favor by giving him this and that, but we merely made him unemployable."

Jones's blue eyes fix me against a background of walls paneled in jarrah wood and a view of the Swan River. "They aren't the same as us. We have to give them the opportunity to come into our society. But at present they don't have the capability to do that. They know it, but our governments don't know it."

To many blacks, and also to many whites, the other race is not likable. For the whites this does not matter; for the blacks it does. I do not think—as I once hoped—that the Aborigines, who were the first Australians, can help very much in the adjustment of white Australians, who are new to their environ, to dynamic and expanding non-white Asia. They are too few, and those who uphold Aboriginal culture are too removed from modern ways. But the wrong exists, and the pain of it does not go away. "Rights" for Aborigines have not canceled out past wrongs, if by that is meant closing the gap between black and white. So white and black Australia remain at odds. As Australia itself changes rapidly—we know nothing of how tomorrow's blacks and tomorrow's Asian-Australians will view each other—the role of Aborigines as an entity in tomorrow's Australia looks doubly uncertain.

ELEVEN

Public Ways

"Marsupials to Parliament," says the spine of volume six of the *Australian Encyclopaedia*. It's only a reference to the span of alphabetical entries, but in parliament you could easily imagine you were observing a wildlife sanctuary. Certainly the politicians *call* each other birds and beasts. "A low sewer rat," says Premier Wran of the National Party chief in New South Wales. Opposition leader John Howard "would make a cat laugh," says Treasurer Paul Keating. Day by day, politicians call each other "dingo," "canary," "bandicoot," and "termite."

"We're having a few problems tonight," Mike Willesee begins his TV show, "and we're not sure we've got a program for you." The TV channel's lawyers are still frantically reviewing an exchange between Willesee and Liberal politician Andrew Peacock in the light of Australia's draconian libel laws. In the end a truncated version of the interview comes over, and to fill out the current affairs show Willesee offers a segment on a struggle for control of a zoo in a New South Wales town. "Well, we've seen the Tamworth Zoo," he closes. "Sorry we couldn't show you as much as we would have liked of the Canberra Zoo."

The atmosphere of Australian parliamentary proceedings—raucous, spiced with clever repartee, larded with gutter language—is half high school debate and half street corner fight. Westminster procedural rules frame the brawling. "The honorable member for Burrumburra is a screeching galah." . . . "Mr. Speaker, the minister for leisure pursuits is not worth his weight in rocking-horse manure."

"Standards have been declining," claims Neil Brown, who was a minister in the Fraser government and is now deputy Liberal leader, "and the turning point was when Hawke, desperate, having not yet made any impact in parliament, lashed out at Fraser, calling him a liar repeatedly with no justification, and refusing to withdraw." Yet years ago, the Liberal foreign minister Paul Hasluck as he sat on the front bench of parliament leaned forward when Whitlam finished a speech and said, "You are one of the filthiest speakers I've ever heard," and Whitlam, who was sipping a glass of water, hurled the contents of the glass into Hasluck's face.

Political style is rougher in Australia than in the U.S.A., where a prevalent patriotism, the power of the city of Washington to inspire awe, and a feeling that America should speak internationally with a single voice all set limits to political invective. Whereas the morning after an American presidential election sees conciliatory phrases about national unity, in Australia the war paint and feathers stay on as politicians vow to go on seeking the total rout of their utterly worthless opponents. But perhaps it's all bark and no bite?

Do you and Paul Keating mean the invective you hurl at each other? I ask John Howard in his Sydney office. "There's a certain play-acting in some of it," says the candid leader of the opposition. "Most politicians are slightly frustrated thespians. It's part of our folklore. In fact, Mr. Keating and I are quite good friends."

Says Don Dunstan, former premier of South Australia, elegant in a jade green open-neck shirt on a summer day: "My fights with Playford [Dunstan's conservative predecessor as premier] were mostly on policy and didn't involve anger." The Labor Party reformer, now head of tourism for Victoria, recalls the days before he rose to the premiership. "In parliament we would spat, then afterwards Playford would say, 'I'll drive you home.' Tom taught me a lot while I sat beside him in that car."

There is a hidden fellowship of a very Australian kind between politicians of all parties. It is a blend of many things: a common love of the amber fluid (though beer drinking by politicians may be on the decline); a tacit agreement to leave each other alone during the many holiday periods; an echo of the mateship tradition that has politicians calling opponents "Jack" and "Harry" in private and in public alike, even as they warn in doomsday terms of what "that bastard" would do to Australia if he got the chance.

Comparable to that in the political arena, the atmosphere of industrial Australia is a blend of bloodthirsty rhetoric, staggering complacency, and underlying buddy-ism—the product of a history in which labor was always in short supply, business became imbued with some of labor's ethos (the reverse of the American experience), and the government was to the fore in economic activity. Here is the Food Preservers Union, which calls the Labor government fascist, leading a strike at the Rosella tomato sauce plant in Melbourne and demanding, in addition to a 5 percent wage rise in parlous economic times, in a land with the shortest working year in the world (229 days), "time off for the workers to attend art classes."

Jim Green, a public affairs officer of a manganese mining company on Groote Eylandt in the Northern Territory, remarks that he's "off tomorrow. You see, we all get a rostered day off each month. It's the best way to bring the working week down to thirty-eight hours according to the award. To reduce each day's working hours further would be too complicated." In Sydney a dispute flares over the strangely irregular appearance of the Australian flag over the towers of the Harbor Bridge. "We can't fly the flags if it's going to involve an overtime payment," says a harassed bridge spokesman in the face of demands by the flag fliers for steep penalty rates on special days.

A crate of Chinese paintings arrives at the Victorian Arts Center for a long-planned exhibition. Opening the crate, a carpenter hits his hand with a hammer. Following its complex rules, the Builders' Laborers Federation will not allow a union replacement—let alone one of the many unemployed young carpenters—to set foot in the Arts Center. The exhibition, with its attendant lectures and receptions, is postponed a month.

Here is a single mother, who has a graduate diploma in outdoor studies and experience in "non-sexist teaching," sending in a complaint to a government unit about discrimination because she can't get a job. The reason could be many things. Real wages may be too high, imposing structural unemployment; as a person the single mother may be a pain in the ass. But she is as certain as night follows day that she is unemployed because she's a woman, and one who "took the trouble to be a mother." She now asks the government to compensate her for these twin "handicaps." And the government does compensate her.

At lunch in Melbourne with Patrick McCaughey, the director of the National Gallery of Victoria, the talk turns to Premier Cain's announced intention to give his state yet one more Christmas–New Year holiday, December 31, in celebration of Victoria's 150th birthday. The plan horrifies business leaders, who estimate they would lose some $80 million in retail trade, with no reduction of their wages bill; to stay open on a declared holiday they would have to pay employees *double time-and-a-half* penalty rates. "Look, no one does much work that day anyway," says McCaughey, favoring the holiday, as if the existence of a string of holidays is an argument to add one more. "God, but the overtime costs for my gallery will be terrible," he adds, holding his head, though not in horror.

"Four or five young people go on the dole getting eighty-eight dollars each," says David Hackworth, the American military hero turned businessman. "Here in Queensland they can rent a nice house for a hundred twenty-five dollars a week, having one bedroom each. Enough is left over for food and drugs—and they surf all day." Adds Hackworth, who runs a restaurant and raises game birds: "We can't get kids to work for us. Where is Australia going to be in twenty years?"

"The New South Wales coal industry is virtually nationalized," I am told by Hugh Morgan, head of Western Mining Company, as he complains about a plethora of taxes and charges that have made the industry unprofitable. "That's classical capitalist exaggeration," retorts Premier Wran when I relate Morgan's gripe. "It's just one of those emotive points that someone can make as they down their fourth port at the Melbourne Club, when they feel a need to exorcise evil spirits. It makes them feel much better to talk that way—to say, 'That fellow Wran stole our marbles.' "

"The major tragedy of this country," remarks Creighton Burns, editor of *The Age* and a World War Two veteran, "is that we had a war on the heels of a big depression. And the war got us out of the depression. We didn't have to get out of it ourselves. If we had have, we might have recovered the inventiveness that we had—or seemed to have—around the turn of the century. In public policy, we apply what they do in America or West Germany or Canada; we haven't really had to think things through for ourselves. It's all derivative here."

After World War Two, Australia emerged without war damage and well poised to sell the world its wool and wheat and dairy products.

Such advantages, plus a growing domestic market provided by immigration, enabled manufacturing to spurt ahead. But after two or three decades these advantages ebbed. Terms of trade went against Australia's primary products, and an overprotected manufacturing sector was too inefficient to innovate and export. An initial minerals boom rescued the Australian standard of living. But iron ore, nickel, other minerals and a variety of energy resources have not proved a panacea. Prices have often been disappointing, and as the world goes high tech, less metal is being used. Since 1970, world demand for steel—once an index of economic growth—has risen only 26 percent, while world gross domestic product has risen 52 percent. Australia's share of world trade has been dropping like a meteor in the southern skies (3 percent in 1960, less than 1.2 percent today).

"It is clear that raw materials do not offer the growth prospects," says John Button, minister of industry, technology, and commerce, with a certain grim deliberateness, "that are needed to sustain the standard of living to which we aspire." "We just have to don a hair shirt," says Senator Gareth Evans, minister for resources and energy, as he tells me of coal mines closing because of soaring wage awards, "silly bloody-minded demarcation disputes" mounted by certain trade unions, an agricultural sector that is "just shot to pieces," and the threat of Brazil to Australia's traditional iron ore markets.

Some Third World countries that compete with Australia are subsidized, in effect, by the International Monetary Fund and the World Bank; they are permitted to dump their products at low prices in order to avoid loan default. So Australia loses out in the not-so-free marketplace. Australia borrows abroad—international debt now represents almost 30 percent of gross domestic product, compared with only 6 percent in 1980—to stave off a fall in living standards. Meanwhile the number of people employed in manufacturing has dropped from 28 percent of the work force in 1965 to 17 percent in 1985. Says Fraser McEwing, publisher of *The Ragtrader* in Sydney: "By the year 2000, the clothing industry—the making of garments and textiles—won't exist in Australia."

When I was at college, some feared that Southeast Asian countries might fail to resist the Communist threat and turn Australia into the "last domino." Today some fear that the capitalist economies of Singapore, Korea, and Taiwan might succeed so well that Australia will be left behind as a white backwater in a dynamic "yellow sea." Malcolm Fraser, speaking more frankly out of office than he did as prime minister, sees a danger that Australia "will continue to fall behind and watch one Asian state after another pass us by [in living standards] over the next twenty-five years."

The Hawke government understands the danger and probably has the intellectual answers to meet it. But does it have the political will? And do Australians *want* to put adventurous growth above middling security? The challenges are not small.

As agricultural exports slow and income levels from tomorrow's mineral export sales look uncertain, how to make Australian manufacturing more competitive in the dynamic Asian region with its low labor costs. How to prevent the entrenchment of a class of bitter drifters—youth unemployed—amounting at present to some 30 percent of their generation. How to balance the demands of the environmentalists with their new religion of awe for nature, and the Aborigines with their demand for the return of land sacred to them, with Australia's need to increase agricultural, mineral, and tourism revenues. In an age of clamor for rights, how to retain a sense of obligations. In the quest for social justice, how to avoid state guardianship which sucks liberty and crushes initiative. As myriad voices claim a share in the pie, how to ensure that the pie is big enough to go around. In the late 1960s, there were four taxpayers for each one person on welfare; by the end of the 1970s there were 2.5 taxpayers for each person on welfare. All sorts of shadows—from despair of the unemployed, to begging, to high-level corruption, to murderous Mafia in country towns—have begun to fall across the public life of the lucky country.

In Melbourne's City Square, as the former Liberal premier Sir Henry Bolte is leaving the platform with the federal Liberal leader Andrew Peacock, after both of them have spoken, a gnarled man on crutches shouts, "Are you sober today, Bolte?"

The former premier stops, turns, and glares. "Who said that?"

"You're drunk," asserts the man.

Sir Henry pokes his leathery face toward his critic. "I'm not."

A tall, resourceful-looking Liberal lady in tweeds takes Bolte's arm and steers him toward a waiting car. "Go away, you bastard," she snaps at the man on crutches.

"There goes a nice Liberal lady," coos the man. His tone changes. "She called me a bastard—the slut."

It is the national election of 1984, the eleventh in twenty years in one of the world's most election-ridden nations, and Australian democracy is expressing itself. The Hawke government faces Peacock's Liberal [conservative] Party, equipped with the most unideological—not to say vacuous—campaign theme the Labor Party has ever had: "Unstoppable, invincible, incredible, unbeatable, undeniable."[1]

There are two other parties of note. The National Party, which used to be called the Country Party, stands for traditional values from the bush. While not opposed to state intervention, it feels the Whitlam sociocultural reforms were a disaster. "The Labor Party," the National Party leader declares, "is the Kentucky Fried Chicken of politics—all left wings and bums." The Australian Democrats are a small party of mostly middle-class trendies who care passionately about peace, the environment, and animal welfare. "Mr. Hawke doesn't care about animals," says one of their candidates, "because they don't have a vote." Influential for some years, froth from the waves of the Whitlam age of reform, the Democrats will probably decline as Australia's mood edges to the right.

The election shows the deep inroads of American political techniques in Australia. The battle is fought in the media, and in American style it is as much the faces and styles of the party leaders as the philosophies of the parties that the voters are choosing between. Far fewer specific policy promises ("a dollar on to your pension, lady"; "ten dollars off your tax, mate") are given than even a decade ago. All parties—and not least the "party of principle," the Labor Party—use market research to identify the issues to be sloganized and sprayed at the people. And the sacred heart of the entire process is not debate, perhaps not even voting, but the endless taking of public opinion polls.

On the glaring summer day of the election I tour the voting booths of Melbourne Ports with Simon Crean, now president of the Australian Council of Trade Unions. This electorate, which Simon's father, Frank Crean, deputy prime minister in Whitlam's government, represented for many years, covers the inner suburbs of Albert Park, Middle Park, and South Melbourne. Young professionals and working-class families inhabit these wide leafy streets.

I go with one of Simon Crean's ACTU colleagues to fetch Margaret Fisher, granddaughter of Scottish-born Labor Party prime minister Andrew Fisher of seventy years ago. "My pension is too low and the tax on it is too high," she tells me as she prepares to mark her ballot for Labor. Miss Fisher has a good word for Malcolm Fraser: "He paid for

1. Peacock was replaced as Liberal leader by John Howard in the spring of 1985.

me to go to a festival in Scotland in 1979." Old people, grumbling
about inflation, vote early at the polling booths in schools, churches,
and halls. They walk by stalls at which church groups and others take
advantage of the day to sell jam, cookies, and handicrafts. Younger
people vote later, on their way to the beach, mostly silently, with an
enigmatic or cynical quip here and there. A girl's T-shirt says, "Don't
Be Caught with Your Plants Down." A boy's says, "Sex Appeal—Give
Generously." (Far away in the outback, 4,000 voters have voting
booths brought to them in the form of twin- and single-engined planes,
with electoral officers at the throttle, at a cost of $50,000, or $12.50
a head.)

Bitterness surfaces over nuclear disarmament. A few prominent
people have left the Labor Party and—joined by Peter Garrett, star
singer in the rock group Midnight Oil, and other artistic figures and
anti-bomb activists—have formed the Nuclear Disarmament Party,
which is "standing" (you don't "run" for office in Australia) for the
first time. A tight-lipped Quaker and longtime peace worker in her
thirties hands out how-to-vote leaflets for the NDP. She is not on speaking terms with her former Labor Party colleagues chatting and smoking
on the footpath a few steps away.

Max Gillies, a hilarious TV comedian whose imitations of Hawke,
Bjelke-Petersen, Peacock, and other politicians are alarmingly good,
comes by to vote at South Melbourne Town Hall, overweight in a pair
of shorts, with a baby in one arm. Like many voters, he politely takes
a card from all the party workers, but his expressive face is at this
moment without expression. Today's election is calm compared with
some passionate confrontations in the eras of Menzies, Whitlam, and
Fraser. "This is the first time I'm not working the booths all day,"
Simon Crean remarks. "I'm playing tennis later."

At lunchtime, as I sit with Frank Crean over corned beef, salad, and
a bottle of Hunter Valley red wine, Simon comes into his parents'
kitchen in a lemon-yellow tennis outfit to fetch cheese scones that his
mother has baked for the afternoon at the tennis club. We chat for a
moment about Wesley College, my old school, now extremely expensive, where Simon's small son is signed up years in advance. I wonder
if Frank Crean's grandson twenty years from now will be voting Labor,
Liberal, or something new and different?

Simon Crean, a rising star in the Labor Party, is a new-style union
leader, poles apart from the grizzled sons of the Depression whom I
knew at the Melbourne Trades Hall in the 1960s. A few weeks before,

Crean and I were standing together at a morning party to observe the U.S. election returns—virtually to celebrate the re-election of Ronald Reagan—at the consulate-general in Melbourne. Waiting for a telecast of the first results, we glanced at our watches to check the time in New York. Crean worked out the U.S. east coast time before I did. "I just had a call from New York," he explained, "from a guy I know asking for an appointment with me next week. That's how I happen to know the New York time."

"From a trade-union official?"

"No, a stockbroker." Crean said yes to the request. Not long ago it was rare for senior Australian union figures to have this kind of American contact. As the Creans and I chat in the kitchen, the topic of the U.S.A. comes up, and on every aspect of it, from the Kennedy family to policy in Nicaragua, Simon is a little more favorably inclined to the U.S.A. than his father.

"It just amazes me," says Frank Crean, who was a member of the Labor Party caucus for decades, "that Hawke could become leader of the opposition after less than three years in caucus." The prime minister has not spent long years in the intense familylike brotherhood and combat of Labor Party life. "No Labor Party leader has ever been so removed from and opposed by the party structure as Hawkie," observes Simon before going off to play tennis.

After lunch I resume my tour of the polling booths and meet an elderly Liberal Party worker. "They're going to move a hospital from our area out to Sunshine, which is wrong," she complains, clinging to local issues in the face of poor national prospects. "We're against the plan for new brothels here," says a middle-aged Liberal woman. "The Labor Party is more open-minded about that sort of thing," she adds, pronouncing "open-minded" gingerly.

I am offered the Liberal ticket by a plump platinum blonde from Tasmania. "We're from the land," she explains, "and so we always vote Liberal." This time she's keen to help the conservative side because the environmentalists have annoyed her. "The socialists pin their notices on trees! They say they're for the environment, but their own messages are wrecking our trees!" This lady, who came to Victoria because of poor job opportunities in the Apple Isle, says that at the technology firm where she works she avoids talking about politics. "Everyone is socialist," she says with a grimace. "It was Whitlam that did it—they all got their education and their start then."

In the safety-net society, supervised by a guardian state, voting is compulsory. You are fined up to fifty dollars if you are over eighteen and fail to exercise your democratic rights! From the legacy of convict society comes compulsory voting. And compulsory voting spurs the advance of market research.

In the evening I go to the local Labor Party's election celebration. By now we know that the Hawke government is back but with a reduced majority. The victor in Melbourne Ports, Clyde Holding, who is minister for Aboriginal affairs, blames a campaign that was too long for the somewhat disappointing result. He and Simon Crean, beer can in hand like everyone else, make speeches, trying to be excited. But Australians are too honest to be good at hype or theatrics. These Labor people are tired and subdued and they do not try to pretend otherwise.

This day half a million Australians (more than the population of Tasmania) vote informal (incorrect ballots). In large part the election has been a battle between Hawke and this void. The Labor Party vote nationwide drops 3.8 percent; the "informal" vote jumps 4.3 percent; most of the rest stays much the same.

To Americans an election is about themselves, but to Australians it's about "them"—the politicians. Few feel an American-type participatory passion. David Kemp, a political scientist at Monash University who for a time worked in the Fraser government, says social science research bears out this impression. "In Australia few people see elections as an important basis for compliance with the law," his surveys have found. More than the citizens of any other Western nation, Australians give the fear of punishment as the main reason for complying with the law. They focus on the law itself, not on the process that made the law. "There is a low awareness of democratic values," concludes Professor Kemp. "The ideological basis of legitimacy is weak." Kemp's surveys found 64 percent agreeing with the statement "Most political conflicts are unnecessary." In a country not threatened from outside, and knowing very little parlous suffering within, the jockeying for place goes on within a vacuum of meaning—tolerated by a bored public.

Somehow Max Gillies's lines on TV seem more memorable than anything the politicians have said. "Mr. Hawke today addressed an audience of household appliances . . ." And, "Mr. Hawke today turned loaves and fishes into an American tracking station."

"What do you *mean* by government?" rasps Lang Hancock in Perth when I inquire his views on current policies. "It's a joke to say the elected representatives of the people are the government." The mining tycoon gives a bitter laugh. "The real government of this country has four arms: The giant bureaucracy, expanding according to Parkinson's law, which no one can sack. The trade union chiefs, who don't change with an election, and who are largely outside the controls of the law. The press, which shapes the opinions of those people who can't think, and that means most people. And the fourth arm is the pressure groups with their hand in the till, obtaining quotas, subsidies, hand-outs." Hancock clicks his tongue in disgust.

"I haven't voted for a while," says my niece Claire Watt as we review the election. She shrugs her shoulders when reminded of the fine for not voting. "The choice between the Labor Party and the Liberal Party is like between brown sugar and white sugar—either way it's sugar. You could get a coalition between them without upsetting their platforms very much."

A few weeks later I talk with Labor stalwart Richard Hall in his Sydney home. "Recently I addressed the Concerned Librarians about the spy issue," says Hall, who is a specialist on the topic of espionage. "A young woman, heavily involved in the Back to the Earth Movement, asked me if I know Jim Cairns, and I said yes." Both Hall and I have long known Cairns, deputy prime minister under Whitlam and for many years the uncrowned king of the Labor Party left. "The woman asked me if I think he's employed by the British secret service to undermine the Back to the Earth Movement." Hall gives a quick, dry laugh. "My God, she asks such a question about the hero of the 150,000 in Bourke Street [a famous anti–Vietnam war march in 1968]! The whole anti–Vietnam war cause has passed away. To the kids today, Vietnam is like *The Guns of Navarone.*" As the old class lines fade and issues become increasingly technical, politics has become professional and bland and well bankrolled—for those outside it, little more than a branch of the entertainment industry—and it does not have much emotional connection to the lives of young people.

"Somehow over Mount Kosciusko you undergo a change," says deputy Liberal leader Neil Brown of his hundreds of flights from Melbourne to Canberra, "and when you step out of the plane in Canberra all problems have become easier to solve. Canberra has even got its own language, unknown to ordinary Australians. Things are 'accessed.' Leaders 'resile' on their policies."

Canberra, where brilliant paper schemes are hatched, is insulated from reality by the cotton wool of bureaucracy, kept company only by nature and liquor. It is not like a city, not like a country town, and not like the outback. Running into Paul Everingham at the Katherine Show, I ask the federal member for the Northern Territory how he found Canberra upon his transfer there from Darwin (where he had been chief minister). "Going to Canberra," he replies, "was like going back to boarding school."

"Canberra is spoiled and incestuous," Malcolm Fraser, who now lives on his farm west of Melbourne, remarks to me disapprovingly. "The media owners ought to send their Canberra reporters away for three years somewhere else," the former prime minister suggests. "Send them to Singapore." He laughs. "Send them to Melbourne or Sydney to get into the real world. The press gallery pretends to interpret government to all of Australia but [they] don't even know how to speak to ordinary Australians."

People far from Canberra quip that in Australia everybody is equal, except the bureaucrats who are well paid to keep people that way. Across the world many capital cities are weighed down by an obsession with politics, but in Canberra there is no industry in town but government. In its national capital you realize that Australia has to be a federation, for Australians cannot identify with such an antiseptic place. Federalism makes for legalism and this—together with the capital's artificiality and the nation's vast distances—explains much in Australian life. The federal system savagely redistributes. Outlying states receive two or three times as much Canberra money per head as the populous states. "I ask honorable members," cried Paul Everingham—the member for the Northern Territory and perhaps the most conservative politician in the national parliament—in his maiden speech, "what is federation about if it is not to assist the disadvantaged areas of Australia?"

The Canberra government has the money, it is said, the state governments have the power, and local government has the problems. "Australia is one of the most overgoverned countries in the world," complains Perth businessman Warren Jones, expressing a view that is common in the frontier states. "Canberra is a bureaucratic jungle and probably one of the greatest mistakes ever made," he adds from his office desk overlooking the Swan River, 3,600 kilometers from Canberra.

Yet if Canberra poses and struts, the delightful thing about Australia is that people elsewhere have the freedom to mock it. Brisbane, Perth, Hobart, and Darwin do not take Canberra more seriously than money requires them to do. Geography, which requires federalism, saves Australia from a stifling centralized establishment that its political-industrial ways might otherwise land it with. These political-industrial ways stem from the nation's origins as a government camp, from Benthamism, and from Justice Henry Higgins's formulation eighty years ago of the worker's "right" to be looked after regardless of conditions in the marketplace.

"Remember," says Greg Lindsay of the Center for Independent Studies in Sydney, "for its first twenty years Australia was pretty much a Communist society." Historian Geoffrey Blainey points out that the convict system was a welfare state system. "In the early nineteenth century it was safer to sail to Australia as a convict than to sail as a free man to America. There were doctors on board the ships."

A key to Australian pragmatism and government-mindedness is that Australians never had to mount a struggle for political power. They have had to concern themselves only with using power to make life more comfortable. The growth *in one decade* of new bodies to which a Melbourne citizen may turn and ask the government to do something for him is amazing. The state level has seen the establishment of an Ombudsman, Equal Opportunity Board, Motor Car Traders Committee, Small Claims Tribunal, Residential Tenancies Tribunal, and a prices branch to the consumer affairs ministry. Federally, the Melbourne citizen has a further array of new bodies to hear and act upon his complaints: Human Rights Commission, Social Security Appeals Tribunal, Commonwealth Ombudsman, Trade Practices Commission, and (for the vast army who are government servants) Grievance and Appeals Tribunal.

Already a quarter of Australian workers are employed by governments, and the newspapers are full of ads for extra positions, far outnumbering, it seems, the positions that business firms advertise. A letter writer to *The Australian* counted that in one issue of the newspaper—in June 1986, amidst an economic crisis—460 government jobs at a total salary bill of $16 million each year were advertised. Similarly there are government notices on page after page soliciting "submissions" to myriad commissions, boards, and inquiries, to help federal or state government wield the baton of supervision.

"It's true that many businessmen fail to speak up for business values," Hugh Morgan of Western Mining says when I ask if he doesn't sometimes feel lonely in his own outspokenness. "It's because they're mendicants, dependent on government handouts." "In this country," says former minister Tony Staley, "business lives with the government of the day. It recognizes that when you get into bed with the government you may get more than a good night's sleep, but get into bed it does.

"Conservatism in Australia is less radical than in the U.S. or the UK," adds Staley, whose views illustrate how far from free marketism many Liberals have been in recent years. "Australians like to see themselves as being in the middle. When I was minister for telecommunications, no one said I ought to sell off Telecom to the private sector. And if I'd tried, I wouldn't have lasted long as minister." Even the National Party, which says it stands for a market economy, small government, lower taxes, and individual initiative, in fact favors few of these things—but rather massive government subsidy and intervention—when it comes to demands on the state by rural Australia, its power base.

"Australians laugh at Americans with all their gadgets," says the acerbic Neil Brown, "but producing these things employs people. Australians don't understand this American dynamism. Here, all is government. Today a grant for 'Artists in the Community,' tomorrow a board set up to assist one-legged colored homosexual immigrants. Ordinary people are unconcerned with the issues the 'new political class' talk about," claims Brown, who joins his Liberal leader, John Howard, in speaking out against big government, sometimes doing battle with elements inside their own party. "These things are just hobbies created by government and various lobbying groups. Polemical reports are produced on this and that by people with degrees in 'media studies,' and then imperious voices ask *why* the report has not been implemented."

Despite these criticisms many ordinary Australians do not object to the busybody state. The Sydney-pragmatic wing of the Labor Party, which today spearheads the political class, stands for political-industrial ways that are rooted in geography and culture. These roots run deep in Australian society.

In the states, as distinct from Canberra, power has frequently been wielded by farmer-politicians. "Bolte was really a farmer," Vernon Wilcox says approvingly of the premier he served. "Playford [who reigned in South Australia for two decades] was an orchardist. Bjelke-Petersen is a man of the land too. The outback has a cleansing effect on the soul," adds the former Victorian attorney general, who himself has a large farm. "People have to be fair dinkum there."

Bjelke-Petersen's idea of a holiday is to go out to his son's property and, with his son on one tractor and himself on another, to sweep aside the scrub. "Feeding the chooks" is his term for press conferences. "On the land you have to use initiative to survive," Sir Joh remarks when I ask about the influence on him of life on the land. "There's no substitute for this kind of experience." An expression of distaste comes to the Queensland premier's mouth. "But look at some politicians down in Canberra. You can see they're just school kids."

The self-reliance and initiative espoused by the farmer-politicians are persistent strands in Australia's political culture but not dominant strands. The norm is government-mindedness from above and a mentality of depending on government from below. Historically there were two traditions, as Blainey points out in *A Land Half Won:* the convict and the free settler. One made for state dependence, the second made for initiative, thrift, and self-help. Today it is the state-dependent tradition that sets the tone for Australian political and economic life.

Here are cinema exhibitors "warning" the government that home video growth threatens them, and demanding that video be restrained. It is assumed that the government should intervene—social trends and market forces be damned. "Make sure your mother gets the fifty percent cab deal," says Simon Crean to the hostess at a dinner party in a reference to a half-price subsidy for elderly taxi riders. "The government spent five million on that scheme last year," the union chief adds proudly.

Here is the federal government giving a massive subsidy to enable Broken Hill Proprietary, Australia's biggest company, to launch cement and steel ventures with China. BHP comes out during 1984 with huge ads hailing the steel agreement as a triumph of Hawke's idea of consensus, whereby government, business, and unions pull together. "I thought it was a little un-BHP," says Brian Rowe, who worked for the company for some thirty years, with a trace of embarrassment. "I mean, to say in an ad how much we owe to the current regime! But it was very clever."

The China steel plans are delayed in 1985, and I ask the prime minister if he's disappointed. "Obviously the concept was right," he replies, "but BHP and the Chinese didn't seem to be able to go that last little bit on price." One would have thought that prices should have been central to the entire deal from the start.

A researcher at the Institute of Family Studies giving a talk on "state help" for those in distress takes as an example the case of a young couple who ran into practical and marital difficulties while building their own house! "Part-time work would help solve many social problems," she goes on to say. "Families find, as in Sweden, that after taxes you do as well with part-time work as with full-time work." Offering solutions to various social problems that all carry horrendous economic implications, she ends by demanding that the state "get rid of poverty," as if that were as simple as getting rid of trash.

I am talking about painters and writers with the director of the National Gallery of Victoria, Patrick McCaughey, and the name of a well-known novelist comes up. "It's wonderful that she's now getting support," he observes as we inspect Australian landscapes, and it comes as a shock to realize that he means a government grant, not support in the sense of a wide book-buying public or any other sort of *reader* response.

If Americans seem to breathe by freedom, Australians can be equivocal about it. "Australians are profoundly uninterested in liberty," bluntly declares Senator Gareth Evans, who was Hawke's first attorney general. "There's no interest in the free speech issue in Australia," says this long-time fighter for civil liberties, "and very little in the fair trial issue." The minister for resources and energy bitterly recalls the difficult career of his cherished draft Bill of Rights: "I knew the public cared little. What's been disappointing is how little the Hawke labor movement cares—most of the Parliamentary Labor Party feels the issue can't win votes, but only lose them. And that reflects the community—there's no concept [of liberty]."

In a harsh land ruled for a long time by a benign colonial power, citizens have seen disadvantages as well as advantages in forthright declarations of freedom. Most of them are Benthamite enough to think that security matters as much as liberty—and liberty's offshoot, enterprise—and one has the impression that young people are even less enterprising than older people.

"The add-ons are destroying industry," complains Warren Jones in Perth. "An allowance because it rained one point and someone got mud on his shoe. Money to get more helmets because the present ones have got a scratch on them. Hawke boasts of the Accord [a pact between government, business, and unions], but the Accord doesn't cover these add-ons." Jones sees a loss of will to work. "People want to get paid for not working, for getting pregnant. They want a special holiday allowance on the basis that they might have worked overtime if they didn't go on holiday." The self-made executive of the Bond Corporation points to fundamentals. "It should be remembered that productivity was what made countries great."

"Australians in general are spoiled," argues Jack Chia, the Singapore businessman who has a Melbourne base. "They were not born with a silver spoon in their mouths, but with a golden spoon!" Chia, who operates in ten countries, is scornful of public policy in Australia. "Tax the rich to pay for the lazy is the Australian system. No politician will change it, because they fear to lose votes." Chia leans back in his chair at his Melbourne mansion. "If Australians worked as hard as Chinese, the GNP here would be three to five times what it is. Perhaps when Australians are cornered they will act differently. At the moment they are not cornered."

"After Hours" and "Work Stoppage" are phrases that haunt me wherever I go in Australia. I find I cannot get a drink in a grand hotel in Melbourne on a Sunday evening because penalty rates make it unprofitable for management to offer service after hours. At the beautiful new blue and ocher Beaufort Hotel in Darwin the cafe menu states that there is a 10 percent surcharge on Sundays and public holidays. It strikes a sour note, and for the visitor to Australia it makes Sundays and public holidays seem dead before he can give them a chance. In Newcastle, a coal city in New South Wales, twenty-two hungry ships are getting no coal because a rail strike frustrates the loading process. The ships, mostly Japanese and South Korean, are switching orders for coal from Australia to South Africa. Yet work stoppages are accepted as a fact of life, like the weather, both by the Arbitration and Conciliation Commission, with its awesome power of compulsory arbitration to set minimum wages, and, more surprisingly, by many businessmen.

In some ways the trade union mentality and the public service mentality are similar. The union leader, putting security before all else, is the mirror image of the Canberra bureaucrat who does the same—and so conformism overwhelms the spirit of enterprise. "The trade unions are the most conservative institution in Australia," says Creighton Burns of *The Age*.

When I discuss with union leader Simon Crean the drastic aging of the Australian population—today the average age is thirty, by the year 2021 it will be thirty-nine—his entire concern is to lock in superannuation benefits for union members before the crunch comes. He has nothing to offer on the size-of-the-pie issue: how tomorrow's pensions are to be financed by a work force that is shrinking as a percentage of the population. "To advocate capacity to pay and market forces," says Crean, "inevitably means that the industrially strong benefit at the expense of those sectors not able to exert market pressure." With all the sharp economic challenges facing Australia, the immensely influential president of the trade union federation offers nothing but unreconstructed Higginsism. Most Australians realize that belts have to be pulled in, but Crean insists that once the unions have achieved a gain— such as 17½ percent extra pay for holiday periods—it is impossible under any circumstances to give it up. Importers lose when the Australian dollar plummets. Exporters lose when metals prices fall. Why should only the unions be exempt from chill winds in the economic environment?

"The belief that Australian people are lazy isn't true," says a very successful Malaysian-born businessman, Lee Ming Tee. "They just need to be given incentive." There is the promise, but there too is the terror. In its small-world cronyism, Australia has grown into what the economists of the 1984 Brookings Institution study, *The Australian Economy,* call a "rent-seeking society."

"Everyone gets a cut in the apparatus of protection," an economist at Griffith University in Brisbane points out. "The shops are closed on Sundays and it's said, 'You're fucking up the tourist industry; the foreigners aren't able to buy their stuffed koalas on a Sunday!' The accused talk back: 'Oh, you're in the bread trade, aren't you? You benefit from the bread marketing arrangement. Oh, you're in milk, aren't you? What about the Milk Board?' " The economist, who is an American, sighs. "No one will cast the first stone."

"Australians are supposed to be rebels," chips in another academic who is listening, "but really we are great conformists. We accept authority." I am reminded of the fatalism induced by the bush that runs through Australian history. The American economist goes on: "There was a whole market strategy in which, historically, protection and racism were intertwined." But that was another era, I say to myself, when Australia was a British outpost. Surely an Australia enriched by diverse waves of immigrants cannot be the same?

"For years at Lizard Island we had no unions," says Sir Sydney Williams, the head of Air Queensland and a major tourism entrepreneur in the north, in his simple Cairns office. "We had a marvelous staff—until one particular bitch complained she didn't get this, she didn't get that. Then the unions came in. The next year our wage bill doubled." Williams, who develops idyllic islands in Queensland because "people have to fly to islands and that puts bums into aircraft," is unsure about Australia's tourism future. "Leisure is our greatest growth industry, but the trade unions are going to root it [screw it up]. It's crazy. I mean, on Lizard Island Sunday is no different from bloody Monday, but we have to pay triple time for Sunday work."

Williams sees overregulation of airlines as a further obstacle to tourism. "We wouldn't have flights between Cairns and Tokyo," he explains, referring to a new service by Qantas and Japan Airlines, "but for Air Nippon applying to come here. Everyone in Canberra was

terrified. Qantas had to get off their bums to hold Air Nippon at bay."
But even Sir Sydney finds geographic reality holding him back from
a free market position. "With open skies," he says, explaining why
he opposes domestic airline deregulation, "Melbourne and Sydney
wouldn't give a bloody damn about us up here in north Queensland."

Tom Burns in Brisbane voices the Labor Party objection that airline deregulation would jeopardize safety. "I'll tell you frankly," he
says, arguing for the superior safety of Australian over American airlines. "I flew around the world once with Pan Am, and the people I
knew in maintenance work in World War Two said to me when I got
back to Brisbane, 'Tom, don't buy a ticket in the casket [Queensland's
lottery]. You've used up all your luck.' "

"God, what medium-sized country is going to survive without an
accord between unions and business?" exclaims Richard Hall, the Sydney author and Labor activist. "Do we want a Scargill situation? Hasn't
anyone heard of Japanese industrial policy?" Part of the point about
Australian public ways is contained in Hall's words. Here is a small
population enjoying the quiet fellowship of its antipodean remoteness.
Where is the incentive or the pressure for change?

"In Australia for a long time there's been an attempt to blame
unions for a lot of the ills of the economy," remarks Prime Minister
Hawke in his Canberra office. "The unfortunate fact is that at times
some unions by their actions have given a basis for that concern." Still,
Hawke puts it to me in late 1985 that the unions have made a greater
contribution to his Accord than has business. "They could do better
in the labor market than they did under the Accord," he claims.

Recently, a minister of the Crown was charged with the crime of accepting bribes in return for the premature release of prisoners. The case
was in Sydney, yet the increasing corruption in Australia is by no means
limited to New South Wales. "Back in the forties and fifties," says Melbourne editor Creighton Burns, "I believed we had an incorruptible
public service. Well, it's been partially corrupted by organized crime."

Who can define corruption, especially in Australia, where power
and wealth have until recently been very timid with each other? The
Menzies era did not lack ruthless operators. John McEwen used the
press to crush colleagues and risked Australia's economic interests to
extract a mite of advantage for his narrow-minded farmers' party. No
one has ever been more cynical in misrepresenting the aims of the
Labor Party than Menzies himself. Menzies and McEwen played their

cards close to the chest, and perhaps we were ignorant of what they might have done for private advantage. Yet I feel the use of power *for profit* was rare in Australia before the 1970s.

"The essence of the Whitlam cultural revolution," says Fraser McEwing, the Sydney fashion publisher, "was a widespread challenge to authority. There is now a backlash against that, but it takes a quiet form. People are leading more self-reliant lives. For instance, they're evading taxes. There's a feeling, if only the government would let me do this, or that, I could get very rich."

"When I came back from the U.S.A.," says Creighton Burns, referring to his promotion from foreign correspondent of *The Age* to the editor's chair, "I was negotiating a salary package with the paper, and the managing director said, 'We have this tax consultant at our service. Why don't you go and talk to him.' I went to see this professional, and he put before me a proposition which, if it didn't break the law, certainly bent it very badly." Burns is wide-eyed. "Here is this man with a big reputation in the law and accountancy giving me this advice with a straight face. In my old-fashioned nonconformist way I was a little shocked. This sort of thing has now become very widespread," Burns adds. Meanwhile politics costs big money, as it never did in Menzies's day, increasing the danger of office and profit seeking drawing too close.

"In our period of sustained prosperity," Burns goes on, referring to the years prior to the 1970s, "the idea that making a lot of money was an easy thing to do, and the natural thing to do, took root everywhere. Then things tightened up, and there was a concentration on how to hang on to what you had—even if you'd bent the rules a bit to get it. The tax man became the target—a tax evasion industry sprouted. Tax evasion became a legitimate thing to do."

It is hard not to associate the corruption with Australia's "rent-seeking society." The marginal tax rate is very high, the incentive to evade taxation is great (because the income tax bears the overwhelming weight of all taxation), and in the pressures of the 1970s human nature caught up with a flawed system. As once on the goldfields, matey hedonism became flecked with a tendency to grab an easy catch.

"Mateship is not universal anymore," says Creighton Burns reflectively. "Not everyone is your mate." Today the mate is the guy who uses his power to help you make a profit, or the guy who uses his money to help you get an appointment, or the guy who commits a crime to help you get money for drugs. To a degree the new corruption is merely an end to innocence as Australia has become a consumer-oriented society. In the decline first of ideology and then of religion that has undermined the cause of Bob Santamaria's National Civic Council one sees, perhaps, a mirror image of the process. "I think politics is about serious things," the Catholic polemicist says sadly as he surveys the "self-indulgent" public life of today. "There are no Catholics in the Labor Party," he observes. He sees "wealthy left-wing trendies" filling the party, which for him was a crusade rather than a vehicle for personal advancement. He dismisses Hawke as the representative of a soft age. "His whole life is an essay in self-indulgence, and that doesn't make for toughness in a crisis." In Santamaria's eyes hype above and consumerism below have changed Australia.

At movie houses a special rate is listed for the unemployed. A new underclass has appeared in the lucky country that for decades considered full employment a possessed gospel—joining an underclass of old people on pensions. Kathy is nineteen, lives in a Melbourne suburb, and has never had a job. She has been unemployed and on the dole since she had to leave school for health reasons at sixteen. "One of the girls here [at the unemployed youths' center] said she'd probably die before she got a job," Kathy says. "Down here you're over the hill at nineteen if you haven't had any experience. You have to be sixteen or seventeen, and then the only work you can get is as a check-out chick."

The Hawke government's Accord between business, unions, and government, achieved by "consensus," expresses a security-minded sense of Australia Incorporated. For a while it spurred economic growth and reduced industrial strife. But one problem with this cozy Benthamism and Higginsism is that significant segments of Australian society are slipping through the net of protection and consensus. At Hawke's Summit—held in Canberra's Parliament House, as if the state as a representation of power groups had replaced the state as a representation of individuals—business and unions moved in symbiosis. In the cloudy heights of Hawke's consensus, the class struggle has become the class waltz; but the young unemployed and many of the aged feel they are losing their political voices.

"Our system of wage determination constitutes a crime against society," says John Stone, who resigned in anger from his post as head of the treasury department in 1984. "Trade union leaders and people preening themselves as 'justices' of various arbitration benches combine to put young people . . . out of work."

"Justice Higgins," says Professor Blainey, in a reference to the pioneer of the Australian living-wage concept, "created unemployment on a massive scale. He said it was better for people not to have jobs than to have jobs that were underpaid. Well, his wish has been granted." The Arbitration Commission is almost a totem in Australian political culture. People boast of it; there are arguments about it that are always won by the commission's defenders. Back in 1964, as a tutor at Melbourne University, I graded the statewide high school exam in social studies and one question ran: "Wage-fixing in Australia should be left to economists instead of judges. Discuss." But despite a thousand discussions the system endures.

There are some young people who prefer not to work; the dole is fifty dollars per week for people under eighteen (rising higher after six months), eighty-eight dollars for those eighteen to twenty (much more for marrieds and those over twenty-one), and it can go on indefinitely. And a minority of economists doubt that youth unemployment would drop substantially if adult wages were less high, and if lower wages for beginning workers were permitted. Nevertheless many economists and many ordinary citizens agree with Stone (who was a schoolmate of Prime Minister Hawke's in Perth) that the high wage determinations by the Arbitration Commission have greatly added to Australia's unemployment problem.

The wages explosion under Whitlam in 1974, equal pay for women, and the second wages explosion under Fraser in 1981–82 together increased unemployment greatly. It is very difficult for an economy quickly to absorb, as Australia did in the 1970s, an increase in the ratio between official minimum wage rates for women and those for men from some 70 percent to more than 90 percent.

To the authors of the Brookings Institution study it seems almost beyond belief that in Australia youth unemployment can be a sort of sealed box, that an army of young people presumably willing to work for less than the judge-determined wage does not "exert some downward pressure on the rate of wage increase." "Making unemployment benefits available to sixteen- or seventeen-year-olds," says former prime minister Malcolm Fraser, "is one of the unkindest things any society could do. For a country like Australia to say to people of that age that the best we can offer you is unemployment benefits is saying something harsh and cruel."

It all goes back to Justice Higgins, to the long-entrenched Arbitration and Conciliation Commission, and in the end to the cultural phenomenon of a conformist approach to trade union membership and a low value put on innovative ways and the entrepreneurial spirit. "You can never give up what you have gained," says Patricia Caswell, a Melbourne trade union official, when I ask if the trade unions could not do more about youth unemployment, "because the redistribution of wages is not controllable." Her solution: "Why don't they get some of the wealth that's in the top fifty families?"

"I don't want to sound cynical about this," says another high trade union official. "But while there are ten percent unemployed, there are ninety percent in employment." Tom Burns in Brisbane remarks, "The pie is there; it's just that some pepole are getting too bloody much of it." The Queensland politician holds to the classic Australian Labor view: "It's not the job of the unions to fight unemployment. The union's job is to fight for its members—and its members generally have jobs."

Meanwhile the Australian middle-class way of running a suburban household as a workshop of Jeffersonian self-reliance is not helpful to the economy. Here is a senior Canberra civil servant, a fat cat as such are called by thinner cats, who paints his own house, builds his own swimming pool, and does all sorts of other jobs that an American on the same salary would pay others to do for him.

A solution for youth unemployment is not in sight but Lady Mary Fairfax has a suggestion. "As in Austria, work and education should be closely linked. Youth should start work part time while they're still at school; then they're more likely to be useful when they leave school and start work." She complains that education is out of touch with economic realities. "Greek, Latin, ancient history—great things, but what are you going to do with them?"

For wealthy Mary Fairfax, this is the one issue that could attract her into politics. "I'd encourage a street trade unionism, a barter system for the exchange of services to make life better."

"I'd have to wish you good luck with the trade unions, Lady Fairfax."

"But the people I want to mobilize are the out-of-work and the retired. They'll help each other. I'd put orphanages next door to old people's homes—they're meant for each other. The Chinese know all about this. Kids need love, and old people are longing to give love."

There are trends and voices that call into question the adequacy of protection, centrally fixed wages, and a general spirit of government-mindedness for tomorrow. Those who want a dynamic and cosmopolitan Australia—as well as those left out of Hawke's consensus—see Higginsism and Benthamism as enemies of tomorrow's Australia.

Small business suffers, many feel, as government and unions and corporations stroke each other. Here is a very successful manufacturer of toiletries in Melbourne, Colbar Proprietary Limited, with sales of $2 million, thirty employees, and a company profit of $100,000. Its managing director, Tom Colcheedas, draws a salary of $35,000. "Look at the net result," says Colcheedas. "The $100,000 company profit, after company tax of $46,000, and personal income tax at 61 percent, is reduced to $22,000." The managing director goes on: "The government gets the following: $650,000 in sales tax (32.5 percent on each toiletry), $100,000 in group tax for myself and employees; $15,000 in payroll tax; $46,000 in company tax; and $32,000 in personal income tax. A grand total of $843,000 in revenue for the government."

Australian youth is tending to the right, as has already occurred in the U.S.A. and parts of Europe. It was a straw in the wind when the Australian Union of Students collapsed in 1984 because it departed from grassroots student opinion. Wagnerian struggles over abstract global ideologies, the trumpeting of 1983 as the Year of the Lesbian, and working with prostitutes' collectives all undermined the Union's standing with students who care mostly about housing, jobs, scholarships, and educational issues.

At times one has the impression that people on the left are cautiously adjusting their view of Australia's traditional political-industrial ways. During our lunch in Melbourne I ask the novelist Helen Garner how she feels about strikes. "Furious—the more so the older I get. A mail strike in Sydney, and no letter from friends for six weeks!" She stops, puts down her fork, and stares at me. "Do you ask everybody that question?" She continues in a measured way: "I try to control myself over strikes, because I know my information is filtered through newspapers hostile to the workers."

There are some new conservatives—classical liberals—who attack the state-dependent tradition in the name of individual initiative. "I have a strong personal grounding in a small-business environment," says John Howard, the cerebral opposition leader and former treasurer in the Fraser government, when I ask how he has escaped the mindcast of government paternalism that affects even his Liberal Party. "I was brought up in an atmosphere where you didn't look to government handouts, and it was almost a sign of weakness to work for the government."

"Deregulating the labor market will be at the top of my agenda," he tells me in his Sydney office in late 1985. "We'll start at the small business end. This will provide people with the freedom to go outside the present system if they wish and make contracts on an enterprise basis. It will involve some reduction in trade union power. It has to be done, though, it really does."

Howard, a rationalist who scorns image-making, and a decade younger than Hawke, feels the wind blows his way. "Middle Australia now regards the excess of power by the unions as being one of the nation's major problems." The energetic bespectacled opposition leader says he believes privatization will be welcomed, "as long as two concerns are taken care of along the way: providing services to remote areas, and ensuring that employees of the large utilities are not unfairly disadvantaged." With a vision of tourism's potential, the Liberal Party leader plans to "deregulate the airlines, get rid of penalty rates, free up the labor market in the tourist area, and get our society onto a twenty-four-hour, seven-day-week basis."

I mention to John Howard that some of Hawke's ministers see a rightward shift of mood and tell me they intend to move further to the right to contain it. "I don't think they'll be able to, though," he comments. "Mondale couldn't."

"Mondale was a prisoner of interest groups," I suggest.

"These fellows are too," rejoins Howard, and perhaps this remains a key point about the Labor Party, even under Hawke. "Mr. Hawke hasn't been a consistent opponent of the left," the opposition leader goes on. "He became president of the ACTU [the national union organization] with the support of the left. Then he became leader of the Labor Party with the support of the right." Howard pauses and smiles slightly. "People who do that, when they fall from grace, that sort of gymnastics tends to be visited upon them."

"The interesting thing about the new conservatives," says *The Age* editor, Creighton Burns, who does not like them much, "is how long it took them to get up their courage to speak out. Would they survive a long period of growth—such as we had from the late 1940s through to the 1960s?" Burns pauses, as if to appeal for agreement. "The call to tighten belts, financially and morally, only has impact when society is under pressure."

The Australian economy remains under severe pressure, and Howard may well be correct that the winds are blowing in the direction of his policies. Just as Whitlam's age of reform reached beyond the parameters of its left-wing political inspiration and became for a season a movement for changes widely favored, so the door may now be open for a market-oriented conservatism to carry Australia with it. Especially if Australians in their millions should come to the conclusion that a safety-net society is a stagnant society.

Regionally, especially in Queensland, there is a real conservative alternative to the left in the realm of social values. Yet Premier Bjelke-Petersen's National Party does not eschew economic interventionism. "Joh's taxed the hell out of the coal miners," complains the head of a Melbourne conservative think tank. "Only in rhetoric has he gone in the opposite direction from [Victorian premier] Cain." This isn't quite fair. The resource-rich frontier states in general do present an alternative to Benthamist state dependency, but they face two severe problems: Within the Australian federation they are hobbled by Canberra; and the markets they need to ensure their progress are not guaranteed.

For the moment in the nation as a whole the Labor Party has the initiative, and interestingly enough office-holding Labor figures have started to utter relatively conservative sentiments. "Yes, it does bother me," says Race Mathews, the Victorian arts and police minister, when I ask if the clamor for rights has not obscured the sense of duty. "This will make me sound like an incipient conservative, but the balance between rights and duties hasn't been preserved, and I don't know how to get it back. Liberation has gone too far," observes this stalwart of the Fabian Society who did much to promote overdue liberation. "The gains were real and vital, and worth fighting to preserve. But somehow you have to strengthen the other side of the balance. You can't make democratic socialism work without a sense of duty and obligation."

"The Labor Party is the natural party of government in New South Wales," says Bob Carr, minister for the environment in that state's government. "We put democracy first," explains Carr, a slim, sharp-featured man with glasses, impeccable in a tan summer suit and a brown silk tie, his cuff links bearing the Australian seal. "We are part of the Western world—that distinguishes us from the left. We stand for increased equality and the abolition of poverty—that distinguishes us from the conservatives. If we look like the defenders of a bloated public sector," says Carr, who is a rising star in the Labor Party, "we would suffer the kind of fate that the U.S. Democratic Party and the British Labor Party have suffered." Gareth Evans, minister of resources and energy, feels that Australia has "come to a watershed" on the question of whether union-won gains ever must be given up. "Broken Hill was the classic example. Gains there—in relation to work practices and so on—were never given up no matter what happened anywhere else in the world. But from now on gains *will* have to be relinquished. You know, if productivity at Broken Hill were doubled, it would still only be two thirds that of Mount Isa." As for recent wage hikes in the coal industry, Senator Evans simply observes grimly: "The result will be some mines will go to the wall."

"What are the unchanging principles of social democracy, John?" I ask Senator Button, the minister for industry, technology, and commerce. The phone rings like an alarm bell to match the look of alarm on Button's face. "You bastard, what a question!" he grunts as he stumps across the room to answer the phone. "Thank God you called," he says into the receiver. "An old friend just asked me to define the unchangeables of socialism." He laughs. "At least I have a few seconds to think of something." Indeed it is hard even for a brilliant man like Button to name much that is unchanged between social democracy of the Hawke era and most of what came before.

He points to three large achievements of the Hawke government's first years—relations with Asia, steps toward economic realism, some redistributive measures—but his definition of social democracy is not a sharp one. "A fair share for everyone. Equality as far as possible. Participation of people in the political process as much as possible. Damping down the most brutal forces in society that might disrupt those three." Button stops and looks at me. "It becomes harder and harder to adjust these things in a world whose technological capacity changes so rapidly."

Button, a flinty, cheerful man, is one of the most experienced and canny members of the Hawke inner group. In a typically discreet maneuver, he masterminded the switch of Labor Party leadership from Bill Hayden (now foreign minister) to Hawke in 1983 by persuading Hayden to resign quietly. "Had there been a fight about it," Button tells me, "that would have led to an instant election by Fraser, and during the campaign the Labor Party would have been perceived as once again in a terminal state due to internal squabbling." Button sighs and crushes a cigarette to a smoky end. "I was accused of playing my cards very close to my chest and I'm glad I did." He believes the Labor Party's tearing itself to pieces in public is a thing of the past.

Minister Button, who is the architect of the government's belated attempt to coax Australian industry into postures more competitive with the dynamic economies of Asia, believes Australians "were a bit indulgent with ourselves in the 1960s and 1970s." He is scornful of Australia's "banana mentality cultivated by protection and policies such as offsets [requiring foreign firms to buy back Australian products to offset part of any sale to Australia]," to quote a memo of his to the prime minister. "A Danish chemical company lost interest in Australia," he reported sadly to Hawke, "when it found out the price of shipping from Perth to Sydney." Instead of protecting inefficient industries, such as consumer electronics, Button wants to select those industries where Australia enjoys "comparative advantage," and put money into research and development and export incentives to help them soar. He thinks it may take ten years to get manufacturing onto a "sophisticated footing." Even that seems optimistic.

Button has more than once ruffled the feathers of education leaders by telling them they ought to think ahead ten years to the needs industry will have—or not have—for trained young people. Whether Australian education can rise to the challenge of the Hawke-Button restructuring is a big question. In Japan, 90 percent of seventeen-year-olds study, in the U.S.A., 80 percent, in Australia a mere 40 percent. It shows, and it will show even more tomorrow.

Nor is John Button always a darling of the trade unions. "The labor market is very regulated and rigid," he confesses in acknowledging the need for reform, "but in this country institutional changes have got to be accompanied by attitudinal changes. It's a slow drip process." He doesn't believe in leave loading—17½ percent extra pay during holidays—but he feels he can't denounce it root and branch. Button also sees dangers in Hawke's egotism, but he believes Hawke's ideas of consensus and the Accord have introduced a new spirit of flexibility and accommodation to Australian political-industrial life. "It's a new era," he sums up. "You know the Whitlam government devoted its entire energies to working out how to spend money, and virtually no energy—as we have been spending so much—in working out how to create wealth."

Will Australia be a republic if the Labor Party stays in office for a decade? Button laughs. "You know this issue is a lot of bullshit. I'm a republican, but it just doesn't fuss me now as it used to."

"Because you're in power?"

"No, no. Because the system we have is not as offensive to me now as it used to be—you understand what I mean?" I am not sure I do understand what Button means but he goes on to relate a revealing incident.

"I went to a big football match in Melbourne recently with my son Nick," says the minister as he puts his feet on a coffee table, "and at the start 'Advance Australia Fair' was played. Everyone stood up except Nick." Button said to his son, "Get up, for Christ's sake." And Nick said he wasn't going to. When Button resumed his seat he asked his son, "What was that all about?"

"I'm not going to get up for that sort of thing. It's nationalistic."

Button, whom I have known for twenty years, ever since we were associated in the early efforts to help Whitlam reform the Victorian Labor Party, says he was angry with his son. "Don't you understand," he said to the youth, "that for twenty years I fought to get rid of that other silly fucking song, 'God Save the Queen'? We succeeded after a big struggle. We may not have found the best replacement, but we did it. And the moment we achieve it, for the new song you don't bother to stand up!"

Button puffs on another cigarette, and in his eyes, blue like a Victorian autumn sky, there is an amused look of "That's the way things are," and perhaps a touch of regret at the generation gap, and at the way you fight for something and it turns out to mean little to those who behold the results.

"I wonder how Whitlam will cope with Paris," mining executive Hugh Morgan remarked to Prime Minister Hawke at the races not long after the appointment of Whitlam as ambassador to UNESCO had been announced. Hawke growled back, "I wonder how the Parisians will cope with Whitlam." Hawke and Whitlam have never thought terribly highly of each other, and Hawke's government is as different from Whitlam's as from Fraser's.

Back from Paris for a visit to promote his newly published memoir in 1985, Whitlam was asked what he thought of Hawke after twenty-eight months in office. "Given time, he will equal my government," he replied of the prime minister he was then serving. (Whitlam's government lasted thirty-five months.) In Paris in mid-1986, when the Hawke government was facing severe economic disappointments, I asked Whitlam how he felt about Hawke's well-known past criticisms of his talent for economics. "Hawke never says anything about my economic prowess because he knows I won't make comments about his," Whitlam replied. "We each see advantage in skirting round that issue."

"A cabinet colleague of Hawke's said to me yesterday," Neil Brown remarks, "that the great contribution of the Whitlam era is that it has taught us what Labor should not do in government." Hawke governs by doing little, whereas Labor governments have tended to govern by bristling with activism. Whitlam, an original man, threw much that was new at the Australian people, and Hawke isn't sure the people want too much of that.

Whitlam's Labor Party was surprised at its possession of power; Hawke's Labor Party likes its power. "It's a young ministry," says Mick Young, special minister of state, of the Hawke government in late 1985, "and all are anxious to stay there. We're a second-term Labor government that's in a good position and going for a third term. No previous Labor people have been in that position. If we govern correctly we can be here for quite some time."

"Gough was an awful chairman," remarks Frank Crean—who was Whitlam's deputy for a time—in the kitchen of his Melbourne home. "Bob Hawke is a superb chairman," John Button tells me a few days later. But is Hawke anything more than a brilliant chairman? Does the "silver budgie," as some people call Hawke, mocking his attention to grooming and image, lack intellectual substance?

"John Howard makes the Kama Sutra look positively meager," Hawke says on TV of his opponent. "I mean he's got so many positions you can't keep up with him." If Howard is a man who sprouts ideas and policies, Hawke seems to have few positions. He offers less a set of policies than a method of harmonizing the various interests, plus himself as harmonizer-in-chief. Of the economic summit he mounted soon after winning office, which led to the Accord, he recalls, "The Australian people put their trust in me and that approach, and it worked."

Some say he is dominated by a faceless staff, which no one ever said of Whitlam. Hawke goes into a restaurant, runs the story, accompanied by his crowd of advisers. "What would you like, Prime Minister?" "Give me steak and eggs." "What about the vegetables?" "They'll have the same." Hawke expects everyone to like him, and he thinks that harmony with almost everyone is possible. His mind has no angles; it is an adaptable mind, and he can talk to anyone about anything with apparent equal interest and ease. To some this makes him a chameleon; Whitlam feels that Hawke has "allowed himself to be patronized." To others he is in the best tradition of mateship.

Bill Hayden, the foreign minister, is a senior and impressive figure who forms the main link between the Whitlam and the Hawke governments. He is privately not a great admirer of Hawke, but he cannot gainsay Hawke's success in winning elections and reassuring a disconcerted nation. As I arrive at the foreign minister's office, a secretary comes out and says, "Bill's not here yet. His plane's late." Hayden bursts in wearing a gray suit and a pink and white shirt and announces that he must "water the horse" before we talk. He is a man of charm and passion. He has the big-featured Australian face and the slightly indrawn Australian mouth.

For Hayden the fundamental issues of race and peace mean a great deal. "Aborigines used to come by," he recalls of his upbringing in a poor area of Queensland, "living in dreadful conditions. White Australia was so patronizing and oppressive toward them." Although Hayden has been part of the peace movement since the 1950s, he talks as a man who has found peace elusive. He seems a little weary of the world's many faults and one can't help wondering how much of this is due to the tragedies of international relations and how much to his nagging disappointment at having been displaced as leader of the Labor Party by Bob Hawke. He sums up Australia's international assets realistically: "We're not big enough to be a threat to anyone. We have ties, especially with the U.S.A., that are widely respected. We have access to advanced technology."

After our chat in his office Hayden takes me along to a luncheon he is giving in honor of a visiting Chinese minister at a restaurant on Canberra's outskirts. As the Chinese finishes proposing his toasts, Hayden digs the interpreter in the ribs. "And . . . and," he whispers, a hand to his mouth, and pushes a card at the young man. I am seated close enough to read the typed words on the briefing card, which call for a toast to "Her Majesty, Queen of Australia." The Chinese corrects the omission. Hayden murmurs loudly as he puts down his wine glass after drinking the toast, "Good Queen Bess, God bless her!"

What does the foreign minister feel when he walks into the Australian embassy in Washington and the first thing he sees is the Queen's picture? "I have developed an immunity syndrome," Hayden says. "If the Poms pay for it," he adds with a grin, apparently referring to the monarchy and its functions in Australia, "I don't lose a lot of sleep over the Queen. There are more important things to be done. If we became a republic tomorrow, it's not going to end poverty in Australia." Hayden stops. "Are you going to write this stuff up with direct quotes?" He laughs.

As we come out the front door of the restaurant on a hill high above the capital, the foreign minister takes me aside. "The cultural tendency to want to be liked is breaking down a bit but not totally," he stresses. "It's part of the Australian character to sentimentalize, to respond warmly at a cultural level. We dub a tie a 'special relationship' at the drop of a hat," he adds in an apparent reference to the alliance with America. We reach his car under a blinding sun. "But there's no such thing in international relations—if you mean by it mateship, sticking with someone through thick and thin. It's a cold hard world. If you don't look out for number one, you may be left high and dry."

"For too many years," says Treasurer Paul Keating, who collects French antique clocks and one day may succeed Hawke, "the Labor Party behaved as though there wasn't a middle class." That changed in the Hawke era, and class polarization has all but disappeared within the world of the Australian political elite.

At a Melbourne party Simon Crean goes to introduce me to Geoff Allen, an executive of the Business Council, but it turns out Allen and I were schoolmates at Wesley College. "Geoff stayed with the side," says Crean with a grin. That kind of reference to class—a Wesley boy leaving the side by going into the Labor Party—is rapidly becoming rare, and Simon Crean's remark was a slightly awkward joke.

"How can you say a tax on the use of swimming pools and restaurants is regressive and inflationary," Crean asks rhetorically at a dinner party in the home of a former Wesley College teacher of mine when the conversation turns to indirect taxation, "for the kind of people we represent?" It is a piquant choice of words; the new political class in the Labor Party uses those swimming pools and restaurants, but the "people we represent" mostly don't.

"Class in Europe is to do with your birth," Neville Wran tells me candidly, "but class in Australia is to do with your clout." The New South Wales premier puts his finger on a fluidity that has long existed in Australia. "You can start off on the wrong side of the tracks in Australia—for me the best thing about coming from the working class was getting out of it—and yet become a scion of society in fairly quick time, if that's what turns you on."

"The right wing of the New South Wales Labor Party," comments Richard Hall of Wran's wing of the party and Prime Minister Hawke's power base, "is trying to make the Labor Party like the U.S. Democratic Party." Hall criticizes the change. "The Hawkites try to counter the left, which has its own far-left overseas models, by making a model of the Democrats. It's this terrible Australian problem that you are not valid till you have an overseas reference point. I said to a guy in the New South Wales Labor Party right," Hall goes on, " 'You can't take morality out of the Labor Party, mate.' " There are many who feel that Hawke is selling out Labor principles. The Hawke era is materialistic, they say. The consensus technique gives an imprimatur to apathy. If you're passionate you're regarded as a fool or a traitor.

"I know a lot of people who think back fondly to the Whitlam days," says George Negus, "because then values were involved."

"But doesn't the Whitlam sociocultural revolution go on, George?"

"It does, but in spite of, not because of, the Hawke government."

Yet Hawke hasn't really taken morality out of the Labor Party. In an age that required a fresh approach for the sake of the nation's standard of living, he has given a skillful new expression to an old tradition of class-transcending chumminess. Hawke speaks to a working-class group, and he sounds one way: "We'll get the bloody Yanks to do what we bloody well *want* them to do." He jumps into his car, goes to an employers' group, and the accent is different, the manner has changed: "The American people stand with us." There is something beyond class, indeed beyond politics, about his appeal.

"From my early days I knew a cross section of people," Hawke himself recalls in his office at Parliament House in Canberra as we talk of his upbringing in a Congregational manse in Western Australia. "Because that was the nature of the church. So as I grew up I easily mixed across classes and groups. I've never been seized by any sense of class hatred or that sort of thing." In a household that knew neither affluence nor poverty, there was a moral vision of the world which assumed common ground existed.

Hawke is a handsome man with a spectacular head of silver hair, large eyes, and sensual hands. Just back from a Commonwealth conference in Bermuda, he is deeply tanned but has a cold. He speaks quietly and slowly and remains seated with his arms leaning heavily on the desk in front of him. He is an extremely engaging person who gives the impression that his pilgrimage through life is a matter of intense fascination to himself. His theme word seems to be "together," an update of mateship. It pertains to process rather than to goals, as does the word "path" which he favors.

"Any politician in Australia who thinks he can decide himself what's best for the country and then seek to impose it," the prime minister remarks, "is destined for a very short tenure in office." Hawke tries to strike a balance between reading the public mind and shaping it. "The secret is to understand the basic aspirations and attitudes of the Australian people, and then try to see how your own policies and concepts can be linked to those aspirations." One recalls that the cry for ideology has nearly always been a voice in the wilderness in Australia.

Prime Minister Hawke appreciates that the 1970s brought a watershed in the Australian political economy. "The Australian economy had to be turned around," he says of his overriding priority when elected to office in 1983. He does not blush to say that the private sector was and is the key to this. "Seventy-five percent of the jobs in Australia are provided by the private sector," he points out as he leans even further over the desk and thrusts forward his head with its silver mane. "And if you don't have a healthy and prosperous and growing private sector, you're not going to have a healthy economy."

Hawke tells me he sees something profound in the recovery of the mid-1980s despite its incompleteness. "What I was trying to say to Australians was that the world no longer owes Australia anything. You see, attitudes, assumptions, and expectations are always formed by a previous generation's experiences. From the start of World War Two, through nearly two generations, that experience was full employment, steady if not spectacular growth, and sustainable levels of inflation." The prime minister draws a hand across his hair. "Now all that was in a factual sense shattered once you got into the 1970s."

I ask Hawke if the enormous stress since the Whitlam years on people's rights is matched by a sufficient stress on obligations. "It's a good question," he replies quietly. He sighs, and then links the question to his grand theme. "It's so easy to see how you immediately benefit by a particular government decision, without understanding that in this world in which we live no one decision, such as raising pensions, can be taken except at a cost elsewhere."

Hawke believes that the crisis of the 1970s was a springboard to the acceptance of a new form of compromise in Australian industrial life. "Because of the very bad economic situation the world was in, there was a very significant response to my call to understand that there are obligations as well as rights." He stops, and his eyebrows rise. "Having said that, I don't want to leave the impression that we've got a totally responsive and responsible society. We haven't."

In Hawke's vision of a revamped Australian political economy, the much-needed sense of obligation would be based on national pride. Hawke resembles Menzies in his ability to unite the nation and satisfy the public with symbols. Menzies took Australians beyond depression and war to a "house and garden" security. Hawke is trying to take Australians beyond politics itself to problem solving by consensus plus a misty nationalism. He spreads the words "Australian" and "the Australian people" around like tomato sauce on a saveloy.

"It is a popular sport to mow down the tall poppies," Hawke remarks when our conversation turns to the topic of national spirit, "but I wouldn't say we've been a self-deprecating country. Where the self-deprecation comes in is that perhaps Australians haven't sufficiently realized the capacity they have to go out into the tough, competitive world markets and beat everyone. There's a feeling that perhaps the Yanks, the Japanese, or the Germans are always going to do things better than we will—and it's not justified a lot of the time."

Hawke comes with me to his office door. He is not a tall man and he is slightly hunched as he walks, neck pushed forward as if in maximum endeavor. I leave Parliament House reflecting that Australia's ever-worsening terms of trade must surely push the nation to further re-examine its political-industrial ways. Prime Minister Hawke's caution about the future seems prudent as during 1986 strikes proliferate, the Australian dollar sinks to historic lows, inflation stands at double that of some of Australia's export competitors, current account deficit is at a record high—and as through it all the trade union leadership insists that what has been gained can never be given up, and pushes for an expansion of employer-financed superannuation. I wonder if for Bob Hawke the fun may be going out of politics.

Fixed in the mold of academic achievement and competitive behavior—he took degrees from the University of Western Australia, Oxford, and the Australian National University before entering the trade union movement—Hawke in more recent years has been softened and broadened by the influence of his family. "Earlier on perhaps his vision was a little restricted," Hazel Hawke remarks in a sitting room of the prime-ministerial residence. "I and the children have differed, to a degree, from his clear-cut attitudes to things." (A Hawke daughter has had problems with heroin. A son devotes himself to Aboriginal advancement in a remote part of Western Australia.) "Over the years," Hazel Hawke goes on of her husband, "he's come to appreciate the softer things, some of the interests our children have developed. He's come to see that there are all sorts of fields of excellence."

While there is argument as to how much the Hawke government has done, and questions about Hawke's courage on the tough economic issues, there is little doubt that his government's *methods* have generally been skillful. No Labor prime minister in Australian history has had better relations with business than Hawke. And no prime minister of any party has had as good relations with both the unions and business.

"The Hawke government," says Tony Staley, who more than any other person helped Fraser to become leader of the Liberal Party, "is Fraserism with a human face." Hawke espouses business values, praises Washington's policies, talks of restraining government expenditure, and tells the trade unions (in public at least) that 50 percent of a tiny pie is less desirable than 20 percent of a huge pie. "I could never in my life vote for the Labor Party," says Brian Rowe, the retired BHP executive, "but, look, Hawke is good for Australia." He bangs his fists together. "Under Fraser we'd be having *confrontation* on everything." Likewise the nation still feels moderately secure with Hawke. It criticizes him, but often it does so with a proprietorial air, as if he belongs to them, will take care of them, and should sometimes be told when he makes a mistake.

For all the recent changes spurred by realists like John Button, for all the eager hopes that devaluation of the dollar will work miracles for export income, and for all Hawke's political brilliance, the economy of Australia is saddled with limitations imposed by its geography and social history. Its remoteness, which affects trade, tourism, and ways of thinking; its small domestic market; its federal system; a legacy of prison colony origins; the tradition of centralized, semi-judicial wage fixing; scars on the national psyche from past depressions; and its state-dependent mentality. These things are not to be changed overnight.

"When we were writing the 1969 and 1972 platforms," recalls Race Mathews of his years working for Whitlam, "even in 1974, there was scarcely a national policy issue to which the solution wasn't clear. Expensive, yes. Administratively complicated, perhaps. Maybe a problem of winning consent." He looks up from his grilled barramundi in the dining room of Parliament House in Melbourne and sighs. "Today a soluble problem is a rarity."

The Victorian arts and police minister sees two reasons. "A fundamental change in the national agenda," for an era in which economic growth cannot be taken for granted. "And the Labor Party has grown more sophisticated on policy analysis." To Mathews the cries of the ideologists do not seem relevant to the Labor Party of the 1980s. "The party is off with the fairies," he says with a shrug, referring to the Labor Party in Victoria, where the left wing still flaps. "Mainstream political parties just can't deal very well with millennialist positions," he observes. Today's Labor Party under Bob Hawke does not intend to be off with the fairies.

"Politics has druglike qualities," Premier Wran says to me not long before his retirement. "It's almost an end to life in itself." The figures of the old Labor Party lived for politics. Those in the new one of today live by politics. The Hawke Labor government is determined to stay in the mainstream, and from there, if its political debts and ties permit, edge Australia toward an urgently needed economic dynamism and competitiveness.

TWELVE

Sense of the Nation

"Where do you live now?" asks a willowy brunette at Melbourne University's sports center as she reads my application for a temporary pass. When I explain that I have lived in Boston for some fifteen years, she squeals to a colleague at the desk, "Isn't that beaut. He hasn't changed his Australian accent after fifteen years in America!" She issues me a third-semester card several weeks early, without charging me the extra money due.

At the check-out counter of a supermarket in Murrumbeena a lady drops a packet of raisins, and a man with one leg stoops down to pick it up for her. When she thanks him he says, "We all have to stick together for Australia, don't we?" The lady says as she puts the raisins in her bag, "Too right!"

For us students in the 1950s and 1960s, Australia Day was an awkward occasion, something between a bore and a joke. Like the religious instruction class at school, it was not part of our real agenda. There has been a change. On January 26 an unembarrassed consciousness of Australia is in the air. Through the ambiguities—the date really belongs to British history for it marks the whites' arrival in Australia in 1788—the shoots of national confidence push up.

"How did you celebrate Australia Day?" says a man at the bar to his mate, in a recent *Bulletin* cartoon. "I saw Pakistan play cricket against the West Indies," comes the reply, "followed by a nice Chinese meal." The irony is good-humored, and could not have been expressed when I lived in Melbourne. A TV dramatization of World War Two, *The Last Bastion,* grips millions of viewers with its proud Australian view of the 1940s. Contradicting or brushing off British and American criticisms of Australian conduct and policy, this nationalistic series would have been unthinkable twenty years ago.

One evening in 1976 I found myself in the Melbourne Town Hall at a Citizens for Democracy rally observing the first anniversary of the fall of the Whitlam government. Donald Horne, author of *The Lucky Country,* warned from the platform that if Australia did not become a republic "the curtain may come down on our civilization." At a party afterwards I said to a friend, "Define for me Australian civilization." She declined. She and I are less skeptical today.

The Australian capture of the America's Cup in 1983 found many people surprised at the emotional jubilation they felt. After that unexpected and perhaps much needed sporting victory, hundreds of thousands continued—the win came early in the morning, Australian time—to drink and sing and cry. At breakfast time Prime Minister Hawke, soaked with beer and champagne from the cans and glasses of a Perth crowd, said to the nation, "Any employer who sacks a worker for taking a day off today is a bum." Perhaps one should put this down mainly to the sports-craziness that grips isolated communities like Australia.

Yet trappings at least of nationalism arise on all sides. Crowds sing "Waltzing Matilda" at cricket tests, which they never did in my youth. The Boxing Kangaroo of Alan Bond's yachting syndicate and other national symbols adorn merchandise and vehicles. The label "imported" on clothes and foodstuffs has lost its magic drawing power. A new awareness of the significance of a flag has produced competitions and societies devoted to finding a better one for Australia.

By law, radio stations must spend at least 20 percent of their music time on Australian performances. Some fine chefs have turned to indigenous foods—witchetty grubs, yabbies, Moreton Bay bugs, braised galah, nasturtium-leaf sandwiches—which not long ago were despised by city folk. Australian wine, which is very good, is used by some of its admirers almost as a weapon against all other wines. Occasionally the nationalist rhetoric seems silly, as when the Canberra anthropologist Professor Derek Freeman, having published a book criticizing Margaret Mead's work on Samoa and been faulted by American reviewers, termed the debate "the intellectual America's Cup."

Some people scoff at all this and say it has nothing to do with Australia's sense of itself as a nation. "Stage-managed national exuberance," snaps the TV reporter George Negus, "and Hawke exploits it." Say the producers of the rural storytelling musical *A Fruitcake of Australian Stories:* "The people who originally spun these yarns are *naturally* Australian; they are not the sort who make deliberate efforts to be Australian by brandishing an 'I Love Australia' plastic shopping bag."

But most are less critical. "I'm embarrassed by the ballyhoo," says Professor Peter Boyce in Perth of the nationalism surrounding the winning and losing of the America's Cup, "yet I'm pleased that people *want* to make so much of it. I've always been an Anglophile, but in recent years I've made a distinction between fondness for English values and a belief in a separate Australian national interest."

"What impressed me most on my trip to the U.S.A.," recalls Senator Button, the industry minister, "was the Smithsonian museum—a monument to American achievements of which everyone is *so proud.* We've had achievements in Australia, but people tend to denigrate them—to see ourselves only in terms of our sportsmen." Perhaps it is a residual lack of national confidence that brings about the occasional excessive nationalistic gesture.

If politicians understand electors, the trappings express something important, for all political parties bang the drum of nationalism. "Put Australia First," urged the Labor Party at the last national election. "Put Australians First," ran a possibly subtle Liberal Party rejoinder. The National Party included a stylized map of Australia in its party symbol, and featured at its campaign opening Dorothea Mackellar's well-worn and sentimental poem about love for a "sunburnt country."

In defense policy, all political parties have pulled back from the idea that Australia can rely on "powerful friends" for the brain and sinew of defense, and are rethinking defense in national terms, accepting that Australia must take a basic responsibility for its own defense. "I feel alliances are based on shared interests, as opposed to shared values," says Defense Minister Kim Beazley, who eschews sentiment and ideology and puts stress on the concrete defense of Australia's own exposed north. "If the values come with it, that's fine, but the shared interests are fundamental." Beazley goes on candidly: "Because of a vague feeling that we are slightly alien to our environment, most Australians accept the conservative view of defense. There's always a desire to drag into the region people who look like us. Well, we'll never be able to bring back one of our old partners. [Britain's] out for good. And the other one [the U.S.A.] comes in—sensibly enough—on its own terms."

"My foreign policy is a nationalistic one," says Bill Hayden, the hard-driving and passionate foreign minister, in his Canberra office. "I think the chip on the shoulder, the cultural cringe, has gone. Now we're more confident. There's an expectation that Australia should operate on the international plane with some confidence. To be docile toward our great and powerful friend [the U.S.A.] . . . is, I think, fairly discredited in the community."

"Hawke has been more pro-American than Fraser was," observes *The Age* editor Creighton Burns. "You could not *have* a more pro-American prime minister than Hawke." The interesting thing is that Hawke can be pro-American without ceasing to seem the quintessential Australian common man. In his talk with me he brushes aside any qualms about his support for Washington. "It was the Labor Party in government during the last war which forged the Australian-American relationship. This is a continuation of a tradition." Hawke's solidarity with the U.S.A. is not the old fearful and boot-licking type. It's an unself-conscious identification with American interests as being in large part Australia's interests. Hawke hasn't derived any particular inspiration from either Britain or from the U.S.A. "Look, mate, we're Australians," is all Bob Hawke needs to say as Australia's Bicentennial draws near.

My uncle years ago told me that before World War Two the cricket tests were almost the only event—since World War One when he fought in Europe—that gave him a feeling of Australian-ness. Today in Australia one can readily feel a sense of the nation. ABC radio and in a lesser way TV make the parts feel a whole, with their standardized Australian voices telling the nation what the eight governments and their numberless civil servants did today, and their inclusion of far-flung spots in time and temperature announcements. "Good morning," says the Sydney announcer. "It is seven o'clock; six o'clock in Darwin."

When the smoke and smell and unpredictability of bushfires come, Australians are bound together, all reminded, as a Spaniard is reminded by religion, or a citizen of the Middle East by war, of the limits to man's power. Great moments in the performing arts—Joan Sutherland at the Sydney Opera House, a slice of Australian life in a play by David Williamson, the rock group Midnight Oil shouting out the anxieties of the late twentieth century—make Australians feel the connections between themselves and world culture and prove to them that they are making a contribution to it.

At a gala night during 1984, "Awards for Excellence" are announced. They are organized by BHP, Australia's biggest company, fresh from its purchase of the American coal-mine company Utah International, about which event it said, "From today, the Australian flag will fly higher and more boldly in the financial capitals of the world." The governor general, the prime minister, and prominent citizens sit at dinner in the elegant Victorian Arts Center and applaud as Australians are rewarded for courage and skill and hard work. Everything is balanced and magnanimous. An Aborigine and a Jew are among the winners. When a champion of protecting the Daintree rain forest in Queensland against road building rises to receive his prize, the prime minister—who didn't fight against the road—finds it in his heart to clap.

Much of the Australia I knew is turned on its head tonight. The Australian "knocker" tradition is not in evidence. A people used to snarling at each other are at mutual massage. Instead of a mumbling self-deprecation we have eloquent nationalist sentiment reinforced by inspirational music. The togetherness of the Hawke era is as tangible as the necklaces and the cigars and the pavlovas.

Everyone agrees that nationalism has strengthened since the 1970s, but the meaning of this is not so clear because nationalism offers varying points of entry for different people. "Being an Australian is a practical question really," says Patricia Caswell, the Melbourne trade union official. "I like being here; it's my backyard; I understand Australian culture." People who express this kind of national feeling are neither chauvinist nor apologetic. "I don't think we're all that great," observes Caswell, though she acknowledges that in recent years on tariff matters she has become a little more nationalist than she used to be.

For many on the left, pride in Australia was kindled by the overdue reforms of Whitlam's age of reform. "It was the Whitlam *Zeit* that really turned me on to Australia," says gallery director Patrick McCaughey, born in Ireland, when I ask him to date his sense of becoming irrevocably Australian. For others, national pride stems from Australia's freedoms and skills and the contribution the nation makes abroad. "I'm really delighted to see Rupert Murdoch making strides in America," says Chief Minister Tuxworth in Darwin, "and to see John Elliot doing the same in the UK—that's where we ought to be."

"Nationalism as a government PR exercise leaves me cold," says Fraser McEwing, the Sydney fashion publisher. "But going often overseas has made me realize that we're better organized than the East. We have a nice balance between freedom and law." Many have found that foreign travel increases their sense of Australian-ness. "Traveling has made me more nationalistic," says Lady Mary Fairfax. "My nationalism means being good to what has made me."

"Years ago I went and saw the Embarcadero development in San Francisco," says New South Wales environment minister Bob Carr, "and I thought Australia can't do that sort of thing, what a pity. But now we're doing it." From a table in the dining room at Parliament House in Sydney he waves an arm toward the window. "Look at the Darling Harbor development. Look at the restoration of our state parliament, which is better than what's in Sacramento. Look at our Science and Technology Museum, which is the equal of the Deutscher Museum in Munich. Australia's lost its feeling that it could never do anything."

As youths I think we lived always with a consciousness that as a remote people we were deprived of splendors but also safe from the evils of that faster northern hemisphere. At school we memorized a line from an Australian war poem: "True to no crown nor presidential sash." It was both a boast of our democratic bloody-mindedness and a reminder of our distance from danger. "I feel at home here," says a young artist at the Christmas party of a Melbourne publisher when I ask her why she loves Australia. She pours a glass of Orlando Chardonnay for herself, then one for me, and grabs a bunch of grapes. "And I feel that nothing terrible could happen to me here."

Amidst the wood panels and stained glass of the Ormond College dining room, I find myself sitting beside the New Zealand–born master David Parker at high table. As we sip thin soup and hack at roast beef, I ask him about the content of Australian nationalism. "I think it's an innocent joy at being here," replies the Oxford-educated literary scholar.

"We don't express it much," says Stuart Sayers, literary editor of *The Age,* "but we do feel it's the best place in the world." The veteran journalist goes on to characterize a way-of-life sense of Australian-ness. "We're peaceful, don't you think? We vote rather than kill enemies. We're all Aborigines, you know! I mean, the Aborigine can't see the sense in working hard all day; he'd prefer to sit in the sun. Australians approve of this. We only work hard at our gardens."

"Are you an Australian nationalist," I ask former prime minister Fraser, "and what does it mean for you?" The blue eyes are intense and the chiseled face takes on grandeur as the chin pushes out. "Of course I am. And it means simply that Australia is the best country in the world to live in." The satisfaction at "being here," heightened by comparisons made in firsthand contact with other less safe and comfortable nations, perhaps sums up what national feeling means for most Australians. The cry of Robertson's old settler song is still the gist of it: "The land, boys, we live in!"

"I came to Australia on holiday ten years ago," says my New Zealand Maori cabdriver as we drive by lilac jacarandas to Brisbane airport, "and I ended up staying. I became an Australian citizen in the Brisbane Town Hall," continues Rita, who is stout and infectiously cheerful, as we pass the Breakfast Creek Hotel, which served as Douglas MacArthur's headquarters in the 1940s. She was one of 612 people, of whom about half were British. "I cried. My husband said I was silly, but I'm a softie. I was the only Maori there, and you know I just felt good." Rita turns her brown face toward me and smiles broadly. "Yes, we was all made Australian citizens. It took about an aw-a [hour]." As I gather my luggage from the trunk of the taxi, I ask Rita what she most likes about Australia. "The weather." She laughs and falls silent. "I can't say the wages. The people are fairly good—but above all the weather."

Australian nationalism often has taken the form of an attachment to the soil. The people who went into the bush and survived were seen as the real Australians. Unlike in many nations, the elite in Australia were not the focus of national spirit. The city lawyer or trader didn't know how to mend a fence or scratch up a meal in the desert. Until the end of the Menzies era it was common for the political and social elite to be oriented to foreign cultures (nearly always to British) and neglectful of the physical body of Australia. Almost by default the bushwhacker became the nationalist.

The soil was not benign, however. "Most Australians did not love a sunburnt country," writes Blainey, in a reference to Mackellar's poem "My Country," in his aptly titled *A Land Half Won*. "The physical mastering of Australia was swift . . . but the emotional conquest was slow." If Australian nationalism has made a number of false starts, the reason is perhaps the difficulty of unqualified love for a harsh environ.

Yet the soil is still the point of refraction for nationalism in some Australians. Patrick White confesses in his scarifying memoir *Flaws in the Glass* that when he "could not come to terms" with the inhabitants of Australia he "found consolation in the landscape." It is the same for certain people today, not least those who dissent from dominant trends in urban Australian society. "The desert affects me deeply," says Andrea Hull, an executive at the Australia Council in Sydney. "The history of our ancient land mass is extraordinary. And a sympathy with the Aborigines goes with this love of the soil." Expressing a drastic nativism, Hull claims that Australia has "brutalized people not of Anglo-Celtic background into submission to Anglo-Celtic values."

"I'm part of Australia, I'm part of the land," says Winnie Quagliotti, the Melbourne Aboriginal leader. "For all that's happened, I love Australia." She is shocked that I have become an American citizen. "How could you give up your Australian citizenship! It's your roots. How could you do it?" This spirited black woman is the only Australian who has ever challenged to my face my switch of citizenship. "I'm a typical Aboriginal person," says Charles Perkins in his office at the Department of Aboriginal Affairs in Canberra. "Two weeks out of Australia and I'm wondering when I'm going to go home. Remember we're really part of this country." Says the conservative polemicist Bob Santamaria, also associating himself with a feeling for the soil, "I love the country, but I don't admire Australians very much. Central to bush values was the family—and now the family is breaking up."

In a different way the soil seems to have taken hold of the consciousness of a trendy elite. "Our nationalism," says George Negus, a scion of the left-liberal middle class, "includes a new turn to the soil: rural retreats, beach houses." Young professionals move to little towns. "Fresh air, lack of burglaries, and cars driving slower," says a psychologist, explaining why he and his astrophysicist wife moved from Melbourne to live in the bush. A century or so after the ex-convicts and the gold diggers, the middle-class environmentalists in Melbourne and Sydney have begun their own love affair with nature.

Is the soil the real Australia and are the new environmentalists, or perhaps their mirror-image adversaries, the old bushwhackers, the real Australian nationalists? "The only thing that makes Australia what it is is the landscape," says Arthur Boyd, "What else is there?" I keep thinking of the artist's words. Why do people recoil from their *urban* self-image? "For many people environmentalism has become a secular religion," remarks Barry Cohen, minister for arts and environment, as we chat in the Sheraton Hotel at Ayers Rock. "Perhaps their personal lives haven't worked, or conventional religion hasn't worked, and so birds, plants, the worship of nature replaces the need that man has to have spiritual values. For someone like myself, who has a lot of affinity for nature but doesn't see it with fervent spiritualism, these zealots are impossible to compromise with."

A hot embrace of the soil by environmentalists does not put an end to the mysterious ambivalence of Australians about the bush. A beach house is not a farm. A graduate diploma in outdoor studies does not guarantee harmony between its holder and nature. Compared with Greek or Italian or French peasants, Australians, even some who live on the land, arc jumpy or defensive about nature. The excellent film *The Long Weekend* arrested audiences with its account of a couple fleeing the city for the bush, seeking a solution to their problems amidst nature, only to be destroyed by a bush in which they found they could never be other than trespassers. "There seems so little tenderness for soil and plant," observes the poet Vincent Buckley, "so little sense of kinship with beasts, so little sense of the seasons as providing an active metaphor for human life. . . . The land is a breeding ground and a killing ground."

Most Australians never eat snake, goanna, or crocodile, though all are edible. Few Australians—except for country folk like us in East Gippsland—ate the delicious mussels from their rocky coastline until European migrants came and presented them as *moules marinière*. Most Australian gardens tell the same story of derivativeness. English-type gardens give Australian suburbia that air of the old world that surprises visitors who expect the outback to begin at Sydney airport. And the animals in their gaudy ribbons at the Royal Agricultural Show are Europe's animals; absent are Australia's own kangaroo, platypus, and koala bear.

It is true that a sprinkling of Australians living on the frontier have come to terms with the environment. They know how to live in tropical conditions. Very often they have developed a practical fellowship across racial lines. For them the tie with nature is a veritable religion made up half of love and half of grim fatalism. Holding the bush dear is the response they make to its desolateness. Yet Australia as a whole lives with the bush only as a myth. One cannot escape the feeling that the conformist suburbs are a defensive reaction to the untamability of the terrifying bush. "The trimmed gardens of the suburbs show a para-noiac fear of nature," says the novelist Helen Garner as we talk about city and country living, "a terror of its encroaching on you. They are an attempt to keep nature at bay, to keep it out of the cities."

The productive, dynamic, cosmopolitan elements in Australia hold back from a passive, romantic solution to the problem of how to deal with the Australian environ. Some ignore the soil. "I find the outback a bore," says Sydney publisher McEwing. Others subsume it within the perspective of economic development. "We dig or we die," says the mining tycoon Lang Hancock in Perth. Despite the dominance of a smart new urban middle class, Australia's problem with nature will not go away, because the power of nature over Australians is not going to go away. Nor does history recede quickly. It seems to me that Aus-tralians are uncertain about their relation to nature in part because the land was for millennia the Aborigines' land. A consciousness exists that white Australia's assumption of its terrain was at another people's expense.

Fay Zwicky, the Perth poet and essayist, loves the countryside and the seaside as a place of enjoyment, but she cannot romanticize the soil. As we talk in her living room on a golden afternoon, I put it to her that the indifference of a harsh environ has made Australia a hos-pitable place for the immigrant; in alienation there is equality. "But I feel indifference is not that benign," objects Zwicky, "and it can be a killer—a defeat of the human." She pours a Houghton's white Bur-gundy and lights a cigarette. "What you call indifference," she reflects, "I would call a refusal to know what one's fellow man is doing." She pauses. "I suppose it's true that not caring saves you from vast ideo-logical upheavals."

Zwicky does not like the current nationalism. "It's jingoism. It reminds me of the way people used to stare at immigrants on trams when they spoke a foreign language. One day when I was young I was in a tram, knitting in the European style. A woman leant over me and said, 'Little foreign girl, are you?' With how much curiosity, how much malevolence, I'll never know; but I was singled out as a foreigner."

"We were sitting there," Zwicky recalls of one of the cultural com-mittees that is planning for the 1988 Australian Bicentennial, "trying to plan the promotion of Australian studies in high schools. There was a great deal of coercion in the terminology used about Australian iden-tity. A monolith of Australianism was being pushed. Once again we were obliged to flog this national identity horse until, my God, it was raw and bleeding in front of us!" Fay Zwicky laughs. "I'm so sick of this question, and yet we're still confronted with it, because we don't know the answer."

The trail of Australian nationalism in the 1970s and 1980s leads me to the arts. Here Australia's sense of itself seems most striking. A large percentage of the many Australians who have felt a heightened pride in Australia over recent years mention the flourishing of the arts as an important reason.

"People are no longer embarrassed about being Australian," says Barry Cohen, the Hawke government's arts minister. "They're proud of their accent. They're proud of their indigenous heritage. And if one industry is to be singled out for building our self-esteem, it's the film industry." This affable middle-class Labor figure goes on: "Whilst there's a lot of crap being produced in the Australian film industry, every now and then we come up with a film of international class that compares with the best in the world. Prior to that our self-esteem came only through our sportsmen."

"Our nationalism has been given a tremendous boost by the renaissance of the film industry," echoes opposition leader John Howard. "As a child I had visions of New York because I saw many American movies. Today children are growing up with visions of Australian cities and the Australian bush because of what they see on the box and the screen."

In the Whitlam era, culture became the backbone of national pride. The strengthened feeling that an Australian item was not necessarily inferior to an imported item more often involved films and paintings and plays and novels than it did products from factory and farm. People became convinced that Australian experience was interesting in its own right as artists skillfully held up a mirror to that experience. It helped that Patrick White won the Nobel Prize for Literature just at this time.

"For me the Whitlam period was the key to the crumbling of Australian self-deprecation," says Craig Munro, author of a biography of the controversial nationalist of the 1930s, P. R. Stephenson, and an editor at the University of Queensland Press. "The 1970s were like the 1930s and the 1890s: a [nationalistic] combination of the cultural and the political. Whitlam was very good at this—better than Hawke is."

That large state subsidies came to fuel the arts—even under the conservative Fraser government that followed the Whitlam whirlwind—suggests how important film, drama, painting, music, and literature have been as vehicles of national pride. "To a great degree in recent years we have had bipartisanship toward the arts," says Tony Staley, who as minister assisting Prime Minister Fraser on the arts was responsible for setting up a community arts program. "In a small country, government must support film and the other arts."

The arts have become a lifeline to a national identity that cannot yet be taken for granted. Factory walls get brightened by murals done by community artists paid by the taxpayer. Writing books becomes a viable job—thanks to Canberra's grants—for the first time in Australian history. In two years under Whitlam the Literature Board awarded 269 fellowships to writers, compared with a total of 207 fellowships (mostly much smaller) in the *thirty-four previous years* of the existence of the board's predecessor. "Ten years ago twenty percent of the books sold in Australia were Australian," Craig Munro tells me, "while today more than fifty percent are."

It was less that nationalism was born or that Australia came of age in the 1970s—it's never as clear-cut as that—than that the nation's sense of itself changed. Instead of centering on the bushman and the Anzac, the self-image began to reflect the dominance in Australia of an educated urban middle class of diverse ethnic backgrounds. "When I took over *The Bulletin,*" says Donald Horne, "I deracialized and debushed it." At the time this was considered an anti-nationalist step. A few years later, when Horne in his classic *The Lucky Country* held up a mirror to a pluralistic urban Australia, the book was seen as nationalist.

When I was in my last year of high school at Wesley College a mere 30,000 university students existed in Australia. Two decades later, in 1975, there were 150,000. In a similar period the number of graduate students rose twentyfold. As the specialists, teachers, and administrators proliferated, the Labor Party, perhaps the most nationalistic of the parties, was transformed. "When I joined the party in 1964," arts minister Barry Cohen remarks during our chat at Ayers Rock, "as a small businessman with a middle-class background I was a rarity. Today the rarity is the hard hat." It is not that Labor figures like the dashing Cohen (or Premier Brian Burke in Perth, a former journalist, or Premier John Cain in Melbourne, a lawyer) are more Australian than the union veterans who used to dominate the Labor Party; but their rise has altered the dominant Australian self-image.

The crocodile poacher that Paul Hogan created in his film *Crocodile Dundee* is cherished in some corner of the Australian soul, and Australians like to play up the bush image for receptive foreigners, but the concerns of the post-Whitlam middle class are far from the world of Mick Dundee.

The educated, urban, ethnically diverse middle class elected the Whitlam government, and Whitlam began the funding of the arts that celebrates the arrival of this middle class. Whitlam in a talk with me in Paris in 1986 spoke of a double link between the arts and the spirit of national pride. "There was an amazing burgeoning of the novel and of film, and a great number of visual artists came back to Australia from abroad." The former prime minister, who tells me of his pleasure that arts minister Barry Cohen has just invited him to be chairman of the Australian National Gallery, believes his policies complemented this surge. "Equally significant, we set out to make the arts accessible to people irrespective—or nearly so—of geography or means."

In a touching novel of some years ago, *My Brother Jack*, George Johnston juxtaposes a traditional Australian, Jack Meredith, a patriotic, narrow, decent, unambitious man, with a new and more sharp-edged figure, his brother Davy, a traveled, hard-driving journalist. Jack is a kind of backdrop for the story of Davy, who feels guilty at times about his success and about his treatment of his wife and his brother. That not Jack but Davy is the focus of the novel can be seen as foreshadowing a basic shift of the center of gravity in Australian society.

Until the late 1960s, even the leading theater companies in Melbourne and Sydney did only one Australian play a year, at most, and Australian playwrights were caught between two models. They created either pale imitations of the British drawing-room comedy or pale imitations of the American musical or social drama. Then a complete break with tradition occurred, centered on the La Mama Theater in Melbourne—once a shirt factory and before that a brothel—and the Nimrod Theater in Sydney, now The Stables. "Wanted: A Display of Shanks," wrote the playwright Jack Hibberd, in a manifesto of 1970 that drew together the threads of change. He called for a "rich, ribald, and relevant" theater that would carve through "the tallow of current taste and lay bare the bone . . . the real myths and mores of our society."

"The new drama was aggressively and unapologetically Australian," says the longtime *Age* drama critic Leonard Radic as we chat in his Melbourne living room. "It capitalized on the extravagances of

Australian speech and slang. What it lacked in polish and in English-style refinement, it more than made up for in exuberance and energy. The whole group of writers and actors," explains Radic, "were educated middle class—unlike Ray Lawler [author of *The Summer of the Seventeenth Doll*] and others of the previous generation who had just come up through the theater. And they were the Vietnam protest generation." So in plays like *Don's Party,* by David Williamson, the urban middle class began to see not the bushman and Anzac of yesterday but the people around them—the ocker, the earnest professional, the salesman, the Labor Party intellectual.

I mention to Radic, a cosmopolitan figure of Yugoslav extraction, that I have just seen *A Fruitcake of Australian Stories* and *The Castanets,* two hearty, sentimental cabarets that seem in different ways to express the bush tradition. "You can still project that image," says Radic with a faint smile. "In urban society there are people prepared to swallow it. It sits comfortably, and you can feel good about it." Then Radic becomes slightly agitated. "But multiculturalism and postwar immigration have changed the face of Australia. The Manning Clarks and others who propagate the bushman tradition, the tradition of Paterson and Lawson, they're fifty years behind the times. That tradition is now embarrassing to most Australians."

Which does not reduce the appeal of *Crocodile Dundee* as a mirror to Australia for audiences in New York and Paris. Nor does it keep Australians from flocking to enjoy Barry Humphries, a mordant humorist who plays upon nostalgia for a simpler age. Humphries will not let Australians let go of their self-deprecation. Just as the bushman and the digger reflect a world of dashed hopes, so in Humphries's characterizations no poppy is allowed to grow too tall, no motive to prove pure, no dream to be fulfilled. Audiences seem to delight in having Humphries show them that everything in Australia is either flawed or of foreign inspiration. Equally, Humphries coaxes his devoted audiences to indulge their mixed feelings about the social changes that have occurred since the Menzies era. Many Australians like to finger this past because they feel uncertainty as to the future. "I looked up 'Aborigine' in the dictionary," one of Humphries's old characters says. "It said 'original inhabitants,' so Betty and I must be Aborigines." Says a Humphries character about a group of young people: "Being unemployed, they all had cars."

While I am in Sydney, The Stables goes up for sale. "In our bruised and troubled age," comments the writer Bob Ellis, by way of explanation, in the *Sydney Morning Herald,* "people seek from theater not so much a play as a foyer, one with drinks and carpets and plush conversation. We needed a drink in the Fraser years. We need it no less now." Acknowledging many troubles in the Australian theater, Leonard Radic criticizes the company at The Stables for trying to save its fortunes by producing *Arms and the Man.* "I mean, a Shaw-led recovery? The mind boggles. Who could be less relevant than Shaw to Australian society today!"

Some theater groups have also suffered as good actors and writers switched into film. "With all that," Radic sums up, "a revolution has occurred. No longer do we talk about Australian plays as such. They're part and parcel of the repertoire along with everything else." He refers to the force behind all this. "The funding authorities expect that a group like the Melbourne Theater Company will include twenty-five to thirty percent Australian material. If a group falls below that quota, funding is probably affected."

Bursts of nationalism have been frequent in Australia since the 1890s. Just before he died at the start of the Hawke era, Xavier Herbert recalled the World War One era: "There was all this bullshit about the Empire and then about 'Advance Australia Fair.' And people used to go around with little kangaroos and pendants and little maps of Australia. They were very chauvinistic, while still being very colonial." But the recurrent vision of nationalism often has turned out to be a mirage. A coming of age was announced many times. Republicanism rushed to center stage and meandered back into the wings. Despite the new sense of the nation expressed in the arts, the paradox about nationalism is that it is seductive but it doesn't always satisfy. It may be a crutch; it is not a destination.

Painting, more than any of the performing arts, has been under pressure to typify Australia. Nature has virtually been God in Australian history, and it has fallen to the painters above all artists to give people a symbolic handle on their mighty but unknown master. A unique landscape has been the Australian artist's great opportunity, and sometimes his straitjacket. The first wave of fine Australian painters—Tom Roberts, Arthur Streeton, and others of the Heidelberg School during the 1890s—heavily imitated French impressionists. But their achievement was taken to be a nativist one because they captured the light and space and color of the Australian soil.

Painters have been required to serve the need of the Australian psyche for a taming of the outback environment. In recent decades, Sidney Nolan in his Ned Kelly paintings, Fred Williams in his depictions of the Pilbara, and others have done this brilliantly, as Streeton and Roberts did before them. It took a long time—the whole of the nineteenth century—for painters to stop painting oaks even when gums were before their eyes, but they have generously made up for lost time. Only in Australia, I suppose, would a great painter fly in an aircraft and sketch at the plane window, as Nolan did over central Australia.

"There's a fatal insecurity," laments Patrick McCaughey at his gallery in Melbourne, "in the desperate desire to be recognized abroad for being distinctive." In walking that road the Australian artist, in McCaughey's view, destroys himself. "Benefit the career and ruin the vocation," he says with a didactic flourish. The heart of the problem, in McCaughey's view, is the tendency to "melodramatize the Australian experience, to make myths, to grab for the sublime." He sees only Fred Williams as a major exception.

Meanwhile the Australian public goes on treating the landscape as the one real topic of Australian art. People do not seem to want their artists to depict urban life with its psychological drama and social tensions, though Peter Booth and Mike Parr and others have begun very ably to do this. "There is a certain innocence about being an Australian," Nolan has said. "It is being part of a dream which hasn't been shattered or burnt out." George Johnston's Jack Meredith lives on in the mind, even as his brother Davy inherits the earth.

Yet even in art, if less so than in the performing arts (and more so than in literature), a nationalist phase turns out to be a mirage so far as the painters themselves are concerned. Young painters frequently express a brooding melodrama that does not seem particularly Australian. "Far from being locked up in legend," writes Mary Eagle of Australian painting, arguing against dwelling on national identity, " 'Australianism' is a flavor no sooner recognised than dispersed."

For some people Aboriginal art is made to fulfill the role of a distinctive Australian-ness. "I had a road-to-Damascus experience," says Patrick McCaughey. "I was walking back after lunch one day and I saw a group of Aboriginal children—from Bathurst Island near Darwin—coming out of the gallery. I felt shame that they had walked around the entire National Gallery and not seen one stick, stone, or feather of Aboriginal art."

McCaughey set out to change this. "I went to Alice Springs, and I drove out into the bush; there was no question I was in a sacred landscape." The gallery director wears a severe expression. "All my life I'd been making judgments about bark paintings on the basis of the most tawdry tourist-trade art. I had never gone and looked at the real stuff. I'd made up my mind about Namatjira only from putrid reproductions in books. It was a terrible kind of cultural racism." Today there is a section of McCaughey's gallery devoted to Aboriginal art. It is sponsored by a Japanese carmaker.

The multicultural urban young people of the 1970s filled Australia's unique "live venue" pubs to hear popular music that mixed bush images with modern life images. In the early 1970s pop and rock music was self-consciously Australian as songs like "Down Under" from the group Men at Work swept the pubs of Sydney and Melbourne. The Goanna group came up with "Solid Rock," a hymn to Aboriginal land rights, and "Let the Franklin Flow," about the environmentalists' opposition to a plan to dam the Franklin River in Tasmania.

Today most pubs echo with an amorphous music that transcends any one nation's spirit and often is apolitical. "You see, we've lost our inferiority complex," says Paul Turner, a music entrepreneur. "Billy Thorpe would never have written a song about Vegemite sandwiches." Groups like Midnight Oil are playing almost metaphysical songs with a flavor of pessimism and resignation that is common to youth's tastes in much of the West.

In film, the paradox of nationalism and the arts is at its sharpest. "The Australian filmmakers," remarks Craig Munro, the Queensland editor and biographer, "are no longer having to prove their Australian-ness in order to do what they want to do. When you're accepted, nationalism breaks down; the need to assert nationalism falls away." He feels that the Australian film industry has, as it were, caught up with the mirage of nationalism—which literature with its occasional jumpy parochialism hasn't done.

Of course the foreign world may like Australian films precisely because they offer myths that melodramatize the Australian experience. "An American visitor said to me after seeing the film *Picnic at Hanging Rock*," recalls Stan Mellick, the Brisbane literary critic, " 'What is the symbolism of the lizard lying on the rock in the sun?' " Mellick laughs. "I said, 'Jesus, nothing. Australian lizards always lie on rocks in the sun!' " A strain of innocence probably makes some Australian films—such as *My Brilliant Career*—appealing to Americans who see few home-grown films about innocence. "Our films gave Americans a vision of a simpler world," reflects Barry Jones, minister for science and technology, as he surveys for me the cultural scene. "The typical protagonist in an Australian film is very unsure of what he wants to do. It's a bit like Mark Twain's *The Innocents Abroad* or the Henry James novels where you've got a rather simple, guileless central character who moves into a complex situation."

"I am more patriotic than most Australian filmmakers," claims Paul Cox in his headquarters at Albert Park, a leafy inner suburb of Melbourne, "because I've stayed here. I mean, I could be splashing in a pool in Hollywood now."

A quiet man with unruly hair and a mustache, Cox came to Australia from Holland in 1963. "I landed in Melbourne by accident," he recalls with a laugh. "I wanted to go to Sydney, but the immigration authorities put me on the wrong list. Now I love Melbourne because it has seasons. I can see the leaves dropping in autumn. I can smell the spring." Both of Cox's recent successes, *Man of Flowers* and *My First Wife,* are set in Melbourne.

"The first time I felt at home in Australia," Cox remarks, "was in the Whitlam period. He was a man with compassion, intelligence, vision—and a certain degree of madness." To Cox Australia is "an amazing country," which he contrasts with a Europe that "cannot move anymore, a civilization that has come to a grinding halt." Although Cox more often uses music as a starting point for a film than he uses landscape, it is important to him that there is "a vast land behind me."

But Cox's films do not make a persona of the Australian natural environment. Films that do are mostly historical and not contemporary like Cox's (the lighthearted *Crocodile Dundee* is an exception). He is not enthusiastic about nationalism. "The more I say I'm Australian and proud of it, the more it makes me feel a potential aggressor—as if there's something to defend." Cox's resonant voice stops and I hear the cars gliding by a window behind his small black desk. "The more I understand the world, the less I want to belong to any particular country."

Yet this Dutch-born man of the city is absolutely Australian, and perhaps no one in the arts has captured as well as he the inner life of the contemporary Australian middle class. "I was amazed at the success of *My First Wife,*" he observes of this torrid film about the breakup of a suburban marriage. "I thought it would run in Melbourne for only a week or two. Years ago I made thirty or forty films. I put them on the shelf because there wasn't an audience for them. I haven't changed, but now all of a sudden my films are very commercial."

The Australian filmmakers who have gone off to Hollywood after doing well in Australia have proved again the mirage of nationalism. Just when they established for the world their Australian-ness, they lost it in the clouds of their success. Cox, on the other hand, in the intense but measured world of Melbourne, is simply not concerned with the Australia-foreign dichotomy.

"I think people are desperately alone," he says softly. "I stubbornly believe that people are starving for a bit of humanity." He stops and sighs. "I can't make political films anymore—I get too angry. All I can do is to make people more aware of their humanity. Film is so powerful that I have an extraordinary obligation—to make people come out from the film and want to discuss something about their life, to touch somebody, to love or weep." Cox, whose jolting films eschew the great Australian myths, goes on to demarcate the terrain of his art: "The inner world of the individual is what concerns me; it's like the roots of a tree, which we never think about because we never see them, but they give the tree its life. And sometimes the inner world of the man who delivers the milk is far richer than the inner world of Mr. Hawke, or whoever." Paul Cox is a splendid example of what the new Australia's quest for confidence and pluralism can produce.

One day I am riding through the center of Perth and a cabbie, in the friendly Western Australian way, is giving me a modest, informative commentary. At Australia Place we come upon a glistening new tower and he mentions the name of the company whose offices are within it. Unfamiliar with the name, I ask if the company is a purely Australian one. The driver, Perth-born and middle-aged, looks at me almost sharply. "Is anything purely Australian anymore?"

Many wise Australians are relaxed about all this. "I'm an anti-nationalist," says Justice Michael Kirby in Sydney. "I'm against false efforts to raise provincial pride, which has been a curse in the twentieth century. Some people even strive to distinguish us all the time from New Zealanders!" Although Professor Leonie Kramer envies the "sense of real pride Americans have in the whole variety of American achievements," she does not wave the flag of nationalism. After her experiences as head of the broadcasting authority she concludes: "Australian nationalism is a form of isolationism; there's a strong component of provincialism in it. I'm against it."

Just as nationalism may be a mirage, so many Australians are mature enough not to really care or even think much about the old dichotomy between Australian things and foreign things. And in Bob

Hawke they have a prime minister who is relatively unconcerned with the Australia-foreign dualism.

Minister of Science and Technology Barry Jones sees an internationalization of science that puts the relation of Australia to the rest of the world in a new light. "After all, there isn't a specifically Australian physics any more than there's Catholic physics or Buddhist physics," he observes. "You have ten Ph.D.s in microelectronics from a certain Australian university, and you find eight of them have gone overseas. Well, that might be appalling, or it might mean nothing at all. What really would concern me was if really exciting things were happening over there and *no* exciting things were happening here. But in radio-astronomy and astrophysics, for example, Australia is at present one of the places to be." The same could be said about a number of fields of medical research.

In a land with a male chauvinist tradition, today it is women who often seem best able to transcend Australian self-consciousness. The novelist Helen Garner, having just served on a panel of judges for a writing prize that was not awarded, complains during our Italian lunch in Melbourne of the quality of the new writing on social and political themes. Is there a lack of tension, I wonder, due to insufficient contact between Australia and a wider world? "I'm not sure," she says after long hesitation and a sip of her espresso, "what there is that happens in that wider world that doesn't also happen here."

"I feel rather strangled by Australianism," says Faith Bandler, the middle-aged author of *Welou, My Brother,* in Sydney. "I am not head over heels about Lawson and Paterson. I read them as a kid and I saw them as racist. It's not the kind of Australianism I feel comfortable with. I feel comfortable with Patrick White, who doesn't have the others' arrogance." Bandler, who is a Torres Strait islander, pauses and her deep blue eyes bore into me. "It has been harder for me to wear what was Australian than it has been to wear my blackness. I found a bloody crudeness, a crassness, among those traditional Australian writers." She stops and laughs. "Sometimes I feel a stranger here in Australia. I feel very much at home in Europe. They say we Australian blacks are part of the Third World, but to me there's no such bloody thing as the Third World. There's only one world."

Signs exist that young people can be more relaxed about the Australia-foreign dichotomy than their parents are. My niece Claire Watt loves the Australian bush, various Asian cultures, and British and American rock music, and finds no tension in such eclecticism. An avid reader, she tells me over lunch in a Melbourne restaurant that she can't remember the last Australian book she read. European and American movies nearly always interest her more than Australian ones. She goes camping among the wildflowers, then comes back to Melbourne to worship at a Buddhist temple and later queue up to buy tickets to hear an American guitarist. She thinks it odd of me to try to sort out these categories.

"The way I feel about Australia," says Claire, who is just back from a long, slow trip through Asia, "is that I know it's my home, and I'm glad it's my home. In Australia you can smoke a cigarette in public and not be accused of being immoral. You can go out for dinner in a singlet and shorts."

After our lunch I thought of a moment from the play *One Day of the Year*. Alf, the ex-serviceman father, is fond of mocking his son Hughie and Hughie's friends for "having ideas." At one point he explodes: "You kids aren't bloody Aussies"; and again: "He's done up like a Yank." Hughie tries to express to his girlfriend, Jan, who is from a different kind of home, why he suffocates in his parents' home: "It's just that they're so . . . they're so—Australian."

"Are they?" responds Jan. "They're what it was. We're what it's going to be." And she smiles.

In the end, Australia's new confidence and acceptance of diversity show themselves in the actions and tastes of individuals, not of the nation as a collective, and each generation of individuals, itself very fragmented, is hardly conscious of being part of a particular era. Individuals seek to enrich their lives with items freely chosen without much attention to labels of origin. "To say all Australians are obsessed with footy and boat-racing is to stereotype us," says Justice Michael Kirby. "There are possibly as many who are obsessed by Mahler." Back in the 1950s and 1960s the choice between football and Mahler did not seem quite so free. I suppose that is why Germaine Greer planned her departure from Australia "when I was 12." I suppose that is why some of us rushed abroad to get educated and found it too hard to go back.

All is silver and green, clouds matching the surface of streams gushing through lush paddocks, as I take the Gippsland train east from Melbourne to collect my thoughts in Bruthen. We pass Warrigul, where my grandfather used to teach school, riding a horse in each day from his little farm, surrounded by prosperous-looking farms with fences made of logs painted white. By the Princes Highway boys sell potatoes, onions, and Thorpdale tomatoes. The fat belching chimneys of Yallourn, a pipeline bringing gas back to Melbourne, and the new McDonald's and caravan parks and supermarkets at Morwell all are a reminder of the unlucky timing of Australia's lurch into heavy investment in energy and resources. At the solid British-looking railway stations the tearooms of yesterday have surrendered to high labor costs, replaced by a chaste little food counter on board the modern carriages of the diesel train. I feel a sense of familiarity, yet also of changes in the years since East Gippsland was my home.

As the train moves toward Sale the trunks of half-dead trees with no small branches or leaves—beetles get under the bark, eat the sap, and kill the tree—twist in bizarre shapes, looking in the winter light like so many animals in frozen postures. A barbed-wire fence runs along the railway line and beyond it rises a siding of red gravel. On the northern horizon the mountains, despite the wintry weather, are a brilliant mid-blue. Dairy cattle drink at water holes. At each little railway station there is a tiny wooden dunny with a discreet entranceway built of iron sheets painted in the dull orange color so beloved of the Victorian Railways. Now and then we flash by a wooden church with its paint peeling off.

We reach neat, flat Bairnsdale, which announces its population of 9,900 on a sign at the town's edge. This town where my brother and I used to sell our rabbit skins doesn't feel like the bush anymore—except when the black night envelops you after eight o'clock in winter—as the tentacles of international culture creep around daily life. I stay at the Kansas City Motel, which has quite a different ambience from the old two-storied pubs with verandas and wrought iron balconies and hallways with linoleum and tall ceilings. Nearby is the Lake of China restaurant. The cinema to which we used to drive from Bruthen to watch British movies is closed—victim of American videos—with a notice on its front door, "Bingo Every Wednesday." Everywhere the car dominates life. Even the rural roads are cruised by police with radar to trap speedsters.

But Bairnsdale retains a homely feel. At dinner in the excellent Sir Thomas restaurant I tell the waitress that I am hesitating between the duck and the porterhouse steak. "Porterhouse's lovely—I had it for tea," she volunteers. At a nearby table a local travel agent tells stories from a recent trip to America. "In San Diego, you wouldn't believe it, one hotel room had a bar in it, and another had two double beds."

On the road from Bairnsdale to Bruthen, apple orchards dot the way and an occasional cypress rises above the bottle brush, kookaburras taking up positions on its boughs. Under the trees sit bracken ferns with tough leaves, a menace to farmers as they greedily feed off the soil. Off the bitumen main road, the side roads are ocher-colored gravel, lined with gums. Everywhere there are gray stumps—those same inviting stumps on which we used to sit or lay out the dishes of a picnic.

The township comes into view and it hasn't changed much. The valley still is beautiful with its maize and bean fields, and the noble poplars and the apple box and the low-reaching willows by the river. The undulating paddocks are like lawns as they used to be. Four decades after VJ day, when we rolled down the hill to the Bruthen Inn inside a galvanized water tank, Bruthen is secure and content to fit in with nature's rhythms. My family's house has a red roof now instead of green, but the walnut and bottle brush trees stand guard as before. Where we grew tomatoes there is no garden, just a horse munching grass. Women's liberation hasn't done away with the Ladies' Lounge—separate from the Saloon Bar—at the Bruthen Inn.

The *Bruthen Times* is long defunct and people read instead the *Bairnsdale Advertiser,* which is full of ads for Japanese cars. A video shop has replaced the old family grocer, but the grocer himself, Jack Pollard, eighty-three years old (all of those years lived in the same house), does not look a day older than when in apron and tie he used to smile at me from behind his counter. "The motor car, the chains, and the sales in the Bairnsdale stores killed my grocery business," he says. He remembers well my friendship with Agnes and says Bruthen has no Orientals at present. "There'd be no jobs for them."

Sleeper cutters no longer fill the pub, for three of the four timber mills from my day have closed. Much of East Gippsland is bitter about the environmentalists' attack on the milling industry. LOGGERS AND SAWMILLERS WORK, says a sign in a pub in a neighboring township, GREENIES JERK. Bruthen is on the fringe of tourist routes, but economically it stagnates. Pretty and tranquil, it seems a happy backwater. "There's plans for a marble mine at Benambra," Pollard says as he points toward the ribbon of the Omeo Road. "Processing could be in Bruthen, but the conservationists object and it may never come to pass."

It was isolation that made Bruthen a backwater. The decision to end the railroad from Melbourne at Bairnsdale kept it remote. The mining boom that developed in the nineteenth century sent stagecoaches back and forth through Bruthen and brought it many banks and pubs. But when the boom ended, there was little to replace it. Now that timber milling is in decline, there is little to replace it either.

In front of the freshly painted Mechanics Institute Hall on Main

Street, where the public gardens are beautifully kept, near a couple of shops with their welcoming verandas and a cairn to remember the explorer Angus MacMillan, I chat with an elderly lady whose family name is vaguely familiar to me. Seeking to pluck her identity from memory's mists, I ask her which church she goes to. "Oh, there's only one church now," she replies with a quick smile.

In my day no Aborigines lived in Bruthen—in season they camped by the Tambo River—but today some thirty Aborigines live in and around the township, and Jock Hood, who welcomes me to his home on Main Street, is related to most of them. We sit at a table covered with oilcloth in his parlor as relatives come in and out. Hood, sixty-seven years old and dark-skinned, says making music by blowing on half-torn eucalyptus leaves is dying out. "Only three of us is left in Gippsland that can play a gumleaf," he says quietly. "The kids like guitars and saxophones." On the walls are boomerangs, family photos, Church of England trappings, a picture of Elvis Presley, and maps of Australia. Hood isn't interested in land rights. "The land rights I want is to own the land under this house," he says.

Hood used to pick beans down by the Tambo River and he remembers my father as the Bruthen school headmaster four decades ago. He asks me if I know the origin of my home township's name. I do not, and he explains: "Bruthen Bungul was head of the Aboriginal tribe around here, that's how it got its name." Hood loves Gippsland. "The great thing is you can go fishing, or rabbiting, any time you like. Put a ferret in the burrow and then knock the rabbits dead with a waddy." Sometimes he uses nets, as we kids used to do; sometimes he just relies on throwing the wooden stick. "My favorite way of cooking rabbits is baked. Sometimes I cook swans too. Young swans, and kangaroos." As we walk out into the winter sun filtering through the brown, bare poplars, Jock Hood says, "Why don't you write me a letter from America, and I'll write you a letter back."

Australia is attempting an awkward maneuver: It is trying to solidify a national identity and in the same era to leap to cosmopolitanism—amidst severe economic difficulties. It is possible that race will divide Australians before they have finished building their national self-image. Australia has not had the experience of racial pluralism on the American scale. Many Australians would go berserk, for example, if a Jesse Jackson—or an Asian equivalent—sprang up in an election and questioned predominant white assumptions the way Jackson did in 1984.

There is a more enticing possibility that Australia will handle the double transition to national maturity and racial pluralism with aplomb. The nation has the blessing of a continent to itself. It is far from most dangers. History's timing gives it an opportunity just as parts of the West feel the choices narrowing. Yet the perennial challenges remain: striking a balance between progress and harmony with nature; transcending race feeling with shared social purposes; sculpting public policies that are compassionate without destroying initiative and responsibility. Only if these issues are handled subtly can this unripened society mature to become a major new civilization across the seas.

What is required, beyond a certain minimum prosperity, is the strong presence of both conviction and tolerance, and a belief that they can go hand in hand. Neither trait has been to the fore in Australia— if we take conviction to refer to national confidence, and tolerance to pertain to racial diversity. Nor are Australians used to the idea that one person may be sold on blue, another on red, and that the two of them can accept the disagreement without panic or malice.

My guess is that neither possibility will fully come about. Probably Australia is too easy-going to snarl itself up over race. Probably it is too isolated and slow-moving to become a new America. A blue-sky mentality exists in most Australians, and there is reality as well as self-delusion in it. In some ways Australia is a bit like a Buddhist kingdom of Southeast Asia, yielding to any pressure that makes for survival or happiness. There is a passivity to the culture. Behind the passivity, perhaps, there lie the twin issues of a failure to move on to republicanism and a failure to get away from the historical folk rule that every Australian is owed a good living.

Whitlam took some steps to strip away Britain's residual authority in Australia, but it took the hurricane of his dismissal to sweep him to republicanism. Hawke has dismantled a few more gargoyles from the monarchical edifice. Yet Queen Elizabeth is still the Australian head of state. The governor general still has the power to act as Kerr acted against Whitlam. Although Whitlam has learned his lesson, few Labor figures now push for a switch to a republic, leading one to wonder whether a mature consciousness of the nation really has arrived.

Without oppression, nationalism is never feverish, and Australian nationalism in its various phases has been relatively unforced. Because the pressure on Australia to cast free from all dependence remains gentle, there exists the luxury of graduated options. Full practical and cultural independence can be maddeningly undervalued and riddled with ambiguity. Yet the lack of total national independence could be linked with the tendency not to take full responsibility for the nation's future.

In a recent conversation I found Whitlam lamenting Australia's economic standing in the world. "And it's not as if the people we used to think would look after us are willing to do so," the former prime minister remarked. "We're just not important to them. South Africa's important, but it seems Australia is not." It is difficult for Australians to see that they are unique and to accept that fundamentally they are on their own. Only when they reach this point will national resolve stiffen and bloody-minded sectionalism fade.

Confronting the Australian political economy, the friendly observer finds himself possessed of a bizarre hope: that industrial disputes will go on savaging Australia's prosperity and morale, and that the currency will sink even further, so that a deepened crisis will at last produce a resolve to tackle the economic problems at their roots. For short of this, one fears, the philosophy of "Avoid Hangovers, Stay Drunk" may retain its hold. The familiar tendency of Australians to flail themselves yet do little about the matter that appalls them, to oscillate between panic and self-deprecation on the one hand and complacency on the other, is not dead. The real test of Hawke's nationalism will be whether he can institutionalize Australians' new confidence in themselves. Whitlam ran into the brick wall of constitutional immaturity; Hawke could run into the brick wall of economic immaturity. The "them and us" mentality in industrial relations eclipses altruism and a vision for the future.

But Australia is not in such a desperate situation that horrors are likely to supply what reason has failed to supply. Not within the short term will Australians come to any moment of great inspiration or energizing shock. More likely they will muddle through, failing to keep up with the countries they have been used to matching, but feeling consoled that this is only a relative failure and that life in Australia can continue to be pretty pleasant. If so, they may have to replace the decades-old phrase "lucky country" with a new phrase—"happy backwater."

Of course Australia cannot make its own future as if it were a painter before a blank canvas. The isolation may never totally be overcome. For a long time the smallness of Australia's population will guarantee a role for external cultural influence. British institutions in Australia seem likely to influence the nation indefinitely. And more than some Australians would like, a variety of American influences will perhaps increasingly color the nation—although Australia will never become as Americanized as it once was Britainized. The British and American elements are there, for the most part freely chosen and generally enriching Australia, even as they seem to some Australians to cloud to a degree the full face of a nation still struggling to align body and spirit.

The enduring force of geography ensures that Australia will continue its gingerly steps into the Asian orbit. But this will not be rapid or total. Australia, like Japan, hangs at a tangent to the nearest region. It may over a long period become to Asia what Japan is to the West— the most Asian nation of the West, as Japan is the most Western nation of the East. But I do not see it happening fast enough for tomorrow's Australia to draw from the tension a Japan-style dynamism.

It proves very hard for Australia to join its region. I well remember how Australian racism and blindness to the Asian region seemed unavoidable issues for our student generation. On my first trip to China in 1964, which taught me the geopolitics of Australia's existence, I began to suspect that if we white Australians were to discover our own identity, we would have simultaneously to confront our Asian neighborhood and the racism within our history and society. Yet twenty years later the first part of that task remains unfinished.

Gough Whitlam says reflectively, "It's so difficult for Australians to come to terms with their environment." Malcolm Fraser confesses that while in office he "only gropingly saw the challenge" of Asia, and he believes now that "a revolution in the life of this country" is needed to equip it for a successful role in the region. The idea of Australia joining Asia has sometimes had an unreal emotional dimension to it. "Our destiny is to be with the fastest-growing countries of the Pacific rim," Kim Beazley remarks carefully. "But that doesn't mean all of Asia." The defense minister observes that "decolonization is a distant memory" and that "the international economy is now a very moveable beast."

In some ways the tide may turn a little toward a global, hence Western integration for Australia, rather than a regional, hence Asian integration. The youth of Australia are probably more open-armed toward American and European cultural influences than are their parents. The transformation of communications and other technologies and the endless success of the capitalist economies may make the west coast of the U.S.A., and beyond it the Western world in general, the next direction of expansion for Australia's international links.

The future will no doubt be more ragged than in any schema now envisaged. I doubt that Australia's engaging idiosyncrasies will fall flat before any juggernaut of international progress. And whatever the speed, or lack of it, with which Australia moves to solve its present problems, this unique land, as its spaces slowly fill up with immigrants, mostly from Asia, and as the mysterious pieces of an evolving immigrant community rub and clink against each other, will become one of the most intriguing of the world's melting pots.

Notes on Sources

The sources for this book fall into three categories. Overwhelmingly the principal one is interviews and conversations with people all over Australia during visits totaling eight months during 1984–86. Those who were interviewed for attribution include the following: Jimmy Ah Toy, Alison Anderson, Bruce Bailey, Faith Bandler, Kim Beazley, Joh Bjelke-Petersen, Geoffrey Blainey, David Blenkinsop, Geoffrey Bolton, John Botting, Peter Boyce, Ernie Bridge, Robert Bropho, Neil Brown, Gordon Bryant, Brian Burke, Creighton Burns, Tom Burns, John Button, John Cain, Bob Carr, Patricia Caswell, Jack Chia, Barry Cohen, Ken Colbung, Barry Coulter, Charles Court, Paul Cox, Frank Crean, Simon Crean, Greg Davis, Ron Davis, Pat Dodson, Don Dunstan, Mary Durack, James Eedle, Peter Ellery, Gareth Evans, Paul Everingham, Rachel Faggeter, Mary Fairfax, Alec Fong Lim, Malcolm Fraser, Bruce Gall, Helen Garner, Peter Garrett, Petro Georgiou, Gordon Godber, Bruce Grant, David Hackworth, Richard Hall, Lang Hancock, Steve Hatton, Bob Hawke, Hazel Hawke, Bill Hayden, Fred Hockley, John Hogan, Clyde Holding, Miranda Hornsby, John Howard, Andrea Hull, Ross Johnston, Barry Jones, Warren Jones, Rona Joyner, Bob Katter, Trevor Kennedy, Michael Kirby, Leonie Kramer, Ian Lancaster, Bruce Lawson, Jan Lecornu, Wellington Lee, Race Mathews, Fraser Mc-Ewing, Adrian McGregor, Patrick McCaughey, Terry McMullan, Stan Mellick, Hugh Morgan, John Mulvaney, Craig Munro, George Negus, Leslie Oldfield, Charles Perkins, Tony Press, Winnie Quagliotti, Leonard Radic, Noel Robins, Brian Rowe, Susan Ryan, Bob Santamaria, Stuart Sayers, Charles See Kee, George Shaw, Dennis Simmons, Tony Staley, Bruce Stannard, Roger Steele, Hugh Stretton, Ian Tuxworth, Chris Wallace-Crabbe, Alan Watson, Claire Watt, Gough Whitlam, Margaret Whitlam, Vernon Wilcox, Morris Williams, Sydney Williams, Roger Windsor, Peter Wombwell, Neville Wran, Shaun Wyatt, Mick Young, Galarrwuy Yunupingu, Fay Zwicky.

A few people preferred not to be quoted by name, and a large number were briefly interviewed (for instance, cabbies) without their names ever becoming known to me. In scattered cases pseudonyms are used: the kids at School of the Air (Chapter Eight), John Cheng and Bill Jenkins (Chapter Nine).

Second, some material is drawn from my memories of growing up in Australia and from diary notes of my many visits to Australia and contacts with Australians over the intervening years. The memoir material is very limited and seldom personal: more will come in a future book.

Third, in Chapter Three, on Australian history, and here and there elsewhere, I have drawn on published writings. In particular Chapter Three has utilized and in some cases quoted from the following: Geoffrey Blainey's *A Land Half Won, Triumph of the Nomads, The Tyranny of Distance, Our Side of the Country;* Manning Clark's multivolume *History of Australia;* John Carroll's *Intruders in the Bush;* J. B. Hirst's *Convict Society and Its Enemies;* H. McQueen's *A New Britannia* and *From Gallipoli to Petrov;* Louis Hartz's *The Founding of New Societies;* H. V. Evatt's *Rum Rebellion;* L. G. Churchward's *America and Australia 1788–1972;* Russel Ward's *The Australian Legend;* A. B. Facey's *A Fortunate Life;* Geoffrey Dutton's *Snow on the Saltbush* (Henry Carter couplet).

I have also drawn on Rodney Hall's *The Australians* (a particularly perceptive work); Peter Coleman's *Australian Civilization;* essays by Hugh Collins, Ken Inglis, Geoffrey Blainey, and Manning Clark in *Daedalus,* Winter 1985; the early volume, *Convicts and Settlers,* by an unnamed author; Alan Reid's *The Power Struggle;* Donald Horne's *The Lucky Country;* Maximilian Walsh's *Poor Little Rich Country;* articles in the Melbourne *Age* at the time of Victoria's 150th anniversary by Tom Griffiths, Stuart Macintyre, Andrew Lemon, and K. S. Inglis. The Hawke quote ("The stuff about the meek") is from Phillip Adams in *Australian Business,* August 29, 1984.

Occasionally in other chapters I have quoted published material. The following is a list of those sources that are not obvious from the text itself:

Chapter Two: Conway quote from *The End of Stupor?,* from which I also draw "I don't go to church, but I'm as good as those that do." From Conway's *The Great Australian Stupor* the point about compliments and abuse, and the phrase "upholstered island." Rodney Hall quote from *The Australians.* "Fifty Lovely Hot Puddings" was the discovery of Joan Colebrook. Coleman quote is from his *Australian Civilization.* The 1840s observer quote and the bushmen's chorus are from Ward's *The Australian Legend.* Reflections on skepticism come in part from John Carroll's *Intruders in the Bush.*

Chapter Four: Reid quotes and Menzies's remark at cabinet meeting from *The Power Struggle.* Calwell quote, "Give McMahon a fair go," and McMahon's words about hand in the till all from L. Oakes and D. Solomon, *The Making of an Australian Prime Minister.* Patrick White's words from Graham Freudenberg's *A Certain Grandeur.* Concerning the remark of the assistant secretary of state—a distinguished Asianist and later a brilliant ambassador to Australia—I am aware that when the remark was reported (in a garbled way) in the London *Observer,* without the interlocutor being named, the secretary denied it (letter to *Observer,* April 8, 1973); however, I was the interlocutor and without doubt the slip of the tongue did occur. I was unwilling at the time to speak to the press for attribution about the Kissinger and Green slips of the tongue over Whitlam. *Time* magazine, phoning me, was told the detailed versions of the incidents, but when they could not quote me, they chose not to mention Kissinger's or Green's name (edition of March 26, 1973). Withers-Wriedt exchange and Mrs. Fraser's words from *Kerr's King Hit* by Clem Lloyd and Andrew Clark. *The Age* 1855 quote is from *A New Britannia.* Bligh and Macarthur from Clark's *History of Australia,* vol. 1. Whitlam quip from *Ryde's* magazine, November 1986.

Chapter Five: Hall quote from *The Australians.* Blainey on Syme from *A Land Half Won.* Manning Clark quote from *Melbourne Historical Journal,* no. 2, 1962. Williamson remark to Jane Sullivan in *The Age,* October 11, 1985. Greer quote from Clyde Packer's *No Return Ticket.* Facts and statistics on the two cities in latter part of chapter from a *60 Minutes* program on Channel Nine, Sydney, in 1984.

Chapter Six: Egerton incident from *The Whitlam Government 1972–1975.* Hall quote from *Meanjin,* no. 2, 1984, page 235. Child molesters and drinking from article by George Langley in *The Australian,* November 9, 1985.

Chapter Seven: Pilbara children's words from the anthology *Small Voices in a Big Country,* published by Mount Newman Mining Company. Bruce Grant quote (footnote) from his *The Australian Dilemma.*

Chapter Eight: "Shirts or singlets" quote and "Yeah, pies" both from an article by Michael Lawrence cited in Richard Beckett's *Convicted Tastes.* Herbert quote from *National Times,* January 18–24, 1985.

Chapter Nine: Rodney Hall quote from *The Australians.* NSW police liaison officer's remarks in *The Age,* December 6, 1984. Melbourne police chief's words from *The Age,* December 12, 1984. Miners' Protective League from Clark's *History of Australia,* vol. 4. Minister of home affairs' words from McQueen's *From Gallipoli to Petrov*. Lee Kuan Yew quote from *National Times,* September 13–19, 1981. Mark O'Connor's words from Judith Wright's essay in *Daedalus,* Winter 1985.

Chapter Ten: Whitlam's remark is essentially repeated in his *The Whitlam Government 1972–1975*. Ken Inglis says Namatjira was arrested for drinking alcohol (*Daedalus,* Winter 1985), but various other sources say it was for supplying other Aborigines with alcohol.

Chapter Eleven: Kemp quote from an unpublished paper entitled "The Stability of Australian Polyarchy"; similar points are developed in his *Politics and Authority,* chap. 6, and in his essay "Political Behavior," in J. S. Western and J. Najman, eds., *A Sociology of Australian Society.* Lee Ming Tee's words to Anne Flahvin in the *Sydney Morning Herald.* Stone quote from *Quadrant,* October 1984. Colcheedas story is from John Monks's article in *The Australian.* Keating's words to Geoffrey Barker in *The Age.*

Chapter Twelve: Robertson song is quoted by Clark in his *History of Australia,* vol. 1. Psychologist and astrophysicist moving to country is from *Sydney Morning Herald,* January 26, 1984. Boyd remark, *The Age,* October 27, 1984. Buckley quote from *Cutting Green Hay.* The *moules marinières* point is owed to Richard Beckett's *Convicted Tastes.* Horne quote from his paper "National Identity in the Period of the 'New Nationalism' " (Australian Studies Center, June 1982). Herbert quote from *National Times,* January 18–24, 1985. Mary Eagle quote and Nolan quote from *Intruders in the Bush.* Paul Turner's words from Bruce Elder's article in *National Times,* January 27–February 2, 1984. Greer's words from *No Return Ticket.* The comparison with Japan toward the end is from Bruce Grant's *The Australian Dilemma* and that with Japan's relation to its neighborhood is from Hugh Collins's *Daedelus* essay.

Acknowledgments

My principal debt is to the Australia that shaped me for twenty-seven years: family, the townships of Longwood and Bruthen, Wesley College, Melbourne University, the Labor Party, editors and public figures, friends and foes.

I am also indebted to the hundreds of Australians, some famous and many not, who spoke to me of their lives and their views during the eight months I spent in Australia on four journeys in the years 1984 to 1986. Many of them are listed by name in the Note on Sources. The openness of Australians to talk with a visiting writer is one of their appealing characteristics.

The Promotion Australia division of the Australian government was helpful both within Australia and through its officers in Washington and its library in New York. While in Australia in 1984, 1985, and 1986 I drew much on *The Age, The Australian, The Bulletin, National Times,* and other papers and magazines, and my debt to them is plain in every chapter. While I was in Melbourne, Keith Wong helped me with research.

Parts of the draft of the book were kindly read by Adrian McGregor

343

in Brisbane, Peter Wombwell in Perth, and Peter Farrell in Darwin. Old friends Bruce Stannard in Sydney and Bruce Grant in Melbourne read the whole manuscript. Maureen Davidson in Melbourne and my brother, Peter Terrill, in Canberra went through Chapter One. To all of these I am grateful for corrections and suggestions. The shaping of the book owes a great deal to the gentle authoritarianism of Fred Hills, my remarkably good editor, and the suggestions of his colleague Burton Beals. My literary agent, Barbara Lowenstein, gave wonderful support to the project from beginning to end.

Index

345

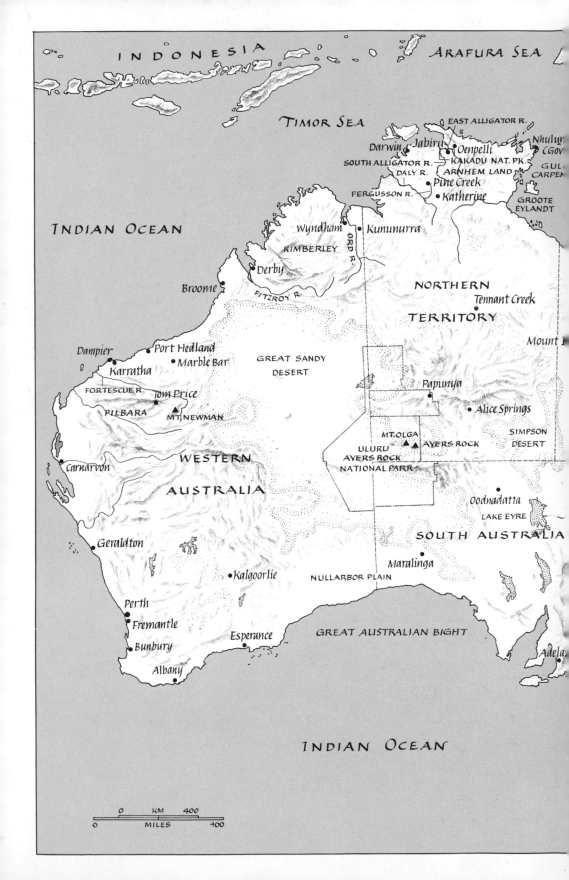